ECUMENICAL
BREAKTHROUGH

DUQUESNE STUDIES
Theological Series   9

ECUMENICAL BREAKTHROUGH

An Integration of the Catholic and the Reformational Faith

by

Herman A. Fiolet

DUQUESNE UNIVERSITY PRESS
PITTSBURGH, PA.
Editions E. Nauwelaerts, Louvain

DUQUESNE STUDIES

Theological Series

Henry J. Koren, C.S.Sp., S.T.D., Editor

Library of Congress Catalog Card Number 71-98548
© 1969 by Duquesne University
Printed in the United States of America

BX
8
.2
F5

CONTENTS

5

8   CONTENTS

PREFACE

This book is a combination and revision of the author's original Dutch works, *Onvermoed perspectief of de Oecumene,* 1963 and *Dilemma doorbroken,* 1965, both published by Paul Brand, Hilversum, supplemented by additional materials. In 1968 the second of these two titles earned the author the triennial Coebergh Prize, awarded by a committee of Catholic and Protestant theologians, for the most important theological contribution to Church unity over the years 1965-1967 in Holland.

Professor Fiolet's book, the committee said, is the "work of a responsible theologian" and "its interest is not confined to his professional colleagues." It envisions the ecumenical problem over a very broad range, while paying special attention to the Catholic and Protestant Churches. From a scriptural basis the author approaches the central issue of ecclesiology and he tries "in particular to determine the relationship between the Church as institute of salvation and the Church as the community of salvation." Going beyond what the dogmatic *Constitution of the Church* "Gaudium et Spes" could attain in this respect, the author approaches the Church in terms of Christology. In his own understanding of the God-man Christ, he "tries to find the model for an understanding of how institution and community go together in the Church." In this way he is able to "transcend the traditional oppositions and to be critical in both directions."

The Committee recommends the method and aim of

Dr. Fiolet's book "as an excellent example showing how contributions can be made to the formation of an ecumenical theology."

Several people have collaborated in the translation of this book. The final revision was made by the undersigned, who bears responsibility for its faithfulness.

Henry J. Koren

INTRODUCTION

"DO NOT RECEIVE HIS GRACE IN VAIN"

The *Ecumene* is a challenge that the Catholic Church of our time cannot evade. In her whole religious life and in her concrete pastoral practice she must show that "promoting the restoration of unity among all Christians is one of the chief concerns of the Second Sacred Ecumenical Synod of the Vatican."[1] It is also a fact that many people belonging to all kinds of Christian Churches are seriously and eagerly hoping that rich fruits will be produced by that concern.

The Catholic Church, in her local congregations, in her ordinary parochial pastoral care and the many other forms of apostolate, in her preaching and instructions, has to realize that the Council must be implemented by a radical change in her practical approach to the other Christian Churches. For the first time in the long, prospectless history of divided Christianity, the Catholic Church has proclaimed her fundamental belief that the Holy Spirit uses also the other Christian Communions as instruments of His saving presence. This declaration rests on the religious insight that "the Holy Spirit, dwelling in those who believe, pervading and ruling over the entire Church, brings about the marvelous communion

1. *Decree on Ecumenism*, no. 1, Walter M. Abbot (ed.), *The Documents of Vatican II* (Herder and Herder, 1966), p. 341.

of the faithful and joins them together so intimately in Christ that He is the principle of the Church's unity."[2]

The Catholic Church realizes that all Christian Communions are not the Church of Jesus Christ in the same way and that, because of the unwholesome ecclesial division, that common life animated by the Spirit of the glorified Lord is unable presently to attain its full stature in this world. But it is certain that the new approach of the Catholic Church to the other Christian Churches will be a dominating factor in the history of the near future.

Until now, when that Church looked at other Churches, she felt she could do nothing more than invite them to return. Basing herself on the honest conviction that she was the one, only true, Church of Jesus Christ because of the apostolic succession, the Catholic Church was unable to recognize any other Church beside herself. To her mind there existed, outside her own bosom, only individual Christians who had separated themselves from the true Church. They were Christians because they "belonged" to the Catholic Church, but in order to become full Christians, they had to be taken in once more into that Church. The Catholic Church considered the separated Christian Communions only as an object for her apostolate. These Communions in turn strongly opposed the Catholic Church because they experienced themselves as a sort of hunting ground for Catholic proselytism.

The divided Christians were, as a matter of principle, unable to recognize one another; they made the Church of Jesus Christ uninhabitable for one another by fiercely and unchristianly combating one another in an apologetic battle about questions of doctrine and ecclesial structures of authority. By unjudiciously invoking the principle that divine truth alone has rights, we gave free

2. *Ibid.*, no. 2, p. 343.

rein to the sin of division. We disrupted the one Church by absolutizing our own way of conceiving and practicing the faith in opposition to the concepts and practice of fellow Christians, as if the decision about what it means to be a Christian and to be Christ's Church coincides exclusively with one uniform Church Order and a Confession, that are valid for all ages.

In our own time we have made the startling ecumenical discovery that the Holy Spirit is not stopped by iron curtains, and that He is everywhere the principle and source of our Church unity. We are not yet able to evaluate the opportunities which that mutual recognition opens up for us, divided Christians, at this historic moment. Still less can we work out immediately the consequences of that new vision. Each one's honest religious concern for the responsibility of his own Church and the strangeness of the wholly new situation in the history of the Church prevent all of us from catching up with the speed of the *Ecumene*.

There are a good number of Christians, however, members of diverse Churches, who realize the historical significance of this moment in the Church's history and they are fearful lest we should fail to make use of the present opportunities. Prompted by their deeply-felt grief at the sight of the present dividedness of Christians, they eagerly seek for an up-to-date response to the Pauline invitation: "Working together with him, then, we entreat you not to accept the grace of God in vain. For he says, 'At the acceptable time I have listened to you, and helped you on the day of salvation.' Behold, now is the acceptable time, now is the day of salvation" (2 Cor. 6:1-2).[3]

It is not surprising that the Catholic Church was last in being affected by this ecumenical movement and that

3. Scripture texts are taken from the *The Holy Bible. Revised Standard Version* (Thomas Nelson and Sons, New York, 1952).

this Church is also most profoundly touched by it. The desire of all Christian Churches for unity constitutes a unanimous appeal to the Catholic Church to integrate into her own ecclesial being the honest protests which in the course of history compelled sincere believers in Christ to separate themselves from her.

The Catholic Church is presently occupied with assimilating the consequences of her discovery that the other Churches are truly instruments of the salvific work of the Holy Spirit. And she cannot stop at the abstract admission of the fact that she no longer conceives the achievement of Church unity as a return of all the separated Christians. In every form of her reflection upon that matter she must show that she does not expect the other Churches to return to the Catholic view.

The Catholic Church must also dare to put her whole historical structure in the crucible of a common ecumenical reflection. She must learn to live with the truth that the Spirit is active also outside her centuries-old exclusive frontiers and that the other Christian Communions, on the basis of their own way of being-the-Church of Jesus Christ, are obliged to put lawful questions to her, which she must honor for her own correction.

Because the divided Christians believe that the Spirit of Christ is the source and active principle of the unity of all Churches in spite of their visible division, they come to realize that they should once more, at this salvific moment, re-examine the possibilities of a visible unification of the Church of Jesus Christ. Because they can now approach one another in a way that totally differs from what was considered the only possibility a few decades ago, they now desire to undertake that ecumenic task with great expectations.

Today the ecumenical encounters of Christians and

Churches are inspired by three entirely new presuppositions:

1. Being-the-Church of Jesus Christ means to live by the salvific reality of the mystery of creation that the Son of the Father became man through the overshadowing of the Holy Spirit.

The divided Christians desire to re-examine their encounters from the standpoint of the central fact of salvation history, namely, that "the first-born of all creation," for the benefit of all men, became "the first-born from the dead" (Col. 1:15-20). Through the inspiring power of the Holy Spirit and for the salvation of all men, the Son has lived His divine being-together with the Father in our sinful humanity.

All Christians know by faith that they are drawn into that salvific reality of the humanity that the Son has in common with us; and this salvific reality is the earthly reality in which the Son has come and continues to come in word and sacrament through the dynamic activity of His Spirit.

The realization that Christians, in spite of ecclesial divisions and differences in the way they live and preach that salvific reality, are nevertheless one as being involved together in that event, has brought the divided Christians together, making them recognize that the others too are Christians and that they too are the Church. Although the people of God, that is still on its pilgrimage, remains divided, those divisions are unable to touch the foundations of Christ's Church, for Jesus has passed through as saving and perfecting the whole human existence.

The discovery that when we meet fellow Christians who belong to other Churches we meet with Christ in an encounter that is animated by the Holy Spirit, makes us

realize more and more that there are more things that
bind us together than things that keep us apart. And
Christians who contradict us are placed on our path
precisely to enable us to become ourselves more fully the
Church of Jesus Christ.[4]

2. *The historicity of human existence and of human
knowledge must always be taken into account in living
the Mystery of the Church.*

All mankind has entered into the salvific reality of
God's love that communicates itself to us through the
humanity the Son has in common with us. But our experience of the faith is always a human translation of God's
permanent Self-communication in Christ, and on that
account, no truths are given to us as eternally human.
Man can never adequately express that experience of the
salvific reality of our being with the Father in Christ. It
remains always a human experience and a verbal expression in a profession of faith which is always marked by
the image of man and the world of one's own time.

The divided Christians have dared to confess their
guilt to one another because they realize they constantly
failed to give due weight to the historicity that marked
their profession of faith in the apologetic era of the past.
That is why they were not able to resist the temptation of
appealing to divine truth in order to make their own
profession of faith and their own Church order so inviolable that they could not possibly be corrected and enriched by other Christians.[5]

3. *The separated Churches need one another for the
task of giving to the ever actual salvific event in Christ a
form that is in keeping with the time.*

The Churches absolutized their own human way of
experiencing and living the reality of divine Revelation;

4. Cf. pages 60-136.
5. Cf. pages 206, 247-248, 283-289.

thus conscience forced them ever farther apart. In their desire to be faithful to Christ they thought it necessary to separate themselves from the others. Through this tragic process their lawful and rich diversity in Christ led to unlawful and sinful division.

The local Churches in ecumenic encounters with others have discovered that they are native manifestations of God's salvific action in Christ, and that they cannot ascribe a divine absoluteness to themselves in opposition to the other Churches.

There is always a danger of schism when a Church indulges in a monologue that tends to give absoluteness to its own views, and this danger can be overcome only by a living dialogue with all the other local Churches. Even when they feel compelled to contradict one another, they cannot forget that through God's coming in Christ they are permanently bound together.

The separated Churches are becoming deeply aware of their responsibility and they realize more and more that they neither can nor may any longer stay aloof from the other Churches. Ecclesial isolation sinfully prevents the Church of Jesus Christ from being fully His Church.[6]

Starting from those three presuppositions in their encounters, the separated Churches now face the ecumenical task of revaluating their conflicting religious doctrines so as to see which ones enrich their being-the-Church or on the contrary maintain its division. Meeting with other Christians has made us realize that we often still are not sure when the others's protest contains an enrichment for our own way of being-the-Church, and where the frontiers that actually divide us are situated. But this very realization has been a source

6. Cf. pages 228-231, 249-261, 302-308.

of unexpected dynamism for the ecumenical movement.

It has been said that many young people are now close to leaving the Church. But might it not also be said that they are opening new perspectives to us if we dare to recognize that they are perhaps close to a new way of being-the-Church? In any case the Churches must take into serious consideration the growing dissatisfaction and stimulating unrest of many younger people. In this we must start from the belief that we have been put together on a road whose destination is as yet unknown. Yet, we have clearly heard the inviting voice crying to us from afar: "Fear not, it is I."

This book would like to facilitate the Church's common exploration of the road that lies before us. It is offered to all Christians who no longer wish to resign themselves to the existing dividedness of Christ's Church.

Chapter One explores the possibilities and limits of the Catholic ecumenical attitude of faith resulting from the breakthrough of Vatican Council II.

Chapter Two considers the starting point of this ecumenical renewal of the Catholic Church: the mystery of God's self-communication in the Incarnation of the Son of the Father through the overshadowing of the Holy Spirit. For God-made-man is the fundamental form of the Father's salvific plan of creation and redemption for all mankind. It is only by ceaselessly reflecting on faith in the light of this central fact of salvation that the Church can prevent the one-sided petrifaction of her human element and renew her appearance in this world. Christian theology and the Christians' way of living the faith must, therefore, learn again to experience all aspects of the revelation as particularizations of the central mystery of faith that God has come to man in Christ.

The remaining chapters attempt on the basis of this biblical testimony about Christ, to transfer the ecumenical dialogue concerning important aspects of revelation from the realm of historical oppositions to that of what it means for us to be Christians today. The internal renewal that is going on in all Churches has removed us so far from the seemingly immovable barriers of the past that an entirely new revaluation has become necessary.

This work does not wish to be more than an attempt to throw light on the centuries-old controversy from the standpoint of our contemporary renewed reflection on the faith. Amidst the dividedness afflicting the Church of Christ it is a modern experiment which endeavors to bring the ecumenical dialogue to a decisive point.

CHAPTER ONE

THE CATHOLIC ECUMENICAL ATTITUDE

1. ECUMENICAL HOSPITALITY

Many Christians desire to live under the one roof of the Church of Christ, but this unity in Christ means no more to them than the unity of those who live under the same roof in a hotel: each one lives secluded in his particular room. Like hotel guests, they don't know one another; they even ignore one another. They have no genuine interest in one another and the thought of being responsible for one another may never cross their minds.

The divided Christians stand, with respect to one point, even one degree lower than those who have rooms in a hotel. Here the guests generally show at least some form of politeness to others. The divided Christians, however, have often failed in the past to manifest even that minimum of kindness in their daily conduct.

During the last decades, however, the image of the Church as a sort of hotel has suddenly undergone a great change. We see guests sitting together in groups in the lobby; they speak about their vacation plans and invite one another for a trip. They dine at the same table and even offer to pick up the check. Upstairs, however, their rooms remain carefully closed to one another. Upon their return from an excursion they may be heard extolling the

advantages of their particular room. These have been
arranged according to their own individual taste, and
they wouldn't think of making any changes, for then they
would no longer feel at home in those rooms. At night
time the doors are firmly shut and each one can be
himself again within his cloistered "home."

The change in the relations between individual Christians and between diverse Christian Churches has been
baptized with the now stylish name of *Ecumene*. Wherever we may go, we hear news about various kinds of
ecumenical activities such as ecumenical discussions, ecumenical symposiums, joint Bible services. But is it not
true that most of the time there was no commitment;
does not each Communion continue its own Christian
life very much like before, after those meetings?

It must be admitted that meeting people "in the lobby"
of the Church can enable divided Christians to better
know and understand one another, and even, in the end,
may make them forgive one another, but this is not the
sort of thing that will produce a true *Ecumene*. All we
can say about such meetings is that they are inter-church
and inter-confessional dialogues. If the divided Christians desire to *live* with one another in a true ecumenical
way, they must be ready to make their own "home" a
place where the others can be "at home."

At the present time we still fail to appreciate the advantage of being truly "received" in the other's home. We
even dislike paying such a visit because we are afraid we
would not feel at home there. Every table and every
corner of our own house are filled with useless souvenirs,
and the place is so clogged up with our cherished quaint
pieces of furniture that we alone can find ourselves at
home there.

That's why we prefer to meet the others elsewhere, in
the open air, and always without any commitment. And

if the question about the peculiar arrangement of our own home should come up, each one wishes that the others fix up theirs according to his own favorite patterns; otherwise we cannot visit them because we do not feel "at home."

When Christians speak about the *Ecumene* they give the impression that their mind is always on the others: by their speaking about their own Church, and bearing witness to their own faith, they wish to teach the others to become different. But in the *Ecumene* it is not primarily a question of the *others* but of ourselves.

The genuine ecumenical attitude prompts us to make a critical examination of the particular shape we ourselves have given to our being-the-Church; it wants to examine the way we ourselves live our Christian life. To what extent does that shape give a pure expression to the integral Gospel which the Triune God has revealed in the historical human manifestation of Christ? The way we live our Christian life perhaps can be explained by historical circumstances but that does not make it objectively justified; hence we must ask ourselves to what extent our way of being Christians is a defensive distortion of that Gospel.

It is to questions like these, examined in all honesty, that the ecumenically-minded desires to give most of his attention. And for this purpose he needs the help of the other Christians, for in them, as in a mirror, he will be able to recognize the countenance of his own Church and at the same time its one-sidedness.

A genuine ecumenical attitude is animated by a spirit of hospitality that wants to make room in one's own Church for everything we discover in other Christians as belonging to authentic Christianity. Hence our encounter with other Christians is not governed by an apologetic combativeness that says: "This is what I have against your way of being a Christian," but we ask with ecumenic openness: "What can I learn from your way of living the faith?" These two aspects in the encounter of divided Christians may not and cannot be separated. For if we separate them we fail to recognize the seriousness of the division that exists among Christians. The genuine ecumenical attitude leads to an approach toward other Christians that differs totally from the traditional apologetic mentality.

It is our intention in this book to contribute toward the development of that spirit of ecumenical hospitality among Catholics with respect to Christians of the Reformation. It is an attempt to bring about a breakthrough in the situation of divided Christianity. This situation used to seem hopeless, for Reformed and Catholic Christians thought it was a matter of conscience for them to maintain the opposite positions that were taken centuries ago; it was, they thought, demanded by their faith. Our study desires to scan new possibilities in our ecumenical encounters for a rapprochement in understanding and living the divine Revelation given us in Christ.

It is evident that we are standing at the beginning of a long and still very dark road. It is still too soon to write a strictly scientific and methodical synthesis. We are merely probing possibilities; this is an "essay" in ecumenical theology rather than a synthesis. But "we must dare to have the courage to be the laborers of the first hour, instead of being harvesters of the eleventh hour."[1]

It is our conviction that it is only a joint reflection of all Christians that can bring about that prudent rapprochement. Hence we feel justified in surveying the road-signs that mark the way Christians believe they can proceed toward the rapprochement. We believe that we

1. F. Thijssen, "Bezinning op Hans Asmussens vragen," *Het Schild*, vol. 36 (1959), p. 63.

can meet other Christians only in a renewed religious reflection upon the Mystery of Christ as it comes to us through Scripture. It is that Mystery, then, that must be the central idea of this book and at the same time dominate all the developments we shall attempt to make.

Even when we do not explicitly mention it, we have constantly kept in mind the way the Reformed Christians have travelled their separate ways during so many centuries, though they are one with us in Christ. In an ecumenical spirit we have looked for and examined the points at which our ways come close and then drift apart again. We have sought to live constantly in the presence of our Reformed fellow-Christians in order to listen to what their witness has to say to us, in order to make it possible for the Reformed tradition to make a genuine contribution to our own Catholic vision of faith.

Catholics may sometimes feel that in this book there is a confrontation of the way Catholics practice their faith with the authentic confession of the Reformed Christians. This may seem to be a dishonest opposition, as if we did not confront the Reformed vision of faith with the Catholic vision, but contrast it with the Catholic way of living the faith; and this would often turn out to the disadvantage of the Catholic Church.

But the Catholic should realize that his way of living the faith has been fed during many centuries by the Counter-reformation of the post-tridentine theology, and that many forms of one-sidedness in the Catholic practice of faith are stubbornly retained precisely because that polemical vision of Revelation cannot be easily modified.

Those who in frequent encounters with Reformed Christians have existentially experienced the power of their protest, know that if we wish to engage in true ecumenical reflection, we must purify and correct every-

thing that is found in the Catholic Church which is the
result of a proclamation based on that Counter-reformation.

The last decades have witnessed a renewal of the
whole Catholic way of thinking both in matters of reflection on our faith and in the practice of that faith. And yet
the Catholic has not reached the end of that road: he has
not yet sufficiently felt the need for listening to the witness of the Reformation, and his encounter with this
witness has not yet been sufficiently intense.

Until that happens, Catholics cannot expect that they
can diminish the protest of Reformed Christians who are
asked to excuse Catholics for being so one-sided in their
practice of the faith. For the sake of attaining to the full
stature of the Christ-Mystery in the future ecumenical
Church, Catholics must confess that particular aspects of
the Revelation have too long remained outside their attention; in consequence of this, their vision of the whole
reality of salvation in Christ became deformed and the
Catholic Church strengthened the Reformation in its protest.

And it is a lame excuse for a Catholic to point out that
the Reformation is also one-sided in its vision of the
Revelation precisely because of its protesting attitude
toward the Catholic Church. Reformed Christians must
also be willing to recognize that the "Ecumene" is a matter of conscience for them and, therefore, an unfulfilled
task of self-examination and self-correction. But since
the ecumenical attitude demands primarily that all examine and reform themselves, Catholics must begin with
themselves: they should not assume an attitude of waiting until the others finally decide to give up their own
one-sidedness.

Just as every genuine hospitality begins with making
one's own house a place where others can feel "at home,"

so must we make our own Church a place where fellow Christians can be themselves.

For the Sake of the One Way Toward Unity

Because only a joint reflection of all Christians will make that rapprochement possible, our study is at the same time aimed at inviting the Christians of the Reformation to study these road signs in Catholic ecumenical thought in the spirit of authentic belief in Christ. This might inspire them with the desire to modify the direction of their approach, which until now has been too one-sidedly a protest against the Catholic Church.

Hence this book necessarily calls for a counterpart presented by Reformed Christians. We can very well understand, psychologically and historically, that the Reformed Christians may be afraid to seriously examine Catholic theology. But ecumenically speaking, is this anxiety justifiable? Is it not sinning against the "Ecumene" when he half-consciously fosters such fears? Will the Reformed Christian dare to show the same openness which manifests itself so clearly among many Catholics: will he have the courage to reflect anew on his own faith in the light of the Catholic view? Here is a pressing question that Catholics today feel obliged to ask their Reformed fellow-Christians: will the Reformed Churches, which leave room for a liberalism that undermines Christian faith, refuse to tolerate in their midst Reformed Christians who, in their reflection on the faith, dare to look earnestly in the direction of the Catholic Church? An outsider sometimes gets the impression that Reformed Churches consider ecumenical-minded Christians as more dangerous than extreme liberals.

The Reformed Christian, too, who is profoundly convinced that he is obliged to help fostering the "Ecumene," must dare to ask himself honestly to what extent the

Catholic witness of faith can enrich his own way of being a Christian. The Reformed Christian should recognize the sincerity of our intention when we put the perhaps painful question to him: Are the Reformed Christians aware of the fact that when they anxiously reject the Catholic Church, they are putting obstacles in the way of the "Ecumene"? Once again, it is only by the open-hearted reflection of all Christians that the road will be prepared for the eagerly desired unity of Christ's Church. That is why we desire to repeat here the call Hans Küng made with sincere ecumenical emotion, a call addressed to all divided Christians to enter that one road that leads to unity:

> We should like to beg our Protestant brothers, *all* our Protestant brothers everywhere, that they will, on their side too, keep themselves open towards the Catholic Church and the demands she makes, and come to meet us in brotherly love. We shall have to count on this kind of openness and this kind of coming half-way, if what we ourselves do for the sake of reunion is to have any meaning.
>
> How can Catholics and Protestants come together? We said before, through a renewal of the Church. But this does not only mean a Catholic reform doing justice to all that is valid in Protestant demands. It also means a *Protestant reform doing justice to all that is valid in Catholic demands.* It does *not* mean playing down the truth, soft-pedalling our differences, making false syntheses and easy compromises, but self-searching self-criticism, self-reform—in the light of the Gospel of Jesus Christ, and with our separated brothers in mind.
>
> If Catholics carry out Catholic reform and Protestants carry out Protestant reform, both according to that Gospel image, then, because the gospel of Christ is but one, reunion need not remain a utopian dream. Reunion will then be neither a Protestant "return" nor a Catholic "capitulation," but a brotherly *approach* from both sides, with neither consciously calculating, on the other's be-

half, which of them has more steps to take; an approach penetrated through and through with love, and wholly determined by truth.

Will there be *on* both sides—among Church leaders, theologians and lay-people—enough men of goodwill, ready to go, step by step, along a road which is going to be neither particularly short nor particularly easy? We can take courage and hope from the fact that some important steps have been taken already, even by the Catholic Church, for long believed to be without any positive interest in the challenge of the Ecumenical Movement.[2]

So we shall now begin our renewed Catholic reflection upon God's Revelation in Christ with the hope that this book will be received in the same spirit that has inspired our writing, and we dare to look forward to a reply from the side of the Reformed Christians that will be their contribution to the "Ecumene."

Individual Returns Are Not the Objective

A true ecumenical encounter of divided Christians and the endeavor to arrive together at an ecumenical theology must of necessity start with a profound reflection upon one's *own* way of being-the-Church.

On the one hand that encounter cannot and may not be governed by a secret or open desire for the individual "conversion" or "return" of the partner in the dialogue. The ecumenical encounter properly understood is the coming together of divided Christians who knowingly and deliberately remain members of their own Church. On the other hand, however, through that joint reflection upon God's salvific work in Christ, they wish to discover the one-sidedness that is found in their own experience

2. Hans Küng, *The Council, Reform, and Reunion* (New York, 1961), pp. 144-145.

of faith and thus be able to give to Christ's Church a form
that is pure and more complete.

No Compromise But Ecumenical Openness

We must keep in mind that those encounters are concerned with the understanding and experiencing of the
divine Self-Revelation in the salvific mysteries of the historical life of Christ and of His Church. Hence no Christian may take the responsibility for the religious conviction of the other, when he conscientiously believes he
must reject that conviction as a distortion or a mutilation
of the divine Revelation in Christ. Any reunion which is
not born from a common recovery of Revelation's total
reality but from an irenic compromise must be unconditionally rejected as an attempt to merchandise in the
divine truth for the sake of pseudo-unity. In the existing
division the Churches are unable to recognize one another as equal manifestations of the Church of Christ.
This is the objective, sad situation of divided Christianity; the distress of the children of one same Father. This
we know and are painfully conscious of; this we are
aware of precisely in the presence of a de-Christianized
world that cannot see the perspective of Christ because
of our division. In spite of everything, however, we cannot approach one another differently, there is not yet any
escape because our conscience forbids us to manipulate
the truth.

On the other hand, precisely that distress forces us to
meet the other Christians in order that we may listen to
one another's testimony of faith. In such conversations
we must honestly prepare not only to listen to the testimony of the other but to critically examine our own
vision of faith and the way that vision is expressed, and
determine whether it fully expresses and is the pure
experience of the whole reality of Revelation. Every part-

ner in the dialogue must dare to ask himself whether his tradition does not keep alive some pseudo-opposition to the other that is based only on inherited antagonism.

Once again, no Christian may be asked to put into doubt his own confession and his own experience of faith. But what is asked of him is to render an ecumenical service, to dare to consider the possibility that particular facets of that salvific reality in Christ are not sufficiently incorporated in his own confession or that they have until now been experienced with excessive one-sidedness.

A Divine Impossibility

In meeting Reformed Christians, Catholics may not leave them in uncertainty; they must make it clear to them that, according to their own firm religious conviction, it is only by connection with and fidelity to the Catholic Church, that the search for the fullness of Revelation—for which the Catholic is also still seeking—will be guaranteed against human weakness and be prevented from falling into heresy.

After all, the Church has sprung from God's loving initiative that sent us His Son. It is not man who constructs the Church by entering into believing association with others. Hence the Church is not the work of men. It is a constant actual gift of God who, in the Incarnation of Christ has decisively taken hold of the whole human existence. "This is the stone which was rejected by you builders, but which has become the head of the corner. And there is salvation in no one else, for there is no other name under heaven given among men by which we must be saved" (Acts 4:11-12).

The glorified Lord is a very concrete, historical reality, which has taken shape in those whom He has desired to call His own. "Saul, Saul, why do you persecute me?"

(Acts 9:4). Hence it is not the Church, in the first instance, that clings to Christ with possibly failing human
effort, but Christ Himself holds His Church during all
centuries in the grasp of his salvific plan for men. Christ
and His Church from the beginning and for all ages are
inseparably bound together: "The glory which thou hast
given me I have given to them, that they may be one even
as we are one" (Jn 17:22).

The Church, like Christ's Incarnation, is a reality that
God has given us; as such it is not dependent on us men.
For the Church is antecedent to our desires. So, when
man stands before the divine reality of the Church, he is
placed before the twofold choice: to let himself be taken
up into that reality or to leave that Church either in part
or completely.

Hence the opinion of the Reformation that the Church
during the first fifteen centuries of her existence had
slowly become unfaithful to Christ through human weakness expresses something that is divinely impossible. The
whole apostolic testimony of the young Church can be
summed up in one word: "The glorified Lord lives, He
lives in His Church."[3] "With great power the apostles gave
their testimony to the resurrection of the Lord Jesus, and
great grace was upon them all" (Acts 4:33. Cf. 1:21;
1 Thess. 4:14; Rom. 4:24 and 10:9; 1 Cor. 15:1-7).

2. THE ECUMENICAL DISCOVERY OF OUR TIME

It follows that the Catholic must make it clear to the
Reformed Christian that, according to his firm conviction, the full reality of Revelation in this world can become visible only in the Catholic Church because it is to

3. Lucien Cerfaux, *Le Christ dans la théologie de S. Paul*, 2
(Paris, 1954), pp. 57-71; J. Schmitt, *Jésus résuscité dans la
prédication apostolique* (Paris, 1949), p. XI.

her that the authoritative proclamation of the Gospel and the official administration of the sacraments, as earthly expressions of the personal actions of the glorified Lord, have been entrusted.

But the Catholic must make it equally clear that he wants to bear witness to the ecumenical discoveries of our time. They are the fact that the Catholic Church has not yet appropriated in her thought and life the fullness of Revelation's reality, and the fact that the Reformed Churches can make an essential and authentically Christian contribution, with the help of which the Church of Christ in this world will become the manifest revelation of God's Self-communication to man in Christ Jesus.

It is becoming more evident every day that we are now in the midst of a radical evolution of the relationship between the Catholic and the other Churches. It is still impossible to foresee the outcome of that change. At present it is not yet more than a hesitant beginning, though it has received its official approval in Vatican Council II.

The historical significance of this Council has a parallel in the history of the ecumenical movement in non-Catholic Churches, viz., the establishment of the World Council of Churches in 1948. These Churches desired to express by that action their responsibility for an ecumenical rapprochement, and *as Churches* they officially took over the torch borne by individual ecumenical pioneers. Similarly, during the Vatican Council, the Catholic Church as a whole expressed her responsibility for the unification of the Church of Jesus Christ in the world.

During the solemnities that marked the end of the third session, the Catholic Church, for the first time in the long history of the division of the Western Church, addressed also a message of sincere Christian love to the

Churches of the Reformation in the Decree that dealt
with "the Catholic participation in the ecumenical movement."

Since the anathema of Trent that cut off all communion with those Christians, the Catholic Church, following
her conscience, had for centuries only been able to take a
stand *against* those other Christians while inviting them
to return to the one true Church which she is. The
Churches of the Reformation on their part considered it
their duty to reject that invitation unconditionally as
long as the Catholic Church did not show itself ready to
return to evangelical purity. At that immovable front of
apologetic trenches the mutual attacks were numerous
and strong, and any kind of meeting between the
Churches remained impossible.

The whole tension caused by the unfamiliarity and the
hesitation that accompanied the change in attitude toward those Churches discharged itself during the weeks
that preceded that historic moment. But precisely in the
part of the Decree in which the Catholic Church was
seeking for a new approach to the separated Churches of
the West, a number of changes in the text that many
considered regrettable were introduced at the eleventh
hour for the purpose of securing an unanimous acceptance of the Decree by all the local Communions of the
Catholic Church.

For many bishops the Conciliar discussions of the draft-
ing of the Decree were their first personal confrontation
with the confession of faith of those Churches. And
though those discussions were governed by a spirit of
openness and readiness for a rapprochement, which sur-
prised even the observers belonging to the other
Churches, it is precisely in that part of the message that
we can see very clearly the reserve and hesitation at a

first meeting, after centuries of ever-increasing estrangement from the others.

It would not be honest to speak here of "compromise," of taking a middle course between extreme conservatives and extreme progressives that would yield the maximum that could be obtained at that moment. The Catholic Church, at that last moment consciously took a few steps backward because she did not want to appear to be more than she could be in good conscience at that particular time. It would not have been advantageous to the ecumenical movement if her official message had expressed only the view of those who are ecumenically progressive, at a time when the Church as a whole is not yet "at home" with that progressive view.

A number of local Churches, because of various circumstances which are their unmerited advantages, may already have undergone a strong ecumenical development and acquired great ecumenical openness. To preserve the collegial aspect of their Church consciousness, they must resist the temptation of behaving like a vanguard that no longer wishes to synchronize its tempo with that of the rearguard. They would then become ecumenical isolationists and as such would no longer be able to serve the Church. In the Church of Jesus Christ the invitation to "walk a mile with him" must always be answered by a willingness to accompany the others for two miles, even if this would seem like going backward in order to go forward together (Mt. 5:41).

The Christians who belong to other Churches must, therefore, read that message as an effort made by the inquiring faith of the Catholic Church. Having discovered the genuine Christian testimony of those Christian Communions, she desires once more to define her own position in their regard. Precisely in Section II of Chapter

III, it becomes clear that the Decree which deals with the Catholic participation in the ecumenical movement is not a final standpoint: it does not fix the position of the Catholic Church with respect to the other Churches for the coming decades. We must keep in mind the spirit of the Council that wishes to serve as a pastoral guide amidst a renewed religious reflection and experience of faith: the Decree on Ecumenism must be looked upon as the beginning of an evolving ecumenical attitude within the Catholic Church.

The climate within which the Catholic Church offers her message is the unpretentiousness of a first step. On the one hand, she must avoid every form of ecumenical triumphalism. Because the ecumenical idea has made so much progress in the Catholic Church in so short a time, Catholics must keep in mind that they are still at the beginning of that course. On the other hand, Catholics must not find it strange that the other Churches, considering that modest unpretentious step, find it difficult to be satisfied with that decree. This hesitation on the part of the other Churches is not merely caused by the awareness of the extent of the division that exists between Christians in Christ's Church. This division should not be camouflaged when honest efforts are made toward a rapprochement. Precisely in these efforts the others feel obliged to renew their profession of faith, though it is now purified of misunderstandings in that ecumenical encounter. The second reason for dissatisfaction is that the Decree itself leaves many still unanswered questions for the other Churches. After all, it is only the expression of the groping reflection with which the Catholic Church, in her ecumenical development, tries to find an answer to that protest of the Reformed Churches.

Now, however, a liberating perspective has opened in the *Ecumene* because the Catholic Church is realizing more and more that only in our time is she able to discover the genuine Christian value of the protest of the Reformed Christians. And it is only now that she can arrive at the answer that the Council of Trent and the subsequent centuries were unable to give.

The Reformation began in the critical period of transition from the medieval concept of man and the world to that of modern times. Because it was not yet possible to see matters in an historical perspective during the heat of the religious conflict, the Council of Trent was not able to appreciate the evangelical witness with which Luther desired to take up a stand of protest within the Church. The two religious Communions soon were no longer able to tolerate each other and consider themselves as the one Church of Jesus Christ in spite of profound differences in their understanding of the faith; they refused to develop together and to outgrow the crisis together. They hastily condemned each other and became increasingly estranged from each other while invoking fidelity to Christ. The separation was to last four long centuries. And the conflicting parties no longer felt the necessity nor even the usefulness of coming together for an open dialogue between the Churches.

It is, however, symptomatic for the Catholic reappraisal of the Reformation in our time and for the unsuspected "elbow room" that can be offered in an encounter with respect to all aspects of our division, that now, for the first time, it is historically and dogmatically proved that a Reformed Christian who fully subscribes to the protest of Luther and Calvin concerning the central point of justification-by-faith-alone, is not condemned by the declarations of the Council of Trent.

This does not mean a rejection of the Council of Trent. No Church that believes in Christ's fidelity can be asked to renounce as false any one of her dogmas. The Reformed Churches cannot be asked to take the "road to Canossa." But every Church must be willing to reconsider her own confession when, having met other Christians, she realizes she has too one-sidedly interpreted Revelation because she was too engaged in an apologetic defensive and too attached to an ancient concept of the world.

In spite of the negative attitude to the Catholic Church, the Reformed Churches have continued to recognize that Church as the Church of Jesus Christ. On the other hand, the Catholic Church has declared in her Council that the Holy Spirit has continued to use the separated Communions as instruments of His salvation. Must these declarations of mutual recognition not lead to the startling conclusion that none of the decisions that the Churches have taken toward one another since 1517, can be the full expression of the human experience and interpretation of the salvific presence of the Lord? *In isolation from other Christian Communions, no single Church can be fully the salvific instrument of the Lord.* "Is Christ divided?" (1 Cor. 1:13).

Hence when at this time many Christians belonging to diverse Churches refuse to accept as definitive any historical decision regarding their mutual relations, this has nothing to do with the temptation of a pseudo-conciliatory attitude which is ready, for the sake of a make-believe unity, to sacrifice the integrity of the evangelical message.

They know themselves as the pilgrim people of God, for whom Christ's fidelity alone is definitive whereas their own fidelity is always an unfinished task. In their renewed encounter with other Christians after so many centuries of aloofness they have with genuine sincerity drawn up the balance-sheet of their division. And they know that there still remain many unsolved problems that are an obstacle to their unity. At the same time, however, they have discovered how many sham-battles have been waged along immovable frontlines, because the traditional questions and answers did not always reach the profound core of their dividedness.

The unique character of our present ecumenical situation is that we do not know at all where the frontier between our real and our apparent division lies. No church can enter into an ecumenical conversation with the certainty that she can before hand determine which aspects of our religion's dividedness split the Church and which enrich her. It is therefore an asset of our time that in all Churches there appears a growing readiness to place their entire historical shape and structure into the melting pot of the "Ecumene." Called together around the word of God, we now desire to resume the religious dialogue that was interrupted by both parties centuries ago.

A New Basis for Dialogue

The separated Churches should accept the Decree that deals with the Catholic participation in the ecumenical movement as a first effort of the Catholic Church in her search for a renewed response of faith. If those Churches feel unable to listen to that Decree as a first beginning, they will put it aside as a wholly non-committal expression of love. That acceptance of the Decree does not, of course, wish to disarm a priori every criticism that comes from Reformed Christians.

Many Reformed Christians who followed the events of the Council with intense expectations were disappointed; some wanted to withdraw from the dialogue because the final statements of the Decree fell below their own ecumenical idealism. It was easy for them to quote particular texts from the Decree that, at a first reading, seemed to make all further conversation impossible, for it would appear that the Catholic Church placed herself over against the other Churches as the only true Church and apparently demanded the unconditional return of the others.

Such an interpretation of the Decree would amount to saying that the Catholic Church is trying to put a smoke-screen around her secret intentions, and this would naturally act as an obstacle in the way of ecumenism. So it is necessary to point out to those separated Christians what the true intention of that conciliary document is, viz., to constitute an actual beginning of a renewed dialogue.

This does not mean that their criticism should be absent in that meeting with Roman Catholics. We are divided Christians and we cannot speak with or about others without asking ourselves at the same time whether we have understood the others and have done justice to their religious convictions.

When the apologetic monologue has given way to the ecumenical dialogue, the Catholic Church must be willing to accept the remaining criticism on the part of separated Communions, even after the good intentions expressed by the Council, as a positive contribution to the coming *Ecumene*.

This "elbow room" for criticism of the Decree must remain open; otherwise the starting point of the dialogue will become a terminus, an obstacle that will prevent the further development of the ecumenical endeavor during the coming years.

Being aware that the Lord has put the divided Churches on the road to the *Ecumene*, the Catholic Church wishes by this Decree to indicate the conditions for a new religious dialogue. She knows that the road will be difficult and long and that the end is not yet in sight. In many aspects of religious reflection and living the faith, the oppositions and antagonism are still so deeply present that, at the present stage, a conversation about those subjects is scarcely possible. And yet the impasse must be broken by creating possibilities for a new approach.

Here are some of the fundamentals to be kept in mind for that new dialogue, according to that Decree:

1. The recognition of the other "Communities . . . as means of salvation of the Spirit of Christ" (no. 3):
2. The experience of our unity in Christ is a rich pluriformity (nos. 4 and 16);
3. The recognition that there is room for a hierarchy of values in the life of faith and in reflection upon faith (no. 11);
4. The distinction between the content of faith and the formulation of the faith, between experience of the salvific reality and the always incomplete expression of that salvific event (no. 8).
5. Ecumenical conversation on the basis of equality (no. 9).

a. Dialogue on the Ecumenical Level

There is one question that will be supreme during the coming years in the dialogue between the Catholic Church and the Reformed Churches: What is the ecclesial status of the Christian Communions that, since the sixteenth century, have ceased to consider the bond with the Church of Rome a decisive element as a visible sign of their union-in-faith with Christ?

It is only reflection upon that question that can be the first step on the long road which, for the first time in the history of the divided Church, the Churches now must follow together. *For it is only in the perspective of the other Churches' "Churchness" that a real dialogue is possible*, a dialogue in which the real oppositions are clearly exposed to one another and a joint answer can be formulated as a mutual corrective and enrichment.

In the background of the Decree on Ecumenism stands the renewed Church-consciousness of the Catholic Church, as she has expressed it in the Constitution on the Church of the same Vatican Council. This Constitution manifests a liberation from the one-sided juridical-hierarchical way of experiencing the Church-mystery that came to shape her in the process of an apologetic and defensive struggle. This view of the Church with its rigidly juridical approach inevitably led to the condemnation of the Reformed Churches as erring and illegitimate deviations. In the renewed reflection, the Church is now pictured as the People of God that is already saved in Christ but still on the road to fulfillment in Him.

The lasting significance of the Decree on Ecumenism is that it creates room in the Catholic Church for putting the problem of the "Ecumene" within its full *ecclesial* dimensions. This Decree no longer follows tradition, addressing itself to individual Christians who have broken away and are invited to return to the one true Church, but it turns to the other Churches asking for a dialogue. The Catholic Church may not yet have been able to give a satisfactory answer, but she has caused a break-through in the dilemma that has kept Reformed and Catholic Christians apart for centuries.

On the one hand, because Christ is faithful to His Church, every break in the ecclesial Communion is also a separation from Christ. And restoration of the grace of the bond with Christ can be attained only through a return to a full communion within the Church.

On the other hand, because the Church, as the people of God that is still on pilgrimage, experiences her salvation in Christ in a sinful "broken" condition, no single Communion can claim to be *exclusively* the Church of Jesus Christ. It is only by putting themselves jointly under the judgment of the word of God that the divided Christians can become jointly the Church of Jesus Christ.

The Catholic Church and the Reformation have in the past given exclusive attention to one of those two horns of the dilemma, and starting with a monologue from one of those horns, they have also refused to engage in any genuine dialogue.

The *Decree on Ecumenism* has done away with that predicament in which the Catholic and the Reformed Churches found themselves by the fact that the Catholic Church no longer identifies herself *exclusively* with the Church of Jesus Christ. In this way she opens for herself a view of the genuine ecclesial values that belong to the other Christian Communions. For, in spite of all the things that keep Christians divided, it is the Spirit who guides all to faith in Jesus Christ and binds them together in the one Community of His Church. "It is the Holy Spirit in those who believe, pervading and ruling over the entire Church, who brings about that marvelous communion of the faithful and joins them together so intimately in Christ that He is the principle of the Church's unity" (Decree, no. 2).

One and the same Baptism is the salvific sign and seal which guarantees that the Holy Spirit permanently makes this people called by God the Church of Jesus Christ: "All these justified by faith through baptism are incorporated into Christ. They therefore have a right to be honored by the title of Christians, and are properly regarded as brothers in the Lord by the sons of the Catholic Church" (no. 3).

Divisions in the Church of Jesus Christ cannot reach the foundations, for the Holy Spirit is actively present in all Christian Communions as the principle of ecclesial unity. That is why the Catholic Church recognizes that "some, even very many, of the most significant elements or endowments which together go to build up and give life to the Church herself can exist outside the visible boundaries of the Catholic Church: the written word of God; the life of grace; faith, hope, and charity, along with other interior gifts of the Holy Spirit and visible elements. All of these, which comes from Christ and lead back to Him, belong by right to the one Church of Christ" (no. 3).

Not only does the Catholic Church recognize the bond of faith that binds individual believers to Christ; she also recognizes that the separated believing Communions participate truly in the Mystery of the Church of Jesus Christ, when she declares that the "liturgical functions" of the proclamation of the word and the administration of the sacraments "can truly engender a life of grace, and can be rightly described as capable of providing access to the community of salvation" (no. 3).

The Catholic Church has placed herself on the ecumenical level and made herself an acceptable partner for conversations in the ecumenical movement by the fact that she has in fact subscribed to the Declaration of Toronto: "The Churches recognize in the other Churches elements of the true Church."

All those who know the history of the ecumenical movement realize what a long road the Catholic Church has had to walk so that from her first answer to the ecumenical movement in the Encyclical *Mortalium Animos* (1928) she was able to reach the declaration of the Second Vatican Council that reads: "These separated Churches and Communities, though we believe they suffer from defects already mentioned, have by no means been deprived of significance and importance in the mys-

THE CATHOLIC ECUMENICAL ATTITUDE

tery of salvation. For the Spirit of Christ has not refrained from using them as means of salvation which
derive their efficacy from the very fullness of grace and
truth entrusted to the Catholic Church" (no. 3).

This Declaration would be unattractive if the Catholic
Church simply identified herself with the Church of
Jesus Christ. Many Reformed Christians have understood
those words as expressing such an identification, and it
was to them as if one hand took away what the other
hand had given. But in the very introduction of that
Decree we read that "almost everyone longs that there
may be one visible Church of God, a Church truly universal" (no. 1). The original Latin text speaks of *sit,* that it
may be truly universal. A proposal to change that word to
est (is), which would mean that the Catholic Church
already fulfills the expectation of the ecumenical movement, was rejected during the conciliar discussions.

We notice the same care to prevent that exclusive identification which would put a major impediment in the
way of the ecumenical movement, in the *Constitution on
the Church* that remains the background for the *Decree on
Ecumenism.* The original project of the *Constitution on
the Church* proposed the following profession of faith:
"the one Church of Jesus Christ . . . *is* (*est*) the "Catholic Church" (no. 8), but that term *is* (*est*) was deliberately changed into *subsistit in* so that we read at present:
"This Church, constituted and organized in the world as
a society, *subsists in* the Catholic Church." And the
Council did not grant the wish of some to return to the
original text.

Insiders of the Secretariate for the fostering the Unity
among Christians, which was so greatly involved in the
conciliar discussions concerning that Decree, have declared explicitly that great care was taken in the writing

of the text that the Catholic Church of Jesus Christ should nowhere be simply identified with the Roman-Catholic Church.

Hence when the *Decree on Ecumenism* speaks about the separated Communities that have broken the unity of the Catholic Church, it is not simply the Roman Catholic Church that is meant:

> Our separated brethren, whether considered as individuals or as Communities and Churches, are not blessed with that unity which Jesus Christ wished to bestow on all those whom He has regenerated and vivified into one body and newness of life—that unity which the holy Scriptures and the revered tradition of the Church proclaim. For it is through Christ's Catholic Church alone, which is the all-embracing means of salvation, that the fullness of the means of salvation can be obtained. It was to the apostolic college alone, of which Peter is the head, that we believe our Lord entrusted all the blessings of the New Covenant, in order to establish on earth the one Body of Christ into which all those would be fully incorporated who already belong in any way to God's People (no. 3).

The Decree declares that the unity of the Church of Jesus Christ is present *in a different way* in the separated Communities than in the Roman Catholic Church: they "are not blessed with that unity which Jesus Christ wished to bestow on all. . . ." It does not say that unity is not present in them, nor that unity is present in a perfect way in the Roman Catholic Church.

Similarly, this Decree speaks nowhere about the traditional "return." Although the Catholic Church knows that she is the Church of Jesus Christ, in the ecumenical encounter she has so well learned to understand her own task and tried to become what she is in Christ, and on the other hand has learned so well to appreciate the ecclesial value of the other Christian Communions, that she can-not simply present herself to those Churches as being the realized *Una Sancta,* the One Holy Church.

For she too knows that she is the people of God that is still "away from the Lord" (2 Cor. 1:3,6) and a pilgrim-age to the "Father's house" (Jn 14:1-5). She likewise cannot be fully the Church of Jesus Christ: "Jesus Christ wishes His people to increase under the influence of the Holy Spirit . . . as she (the Church) makes her pilgrim way in hope toward her goal, the fatherland above" (no. 2).

The Church on earth is the people of God that is still in the condition of "self-emptying" which Christ took in his vicarious function on behalf of all men and from which He passed on to glorification with His Father. This is a condition this people has still to endure; the Church "bears in her own body the humility and dying of Jesus (so that she) may daily be more purified and renewed, against the day when Christ will present her to Himself in all her glory, without spot or wrinkle" (Eph. 5:27; Decree no. 4).

Unity, holiness, catholicity and apostolicity are already given in Christ to the Church, as gifts that are at work in her, but they are at the same time a task committed to her, and this she can fulfill only by constantly correcting human sinfulness through the power bestowed on her in her encounter with her Lord: "Every renewal of the Church essentially consists in an increase of fidelity to her own calling. Undoubtedly this explains the dyna-mism of the movement toward unity. Christ summons the Church, as she goes her pilgrim way, to that contin-ual reformation of which she always has need, insofar as she is an institution of men here on earth" (no. 6). "If the faithful are true to this course of action (exercising charity in all things . . .) they will be giving (in the ecumenical dialogue) even richer expression to the authentic catholicity of the Church, and, at the same time, to her apostolicity" (no. 4, par. 7).

By failing in that task and not manifesting fully what she is in Christ and what she can constantly be through Him, the Church is, herself, the cause of their inner division. She has made it necessary for individual Christians and for entire Communities to take a protesting stand against her sinful shortcomings. And because she has not paid proper attention to that protest that was dictated by faith, she has driven them to become dissenters who sadly live apart.

Hence a mutual confession of guilt is the condition for a united Church: "St. John has testified, 'If we say that we have not sinned, we make him a liar, and his word is not in us' (1 Jn 1:10). This holds good for sins against unity. Thus, in humble prayer, we beg pardon of God and of our separated brethren, just as we forgive those who trespass against us" (no. 7, par. 2). For there can be no ecumenism worthy of the name without a change of heart. For it is from newness of attitudes (Eph. 4:23), from self-denial and unstinted love, that yearnings for unity take their rise and grow toward maturity (no. 7, par. 1).

b. Unity in Pluriformity

By recognizing the ecclesial character of the separated Communions, the Catholic Church has made an important contribution to the betterment of the interconfessional climate and she has opened the way on the ecclesial level for a genuine ecumenical dialogue "on an equal footing" (no. 9).

We now leave room in our ecumenical dialogue for the proper character of the Churches because we now see that the unity of local Communions and of individual

Christians can be lived only in a rich pluriformity: "While preserving unity in essentials, let all members of the Church, according to the office entrusted to each, preserve a proper freedom in the various forms of spiritual life and discipline, in the variety of liturgical rites, and even in the theological elaborations of revealed truth" (no. 4, par. 7).

Vatican Council II, which was itself a manifestation of a unity-within-a-rich-variety, discovered that the strong tendency to impose a Western-Latin uniformity upon local Communions has been an obstacle in the way of being truly the Church of Jesus Christ in our own day. And an unsuspected perspective is opened for the "Ecumene" when the Council recognizes that that tendency to uniformity is also responsible for the division of the Church: "From the earliest times, moreover, the Eastern Churches followed their own disciplines, sanctioned by the holy Fathers, by synods, even ecumenical Councils. . . . Such diversity . . . only adds to her (the Church's) comeliness. . . . This sacred Synod declares that the Churches of the East, while keeping in mind the necessary unity of the whole Church, have the power to govern themselves according to their own disciplines. . . . Although it has not always been honored, the strict observance of this traditional principle is among the prerequisites for any restoration of unity" (no. 16, par. 1).

It is only when what is proper to local Communities is fully recognized that being-the-Church of Christ can be experienced as a dialogue in which the various Churches can constantly correct and enrich one another, and all aspects of that Church-mystery can become fully revealed.

This rediscovery of the necessary diversity within the unity of Christ must prompt the Catholic Church to revaluate the ecclesial character of the separated Communities. She can no longer engage in a monologue issuing from Rome that, by making the Church uniform, prevents Communions in East and West from being "at home" in her. She needs the other Communions in order to function fully as the Church of Jesus Christ.

On the other hand, the separate Churches must realize that the dialogue between local Communions presupposes a center by which the native diversity can become legitimized. Because they have been isolated from one another for centuries, they are atrophied and do not possess the fullness of being-the-Church of Christ.

c. Hierarchy of Values

Because the Catholic Church and the Reformed Churches have lived so long in estrangement from one another, there came about an ever stronger and sharper one-sidedness in the life of faith and hence also in the reflection upon the faith. In the apologetic struggle particular aspects of the salvation-mystery were often so one-sided by exaggeration that the opponents seemed to be perfect strangers rather than fellow-Christians.

Yet we ought to remember that, as Christians, we are secure together in the salvific work of Christ who is the only and the absolute foundation of our salvation. In experiencing and reflecting upon that salvific event it is quite natural that certain aspects will be put in the foreground by one while another does not give them that central position. But in an open encounter with one another neither will be ready to deny the value of those aspects.

If we wish to avoid enforcing an amorphous uniformity upon others which will tend to division within the Church, we must live our unity at the center of God's salvific activity with us in Christ and His Spirit; but we must at the same time leave to others the freedom in

Christ to experience the encounter with Christ according to their personal development and national or racial character.

Some have considered this liberating insight the most important contribution of the *Decree on Ecumenism* to the ecumenical movement: "When comparing doctrines they should remember that in Catholic teaching there exists an order or 'hierarchy' of truths, since they vary in their relationship to the foundation of the Christian faith. Thus the way will be opened for the kind of fraternal rivalry to incite all to a deeper realization and a clearer expression of the unfathomable riches of Christ (Eph. 3:8)" (no. 11, par. 3).

d. The Content of Faith and Its Formulation

As ecumenical encounters multiplied on both the pastoral and the theological levels, the divided Christians have had the courage to confess that the way they have experienced and interpreted their own confession has borne the marks of the ghetto, a ghetto within which each Communion felt obliged to cloister itself.

In the past we have exaggerated the oppositions and differences that existed between us because we failed to understand and caricatured the views of the others. Out of "fidelity to Christ" we absolutized the formulation of our confession and exalted it so much that it could no longer be corrected or enriched by other confessions. A quick reference to one's own dogmatic or confessional writings was often considered sufficient to dismiss the opponents.

In conversations with others there is still too little effort to look beyond formulations that are often one-sided and seek for the authentic content of our faith in which we are much more united than we suspect. We have often lacked the humility which is needed to recog-

nize that our own confession is too closely tied to past
phases of history and culture, and particularly marked by
defensive features.

The Churches stand before the task of re-opening the
dialogue that was broken off long ago and that should
enable them to overcome their state of dividedness from
within:

"Christ summons the Church, as she goes her pilgrim
way, to that continual reformation of which she always
has need, insofar as she is an institution of men here on
earth. Therefore, if the influence of events or of the times
has led to deficiencies in conduct, in Church discipline,
or even in the formulation of doctrine (which must be
carefully distinguished from the deposit itself of faith),
these should be appropriately rectified at the proper moment.

"Church renewal therefore has notable ecumenical importance. Already this renewal is taking place in various
spheres of the Church's life: the biblical and liturgical
movements, the preaching of the word of God, catechet-
ics, the apostolate of the laity, new forms of religious life
and the spirituality of married life, and the Church's
social teaching and activity. All these should be considered as favorable pledges and signs of ecumenical progress in the future" (no. 6, par. 2).

3. A NEW MENTALITY

Hence, in the light of that ecumenical discovery the
Catholic Church must first of all earnestly and carefully
reflect upon her own way of proclaiming the faith and
her own life of faith as the human appearance in which
she brings the divine Revelation to the world.

The Catholic Church takes the sin of division very
seriously. She does not confine herself to asking the separated Christians to make allowances for human weak-

nesses with respect to her one-sidedness. She wishes also to ask herself to what extent her human appearance in her arduous course through history and through the cultures of many peoples has been infected by possible limitations and one-sidedness, so that she became a dogmatic and practical scandal to the other Christians who, with the best will in the world, are not able to recognize in her the fullness of divine Revelation. With this honest openness she wishes to look in the mirror of the Reformation witness of faith in order to discover the one-sidedness which disfigures her own countenance.

Secondly, the Catholic Church, in her ecumenical witness, wishes to openly declare that, at the split of the sixteenth century, the Reformation took with it authentic elements of the full Revelation and that these elements are more consciously and more personally experienced and lived in the Reformed Churches. She wishes to acknowledge that she failed to understand the religious need which gave rise to the sixteenth century Reformation, and that nervous attention to the threatened aspects of her own experience of faith led her to see two views of the Revelation in too sharp a contrast.

The Catholic Church, therefore, in this century of the "Ecumene" desires to ask the Reformed Churches to recognize, together with her, the tragedy of Christianity's divided history. Since the sixteenth century we have been estranged from one another through the caricatures we then made of one another. Four hundred years of battle from pre-established positions and fixed trenches, without hope of victory on either side, have tired us out: we possessed neither the will nor the possibility to become acquainted with one another in personal encounters. The picture which we formed of one another in the sixteenth century has for four centuries poisoned our relationship and nourished our mutual animosity.

Today, however, we must ask whether a continuation of these battles would not be quixotic in many respects. Does an authentically Christian conscience really still force us to take such sharply antagonistic positions? At the least, every Christian, every Catholic and every Reformed Christian, is conscience-bound to develop a new picture of the other's conviction, one that is as objective as possible. Each one will have to resist the tendency to let himself be guided in this by the almost ineradicable prejudices of the past. Only then will true ecumenical dialogue be possible with respect to the differences that still separate us in our understanding of the Revelation. The Reformation can make her own authentically Christian contribution to this dialogue for the purpose of letting the Church of Christ in this world attain her full stature as the "Ecumene."

Our Oneness in Christ Is Also Visible

It is of the utmost importance in that encounter of faith that the Catholic Church remain always conscious of the fact that Reformed Christians are not "strangers" to her. First of all, by the fact that we mutually accept the validity of baptism, the Catholic Church professes also that our Reformed fellow-Christians stand in the salvific sign of the salvation-mystery of Jesus Christ. According to the testimony of St. Paul (Rom. 6:3-11), Christ through His solidarity with our sinful humanity has in and through baptism also died, been buried and risen in those fellow-Christians. Hence we recognize them as co-redeemed in Christ and as having been marked as such in baptism; and we wish to meet them as such. Their baptism too has salvific power. Because all Christians through one baptism share in the same life of Christ, the Lord who ascended to Heaven lives His glorified life also in them. This glorified life in Christ pervades their Christian existence, their thought and their experience of faith.[4]

But the Catholic Church must go farther than that. Because baptism is the visible sign and the sacrament of incorporation of all believers in the visible Church of Christ, this participation in the glorified life of the risen Lord takes shape also in the Reformed Churches and in their traditions.[5] Now the Church takes shape where there is a living bond with Christ. As a consequence, the Reformed Christians and the Reformed Communions live by the eternal actuality of Christ's salvific deeds-for-us precisely because and in the measure that the three elements of the visible Church—baptism, faith and apostolic authority—are clearly present. The Catholic Church will have no difficulty in recognizing that these elements exist in the Reformed Churches.

First of all, the baptism that is administered in the Reformed Church is the visible ecclesial foundation for the reception of the other sacraments. The Reformed Christian has the basic capacity with respect to all sacraments.

Secondly, faith in Christ takes shape in the Reformed Churches in their scriptural preaching and profession. These Churches recognize Scripture and the dogmas of the first six ecumenical Councils as authoritative and authentic interpretations of Scripture.

Thirdly, it is true, of course, that there is no formal recognition of the apostolic authority of the Church. But

4. F. Haarsma, "De geldigheid van de Doop in niet-katholieke Kerken," *Tijdschrift voor Theologie*, I 1961, pp. 170-171; M. Thurian, "L'unité visible des chrétiens," *Verbum Caro*, 57 (1961), p. 14.

5. V. Morel, "Le corps mystique du Christ et l'Eglise catholique romaine," *Nouv. Rev. Thom.*, 70 (1948), pp. 703-726; A. Liégé, "L'appartenance à l'Eglise et l'encyclique 'Mystici Corporis Christi' ", *Revue des sciences phil. et théol.*, 32 (1948), pp. 351-358.

the Reformed Churches are seeing more and more clearly that the ecclesial preaching is subject to the judgment of Christian tradition. This recognition by the Reformed Communions of the authority of the Church is confirmed by a view that, recently, has increasingly penetrated into Catholic consciousness, namely, that Christ gave His commission and power to His apostles *within* the believing community of the Church.

It follows that the hierarchical authority to preach functions, not above the Church, but only in organic connection with the faith of the whole Church. This general priesthood of the faithful is a real element in the achievement of the commission given by Christ. When the Reformed Christian sees the particular office blossom forth from the general priesthood of all the faithful, the Catholic need not reject that office and the confirmation of that office as void and meaningless gestures. Catholics can recognize also in the Reformed office a form of the apostolic office because of its bond with the tradition of the Church and the function of the general priesthood.

From these considerations two important conclusions can be drawn that open new perspectives in the ecumenical encounters of the divided Christians:

First, the Catholic Church can recognize that the Reformed Christian is a member of the Church and that the Reformed Communions are visible forms of the Church of Christ.

Secondly, the Catholic Church will have to add that the membership in the Church possessed by the Reformed Christians cannot fully develop and that the Reformed Communions are not in a full living communion with the apostolic kerygma through a formal recognition of the apostolic succession.[6]

6. Hans Asmussen and Wilhelm Stählin, *Die Katholizität der Kirche,* Stuttgart, (1957).

But this restriction does not do away with the fact that the already present unity of the Catholic and Reformed Christians—through the visible sign of baptism, faith and office—is the common foundation upon which *both* are called to bring their genuine Christian heritage into the ecumenical encounter: "pieces that have broken loose from the gold-bearing rock also contain gold" (Pius XI).

Hence the Catholic Church does *not* ask from the Reformed *an unconditional return, nor a capitulation, but that both may grow closer to each other on the basis of their unity in Christ and for their mutual enrichment.* The Reformed Christian ought to know that in thus growing toward unity "he is not asked to sacrifice anything of what God's grace has until now developed as a patrimony of salvation; on the contrary, this will be brought to full accomplishment and completion."[7]

The Catholic Church desires to practice the utmost openness toward the Reformed Churches and firmly hopes that he who is our common Lord will crown the effort made with so much faith by leading us to our visible unity in Christ and the reunion of the Churches in a full "Ecumene."

4. ON THE WAY TO UNITY THROUGH RENEWAL

In this ecumenical century we are now standing at a turning point in the hopeless struggle between divided Christians. There are now possibilities for Catholic and Reformed Christians to find one another, not by continued calling back the separated brethren without doing anything ourselves, not only through moral reformation, but by a genuine renewal of the Churches.

The Catholic Church can fulfill in herself the just

---

7. *Instruction of the Holy Office,* December 20, 1949.

desires of the Reformers and thereby make herself a place where all Christians are "at home." The Churches of the Reformation can realize that the renewal of their religious thinking will constitute a necessary contribution to the fullness of Christ's Church.

> Hence in the 'Ecumene' it is not first of all a question of external reunions, as if we could be simply satisfied with the lessening of the number of Churches. It is rather a matter of a restoration in depth, a qualitative rather than a quantitative change. It is a question of re-discovering an all-embracing vision and experience of God's one plan for mankind, of the place of the Church in it and of the wonder of restored life that Christ accomplishes through her. When that is restored then reunions will occur of themselves.[8]

We cannot bring about the *Ecumene* with less than a Christian dividedness by taking refuge in the ideal of the invisible Church of Christ, in which the unity would already be found:

> It is entirely wrong to look upon the spiritual unity mentioned in John 17, as an invisible unity, as a Platonic idea or a beautiful sentiment, that is hidden in the hearts of the believers, but that does not find any concrete expression in their social life and their witness. The world will believe on the basis of the Church's unity. It must also know through that unity what God has done in Christ. And this cannot possibly take place if the unity is an abstract idea or remains a secret conviction in the hearts of men.[9]

8. H. van der Linde, *De komende oecumenische Kerk,* Serie Verkenningen (Utrecht, 1956), p. 14.
9. W. A. Visser 't Hooft, *The Pressure of Our Common Calling* (London, 1959). Cf. also Jean Jacques van Allmen, "L'attitude chrétienne devant le schisme de l'Eglise," *Verbum Caro,* 53 (1960), pp. 14-29; Ernst Kinder, "Evangelische Katholizität, Zum ökumenischen Horizont der evangelisch-lutherischen Kirche nach Gedanken von Werner Elert," *Kerugma und Dogma,* 6 (1960), pp. 81-82.

We cannot bring about the *Ecumene* with less than a complete renewal of our reflection upon, and our living of, the faith.

Having shown in these considerations that in the Catholic Church there is a possibility of and a readiness for renewal, we must now follow the road of renewing ecumenical reflection.

CHAPTER TWO

OUR INVOLVEMENT IN THE SALVATION MYSTERY THAT THE SON OF THE FATHER IS OUR FELLOWMAN THROUGH THE SPIRIT

When there is a violent storm and the crew who man the rescue-vessel see a ship in trouble, they leave the security of their own homes; animated by a spirit of solidarity with the stricken sailors, they risk their own lives to save their struggling fellowmen and to bring them back to their families. So did the Son of God leave His Father's house to live His perfect being-with-the-Father within the deadly situation of being-with-sinful-men; and this He did to draw them all into the Father's salvific plan for all creation by the humanity the Son would share with us through the Holy Spirit.

> Though he was in the form of God . . .
> he emptied himself,
> taking the form of a servant,
> being born in the likeness of men.
> And being found in human form
> he humbled himself and
> became obedient unto death,
> even death on a cross.
> Therefore God has highly exalted him
> and bestowed on him the name
> which is above every name . . .

60

to the glory of God the Father:
Jesus Christ is Lord (Phil. 2:6-11).

GOD'S SALVIFIC PLAN FOR CREATION IN CHRIST

In his Letter to the Ephesians St. Paul reveals a grandiose view of the completion of God's salvific plan for man and his world, in the mystery of the Incarnation of the Father's Son:

> You have heard of the stewardship of God's grace that was given to me for you, how the mystery was made known to me by revelation, as I have written briefly. When you read this you can perceive *my insight into the mystery of Christ*, which was not made known to the sons of men in other generations as it has now been revealed to his holy apostles and prophets by the Spirit; *that is, how the Gentiles are fellow heirs*, members of the same body, and partakers of the promise *in Christ Jesus* through the gospel.
>
> Of this gospel I was made a minister according to the gift of God's grace which was given me by the working of his power. To me, though I am the very least of all the saints, this grace was given, to preach to the Gentiles the unsearchable riches of Christ, *and to make all men see what is the plan of the mystery hidden for ages in God* who created all things; that through the church the manifold wisdom of God might now be made known to the principalities and powers in the heavenly places. *This was according to the eternal purpose which he has realized in Christ Jesus our Lord*, in whom we have boldness and confidence of access through our faith in him. So I ask you not to lose heart over what I am suffering for you, which is your glory.
>
> For this reason I bow my knees before the Father, from whom every family in heaven and on earth is named, that according to the riches of his glory he may grant you to be strengthened with might through his Spirit in the inner man, and *that Christ may dwell in your hearts through faith;* that you, being rooted and

grounded in love, may have power to comprehend with all the saints what is the breadth and length and height and depth, and to know the love of Christ which surpasses knowledge, *that you may be filled with all the fulness of God.*

Now to him who by the power at work within us is able to do far more abundantly than all that we ask or think, to him be glory in the church and in Christ Jesus to all generations, for ever and ever. Amen (Eph. 3:2-21).

1. THE INCARNATION OF GOD'S SON AS COMPLETION OF GOD'S SALVIFIC PLAN FOR CREATION

a. *Creation as a Salvific Event*

Already in the Old Testament the creation of man and his world are described as a salvific event, as a Divine Self-communication to man. For "God created man in his own image . . . Let us make man in our image, after our likeness" (Gen. 1:26-28).[1]

This biblical concept of man must not be understood as expressing a *static* condition, as if man were like God in his spiritual powers of mind and will and his human spirit were a created image of the divine Spirit. That formulation, however, is found in the Catechism of Trent, "He formed the *soul* after His own image and likeness."

When Scripture calls man the image of God, it desires to express the functional relation that exists between God and man. The image represents the original, it makes present the one who is represented, and tends dynamically to constantly realize an actual encounter of man with the person that it represents. Hence Scripture desires to say that man must experience his existence as a

1. H. van den Bussche, "L'homme créé à l'image de Dieu," *Collationes Gandavenses* (1948), pp. 185-195; P. Humber, *Etudes sur le récit du Paradis et de la chute dans la Genèse,* (Neuchâtel, 1940), pp. 154-175; P. de Haas, *De schepping als heilmysterie,* Den Haag, (1962), pp. 165-173.

continuous actual encounter with God. By the fact that man is created in God's image and likeness a perspective is opened with respect to the mutual relation between God and man—the God who constantly calls the world to being together with Him in His Covenant, and man who experiences that Covenant as the ultimate purpose and the full realization of creation.

What is entirely unique in the faith of Israel is that it is based on the fact that the absolutely transcendent God is forever actuating man, making him realize himself immanently as a creature that gives a personal response to God. God is constantly calling man to existence and is continuously occupied with his salvation, so that man may enter and remain in a personal Covenant-relation with God.

Hence when Yahweh publicly manifests Himself to Moses as "I am who I am" (Ex. 3:14), this scriptural expression contains no philosophical connotation. This "being" of God must be understood as a divine being with His People: Yahweh is there for Israel. He reveals Himself to His people as a helping Presence, as a saving Almighty Power. It is only in the profound experience of that saving Presence that Israel knows its God.

On the other hand, Scripture shows clearly that man is not one creature among many other creatures that have merely a relationship of being to God. Man alone is a person; and he alone, as a personal response to his realization that he is always dependent upon God, is the center of the whole creation. Man, then, is not first created and after that endowed with grace. He is not first given a neutral existence, after which he is called to a choice for God. But man's very existence is a being-constantly-called by God; he is constantly invited to be and live together with God.

The Covenant between God and man is, therefore, the

intimate foundation, the meaning and purpose of creation. And creation is the external ground of the Covenant, the realization of the Covenant. Creation is there
because God desires to enter into a Covenant with man.
Men exist because God constantly calls them to the Covenant. And when Yahweh reveals Himself in His word and
in His salvific action, He makes man discover his existence more and more as the experience of living in the
Covenant.

Those biblical ideas are contained in the expression
"created in God's image and likeness." Human existence
refers to God, it has a similarity with God because man
as a person in his conscious living of the Covenant,
actualizes the meaning of God's self-revelation in creation and in his own existence. In the created world, man
is the immanent representative of the transcendent God.

The full meaning of that Old Testament pattern of
creation, however, is revealed only in the New Testament, namely, in the mystery of the Incarnation of God's
Son as the completion of the Covenant of God with His
creation, as the perfect being-together and living-together
of God and man.

In the epistles of St. Paul, in the Gospel, in the epistles
of St. John and in the epistle to the Hebrews we find the
profession of faith of the young Church to the effect that
He who is the center of the whole salvific history of God's
creation in the salvific events of His human life, is also
involved in the creation of man and of his world.

b. The Salvific Function of the Word Destined to Become Incarnate as the First-Born of All Creation

Christ, as the "Word destined to become man" (*Verbum incarnandum*), as the Word that was destined from
all eternity to live among us in human form, is the
"image of God" according to which God created man. "He

is the image of the invisible God, the first-born of all creation; for in him all things were created, in heaven and on earth. . . . All things were created through him and for him. He is before all things, and in him all things hold together." He is the "mystery hidden for ages and generations but now made manifest to the saints" (Col. 1:15-17).[2]

When Scripture speaks of the pre-existence of Jesus, it does not wish thereby to express His unity of nature with God, or His divine nature, but His oneness with God in the activity of Revelation. Hence it is a question of the salvific function of Christ in the creative act of God: The Father "has made known to us in all wisdom and insight the mystery of his will, according to his purpose which he set forth in Christ as a plan for the fulness of time, to unite all things in him, things in heaven and things on earth" (Eph. 1:9-10).

Christ is the ideal of God's creation, the original pattern of our human nature and the prototype of all human existence. "As he chose us in him before the foundation of the world, that we should be holy and blameless before him. He destined us in love to be his sons through Jesus Christ, according to the purpose of his will" (Eph. 1:4-5). In the Father's salvific plan for the Incarnation of His Son, all men were, all together, and from all eternity, in God's thought; and God willed and loved them.

The mystery to which creation is oriented and that made the Old Covenant tend constantly to an ever greater experience of that dynamic force, is the Father's eternal salvific plan: He willed to communicate Himself wholly to man in His Son who was to become man for us, and He desired in this way to complete creation and make it attain perfect being and living with Him.

2. J. Bonsirven, *Théologie du Nouveau Testament*, (Paris, 1951), p. 272.

Hence all men find the reason for their being, the inner vitality of their life and the final purpose of their life's task in Christ in the likeness of their humanity to that Ideal: "For those whom he foreknew he also *predestined* to be conformed to the image of his Son, in order that he might be the first-born among many brethren" (Rom. 8:29).

Man was created after the pattern of Jesus Christ. Man owes his existence to the Covenant, to God's creative love that wishes to be represented in a creature which can experience that likeness to God in a personal response of love. If this is so, Christ, who is the perfect response of love, is the model of every human union with God. To whom can the Father communicate himself more completely than to the Man who is His Son?

Divine Love that inspired the creation of man is directed to the human life of the Son, in whom the full realization of union of God and man is attained. Creation, as Covenant with God, is interiorly propelled to the sharing in our humanity by the Son, whom the Father has predestined to be Lord of all that exists, and through Him He has also made the universe: "He appointed his son heir of all things, through whom also he created the world. He reflects the glory of God and bears the very stamp of his nature, upholding the universe by his word of power" (Heb. 1:1-3).

This New Testament profession that the world was created through Christ and is permanently called to existence through Him, is the full unfolding of the creation-hymn of Genesis 1, which reveals to us that everything was created by God's mighty word. Every stanza of that hymn begins with the majestic words: "God said."

The view of faith that God's persevering creative act is a Covenant activity, a divine Self-communication to His creation, led already in the Old Testament to a personification of God's word that sounds clearly in Isaiah:

> For as the rain and the snow come down from heaven,
> and return not thither but water the earth,
> making it bring forth and sprout,
> giving seed to the sower and bread to the eater,
> so shall my word be that goes forth from my mouth;
> it shall not return to me empty,
> but it shall accomplish that which I purpose,
> and prosper in the thing for which I sent it (Is. 55:10-11).

The full personification of God's creative word, however, is revealed only in the prologue of St. John's Gospel, in which the perfect unity between the incarnate and the pre-existent Jesus is professed:

> In the beginning was the Word,
> and the Word was with God,
> and the Word was God,
> He was in the beginning with God;
> all things were made through him,
> and without him was not anything made that was made.
> In him was life,
> and the life was the light of men (Jn 1:1-5).

Although John speaks about the Word, as "being" with the Father, actually there is question of the "function" of the Word in the creative activity of God. The words "In the beginning" clearly refer to the account of creation in Genesis, but this is now revealed in its Christological dimensions: the being of the Word is God's salvific activity in His creation, is God's Self-communication to man. For the Word does not stand as God alongside of God. Neither is He inferior to God. But the Word is with God: He is given together with the creative act of God. He is God who reveals Himself in His creation. He is God in His salvific activity with creation: "all things were made through him." That is why He is life, the permanent actual foundation of all that exists.

The whole creation is there because it is permanently willed in Christ by the Father, because the Father loves it as the Christ-mystery that completes itself in time and space. In Christ the Father recognizes creation as a response to His love, because the Word has irradiated the earthly reality with His light and is occupied in leading it to the Father in an increasingly greater likeness to Himself.

In that very beginning of his Gospel, John inserts the theme that will be the dominant of his whole Gospel: Jesus brings us the true, the complete word of God, because He is Himself the Word of God from all eternity. The word of God that is proclaimed by Jesus is at the same time the Word of God lived by Him. That is why there is a profound meaning in the words of John when he recalls that Christ said "if you continue in my word" (Jn 8:31), "if any one keeps my word" (Jn 8:51), and that He promised eternal life to those who listened to His word. It is also in that perspective that we must see the unity of the figurative meaning of the bread as the word of God, and the literal meaning of the bread as the eucharistic self-communication of Jesus in John 6. Paul refers to a similar meaning when he speaks of the "word of the cross" and the "word of reconciliation."

On the basis of the rich meaning that the "word of God" has in St. John's Gospel, the clear parallel between the first words of the story of Genesis and of the Prologue of that Gospel acquire unsuspected dimensions. Here is revealed that the primary aspect of the Incarnation of God's Son is the completion of creation.

The Old Testament consciousness of creation was not the result of a philosophical reflection upon the existence of the world, but it came from the profound experience of God's activity in the Covenant with His people, from the impact of God's intervention in the life of the People of Israel. It is not to man's origin but to his destiny that attention is primarily given; God creates for the purpose of entering into a personal relationship with man.

In His first Self-revelation to Moses God showed Himself as always present to His People, as the divine "being with" man and his world. But it is only in the mystery of God sharing our humanity in Christ that it becomes clear that creation is not merely a matter of the existence of a creature but a matter of man's presence to God, of his "being with" God: in the Father's Incarnate Son man has become a child of the Father.

John makes human existence transparent as a salvific event on the basis of creation as completed in the Christ-mystery; to be created means to be called to be-with-God in and through the Second Person of the Triune God who is, at the same time the "first-born of all creation": Jesus Christ through the bond of love of the Holy Spirit lives as Son by His being-with-the-Father and as the prototype of all human existence gives all men "power to become children of God" (Jn 1:12). This same God Incarnate is both the destiny and the origin of all creation. In the one Person who enjoys the human as well as the divine way of existence we can see God's most profound intention in creation, namely, a perfect personal being together of God and man. This orientation of man to such a personal union of being with God, John expresses when he shows Christ's salvific function.

The connection of the two ideas, that the Word is with the Father and that the Word calls creation to existence precisely as living through the Father, shows that it is not a mere matter of recalling the creative acitivty of the Word, but there is also the question of the orientation of all creation to the Father through the Word. Jesus, as the

Word destined to become man, is the life, the life-princi-
ple, the inner life-force of all existing things precisely
because he is with the Father.

All men live by an inner likeness to Him, who is their
most profound foundation of life; and in Him they stand
oriented to a being-with the Father. But man can discover and experience that inner orientation of his existence only in a personal encounter with Christ. For He
alone, in His Incarnation, has cast a divine light on our
existence, and only through Him can man overcome the
darkness, the sinfulness and the meaninglessness of an
existence that is shut up in itself.

It follows from that Johannine view of creation as a
salvific act in Christ, that creation has essentially religious dimensions. Because the Word in His being-with
the Father is the inner life, the inner foundation of creation, man's existence essentially is already a grace. When
we say that God has created man, this does not mean
that He once at the beginning has given existence to
man, but that He permanently calls him to existence.
Man is not an object amidst other created things. For
man alone is a person amidst the totality of creation. He
is not a "be-ing" but actually a "being-for," a being-di-
rected to the other. He is permanently directed in freedom to being-together with God.

True, it is only in an encounter with Christ in word
and sacrament that man can arrive at a conscious personal experience of that being-with God; similarly, he
can ultimately experience his perfect likeness to the glorified man Jesus Christ only in his own resurrection.
Human existence, nevertheless, is never neutral and
never exclusively sinful. For in the measure that human
existence is lived in obedience to conscience as the experience of being-present to God, it is already grace in
Christ. The encounter with Christ is given together with

human existence reflexively or non-reflexively, experienced sacramentally or anonymously.

The salvific function of the Word destined to become incarnate as the First-born of all creation, can be professed in this way: we owe our existence constantly to Christ and in Him that existence is oriented to the Father; "there is one God, the Father, *from* whom all things, and *for* whom we exist, and one Lord, Jesus Christ, *through* whom are all things and through whom we exist" (1 Cor. 8:6).

c. The Salvific Function of the Word Incarnate as the Perfect Living of God's Plan of Creation

As the Word Incarnate, who in the fullness of time (Gal. 4:4) appeared in our human form of creation, Christ took our human mode of existence into the unity of his divine person (2 Tim. 1:9-10).

Christ lived His co-existence with the Father in His human life for us, that is, in our place and for our benefit. And in this being with us He has effected in all mankind an inner orientation and grace-filled destiny to Himself.

Christ is not only the "image of the invisible God" according to whom man is created, He is not only the "First-born of creation" (Col. 1:15), but He is also the God who is a perfect fellowman: "The goodness and loving kindness of God our Savior appeared" (Tit. 3:4-7). Christ, as the Word that was destined to become man, is not only the inner dynamic pattern of creation that from the beginning has constantly moved man to an increasing awareness of his encounter with God in the Covenant; but He is, precisely as God-man-with-us, for all men the highest realization of human existence as created after God's image.

That is why the salvific mystery of the Incarnation is

in the first place the completion of creation. For Christ,
as the Son of the Father become man with us, lived His
transcendent divine life in union with the Father in an
immanent free human self-realization for our benefit:

> And the Word became flesh
> and dwelt among us
> full of grace and truth;
> we have beheld his glory,
> glory as of the only Son from the Father . . .
> And from his fulness have we all received,
> grace upon grace (Jn 1:14-16).

The Word, destined to become man and which has
molded creation interiorly for being together with the
Father, appeared in the Incarnation as the perfect creature. The Son of God, by living among us as a perfect
fellowman, has revealed to us that creation is a human
being-together-with-His-Father: "We have beheld his
glory, glory as of the only Son from the Father" (Jn
1:14).

The three divine persons live the unity of their divine
life in a personal surrender to one another, in existing
with and for one another. Christ, in His Incarnation,
lived His Sonship through the Holy Spirit, in a complete
self-surrender to the Father. He thereby has given a creatural expression of the inter-trinitarian life: "In him the
whole fulness of deity dwells bodily" (Col. 2:9). And
precisely because the Son lived His personal surrender to
the Father through the dynamic love of the Holy Spirit in
a human way, He has completed and fulfilled creation as
man's being together with God.

The mystery of the Incarnation of God's Son reveals to
us the most profound dimensions of our own human
existence. Only through togetherness with others can
man realize himself in this world. Human existence does

not consist in "being-there" but in "being-*for*," it is being a person who is really oriented to being with others, to interpersonal communion that enables him to become himself.

In Christ as being with us as a fellowman we see a sign of our being together with God. In Christ the other's *you* becomes visible as the divine "You." As we encounter the man Jesus Christ, we can live our human fellowship with Him as a permanent encounter with His Father who has become our Father.

When man, in his daily intercourse with his fellowman, transcends himself in order to realize the possibilities of his human life by being at the disposal of others, this efficacious love for others in Christ becomes the sacrament of his encounter with God. The sovereign, transcendent love the three divine Persons have for us, has received in Christ an interhuman and intraworldly form, and it is only in fellowship with others that it can be responded to: "If any one says, 'I love God,' and hates his brother, he is a liar; for he who does not love his brother whom he has seen, cannot love God whom he has not seen" (Jn 4:20).

In Christ's Church the love for the Father through the power of the Holy Spirit is translated into a mutual love that forms a community of men. In the encounter with Christ man transcends his love for his fellowman. It becomes a lived love for God. For "the divine infinity, as a consequence of the Incarnation, has been transformed into a universal presence of the Christ-mystery. All the good I can do—'*opus et operatio*'—is actually, through some inner aspect, taken up into the reality of the glorified Christ."[3]

Christ, by His being together with man, has given all

3. P. Teilhard de Chardin, *Le Milieu divin* (Paris, 1957), p. 150.

men the real possibility to live their human life as being together with God. In the encounter with Christ, God, in a transcendent act, makes man His partner in a Covenant, and as such man experiences his freedom as the self-realization of God's salvific plan for his life in Christ. Man must, deliberately and with a complete commitment of his whole person, fulfill that divine project that calls for our life in Christ.

In virtue of his encounter with Christ, man is called to the noble life-task of modelling his whole existence in accordance with the ideals, thoughts, and desires that dynamically animated Christ's human life during His historical sojourn in Palestine and that continue to animate Him in His glorified life with the Father.

To live a Christian existence means to become consciously what one already is in virtue of being created in the likeness of Christ. It means to learn to think His thoughts, to live by the eager expectations that gave a dynamic inspiration to His life, to learn to love what He has loved in His unconditional self-surrender.

In an encounter of faith with Christ man constantly enters into an I-You relation with Him. He does not only experience Christ as the Other, as the Incarnate Son of the Father who reveals to Him God's will with respect to the orientation of his life. But he experiences Christ also as a presence. For to the extent that he consciously lives his human existence on the basis of that encounter with Him, he discovers the likeness to Christ of his human existence.

The being-in-Christ determines all his thought, volition and love. "Have this mind among yourselves, which you have in Christ Jesus" (Phil. 2:5). And the more radically a Christian lives his union with Christ, the more intensely he becomes himself and realizes and fulfills the meaning and the task of his human existence: "The life I now live in the flesh I live by faith in the Son of God, who loved me and gave himself for me" (Gal. 2:20).

Because human life is a being-together with God, man experiences his existence as a dialogue, as being spoken to by God and being called to give a response. It is in this that the essence of human freedom is found: it is in that dialogue with the Father, in the forever actual encounter with Christ, that man discovers the real possibilities of God's salvific plan concerning his existence, and that he realizes himself. "I know my own and my own know me, as the Father knows me and I know the Father" (Jn 10:14). Hence, since the time that God's Son became man we can no longer speak about love toward God without calling man to make a true act of faith.

In the light of the perfect response of Christ, the fundamental type of creation, man cannot be content with exercising that act of faith by merely extending an empty hand and doing nothing but receiving gifts; he must exercise it by actively trying to live a Christlike life. That is, he must live his human life the way Christ constantly embodied His being the Son of the Father in a perfect living of our humanity. God's grace in our behalf is an incarnate grace; it can be lived only in genuine human fellowship and in the realization of earthly values.

2. THE INCARNATION OF GOD'S SON AS THE DELIVERANCE OF SINFUL CREATION

Consequently, when Christ came into the world, he said,
"Sacrifices and offerings thou hast not desired,
but a body hast thou prepared for me;
in burnt offerings and sin offerings thou hast taken no pleasure."
Then said I, "Lo, I have come *to do thy will*, O God!". . .
And by that will we have been sanctified through
the offering of the body of Jesus Christ once for all (Heb. 10:5-10).

The salvific mystery of the Incarnation of God's Son is in the first place the completion of creation. But because that mystery is achieved in a sinful creation, which frustrated the execution of God's salvific plan by the negation of Christ, that fulfillment of creation in the mystery of the Incarnation is at the same time creation's deliverance and redemption: "The power of God, who saved us and called us with a holy calling, not in virtue of our works but in virtue of his own purpose and the grace which he gave us in Christ Jesus ages ago, and now has manifested through the appearing of our Savior Christ Jesus who *abolished death and brought life and immortality to light through the gospel*" (2 Tim. 1:9-10).

a. Sin as the Negation of Christ

Man has frustrated the God-given power of his human existence to realize himself in Christ, to live and experience personally in his life what he already is in Christ. His deliberate refusal to live his human existence in a Christ-like way runs counter to God's salvific plan for creation as it manifests itself in the Incarnation of His Son.

Man has opposed his own ideal to God's ideal of human existence. He wished to be equal to God (Gen. 3:5), to be his own law and to determine for himself the aim and orientation of his life.[4] He desired to determine himself what is good and what is evil for man and to be guided in this by his own self-chosen ideal of life. He did not wish to be "at home" with God in the Covenant but to be "at home" with himself. Thus he closed the door on the openness to God contained in his existence and was hopelessly thrown back upon himself. "God created man

---

4. Cf. St. Lyonnet, *De peccato et redemptione*, vol. I, *de notione peccati*, (Rome, 1958); O. Protksch, *Theologie des alten Testamentes*, (Gutersloh, 1950), pp. 632-653.

for incorruption and made him in the image of his own eternity. But through the devil's envy death entered the world, and those who belong to his party experience it" (Wis. 2:23-25).

It is only in the light of God's Covenant with his creation and of human existence as the encounter with Christ that the true dimensions of the mystery of sin become visible. Sin is not experienced in its essence as long as it is exclusively seen as a transgression of God's law, as if man could only become conscious of his guilt with respect to God when a concrete deed is a rejection of God's revealed will. For Scripture sin penetrates much more profoundly into man's existence. Sin is the *situation* in which human existence is empty of God: there is a "separation between you and your God" (Is. 59:2). Sin is the deliberate refusal to live the human existence as the encounter with Christ.

For this reason the Bible can only see the sinful deed, the transgression of God's law, as the inevitable consequence of the all-encompassing fallen condition afflicting human existence through man's radical revolt against God: "Therefore God gave them up in the lusts of their hearts to impurity" (Rom. 1:24-32). For this reason the full dimensions of the sinfulness of man's own existence escape human experience: sin must be believed. The experience of sin is an experience of faith. The consciousness of the guilt embodied in human existence is a religious attitude in which man, in the light of God's revelation in His Covenant and in the mystery of Christ, discovers that in his whole internal attitude of life he is turned away from God, that he continually goes his own way and follows his own ideals.

Isaiah saw his own sinfulness in this light of faith when, called by Yahweh, he discovered that his own existence should be a being-together with the holy God, whose glory must find a creatural reflection in man's experience of creation as the Covenant with God: "Holy is the Lord of hosts; the whole earth is full of his glory." In experiencing the contrast between this divine mandate and the actual turning away of his existence from God, Isaiah could only exclaim: "Woe is to me! For I am lost" (Is. 6:1-5).

Peter also experienced his own sinfulness when during the miraculous catch of fish he encountered God in the man Jesus Christ and discovered in this encounter also God's salvific plan for his own human existence. He could only react to this experience by saying: "Depart from me, for I am a sinful man, O Lord" (Lke 5:8).

Man only experiences sin when the Covenant and the encounter with Christ throw light on the transcendent dimension of his existence and when in the light of faith his own deeds, motives and ideals are unmasked as an often heavily camouflaged refusal to serve God, as a continued secret revolt against God. In sin, as the lived negation of Christ which his life is, man has chosen to be left to his own resources, to be left in lethal aloneness, to be abandoned by God. He has let go the God who in the encounter with Christ is the lasting fountain of life and he thus has delivered himself to death: "Then desire when it has conceived gives birth to sin; and sin when it is full-grown brings forth death" (Jm. 1:15). Man's lonely existence consumes itself, as a fire that is no longer nourished, and burns itself out in his being-dead-for-God.

The full extent of the mystery which sin is lies expressed in the scriptural admonition: "Remember that you were at that time separated from Christ, . . . having no hope and without God in the world" (Eph. 2:12). The essence of sin is revealed to us here in terms of the Christ-centered character of human existence, the uni-

versal orientation of the whole of creation to the incarnate God Jesus Christ: "The light shines in the darkness,
and the darkness did not overcome it" (Jn 1:5).

Man destroyed his being-created to God's image and
likeness, his being like unto Christ, through his sinful
rebellion. What now dominates his deeds and his ideals
is not a personal surrender in Christ to the Father but the
proud attempt to be like unto God (Gen. 3:5). "The true
light that enlightens every man was coming into the
world. He was in the world, and the world was made
through him, yet the world knew him not. He came to his
own home, and his own people received him not." (Jn
1:9-11).

Although sinful man in his negation of Christ continually takes away the foundation of his existence, God
continues to hold fast to him because man's existence is
orientated to its fulfillment in the mystery of Christ. God
still wills sinful man as His partner in the Covenant.
Man's orientation to Christ is the only reason why he
continues to exist in spite of the lethal power of his sin.
This is why those also who do not receive Christ are
called "his people" by John.

The biblical story of the Flood teaches us two things.
On the one hand, man, by his refusal to respond to God's
creative word of the Covenant has lost the reason for his
existence. Man is created for this Covenant. This Covenant is the whole reason for his existence: hence being-
man as being-a-person is essentially a being-called, invited to be together with God. Without adherence to the
Covenant man's existence is not only meaningless and
absurd but also a non-being. Man who is to be together
with God cannot live alone, for "how would anything
have endured if thou hadst not willed it?" (Wis. 11:25).
God's act of creation does not call something into existence once and for all "at the beginning," but is a continu-

ous calling into existence. Because God continually "calls into existence the things that do not exist" (Rom. 4:17), man has a relation of radical dependence to God. Being no longer called by God means not to exist any longer.

From the viewpoint of the Bible, therefore, death cannot be seen as a punishment that is not inherent in sin. By virtue of the holiness proper to the divine Partner in the Covenant and the absolute dependence of the human partner, sin is in itself lethal. The story of the Flood merely makes the essence of man's fall into sin manifest as man's ontic suicide.

On the other hand, this same story also reveals the new dimension of God's salvific will: His faithfulness to his plan of salvation for creation by virtue of this plan's inner orientation to its fulfillment in the mystery of Christ: "God is faithful, by whom you were called into the fellowship of his son, Jesus Christ, Our Lord" (1 Cor. 1:9). Since man's refusal of the Covenant, God's salvific will with respect to man contains a twofold mystery:

1. Through the wholly gratuitous loving initiative of His creative will, God makes man be in Christ as His freely responding partner in the Covenant.

2. Even in man's lethal refusal God continues to hold man in the loving grasp of His salvific plan, for the sake of the completion of creation in the glorified man Jesus Christ as the first-born of all creation.

Sinful man owes his existence to God on a twofold ground: in the Covenant of Creation he owes his existence to God's will of salvation, and in the Covenant of Redemption he owes it to God's mercy. Man does not live solely in the world of the Covenant of Creation, but he also lives his existence in the world of the broken Covenant—the world of original sin—in which he is kept in existence solely by the grace of the Covenant of Redemption in Christ, which began with the promise of the

Redeemer in the "proto-gospel." The world in which man lives is not only continually called forth from nothingness by God, but is also uninterruptedly being redeemed from the destructive power exercised by man's sinful rebellion, which continually estranges him from the reason and the ground of his existence.

Sin not only disturbs man's orientation to God in Christ but also does violence to his conformity to Christ in his psychical and physical existence: " 'Is it I whom they provoke?' says the Lord God. 'Is it not themselves, to their own confusion?' " (Jer. 7:19). The inevitable consequences of sin are not only the disorientation of man's willing, thinking, strivings and passions, but also sickness, suffering and death. The latter are so obviously consequences of sin in scripture that in the first phase of the Old Testament history of salvation, when the idea of resurrection was still lacking, they gave rise to an anxious problem (Job).

Because man's existence is modelled after Christ who, as God-in-human-fellowship-with-us, is the first-born of all creation, man is a corporeal-spiritual being who through sin has turned away from God in his totality and who, therefore, in all the manifestations of his life is marked by death. Sin extends just as far as man's existence: the disharmony in man's relationship with God disturbs the whole of man's existence in this world. The orientation of man's will to itself through sin has as its necessary consequence that the whole of human existence is lowered: it leads to a change in man's being, an ontic disintegration, for sinful man can no longer live his conformity with Christ in his actions and his ideals.

Sin has given the form of death to man's entire physical-psychical existence. For this reason death should not be seen as an external punishment but as a revelation of what sin really is, as the inevitable end to which this sinful human existence is orientated through its fall from its divine elevation in Christ.

b. Sin as a Mystery of the Covenant

In sin the Christian is confronted with the inexplicable mystery of how man can freely turn away from the God on whom he is wholly dependent. The traditional explanation of the presence of sin in creation appealed to God's permissiveness. God created man a free person to such an extent that He realizes man even when man turns away from him. In this explanation physical evil served to explain the presence of moral evil: physical evil was a sign that, in spite of God's action, the creature's activity is so much his own that God's plan of creation can fail. God does not will evil but permits it because good comes from evil: it manifests His justice and especially His mercy.

If, however, creation is exclusively seen from the one-sided standpoint that God gives existence to the creature, the problem of man's freedom with respect to God's absolute sovereignty becomes insoluble, and sin as the denial of God becomes an inexplicable mystery. In the order of creation there is no room for sin: as a creature man cannot be sinful, and as a sinful creature he cannot exist. Through sin man, who continually owes his existence to God, takes away the ground of his own existence. If sin is viewed as a mystery of creation, God would become the author of sin, for God gives reality to sinful man.

Sin, however, is not a mystery of *creation* but of the *Covenant*. The Incarnation of God's Son reveals to us that man realizes his existence in freedom, he realizes his being-man in the encounter with Christ as being-together with God. Christ is not God *and* man, His human activity does not stand over against His divine action, but he lives His divine life as the Son of the Father in His human actions.

In Christ it becomes evident to us that man's existence is a being-of-God and being-to-God: man's relationship to God is not solely a relationship of being but ultimately a personal relation, a relationship of love. The inner ground of man's existence is God's Covenant in the man Jesus Christ. Christ is the completion of creation, precisely because in Him the Father has brought His Covenant with man to full realization. In Christ, the Emmanuel, the "God with us," has become a human reality.

Thus it is only in the continual encounter with Christ that man can realize all the possibilities of his existence as God's partner in the Covenant. Viewed in this salvific dimension, sin appears in an entirely new light as a frustration of the Covenant. Just as the loving response, so also sin is a free deed of man in the Covenant, it is a deed of a partner in the Covenant: "Let no one say when he is tempted, 'I am tempted by God'; for God cannot be tempted with evil and he himself tempts no one; but each person is tempted when he is lured and enticed by his own desire" (Jm. 1:13-14).

Sin is a deed of man as a partner in the Covenant:

> Do not say, "Because of the Lord I left the right way";
> for he will not do what he hates.
> Do not say, "It was he who led me astray";
> for he has no need of a sinful man.
> The Lord hates all abominations,
> and they are not loved by those who fear him.
> It was he who created man in the beginning,
> and he left him in the power of his own inclination.
> If you will, you can keep the commandments,
> and to act faithfully is a matter of your own choice.
> He has placed before you fire and water:
> stretch out your hand for whichever you wish.

Before man are life and death
and whichever he chooses will be given by him (Sir.
15:11-17)

The mystery of sin, then, consists in this that man,
who owes his entire existence to the Covenant and who
through sin, his breach with the Covenant, takes away
the reason for his own existence, nonetheless exists and
continues his sinful existence. This existence of the sinful man cannot be explained in terms of his creature
relationship to God, for a sinful creation is a contradiction. In the order of creation sin, as the turning away of
the totally dependent creature from God, would simply
be suicide.

Sinful man can only be explained in terms of the love
of the God of the Covenant as the inner ground of creation. He does not permit sin, but He still wills sinful man
as his partner in the Covenant: "Where sin increased,
grace abounded all the more" (Rom. 5:20). Because man
is orientated to God in Christ, sin is not yet able to work
out its lethal power. The existence of sinning man is a
pure grace of the Covenant, it is the existence of a man
who strictly speaking, can no longer exist.

The problem of how sin can be harmonized with God's
creative power is a pseudo-problem, and the answer that
God permits sin is even more inappropriate than the
problem. Because God's creative power is essentially directed to the Covenant, it lies, so to speak, beyond the
"range" of sin. For, in spite of the destructive power of
sin, God continues to hold fast to sinful man as His
partner in the Covenant. This is not the same as "permitting" him to sin. God does not preserve sinful man in the
neutral "zone" of creation, for as a creature sinful man
can no longer exist. But, even in man's sinfulness, God
continues to speak to him and to call him by a pure grace
of the Covenant. For this reason man continues to exist

as a possible partner of the Covenant, until creation will be completed in the final fulfillment of the mystery of Christ: "God has consigned (preserved in existence) all men to disobedience, that he may have mercy upon all" (Rom. 11:32).

When the mystery of Christ has been brought to fulfillment, sin will be able to exercise its lethal power upon man in a definitive way. Man's eternal rejection consists in the definitive and uncamouflaged "fixation" of this sinful situation. Abandoned by God without any hope, man will then be delivered up to his continual self-destruction. This does not mean, however, that God leaves sinful man to his fate and that hell is a situation in which man is finally able to be himself. A rejected creature is impossible. Moreover such a view of man's rejection is contrary to God's creative love.

If, then, the rejected man continues to exist because God continues to will him, God does not will him as rejected. Just as God continues to will the sinful men as His partner in the Covenant, so also does He will the rejected man as His partner because for all eternity he is included in the Father's love of Christ. All men stand forever before the Father in Christ as the First-born of all creation: "I have loved you with an everlasting love; therefore I have continued my faithfulness to you" (Jer. 31:3).

The rejected man continues to be wholly orientated to God by virtue of his being-created toward Christ, and in his being-together with Christ he has the possibility to realize God's salvific plan for his existence and for the fulfillment of all his human powers. But, at the same time, the rejected man continually frustrates his conformity with Christ through his negation of Christ. It is not God's absence but precisely God's creative presence to His creature through the latter's essential orientation to

Christ that makes hell truly hell. For man will not experience his eternal rejection as a creature abandoned by
God, but as a sinful and definitively rejected partner of
God's Covenant. Hell does not consist in God's absence
but in the fact that God's presence in the conformity with
Christ of man's existence is experienced as the absence
of God because of man's definitive and uncamouflaged
negation of Christ.

But even sin cannot make creation drop out of God's
hands and it cannot yet fully exercise its deadly power.
For the world, even amid sinfulness, remains always
God's creation. It remains the predestined place in which
the mystery of the Incarnation is accomplished. The salvation history of the Old Testament is animated by the
increasingly clearer inner orientation of creation to
Christ; and in the New Testament man lives, consciously
or still unconsciously, toward the full manifestation of
creation's completion in Christ.

Sinful creation preserves an inner core of goodness
because God continues to will creation in order to complete the Covenant He made with creation, in Christ.
Although sinful man misuses the intrinsically inexplicable continuation of his existence to live in rebellion
against God, God remains faithful to man, in Christ, in
spite of all human unfaithfulness.

Sinful man and his world, then, retain goodness because they are predestined to be the room within which
God's self-communication in Christ will become a full
creatural reality. Hence there can be no question about a
"neutral" sort of divine Providence in which sin becomes
a contradictory mystery, i.e., God does not preserve the
world in existence because it simply happens to be a
world He once created. For the whole of creation is permanently oriented to togetherness with God, in Christ, in

spite of the contradiction of sin and its deadly turning away from God: "For he has made known to us in all wisdom and insight the mystery of his will, according to his purpose which he set forth in Christ as a plan for the fulness of time, to unite all things in him, things in heaven and things on earth" (Eph. 1:9-10).

Even in her sinfulness, creation retains an inner goodness and earthly values; sinful man retains the capacity of being spoken to by God. His likeness to Christ, his being-created after God's image and likeness, man cannot renounce even in his sinful situation. And here is no question of an eternal likeness, of a copy that man can make through his own powers, but the whole of creation has an inner connection with Christ. "This orientation to Christ, and in and through Him to the Father, for man and for his world, means an elevation of which man is incapable by his own powers, although it implies at the same time the richest possible fulfillment of man's inborn natural desire for perfect happiness. That is why that elevation is a pure grace of God, the fruit of His free love."[5]

c. Christ's Solidarity with Sinful Man

Within the evil situation of sinful mankind, God has led His creation to fulfillment by means of His suffering and rising Incarnate Son. He who was predestined as the "first-born of all creation" (Col. 1:15) has, for the benefit of a lethally powerless creation, become "the first-born from the dead" (Col. 1:18), "the first-fruits of those who have fallen asleep" (1 Cor. 15:20).

The Incarnation is God's response to centuries of eager expectation in the situation of a broken Covenant: "But

5. J. C. Groot, "De vestiging van het Rijk Gods," *Jaarboek Kath. Theol. in Nederland,* (1958), p. 97.

our commonwealth is in heaven, and from it we await a Savior, the Lord Jesus Christ, who will change our lowly body to be like his glorious body, by the power which enables him even to subject all things to himself" (Phil. 3:20-21). The mystery of salvation contained in God's entrance into our sinful human relationship is summarized by St. Paul in the words: "Jesus, our Lord, who was put to death for our trespasses and raised for our justification" (Rom. 4:25). If we wish to understand the mystery of salvation in its most profound dimensions, and realize what it means for mankind as a whole and for every man personally, we must try to understand the scriptural ideas of *solidarity* and of the *vicarious role* of the Servant of Yahweh.

At the baptism of Jesus in the Jordan "when Jesus also had been baptized and was praying, the heaven was opened, and the Holy Spirit descended upon him in bodily form, as a dove, and a voice came from heaven, 'Thou art my beloved Son; with thee I am well pleased' " (Lke 3:21-22). In this self-revelation, the three Divine Persons declared the salvific plan of their love in the Incarnation of the Son. This moment at the beginning of His public life was decisive for Christ's self-awareness. For those words are the introduction of Isaiah's prophecy about the suffering Servant of Yahweh: "Behold my servant, whom I uphold, my chosen, in whom my soul delights; I have put my Spirit upon him" (Is. 42:1).

While the other Jews went to John to be baptized for their own sins, Jesus listened to words that indicated that it was not for personal sins that He let Himself be baptized, but that He was appointed to take on the task of the suffering Servant of Yahweh. From that moment Jesus knew that the prophecy of Isaiah had been fulfilled in Him and that He would deliver all sinful mankind through His vicarious suffering:

And the Lord has laid on him the iniquity of us all . . .
It was the will of the Lord to bruise him; . . .
by his knowledge shall the righteous one, my servant,
    make many to be accounted righteous:
and he shall bear their iniquities . . .
Therefore I will divide him a portion with the great,
and he shall divide the spoil with the strong (Is. 53:6-12).

Christ's words reveal to us how He Himself experienced His own baptism: "Are you able to drink the cup that I drink, or to be baptized with the baptism with which I am baptized?" (Mk 10:38). "I have a baptism to be baptized with; and how I am constrained until it is accomplished" (Lke 12:50). From the time of His baptism, Jesus saw the course of His life clearly outlined before Him. The word of John after Christ's baptism stands like a motto written above His life's task that He had freely accepted from the Father: "Behold, the Lamb of God, who takes away the sin of the world: (Jn 1:29, 36).[6] The Old Testament reveals a typical development in the idea of the vicarious function: whereas that function was first assumed or borne by a whole people or community it was more and more borne by a few; salvation history from being concentrated upon all creation, all mankind, is finally concentrated upon one.[7]

Jesus deliberately assumed the task of vicarious suffering for the benefit of all men: "he was numbered with the transgressors" (Is. 53:12), "I tell you that this scripture must be fulfilled in me" (Lke 22:37). We likewise see a manifestation of His awareness that He was the *Ebed Yahweh* in Christ's thrice repeated explicit prophecy about His suffering, death and resurrection: "And he

6. *hamnos thou Theou* is a variant of *pais Theou*, which is the Greek equivalent of the Hebrew *Ebed Yahweh*. Cf. H. W. Wolff, *Jesaja 53, im Urchistentum*, 2nd ed., (1950), p. 86 ff.
7. O. Cullmann, *Christus und die Zeit* (Zurich, 1952).

began to teach them that the Son of Man must suffer
many things, and be rejected by the elders and the chief
priests and the scribes, and be killed, and after three days
rise again. And He said this plainly" (Mk 8:31-32).

But it is in Christ's words and actions at the Last
Supper that we hear in all its fulness the theme of the
Ebed Yahweh, the Servant of Yahweh, who by his vicarious suffering will restore God's Covenant with His people
and with all creation as the Mediator of the Covenant. St.
Paul opens his account of the institution of the Eucharist
with the words, "on the night when he was betrayed"
(1 Cor. 11:23). There is here a clear reference to the
Isaiah-prophecy, concerning the Servant of God who is
delivered to death because "he bore the sin of many" (Is.
53:12).

The words that we find repeated in the Synoptics, "this
is my blood of the Covenant, which is poured out for
many" (Mt. 26:28; Mk 14:24), are the most pregnant
synthesis of the vicarious sufferings of the *Ebed Yahweh*
(Is. 53:4, 10). Also in the repeated command, "do this in
memory of me," there is question of the permanent salvific activity of the *Ebed Yahweh* who is humbled for the
sins of all, but who is exalted precisely because of His
obedient humiliation for the salvation of all: "By his
knowledge shall the righteous one, my servant, make
many to be accounted righteous . . . He bore the sin of
many and made intercession for the transgressors" (Is.
53:11-12).

And in the words pronounced over the cup: "This is
the chalice of the New Covenant in my blood that shall
be shed for many" we see a reference of the Covenant to
the *Ebed Yahweh*, whom "I have given you as a covenant
to the people, a light to the nations (Is. 42:6), "and given
you as a covenant to the people" (Is. 49:8). And this

Covenant will be new, "new things I now declare" (Is. 42:9).

In the scriptural testimony about the institution of the Eucharist, all aspects of the task of the *Ebed Yahweh* are actively present: there is pain and resurrection for the benefit of all, and by it the broken Covenant of God with His creation is repaired and made complete in Him.

d. The Man Who Offered Himself for the Salvation of All Men

When the New Testament sees Jesus as the fulfillment of the prophecy of the *Ebed Yahweh*, it also connects with this the idea of the High Priesthood, by which the full stress can fall upon the deliberate and free acceptance of the sacrifice of his life. "So Christ, having been offered once to bear the sins of many" (Heb. 9:28), is at the same time the High Priest who is offering and the Servant of Yahweh who is offered for all. He is the One who offers Himself for the salvation of all, because, as He perfectly executes God's salvific plan for man, He brings all mankind to completion.

"It was fitting that he, for whom and by whom all things exist, in bringing many sons to glory, should make the pioneer of their salvation perfect through suffering" (Heb. 2:10). By growing in complete accord with the Father's will, He can lead all men to moral perfection: "For a single offering he has perfected for all time those who are sanctified" (Heb. 10:14). He knows our human existence from within. He knows what occupies us each day and in diverse circumstances. He has experienced the constant threat to human life just like ourselves, and come in close contact with sin. The Synoptic Gospels speak about the temptation of Jesus. But there the temptation remains external as it were. It does not touch Jesus. The Epistle to the Hebrews tries to make us penetrate into the salvific significance for us of Christ's temptation. "In the days of his flesh, Jesus offered up prayers and supplications, with loud cries and tears, to him who was able to save him from death, and he was heard for his godly fear. Although he was a Son, he learned obedience through what he suffered; and being made perfect he became *the source of eternal salvation* to all who obey him, being designated by God a high priest after the order of Melchizedek" (Heb. 5:7-10).

We are not permitted to speak about Christ being able to sin. He has not sinned nor could He sin: "he has in every respect been tempted as we are, yet without sinning" (Heb. 4:15). But He has experienced sin, not only formally but also really, precisely because He desired to be one with us: "He is not ashamed to call them brethren" (Heb. 2:11). Christians generally do not sufficiently realize and appreciate the reality of Christ's temptation. And yet we stand here at the salvific center of our encounter with Christ. It is precisely in this experience of sin that the salvific meaning of His sinlessness acquires its full perspective: "Therefore he had to be made like his brethren in every respect, so that he might become a merciful and faithful high priest in the service of God, to make expiation for the sins of the people. For because he himself has suffered and been tempted, he is able to help those who are tempted" (Heb. 2:17-18).

For us Christ struggled with our will in its rebellion against God, by making the Father's will the core of his own freely chosen sacrificial death. And in the struggle to bring this supreme sacrific to the Father on behalf of all, He raised all to perfection. Christ had to suffer with all men in order to be able to become for all the cause of eternal salvation. Precisely because Jesus as the First-born of creation has sanctified our life in the growing sanctification of His human existence, the Letter to the

Hebrews constantly repeats the word *ephapax*, "once and for all": by the definitive and decisive act of His supreme obedience He has "once and for all" realized the salvation of all men. "By that will we have been sanctified through the offering of the body of Jesus Christ once and for all" (Heb. 10:10; 9:26; 10:14). The salvific act of the High Priest has an eternal value for men of all times and countries. That act cannot nor need it be repeated. It is the center of human history, the decisive central point of all times.

e. Adam as the Anti-Type of Christ

Christ became one with us sinful men. Being profoundly conscious of His saving mission in this world He preferably calls Himself the Son of Man. "For the Son of man also came not to be served but to serve, and to give his life as a ransom for many" (Mk 10:45).

When Jesus speaks about Himself as the Son of Man, He does not only wish to express thereby His earthly task as the *Ebed Yahweh* to complete, by vicarious and supreme obedience, in His human existence God's salvific plan for the benefit of all men. He points also to His eschatological function as the Judge of all men, that puts the whole of creation under His jurisdiction in virtue of His vicarious life.

There is an evident parallel between the consent to temptation of man on the morning of his existence and Christ's victory over temptation in the desert at the beginning of His public life. He gave the Father unconditional obedience in contrast with the disobedience of Adam. In this parallel we can see an expression of Christ's awareness that He is the Image of God after which God created man. Christ accepted to experience the temptation of sin as part of the Father's salvific plan. He thus manifests Himself as the Word of God that became man in the fullness of time in order to show fidelity to the destiny of human existence as image of God and vicariously fulfill the commission that man had refused to accept.

The Son of Man stands in a twofold relation to Adam. *Positively,* He shares with Adam the common task of being the image of God, by living His life as a being-to-gether-with-God in the Covenant. It is only in Christ as God who perfectly shares our humanity, that this ideal of creation reached its complete fulfillment; the Incarnation of the Son of God is primarily the completion of creation. The other relation is *negative.* In contrast with Adam's refusal of the Covenant, Christ put vicarious obedience in His human life, and thereby restored God's salvific plan for creation: the Incarnation is at the same time the salvation of man and of man's world. "The first man Adam became a life-giving spirit. But it is not the spiritual which is first but the physical, and then the spiritual. The first man was from the earth, a man of dust; the second man is from heaven. As was the man of dust so are those who are of the dust; and as is the man of heaven, so are those who are of heaven. Just as we have borne the image of the man of dust, we shall also bear the image of the man of heaven" (1 Cor. 15:45-49).

St. Paul sees the whole salvation history from the standpoint of the mystery of the Son of God's Incarnation. The Christ-mystery is already active in the creation of man. The Son of Man is predestined in the creative act of God's love to be the perfect high point of creation as Covenant with God, for the benefit of all men. In the encounter with Jesus Christ, who lived His being with His Father in His being with men, man can live His love for His fellowman and produce earthly values, as a conscious realization of what man already is by virtue of the fact that he is created in the likeness to Christ, namely, the image of God.

Since creation is fulfilled as a Covenant in Christ, we see that God's salvific plan with respect to the creation of man in Adam was an initial realization of the ecclesial community in Christ.

Unfortunately the human partner in the Covenant responded with a sinful refusal. On that account the Covenant, as a beginning in the realization of that Christological dimension of creation came to exist in an unsalutary condition of lethal powerlessness. Though God constantly called man to existence in this unsalutary situation, this call was no longer a reception in Christ's grace. For men can no longer live their lives as being together with God in this unsalutary condition, because their human community has no longer the form of a Covenant lived as human fellowship in Christ, but manifests man's abandonment by God as an all-pervading loveless existence.

Individual men were also abandoned by God because the human community and earthly reality had denied Christ. The possibility of living their lives in Christ as partners in a Covenant was taken away because their interhuman relations and their work no longer appeared to them as an encounter with God.

Over against Christ as the perfect figure of God's salvific plan for His creation stands Adam who is a figure of calamity. He personifies the impotence of the Covenant that was frustrated by man. He personifies the negation of Christ by that calamitous community, a community that was oriented to Christ as the only source of all salvation and was destined to be drawn into the completion of creation in Christ's glorified existence as our fellowman with the Father.

The mystery of original sin consists precisely in this that the actual earthly reality, as the antipode of the mystery of the all-fulfilling human fellowship-with-us of

God's Son, has become the universal source of calamity. All creation is oriented to Christ as the First-born, because Christ has become salvation for man through being our fellowman, and desires to draw all men to salvation through the human community of His Church. Precisely for this reason the earthly reality of human fellowship and of human work has "the power" (cf. Jn 1:12) to become a misfortune for all men through the negation of Christ in man's refusal of the Covenant.

That is why the Son of Man as the divine prototype of mankind entered into the lethally sinful creation, in order to free all men from the situation of desertion by God and complete them as images of God:

> Therefore as sin came into the world through one man and death through sin, and so death spread to all men because all men sinned . . . Adam (who) was a type of the one who was to come.

> But the free gift is not like the trespass. For if many died through one man's trespass, much more have the grace of God and the free gift in the grace of that one man Jesus Christ abounded for many. And the free gift is not like the effect of that one man's sin. For the judgment following one trespass brought condemnation, but the free gift following many trespasses brings justification. If, because of one man's trespass, death reigned through that one man, much more will those who receive the abundance of grace and the free gift of righteousness reign in life through the one man Jesus Christ.

> Then as one man's trespass led to condemnation for all men, so one man's act of righteousness leads to acquittal and life for all men. For as by one man's disobedience many were made sinners, so by one man's obedience many will be made righteous (Rom. 5:12-19).

These words of St. Paul express Christ's consciousness of himself at the beginning of the road on which His Father would lead Him in a sacrificial self-surrender: As the Son of Man and vicariously for the benefit of all men, He would make creation complete the image of God through His obedience as the *Ebed Yahweh:* "You have put off the old nature with its practices and have put on the new nature, which is being renewed in knowledge after the image of its creator" (Col. 3:10). This core of the salvific meaning for us of the Incarnation's mystery, St. Paul expresses in the words: "Put on the new nature, created after the likeness of God in true righteousness and holiness" (Eph. 4:24).

This theme is richly developed in the Christ Hymn of the Epistle to the Philippians:

Have this mind among yourselves which you have in Christ Jesus,
who, though he was in the form of God,
did not count equality with God
a thing to be grasped,

but emptied himself,
taking the form of a servant,
and bestowed on him the name

And being found in human form
he humbled himself and became obedient unto death,
even death on a cross.

Therefore God has highly exalted him
and bestowed on him the name
which is above every name,

that at the name of Jesus
every knee should bow,
in heaven and on earth and under the earth,

and every tongue confess
that Jesus Christ is Lord,
for the glory of God the Father (Phil. 2:5-11).

In the first verse Christ appears as the Son of Man: He "was in the form of God," He was the Image of God. Here is a clear reference to Genesis: "God created man after his own image" (Gen. 1:27). There is no question here, as some translations might suggest, of His divine nature, but of Christ as the prototype and pattern of creation. He alone fully achieves the divine destiny of man, to be the image of God. All men must be transformed to the likeness of Christ who is Himself the perfect image of the Father in virtue of the Holy Spirit: "we all, with unveiled face, beholding the glory of the Lord, are being changed (*metamorphoumetha*) into his likeness from one degree of glory to another; for this comes from the Lord who is the Spirit" (2 Cor. 3:18).

In the verse "(he) did not count equality with God a thing to be grasped" we find an echo of a parallel passage of Genesis:" For God knows that when you eat of it your eyes will be opened, and you will be like God, knowing good and evil" (Gen. 3:5). The sin of Adam consisted in this that he as it were robbed God of the honor that would come from a life of deliberate dependence on Him by autonomously deciding what his human life would be. The Son of Man by living His life of union with the Father in a human way did not rob God of anything. Precisely because He gave a human shape to His divine unity with, and in His perfect obedience to the Father, he fulfilled the task that all men should fulfill, realized the ideal of all human life, namely, that of being an image of God.

In the first and second verses, quoted above, St. Paul sees Jesus as the *Ebed Yahweh* who has been faithful to that task when He emptied His divine form for the benefit of all, and assumed the form of a slave. He who is like the Father accepted to be like to man in man's condition that shows a disfiguration of his likeness to God. And this

He did in order to go to the limit of absolute and unconditional surrender to the Father on the Cross, in contrast
with man's disobedience.

f. Christ's Suffering in Conscious Solidarity with Sinful Man

Desiring to fulfill the design of the Father, namely, to
bring the whole universe, all beings in heaven and on
earth (Eph. 1:9-10), under one Head in Him, Jesus
entered into the situation of sinful man: "Since therefore
the children share in flesh and blood, he himself likewise
partook of the same nature, that through death he might
destroy him who has the power of death, that is, the
devil, and deliver all those who through fear of death
were subject to life-long bondage. For surely it is not with
angels that he is concerned but with the descendants of
Abraham. Therefore he had to be made like his brethren
in every respect" (Heb. 2:14-17).

By desiring to live His being with the Father in our
human way of life that had become subject to sin and
death, He came to take for us the stand we should have
taken, namely, on the side of God's perfect aversion for
sin. By becoming man and "having become a curse for
us" (Gal. 3:13), He made God's wrath against sin descend upon Himself and through His utter struggle with
the deadly power of our disobedience He managed to give
a perfect orientation to our human existence in accord
with God's salvific will, and this He did from within: "For
he is our peace, who has made us both one, and has
broken down the dividing wall of hostility, by abolishing
in his flesh the law of commandments and ordinances,
that he might create in himself one new man in place of
two, so making peace, and might reconcile us both to God
in one body through the cross, thereby bringing the hostility to an end" (Eph. 2:14-16).

The salvific meaning which the Bible ascribes to the

mystery of Christ is foreign to the idea that the suffering of Christ had its source only in an excess of love and that His suffering was not necessary for the salvation of man. The speculative question whether the salvific event of the Incarnation would have occurred if man had not sinned, fails to appreciate Jesus as the First-born of all creation. But even the idea which, without making the Incarnation dependent upon the Fall, cannot recognize the suffering of Jesus as the intrinsic consequence of His solidarity with men, starts from the supposition that a good creation preceded the Fall.

Jesus has fulfilled the divine salvific plan with respect to creation by His obedient living of our human life in a disfigured world. He entered into the unsalutary situation of an as yet unfinished creation that waited for an encounter with God's First-born. Human existence is marked, in its incompleteness, by death as the experience of being abandoned by God in the broken Covenant. By Christ's freely chosen solidarity with God-forsaken man, sin could exercise its deadly power on His life, and Christ's suffering and death became necessary as the full experience of His being-like to man. "He himself bore our sins in his body on the tree" (1 Pet. 2:24). Our sinful human existence brought Him to Calvary where "He has cancelled the bond which stood against us with its legal demands; this he set aside, nailing it to the cross" (Col. 2:14).

On the eve of His Passion, He Himself pointed to His suffering and death as the consequence of God's salvific plan: "I tell you that this scripture must be fulfilled in me" (Lke 22:27). And speaking to the disheartened disciples of Emmaus He stressed likewise, basing Himself on Scripture: "Was it not necessary that the Christ should suffer these things and enter into his glory?" (Lke 24:26).

If we wish to realize fully the salvific meaning which

the mystery of the Incarnation has for us, we must dare to become familiar with the thought that Christ, during His sojourn in Palestine, in a definite respect did not wish to be "with the Father," precisely because He wished to be like us for the sake of our salvation. "While we are at home in the body we are away from the Lord" (2 Cor. 5:6). Now, "the Word became flesh and dwelt among us" (Jn 1:14). That is why "for our sake he made him to be sin who knew no sin, so that in him we might become the righteousness of God" (2 Cor. 5:21).

Here we stand before the perfectly impenetrable mystery of the Incarnation of God's Son, namely, that although Christ was personally without sin, for our sake He lived in our situation of estrangement from God! One who in every respect has been tempted as we are, yet without sin (Heb. 4:15), "for our sake he made him to be sin who knew no sin" (2 Cor. 5:21). We shall never be able to understand that divine-human tension in the Christ. But Scripture forbids that we take anything away from the full salvific significance of the reality of His being-man with us, in our desire to "safeguard" His being-God with the Father. Because of that salvific significance of the Incarnation, we must dare to define so sharply the full reality of Christ's two ways of existence that they become almost unbearable. Basing ourselves on Scripture we must dare to reflect with faith on what it means for us that Christ is truly God *and* truly man. "The question is not that one subject acts in both natures, but we are concerned with their mutual communion. For the Son of God exercises His *divine* power in and through *human* nature and that fact is based on the same relation that permits us to say that even human weaknesses are actually proper to the Son of God."[8]

8. A. Hulsbosch, "De genade in het Nieuw Testament," *Genade en Kerk* (Utrecht, 1953), p. 41.

Hence Jesus has fully experienced on the Cross what it means to be man, that is, to be a sinner before God. "Sending his own Son in the likeness of sinful flesh and for sin, he condemned sin in the flesh" (Rom. 8:3), that is, in the man Jesus Christ, by annihilating his body on the Cross. Never has a man so existentially experienced the distance between the holy God and sinful man in his own life and fathomed the depth of sin, *as the man who was God.*

His cry upon the Cross: "my God, why hast thou forsaken me?" (Mt. 27:46) was the cry of man's way of being that He had made His own; it was the exposure of our sinful situation before God, into which He descended for our sake. Pilate unconsciously revealed the profound salvific meaning of that mystery of suffering when he said: "Here is the man" (Jn 19:5). So does God see man. His suffering was the manifestation of God's judgment on our sinful humanity.

Hence Christ not only desired to take upon Himself the punishment for sin, and the consequences of sin, for our sake, but He desired to accept sin formally, because He desired to experience our own human estrangement from God, as His own way of existence. Although "in him there is no sin" (Jn 3:5) as a personal misdeed, He was personally involved in man's inner guilt before God because He experienced His divine life in a human way.

3. **THE INCARNATION OF GOD'S SON AS THE GLORIFICATION OF CREATION**

"When the days drew near for him to be received up, he set his face to go to Jerusalem" (Lke 9:51). These words reveal to us that Christ's earthly life was a passage in our name and in our behalf to His glorification. Good Friday was no terminus of that way but it was a moment of that glorification. Hence his departure in death and

His exaltation in the Ascension may not be understood in a spatial way; they must be experienced in their salvific meaning for us as a pass-over from our sinful human situation to the glorification of our human existence in Christ with the Father.

For this glorification is accomplished within the confines of His human way of existence. It is the fulfillment of His prayer: "Father, glorify thou me in thy own presence with the glory which I (as the first-born of creation) had with thee before the world was made" (Jn 17:5). It is only in the resurrection, the ascension, and the sending of the Spirit that His solidarity with sinful man blossoms forth and opens up its full perspectives of salvation, and only therein does the Incarnation of God's Son reach the high point of His salvific function: by His life in perfect obedience, by His passion and death, by His resurrection, ascension and the sending of the Spirit, He has raised and led up to the Father our own human existence, and exalted it to a glorified existence with the Father. "The glory which thou hast given Me I have given to them, that they may be one even as we are one" (Jn 17:22).

Christ remains man and in His glorified human existence He is for all men the permanent principle of their pardon and grace. "For it was fitting that he, for whom and by whom all things exist, in bringing many sons to glory, should make the pioneer of their salvation perfect through suffering. For he who sanctifies and those who are sanctified have all one origin. That is why he is not ashamed to call them brethren" (Heb. 2:10-11).

Christ is the first man totally oriented to God who has taken all men with Himself out of their condition of abandonment by God, into His own glorified communion with the Father. "We know that we have passed out of death into life, because we love the brethren" (1 Jn

3:14). "For since we believe that Jesus died and rose again, even so, through Jesus, God will bring with him those who have fallen asleep" (1 Thess. 4:14; cf. 1 Cor. 6:14-15; Rom. 8:11; Eph. 1:3-10).

That is why the new and definitive Covenant between God and all men is concluded in the glorified man Jesus Christ. "He is the mediator of a new covenant" (Heb. 9:15). He has given all men, in the encounter with Him, the possibility to obey the Father as He became obedient to the Father. "Although he was a Son, he learned obedience through what he suffered; and being made perfect he became the source of eternal salvation to all who obey him, being designated by God a high priest after the order of Melchizedek" (Heb. 5:8-10). In him is salvation for all definitively present. "Jesus has gone as a forerunner on our behalf, having become a high priest for ever after the order of Melchizedek" (Heb. 6:20).

Because He has brought to completion God's salvific plan with respect to the creation of man and has done so for the benefit of all, He is our mediator, our permanent intercessor with the Father. "He holds his priesthood permanently, because he continues for ever. Consequently he is able for all time to save those who draw near to God through him, since he always lives to make intercession for them" (Heb. 7:24-25). But at the same time the definitive completion of creation is already actively present in Him: "So Christ, having been offered once to bear the sins of many, will appear a second time, not to deal with sin but to save those who are eagerly waiting for him" (Heb. 9:28).

In this scriptural testimony the salvific presence of the glorified Lord is the permanent actual center of human history. In this saving presence with men of all times and all countries we have not only the perpetuation of the past as His decisive intervention in man's sinful situation, through His vicarious passion and resurrection, but God's future definitive judgment concerning the believing response of man is also already being fulfilled amidst the broken relations of the covenant of creation.

In the last verses of the Christ-Hymn of the Epistle to the Philippians, Jesus appears as the *Kyrios*, the glorified Lord:

> Therefore God has highly exalted him
> and bestowed on him the name
> which is above every name,
> that at the name of Jesus every knee should bow,
> in heaven and on earth and under the earth,
> and every tongue confess
> that Jesus Christ is Lord,
> to the glory of God the Father (Phil. 2:9-11).

In this liturgical hymn the first Christian communities professed their belief that Jesus, in virtue of His accomplished task as the Son of Man—as *Ebed Yahweh*—has received universal dominion over all creation. The young Church saw the event of His resurrection, of His glorification with the Father, as the high point in the course of ages, as the completion of God's salvific plan for creation. Death is definitively overcome. The life of the final age, as a being-together in Christ with the Father, has already begun.

The fact of the Resurrection is not a mere divine guarantee; it is also the realization that in Him our human existence *has attained* the fullness of the creative plan which the Father wishes to actualize by calling each human being into existence.

At this high point of His salvific work, the title of *Kyrios* (Hebrew *Adonai*), which belongs to the Father alone, is passed on to Christ. He who had "not counted equality with God a thing to be grasped" was "designated

Son of God in power according to the Spirit of holiness by
his resurrection from the dead, Jesus Christ our Lord"
(Rom. 1:4). The divine and eternal union with the Father He now experiences in virtue of His utter obedience
as a cosmic dominion over creation, as holding the primacy over all and every thing.

The belief that the Father has passed on to the glorified Christ His own name and His own dominion has
far-reaching consequences for our understanding of
Christ as a person. On that account all God's words and
deeds in the Old Testament can fundamentally be attributed to Christ in the New Testament. With the exception
of the name "Father" all of God's names are transferred
to Christ. That is why in the Epistle to the Hebrews
creation is attributed to Christ: "But of the Son he says
. . . 'Thou, Lord, didst found the earth in the beginning,
and the heavens are the work of thy hands' " (Jn 5:30).

It is clear from the scriptural thought that "He is Son
of God in power, as appears from His rising from the
dead" that belief in Christ's divinity does not rest upon
speculative reasoning, but upon the profound experience
of Christ's exaltation, of His dominion over the Church
and over creation. The experiencing of the fact of the
Resurrection is the foundation of the belief that He, who
from the beginning was God's Son, now exercises divine
dominion in the name of the Father.

Here we find the key for the understanding of the New
Testament Christology: we can speak of the Son only in
relation to the revelatory action of God, and not from the
"being" of God. Christ reveals Himself as God to the
extent that the Father manifests Himself in the salvific
events of Christ's life. He is the self-communicating God:
"I can do nothing on my own authority . . . because I
seek not my own will but the will of him who sent me"
(Jn 5:30). The fundamental unity of the Incarnate Son

with the Father consists in the unconditional unity of will: "My food is to do the will of him who sent me, and to accomplish his work (Jn 4:34).

Jesus experiences His inner life as Son of God in the human fulfillment of the will of the Father: "Whatever (the Father) does, that the Son does likewise. For the Father loves the Son" (Jn 5:20). "Father" is therefore identical with "He who sent me" (Jn 8:16). This being-sent is the life of the Son: "If God were your Father, you would love me, for I proceeded and came forth from God; I came not of my own accord, but he sent me" (Jn 8:42). That is why He is never alone, "for he (the Father) who sent me is with me" (Jn 8:29). That is why He returns to the Father after completing His salvific work: "I came from the Father and have come into the world; again, I am leaving the world and going to the Father" (Jn 16:28). The New Testament knows an unbreakable bond between the person and the work of Jesus Christ because it is only from His absolute dominion that faith in His divinity blossomed forth. We can construct a scriptural Christology only upon the experience of Christ's salvific work as manifesting His being together with the Father: "If I am not doing the works of my Father, then do not believe me; but if I do them, even though you do not believe me, believe the works, that you may know and understand that the Father is in me and I am in the Father" (Jn 10:37-38).

This knowing of Jesus through His works shows that the doctrine concerning the divine and the human nature is not a biblical but a Greek approach to the mystery of Christ. In the Church's struggle against heresy it was necessary for her to find an answer to the questions that were asked her from the standpoint of the Greek image of man. But that view of Christ brought with it the inescapable danger that the Church would speak ab-

stractly about the Son's being with the Father and would
isolate His "divinity" from His work of salvation.

Now from that abstract standpoint we do not get a
complete view of the Person of Christ. For in the scriptural testimony the primary question is not about the
"being" of Christ, but it concerns His salvific function.
When Scripture speaks in Col. 1:15-20, Jn 1:1-4 and
Heb. 1:1-3, about the preexistence of Christ as God, this
testimony must be seen in function of salvation history:
"For us there is one God, the Father, *from* whom are all
things and *for* whom we exist, and one Lord, Jesus
Christ, *through* whom are all things and *through* whom
we exist" (1 Cor. 8:6).

Just as the belief in creation did not arise in the chosen
People of Israel from speculative considerations, but
from the profound experience of God's acting through
the Covenant, so has the Church come to believe that He
who is Lord of all and everything, has also stood in a
relation to all and everything from all eternity in God's
salvific plan of creation.

a. The Salvific Presence of the Glorified Lord in the Church

In the scriptural testimony about Christ there is a
unity between His historical work of salvation and His
present salvific actions in word and sacrament. "So must
the Son of man be lifted up, as Moses lifted up the
serpent in the wilderness, that whoever believes in him
may have eternal life" (Jn 3:14).

His glorification on Mount Tabor is not an anticipation
of His resurrection, but the revelation that His glorification is accomplished in and through His humiliation.
That is why Jesus can speak about the hour of His death
as the hour in which the Son of Man is glorified. "Now is
the Son of man glorified" (Jn 13:31). Here we see with
the eyes of faith the typically Johannine identification of

Christ's being raised on the Cross and His exaltation at the right hand of the Father.

Jesus is our mediator and permanent intercessor with the Father precisely as the glorified man, who in utterly emptying Himself by obedience to the Father for the benefit of us all, has experienced His being-equal to the Father, as *man*. "Unless a grain of wheat falls into the earth and dies, it remains alone; but if it dies, it bears much fruit" (Jn 12:24).[9] Because He has actualized His divine being-like the Father in a perfectly *human* way, He is "able for all time to save those who draw near to God through him, since he always lives to make intercession for them" (Heb. 7:25).

This being-mediator for us with the Father has a two-fold aspect: On the one hand Christ represents in a collective way the whole of mankind saved in Him before the Father. "And round the throne, on each side of the throne, are four living creatures . . . behold, a great multitude . . . . before the Lamb. . . . I saw a Lamb standing, as though it had been slain . . . thou wast slain and by thy blood didst ransom men for God from every tribe and tongue and people and nation, and hast made them a kingdom and priests to our God" (Rev. 4:5-9).

On the other hand Christ constantly in a personal way encounters those who are already saved in Him, but who must still become aware of what they already are in virtue of being created and saved in Him: "All authority in heaven and on earth has been given to me. Go therefore and make disciples of all nations, baptizing them in the name of the Father and of the Son and of the Holy Spirit" (Mt. 28:18-19).

And when Jesus connects with that commission the

9. Cf. O. Cullmann, *La royauté de Jésus Christ et l'Eglise dans le Nouveau Testament* (Paris, 1941).

guarantee, "I am with you always, to the close of the age," there is no question of a protective presence of Christ on the occasion of preaching the word and administering the sacraments, but it means a dynamic presence of Christ in the word proclaimed in virtue of His commission, and in the sacrament administered in virtue of power given by Him. The word and the sacrament are personal acts of the glorified Lord: "He who hears my word and believes him who sent me, has eternal life; he does not come into judgment, but has passed from death to life" (Jn 5:24). "I am the living bread which came down from heaven; if any one eats of this bread, he will live for ever" (Jn 6:51).

It is in function of that twofold form of the eternal mediatorship of Christ with the Father that the mystery of the Church must be appreciated and lived. On the one hand the Church is the salvific community of the glorified Lord, the community of all who realize they are already saved in Christ; she is the People of God already sanctified in Him. But at the same time this People realizes that their salvation in Christ is still incomplete from the subjective standpoint; they are still far from the Lord on their pilgrimage toward a complete union with Him.

On the other hand the Church is the salvific instrument of the glorified Lord: to this community at the same time is given the task and the power to preach His word and administer His sacrament, by which Christ personally makes the individual Christian and the whole believing community realize that their human existence is already saved in Him: "And his gifts were that some should be apostles, some prophets, some evangelists, some pastors and teachers for the equipment of the saints, for the work of ministry, for building up the body of Christ, until we all attain to the unity of the faith and of the knowledge of the Son of God, to mature manhood, to the measure of the stature of the fulness of Christ (Eph. 4:11-13).

b. Cosmic Dominion of the Glorified Lord

The first Christians spontaneously connected their faith in Christ as the Lord of the Church with that in His dominion over the whole creation. The Incarnation is not only a question of a totally new encounter between God and man, but also of a new relation between God and earthly reality.

God's coming in the man Jesus Christ *is* a completion of creation. The Word of God "through whom and for whom all things were created" (Col. 1:16), has fully responded to God's salvific plan for creation by living His human life in obedience. By this life of obedience to the Father and His making use of earthly values, He has reoriented the whole of creation Godwards. His saving presence embraced both man and his world in which He gave concrete form to His human existence. In the Son, the heavenly Father fully realized His salvific intentions in the Incarnation by bringing the universe under one head in Christ, by uniting "all things in him, things in heaven and things on earth" (Eph. 1:10).

If the created earthly reality is the space predestined from all eternity within which God will fully communicate Himself through His Son as our fellowman, then creation has an inner orientation to God, in spite of the fatal helplessness resulting from its state of abandonment by God. In the man Jesus Christ who is wholly oriented to the Father, creation can make good its dormant orientation to God and earthly values can fulfill their own salvific function. For "the creation waits with eager longing for the revealing of the sons of God; for the creation was subjected to futility, not of its own will but by the will of him who subjected it in hope; because the

creation itself will be set free from its bondage to decay
and obtain the glorious liberty of the children of God. We
know that the whole creation has been groaning in tra-
vail together until now" (Rom. 8:19-22).

Already during His stay in Palestine Jesus gave earthly
values the power to exercise that salvific function in the
service of the Kingdom of God, when He cured the sick
through contact with His human body, stilled the storm
by His human voice, used water to work the miracle of
Cana and a few loaves of bread to feed five thousand in
the desert. The fact that Jesus manifested His dominion
over all creation in these deeds is evident from the question He asked the lame man: "Do you believe in the Son
of man?" (Jn 9:35) and from the words He addressed to
the paralytic whom He desired to cure: "That you may
know that the Son of man has authority on earth to
forgive sins—he said to the man who was paralyzed—'I
say to you, rise'" (Lke 5:24). It is in this light that John
places all the miracles of Jesus. They are the sign in Him
of the active dominion of God over the whole creation, of
the Kingdom of God realized in the Son of Man.

God has completed creation and the salvation of man
in the human way of existence of His Son. It is as man
that the Son became obedient to the Father through the
power of the Spirit, as man that He suffered, died and
rose again. But it is also as man that He exercises in His
glorified existence with the Father, His dominion over all
creatures. "It has been testified somewhere, 'What is man
that thou art mindful of him, or the son of man, that
thou carest for him? Thou didst make him for a little
while lower than the angels, thou hast crowned him with
glory and honor, putting everything in subjection under
his feet.' Now in putting everything in subjection to him,
he left nothing outside his control. As it is, we do not yet
see everything in subjection to him. But we see Jesus,

who for a little while was made lower than the angels, crowned with glory and honor because of the suffering of death, so that by the grace of God he might taste death for every one" (Heb. 2:6-9). "Let all the house of Israel therefore know assuredly that God has made him both Lord and Christ, this Jesus whom you crucified" (Acts 2:36). We would misjudge the salvific meaning for us of the mystery of Christ's resurrection, if we isolated His glorification from the earthly reality. For man can realize his existence only in and with his world. He can become himself only by realizing earthly values. Now it is precisely because of the self-development of this man who was willed and redeemed in the First-born of His creation, that the Father permeates all human and earthly values through the Spirit of the glorified Lord: all culture, science, technique, the economy, human society and the State. While retaining their own structure, their own inherent norms and their own development in accordance with these norms, they are taken up into the glorified man Jesus Christ in their own value function, for the full breakthrough of the Kingdom of God that is realized in Him. This cosmic salvation is so realistically experienced by St. Paul that he calls the sin against the bodily dimension of our existence a desecration of a temple of the Holy Spirit" (1 Cor. 6:12-20).

The community of all who experience the redemption of human existence and of earthly reality in Christ, is the incipient incorporation of the whole creation in the glorified Christ. The Church is the instrument of the return of creation to Christ. Her sacraments, in which God's salvific word reaches the fullness of its salvific power through the consecration of earthly reality as a saving sign, presage the final age when the whole of creation will be irradiated by the glory of the man Jesus Christ. That the sacraments are an anticipating sign of that final fulfillment of creation in Christ, we can hear in the words of the *Didache:* "Just as this bread was spread over the mountains and became one after being gathered together, so may your Church be gathered from the extreme ends of the earth for your Kingdom."[10]

In the glorification of His human existence Christ has already brought the whole of creation to fulfillment, and His Church, as the community of salvation redeemed in Him, lives already through that glory. But at the same time He continues through the word and the sacrament of the Church as His salvific instrument, to effect that glory in the subjectively-unredeemed men of all countries and times. This tension between what is already fulfilled and at the same time not yet completed, is the real characteristic both of the Church and of the cosmic reign of Christ. Both are localized in the interval between the ascension and the return of Christ.

It is the time of the Holy Spirit who is given to all, after Christ's glorification and His active presence in the establishment of the Church and in the sanctification of earthly values. But the Spirit is at the same time the "guarantee," the "earnest" of the final completion in Christ, toward which man and his world are still looking forward, full of eagerness (2 Cor. 1:22; cf. 2 Cor. 5:5 and Eph. 1:14).

This is the agreement between the salvific presence of Christ in His Church and His cosmic reign in the earthly reality. Both are bound to the limited period between the ascension and Christ's return. Although God's Kingdom is already present in that reign—"the kingdom of God is in the midst of you" (Lke 17:21)—the Church is not the Kingdom of God, and the Christian can experience the

10. J. R. Harris (ed.), *The Teaching of the Apostles,* (Baltimore, 1887), p. IX.

activity of that Kingdom in the rule of Christ over creation only in the darkness of his faith.

Beside that temporal agreement, there is a spatial difference with respect to the salvific function of the glorified Lord in the Church and in earthly reality; the realm of the Christ's cosmic rule does not coincide with the Church. His rule extends to the whole creation and covers all fields of creativity of the human spirit. The Church, however, is not a field alongside these other fields, but she is the center from which Christ exercises His invisible rule over the whole universe. All those fields lie, with their own values, as concentric circles around the most inner circle of which Christ is the central point.[11] Here we see the tension: on one side the Church, as the Body of Christ, is the dynamic presence of Christ, upon earth; on the other side, the Church, like all parts of creation, is constantly subject to Christ as her Head.

c. The Glorified Lord as Eschatological Judge

Because the Kingdom of God is already an active presence of Christ in His glorified human existence, He is also the judge over all mankind and over the whole creation. Not for ultimate reasons, but on the basis of His vicarious obedience and glorification, every man and all human values are already under His juridical power: the Father "has given him authority to execute judgment, because he is the Son of man" (Jn 5:27). This judgment is not only a condemnation ending in a definitive rejection, but it is also already an acquittal in the earthly situation: "the Son of man has authority on earth to forgive sins" (Mk 2:10).

This eschatological commission lies in the prolongation of His earthly work of salvation. From His aware-

11. O. Cullmann, *Christus und die Zeit*, p. 166.

ness of the fact that He represents all mankind in His suffering and resurrection, Jesus attributes to Himself a decisive task in the final event that is already in the process of being fulfilled. It is the "day of the Son of man" (Lke 17:26) after which He comes "in the glory of the Father" (Mk 8:38) and "shall be seated at the right hand of the power of God (the Father)" (Lke 22:69). This sitting at the right hand of the Father expresses the eschatological function of the Son of Man: "Christ, having been offered once to bear the sins of many, will appear a second time, not to deal with sin but to save those who are eagerly waiting for him" (Heb. 9:28). Because the sentence is based upon the salvific work of the *Ebed Yahweh* that forgives sins, the norm of that sentence lies in the attitude of every man toward His fellowman who lives by being constantly called to existence and to salvation by the completed Man Jesus Christ: "As you did it to one of the least of these my brethren, you did it to me," and "as you did it not to one of the least of these, you did it not to me" (Mt. 25:40, 45).

That is why eternal blessedness for the man who is saved in Christ will consist in likeness to Him who has lived His Sonship of the Father in perfect fellowship with man: "when he appears we shall be like him" (1 Jn 3:2). And it is significant that the definitive fulfillment of creation will be accomplished in the subjection to the Father of the Son who became man for the benefit of all men: "Then comes the end, when he delivers the kingdom to God the Father after destroying every rule and every authority and power. For he must reign until he has put all his enemies under his feet. The last enemy to be destroyed is death. 'For God has put all things under his feet.' But when it says, 'All things are put in subjection under him,' it is plain that he is excepted who put all things under him. When all things are subjected to him, then the Son himself will also be subjected to him who put all things under him, *that God may be everything to every one*" (1 Cor. 15:24-28).

4.   A NEW WORLD-VIEW

When the mystery of Christ as the First-born of the whole creation is made central it necessarily leads to radical changes in the view of the world that we have been familiar with until now. In the sixteenth century the Ptolemaic view of the universe was put aside and replaced by the Copernican image of the world. No less revolutionary is the present change from the Copernican to the evolutionary image of the world. The static view of the world will make room for the dynamic salvific plan of God for His creation in Christ. Creation, supernatural endowment, the fall into sin and salvation, are no longer seen as four successive periods in the history of God's creation, but as aspects of the Christ mystery that is active in the whole salvation history and, with evolutionary power, propels creation to its fulfillment.

This evolutionary image of the world opens new perspectives on earthly reality as the room within which the mystery of Christ is accomplished.

First of all, God's act of creation does not consist in giving existence to the world once at the beginning, but in calling the world constantly to a fuller existence in Christ.

God's transcendent act of creation has no history, it has no past nor future. Creation is called forth from nothing in all its reality at every moment because God constantly wills it in Christ. Hence the beginning of the world is in no way privileged, as if that first moment at the margin of the "nothing" alone had experienced the youthful newness of God's creative love. This newness of the permanent call-out-of-nothing to a being-together-with-God in Christ accompanies the creation in its whole existence and is the dynamic power of evolution as it tends to the fulfillment of creation.

This transcendent creative act of God has its terminus in time, it is immanently accomplished in the earthly reality. God creates man and his world in a dynamic evolution toward the fulfillment of the mystery of Christ. This actual creative act of God in Christ is being accomplished *immanently* in salvation history, for man and his world. God constantly makes creation be itself, with its own inborn possibilities and norms. God constantly creates man in freedom for his self-realization in Christ. In the encounter with Christ in word and sacrament, man can constantly experience and understand his life as a being together with his Father.

These inner laws governing earthly values must be recognized, for from its beginning Christ has set the whole creation on the road to the Father; creation has the inner dynamics of its self-development in Christ: "the place on which you are standing is holy ground" (Ex. 3:5). Hence in the Christian view of the world and of history the accent should not be put on the beginning but on the completion of creation which, by way of cosmic evolution, develops toward its fullness in Christ.

Secondly, the preservation of the world by God must not be understood as causing it to continue to exist, but as God's continuing creative activity that brings the world to its self-unfolding, that makes the world be itself in Christ at every moment of its existence. For, in virtue of God's transcendent creative act, creation does not merely receive its permanent existence, but all creatures act also uninterruptedly in accord with the immanent aptitude of their likeness to Christ: in the restless orientation of creation to its fulfillment in Christ, the higher evolves from the lower, and the new proceeds from the old.

Man must experience his being-in-the-world and his being actively involved in this world as an encounter with God, as being personally involved in the mystery of the Incarnation of God's Son. His work in this world and his daily life with his fellow-man are not a neutral occupation that totally lies outside his being-a-Christian, but it is the earthly and human actualization of his being-saved by the fact that the Son of the Father is a fellow-man of ours.

Thirdly, we may not conceive God's governance of the world as a sort of constant competition with human freedom; it is not a constant invasion of and interference with the creation He realized once upon a time (Molina, Bannez), but it is His transcendent, always eternal act of creation that He accomplishes immanently according to His salvific plan in Christ. God is in the actual process of creating this world in a free self-realization, for the sake of fulfilling that plan of creation.

An evolving creation in which all creatures actualize themselves as being constantly called to existence, is a more impressive proof of God's greatness as a Creator than a cosmos in which God repeatedly intervenes from without by a new act of creation. We do not make God appear greater by making His creation look smaller. Through faith the Christian can make the cosmos transparent as a creation in the making, as constantly drawn and moved by the fact that it is already fulfilled in

Christ: "creation, moved by your attraction."[12] For the Son's Incarnation has given to all human values and all aspects of human life the power to cooperate in the fulfillment of God's creative plan.

Fourthly, God did not first create man and then bestow grace on him. Neither must we think of the Incarnation as something intended by God only in order to save man who had become sinful. We must not think that God after many centuries intervened as Savior in His creation through the Incarnation simply because man had fallen from grace through sin.

The continuous and permanent act of creation is a bestowal of grace on man in Christ. In this actual bestowal of man's self-actualization in Christ there is always the danger that man will be unfaithful to the Covenant and deny Christ, but sinful man is continuously called to existence and on that account God is always acting as Savior of man in order to fulfill the Covenant in Christ.

The evolutionary world view is contrary to the conception of creation as finished at the start, and in which then God intervenes from outside without having to do so. When that evolutionary world view is accepted there can be no longer any question of the gratuitousness of grace, for man's very existence, precisely as called to the Covenant with God in Christ, *is* a bestowal of grace.

The supposition that God could create man without calling him to a life of union with Him is a denial of the Christ-centered character of creation, of the cosmic dimensions of the mystery of Christ. The gratuitousness of grace lies in man being constantly called to existence, to being together with the Father of Jesus Christ; it does not consist in bestowing grace on a man who was first neu-

12. P. Teilhard de Chardin, *Oeuvres,* vol. V, p. 205.

tral, then raised to the supernatural order, and later again fell into sin. A "natural" order does not exist in creation as it actually is, and that is why we cannot form a meaningful picture of such an order.

In this Christological view of creation there is no room for the four successive periods of the traditional view of salvation history: the creation of man, his reception of grace, his fall into sin, and his salvation. For God in the Old Testament constantly creates man for the Covenant as the veiled pre-revelation of the Christ-mystery, and in the New Testament He constantly creates him for communion with the glorified Lord. Hence creation, bestowal of grace, fall into sin and salvation are aspects of the Christ-mystery that evolves in earthly reality. Christ, as God-in-fellowship with man, is the perfect human actualization of God's transcendent act of creation. The Incarnation of God's Son is the completion of creation.

In the New Covenant as participation in the glorified life of the Son of the Father, and in the Old Covenant as veiled pre-revelation of the mystery of Christ, God constantly exercises His forever actual act of creation more fully in the free activity of the human community of faith. Man can discover his own history in the encounter with Christ in the Old and the New Covenant, as the story of the ever richer unfolding of God's "grace-full" action with His creation.

That evolution of creation toward its fulfillment in Christ is accomplished in the permanent struggle against the power of sin that tends to annihilate creation. That is why this being-on-the-way-to-fulfillment is at the same time a permanent redemption from sin in Christ. "Our commonwealth is in heaven, and from it we await a Savior, the Lord Jesus Christ, who will change our lowly body to be like his glorious body, by the power which enables him even to subject all things to himself" (Phil. 3:20-21).

In Christ we are given the power to overcome our sinfulness, for, as involved with Him in His total surrender to the Father, we have the dynamic power of the Holy Spirit which propels us also to our glorification: "And we all, with unveiled face, beholding the glory of the Lord, are being changed into his likeness from one degree of glory to another; for this comes from the Lord who is the Spirit" (2 Cor. 3:18).

5. THE REFORMATION TESTIMONY ABOUT THE INCARNATION

In this biblical climate we can see the possibility of a faith encounter with the testimony of Reformed Christians about the central mystery of God's revelation in this world.

a. Concern for the True Humanity of Christ

The Calvinists in their vision of the salvific event of the Incarnation are particularly eager to safeguard the true humanity of Christ. "He who was the Son of God became the Son of man—not by confusion of substance but by unity of person. For we affirm his divinity so joined and united with his humanity that each retains its distinctive nature unimpaired."[13] Referring to the Council of Chalcedon, Calvin fully stressed the distinction of the divine and the human natures in the one Person of Christ.

It is not the divine nature, but the divine Person of the Word who became man. It is in this divine Person that is anchored the unity and, at the same time, the unmixed

13. Calvin, *Institutes of Christian Religion*, bk. 2, ch. 14, no. 1, Library of Christian Classics, vol. 20, Westminster Press, 1960, p. 482.

distinction between the two natures: "Although they have most strongly defended the unity of Person, the Calvinists have also applied to Christ the principle: *finitum non est capax infiniti* (the finite cannot receive the infinite), and they have upheld this not only in Christ's state of humiliation but even in that of His exaltation. In this way Reformed theology acquired room for a purely human development of Christ."[14]

Reformed Christians deny every indirect influence of the divine nature upon the human nature in Christ because Scripture pictures Christ in His helplessness in Bethlehem, His growth in grace with God and men, His growth in wisdom and knowledge, His moral develoment, His life of faith and confidence, His temptations in the desert, and His state of being abandoned by God on Golgotha: "Scripture tells us about the suffering Son of man, the Man of sorrows, who suffers and sorrows and is filled with anxiety, who prays and weeps and is astonished, who longs for, believes and hopes and has confidence."[15]

Reformed theology stresses so much the true humanity of Christ that in reflections on the Epistle to the Hebrews it maintains that Christ, though in fact He did not sin, knew the possibility of sinning.[16]

b. Christ's Work of Salvation

Christ restored the relation between God and man in the reconciliation through His death and resurrection.

14. H. Bavink, *Gereformeerde Dogmatiek* III, Kampen, (1929), pp. 237-238; Cf. G. C. Berkouwer, *Conflict met Rome*, Kampen, (1949), pp. 254-282.

15. B. C. Berkouwer, *De Persoon van Christus*, Kampen, 1952, p. 186. Cf. *Het werk van Christus*, Kampen, 1953, pp. 191-193.

16. O. Cullmann, *Die Christologie des Neuen Testaments*, pp. 93-94; F. W. A. Korff, *Christologie, De leer van het komen Gods II*, Nijkerk (1941), pp. 146-147; P. Althaus, *Dogmatik II*, p. 108; H. Windisch, *Hebräerbrief*, Tübingen, (1931), p. 39.

The Reformed Christian experiences that salvific work that Christ operates in us completely in the personalistic sphere. His encounter with Christ is a person to person relationship; it is not a real unity of life, not a participation in God's life, no more than the divine nature penetrated the human nature of Christ.

Christ has not saved man insofar as He is the prototype of those who "become partakers of the divine nature" (2 Pet. 1:4). For it is not the presence of the Word of God in our human nature that immediately sanctifies Him and, as the "First-born from the dead," penetrates and divinizes the humanity of all who believe in Him. But it is the Holy Spirit who, through the communication of His gifts, sanctifies Him and makes Him capable of accomplishing His salvific work.

That is why "the communication of properties does not consist in a merger of properties, but it is a communication *to* the one person of the Son."[17] "Let this, then, be our key to right understanding: those things which apply to the office of the Mediator are not spoken simply either of the divine nature or of the human,"[18] but are said of the divine Person of the Word.

c. No "Creature Divinization"

When the Reformation approaches the Christ-mystery in that exclusively personalistic way, in which there is question of the unity of person in two natures that remain what they are, and of the encounter of Christ with man who remains a sinner, it does not want to be misunderstood.

17. H. Bavink, *Gereformeerde Dogmatiek* III, p. 294; Cf. G. C. Berkouwer, *De Persoon van Christus*, p. 236.

18. Calvin, *Institutes*, bk. II, ch. 14, no. 3, *op. cit.*, p. 485. Cf. E. Emmen, *De Christologie van Calvijn*, p. 43; W. J. Aalders, *De Incarnatie*, Groningen, (1933), p. 180.

Every vision concerning the mystery of Christ that accepts a direct sanctification of the human nature of Christ and sees that divinization of His human nature as a model for all who believe in Him, must be radically rejected as a "creature divinization."[19] "The Word takes on the flesh. It remains a question of the Word. We are not permitted to divinize the flesh."[20]

This "extra-calvinisticum"[21] that opposes any kind of inclusion of the divinity of Jesus Christ in the human nature, has been developed to its ultimate consequences by Barth. When we call Christ the Revelation of God, this cannot mean that His humanity participates in divine nature. God does not give Himself as a prisoner to man, not even the man Jesus Christ. Even in Him there remains the infinite distance between God and man, for God's presence in His humanity too is a transcendent event, a continually actual activity. Although Christ is the Revelation of God, He is at the same time the manifestation in His humanity of man's nullity before God: "He places Himself as sinner before sinners. He places Himself wholly under the judgment to which the world is subject. He places Himself even there where God can be present only as an asking for God. He takes on the form of a servant. He goes to the Cross, to death. At the summit, at the end of His way He is only negatively great . . . and precisely in that state of negation ('My God, My God why hast Thou forsaken Me') . . . He is the one who fulfills . . . the possibilities of human development . . .

19. Berkouwer, *De Persoon van Christus*, p. 251.
20. B. C. van Niftrik, *Een Beroerder Israels, Enkele hoofdgedachten in de theologie van Karl Barth*, Nijkerk, (1948), p. 72. Cf. *Kleine Dogmatiek*, Nijkerk, (1946), pp. 81-83.
21. The Heidelberg Catechism, pp. 47 and 48; *De Nederlandse geloofsbelijdenis*, art. 19. Texts in J. N. Bakhuizen van den Brink, *De Nederlandse geloofsbelijdenisgeschriften*, Amsterdam, 1940, pp. 169-170, 93-94.

In Him we really see God's fidelity in the depths of Hell. The Messiah is the end of man. Also there, precisely their God is faithful. The new Day of God's justice will dawn with the Day of the Man 'who was lifted up.' "[22]

d. The Concern of the Reformed Christians

That Reformational way of looking at the mystery of Christ manifests the concern to emphasize, in fidelity to Scripture, as much as possible the *salvific* event that God's Son became incarnate. Two aspects are here given full attention. First, Christ has desired to become wholly like us sinful men, though without personally ever committing a sin. Secondly, God acts in Jesus Christ and through His death, in complete obedience to the Father, we can attain to a totally new personal relation to God.

"He (Calvin) has seen to it that the frontier that delimits the human character should not be crossed, not even in Christ. In the Gospel he saw that the riches of Christ lie precisely in this that He had redeemed us as *one of us*. And that is why he has also been watchful in his Christology lest anything that is truly human in Christ should be erased even after this glorification."[23]

The Reformed Christians do not dare to think through to its full consequences the idea that God became a sharer of human nature and desired to live His divine existence among us in a human way, because they think that if we divinize Christ's human nature we impair the Incarnation's salvific meaning for us. Then Christ would have remained so high above us that we sinners would not be able to reach Him. It is only by becoming com-

---

22. Karl Barth, *Der Römerbrief,* Zollikon-Zürich, 1947, p. 72. Cf. G. C. Berkhouwer, *De triomph der genade in de theologie van Karl Barth,* Kampen, 1954, pp. 116-142.
23. G. C. Berkouwer, *De Persoon van Christus,* p. 242.

pletely like to us that He was able to bring us to a new personal relation with the Father.

6. CATHOLIC REFLECTIONS

a. The Demand for Ecumenical Integration

The Council of Chalcedon was faced with the task of defining the mystery of the divine Revelation in the man Jesus Christ for the believer. Fully aware that this mystery cannot be solved even by a mind that is enlightened by faith, the Church in that Council could not nor did it desire to do more than to trace a few clear boundaries in order to protect the believer's living faith in that encounter with God in Christ against the influence of heresies.

Christ lives in the world of His Father and in the world of man. He participates in the divine life with His Father. (He is "consubstantial" with the Father) but He participates just as much in our human life (He is "consubstantial" with us). Hence every theology that detracts from the fullness of Christ's humanity must as strongly be rejected as a theology that denies the true divinity of Christ.

Out of respect for the mystery that Holy Scripture reveals to us here, the Council did not dare to describe the relation between the divine and the human nature in the one Person of Jesus Christ in any but negative terms, without being able to penetrate into the mystery itself. On the one hand, the two natures in Christ cannot be *divided nor separated,* because of the unity of Person. On the other hand, the two natures cannot be *changed nor mingled* because of the qualitatively infinite distance between God and man (Denziger, no. 148).

In the ecumenical encounter we must ask ourselves the following question: if in their reflections on faith the Reformed and the Catholic Christians both desire to ac-

cept that mysterious description of the mystery of Christ
and to respect these clear boundaries, is there anything
then that obliges them to accuse one another of the
heresy of Nestorianism[24] and of Docetism?[25]

The Reformation rejects the divinization of the human
nature of Christ (habitual grace) because this exaltation
would endanger the true humanness of Christ and because it would be in evident conflict with the testimony
of Holy Scripture that speaks of Christ's uncertainty, the
struggle, anxiety, and temptation.

There has been a shift in emphasis in Catholic thought
about the Christ-mystery, so that Christ is seen primarily
as the Son of the Father who wishes to give shape to His
divine Sonship in the obedient living of His whole human
life. We must therefore ask whether it is not possible
ecumenically to integrate the Reformed and the Catholic
visions.

b. Christ's Human Nature May Not Be Made Autonomous

First, the Council of Chalcedon maintains that the two
natures in Christ are not divided nor separated, because
in Him there is only *one* Person, only one "I." The same
Person was able to say: "I and the Father are one" (Jn
10:30), and at the same time, "My soul is very sorrowful,
even to death" (Mt. 26:38). It is the Son of the Father
who in His human existence gives a visible human shape
to His divine unity of life with the Father, who translates
it into human thinking, human willing, and human love.
"The Father who dwells in me does his works" (Jn
14:10).

In our reflections on faith we must distinguish the
divine nature from the human nature ("not mingled, not
changed"), but we may never separate them, because

24. A. Hulsbosch, *De Genade in het Nieuwe Testament*, p. 25.
25. G. C. Berkouwer, *De Persoon van Christus*. e.g. p. 178.

they are the two ways of existing, the two ways of appearing of the one Person. "Two natures exist only in our thoughts and we are justified in conceiving them because there is something corresponding to them in reality, namely, the fact that Christ is both God and man. But the separation we make in our thinking must in no way make us conclude that there is a twofold reality, for Christ is *one*."[26]

Neither the divine nor the human nature in Christ have an autonomous existence. Though they have their proper character and their proper way of acting, they should not be made autonomous. From this follows an important conclusion, namely, that the humanity of Christ does not have an autonomous holiness, because His holy human life is substantially *one* with the divine life of the Word. Once again, it is the Son of the Father who, in that human way of being, lives His divine unity of life with the Father. The human holiness of Christ is the holiness of the Son who translates His love for the Father, in that human existence: "The humanity of Christ is not a separate principle that is receptive to a participated holiness. The humanity is only the measure and the way according to which the Word manifests His own holiness."[27]

When Catholic theology holds that the union of the Person of the Word is sanctifying grace for the human nature of Christ, it does not try to make His humanity autonomous. For by the personal unity with the Word, the humanity of Christ is taken up into the intersubjec-

---

26. A. Hulsbosch, "De hypostatische vereniging volgens de H. Cyrillus van Alexandrie," *Stud. Cath.* 24 (1949) p. 90. Cf. K. Rahner, *Probleme der Christologie heute, Schriften zur Theologie* I, Einsiedeln, (1954), pp. 169-222; A. Grillmeyer, *Het Christusbeeld in de huidige katholieke theologie, Theologisch perspectief* Vol. II, Hilversum, (1959), pp. 61-94.

27. Hulsbosch, *art. cit.* p. 76.

tive relationship with the Father. The Father testified about the man Jesus Christ: "Thou art my beloved Son; with thee I am well pleased" (Mk 1:11). Also as man Christ knows Himself to be the beloved Son of the Father and is constantly in a personal encounter with the Father: "Do you not believe that I am in the Father and the Father in me?" (Jn 14:10).

The love which the Father has for the man Jesus Christ means a giving of grace to His human life. For precisely because in His human nature He experiences His being-the-Son-of-the-Father, He is in this world the revelation of the Holy Spirit who is the bond of love between the Father and the Son: "God anointed Jesus of Nazareth with the Holy Spirit and with power" (Acts 10:38).

Hence Catholic theology stresses in the man Jesus Christ the distinction between the grace of the unity of Person with the Word, and the grace of the indwelling of the Holy Spirit as a distinct reality on the creatural level. But this is not an unjustified attempt to an autonomous entity. For the pneumatic giving of grace to the man Jesus Christ is the permanently actual creatural expression of His human way of living His unity with the Father.

This idea that the grace of Christ is not an autonomous created reality, was expressed by Patristic theology in the words: "It is created by the very fact of assumption."[28] In other words, by the fact that the Son continually takes up the human nature into the unity of His Person, He sanctifies it, He involves it in His unity with

28. "*Nec sic assumptus est, ut prius creatus, post assumeretur, sed ut ipsa assumptione crearetur,*" Augustinus, *Contra sermonen Arianorum*, 86, P.L. 42, 688. Cf. M. de la Taille, "Actuation créée par Acte incréé," *Rev. Sc. Rel.*, 18 (1928), pp. 253-268; "Entretien amical d'Eudoxe et de Palamède sur la grace d'union," *Rev. Apol.* 48 (1928), pp. 5-26.

the Father through the Holy Spirit. Christ's sanctification by the Spirit is His creatural living of His being-loved-by-the-Father.

At the Jordan, John the Baptist received the revelation of the sanctification of the man Jesus Christ by the Holy Spirit: The Father "who sent me to baptize with water said to me, 'He on whom you see the Spirit descend and remain, this is he who baptizes with the Holy Spirit.' And I have seen and have borne witness that this is the Son of God" (Jn 1:33-34).

c. In the Divinization of His Human Nature Christ Remains Truly Man

Secondly, the Council of Chalcedon formulated as a datum of Revelation that the two natures in Christ are not changed nor mingled, because in Christ, too, the qualitative difference between God and man remains intact.

In Christ there is a truly human way of being-God, because the Son of the Father desired to save us precisely through His solidarity with sinful man. "Since therefore the children share in flesh and blood, he himself likewise partook of the same nature" (Heb. 2:14). This being-taken-up into personal unity with the Word means a sanctification, a divinization of His human nature. Christ lives His being-human in a divine manner. "Believe me that I am in the Father and the Father in me; or else believe me for the sake of the works themselves" (Jn 14:11).

That sanctification of Christ's human nature continually raised it above the possibilities of human nature, albeit within the boundaries of created reality. Although Christ's human nature is divinized, He remains truly man. And although He experiences in His human nature the unity-of-Person with the Word, in Him, too, there is no crossing of the boundaries between God and man, still less are they taken away. In the Father's loving initiative that made Him send His Son in our human and sinful situation, God always remains God and man continues to remain man.

Here we stand at the boundaries of the mystery of Revelation and we are not able to make any positive declaration about it. We shall never be able to understand what it means that God became man. But our believing reflection must respect clear boundaries: the divine and the human natures in Christ do not change nor do they become intermingled.

And here we must ask the Reformed Christian what comes to his mind when he hears the Catholic speak about the divinization of human nature. Doesn't he accuse the Catholic, at least in his thoughts, of adhering to some form of pantheism? This question needs to be raised openly, for from this implicit and often unconscious idea comes opposition and it poisons dialogue; it makes mutual understanding most difficult in spite of much verbal agreement.

The rather plastic language used in Catholic theology, and particularly in Catholic piety does not make it easy for Reformed Christians to completely discard that idea of pantheism. But for the sake of ecumenical rapprochement, we ask the Reformed Christians to listen to and examine the testimony of faith of their Catholic fellow-Christian, knowing for a certain fact that the Catholic, too, fully preserves the infinite distance that exists between God and man, and that he respects man's limitations as a creature.

Man, by divine grace, is raised to the supernatural order, insofar as in his encounter with Christ he receives potencies which he can in no way attribute to himself. Here, in the first place, must be mentioned the divine gifts of faith, hope and charity, by which he learns to see earthly values in the light of God, by which he lives in a dynamic tension toward the complete permeation of human relations by the Kingdom of God, and loves the earthly realities that God loves and in the way God loves them. But he remains a man. This divinization remains within the limits of his being-a-creature.

This is also the vision Revelation gives us of the salvific meaning of Christ's humanity. He is not identical with God in the divinization of His human life. Man's rebellious desire to be equal to God constitutes precisely the nature of sin. Christ desired to be equal to us men, in order to make us equal to the divinization of his human nature. He, too, stood as a recipient before God, as a man who had received grace from God. But He received that divinization of His human nature in the permanent unity-of-Person with the Word. We receive grace constantly from Him in a participated, imperfect but nevertheless real way.

d. Christ is Truly Man

Thirdly, the Son became man. Human nature is His way of appearing to us, His way of existing in our human relationships. He has desired to be God among us in a human way.

Hence His human knowledge is no participation in divine knowledge, making Him know everything that the Father knew. Christ Himself testifies: "But of that day or that hour no one knows, not even the angels in heaven, nor the Son, but only the Father" (Heb. 5:8-9; cf. Lke 2:52). "If we were to speak of communication and participation, we would thereby make an autonomously thinking subject out of His humanity, and destroy the unity of the Godman."[29] In Christ's human knowledge,

29. Hulsbosch, *art. cit.* p. 71.

too, we must maintain the unity of Person of the human nature with the Word. Christ knew God and God's salvific intentions in a human way; hence His knowledge was subject to human development—"And Jesus increased in wisdom and in stature"—and human limitations.

Christ, during His earthly life, reached religious perfection through sanctification of His will. By utter obedience to His Father He sanctified Himself: "Although He was a Son, he learned obedience through what he suffered; and being made perfect he became the source of eternal salvation to all who obey Him" (Heb. 5:9-10). This sanctification of His human nature does not stand independently alongside the sanctity of the Word, but it is the very divine life of the Son that reveals itself in a human way and hence was able to become more perfect in a human way. It is in temptation that we get the clearest understanding of the mystery of the Son as living in a human way. He experienced His Sonship in a human way when He underwent temptation. And in becoming wholly victorious over temptation, He showed His ability to give shape in a divine way to His humanness.

In the temptation we see clearly that His likeness to us is not merely external but that it touches His whole human existence: "For we have not a high priest who is unable to sympathize with our weaknesses, but one who in every respect has been tempted as we are, yet without sinning" (Heb. 4:15). "Therefore he had to be made like his brethren in every respect, so that he might become a merciful and faithful high priest in the service of God, to make expiation for the sins of the people" (Heb. 2:17). In a clear parallelism with the first man who refused to serve God because he desired to live for his own greatness, Jesus at the beginning of His public life was led into the desert by the Spirit and experienced the temptation to found an earthly and political kingdom: "All these I will give you, if you will fall down and worship me" (Mt. 4:9). To that threefold temptation corresponds the thrice repeated prayer in Gethsemane to remove the Passion from Him: "My Father, if it be possible, let this cup pass from me" (Mt. 26:39; cf. Heb. 5:7).

If the Christian refuses to reduce the testimony of Scripture to empty words and to take away from it all salvific meaning, he may not deny the reality of temptation in Christ's life out of lack of faith. It is typical that the Gospel mentions at the end of the temptation in the desert that, "when the devil had ended every temptation, he departed from him until an opportune time" (Lke 4:13), and that Christ reacted sharply to every attempt to make Him manifest His earthly greatness" (Mt. 16:23).

And yet though Christ experienced the reality of temptation, He did not nor could He fall for it. For while experiencing the invitation of sin, He experienced also the invitation of the Father. He desired to be the Son of the Father in being truly man. He has desired to experience and live His being-like-the-Father in His being-like-to-us.

e. True God in a Truly Human Form

The Reformed Christians and the Catholics accept the revealed datum that Christ is true God and true man. And yet they have grown apart in their religious reflection upon the Christ-mystery. The shifting of stress that is now seen in Catholic theology is intended to free the approach of faith to that mystery from all danger of seeing the divine and the human nature in Christ as autonomous principles. *Christ is truly God in a truly human form.*

Is there not here a possibility to ecumenically integrate

the Reformed and the Catholic vision? And would it not be possible to take this as a starting point from which a further perspective could be opened with respect to the salvific consequences of Christ's solidarity in relation to the bestowal of grace upon man: "and being made perfect he became the source of eternal salvation to all who obey him" (Heb. 5:9-10)?

CHAPTER THREE

THE MYSTERY OF THE CHURCH AS BEING TOGETHER WITH THE FATHER THROUGH THE POWER OF THE SPIRIT OF THE GLORIFIED LORD

1. THE SELF-CONSCIOUSNESS OF THE APOSTOLIC CHURCH

Jesus Christ, during His historical sojourn in Palestine, was the one in whom the Triune God's presence in His creation took the form of full fellowship with man. In the Incarnation of the Son of the Father through the overshadowing of the Holy Spirit it is fully revealed to us that creation in its immanent self-development is from the beginning a salvific event, a divine Self-communication to man.

Man is created after God's image and likeness (Gen. 1:27). The profound dimensions of that Old Testament plan of creation become manifest in the central salvation mystery of the New Testament: the utter solidarity of the Son of the Father with the whole of mankind is the fulfillment of the Covenant to which the Father keeps calling His creation. For in the human life of Jesus Christ is accomplished the perfect being-together and the most intimate living-together of God and man.

That (the Word) which was from the beginning (of creation),

which we have heard, which we have seen with our eyes,
which we have looked upon and touched with our hands,
concerning the word of life—
the life was made manifest, and we saw it,
and testify to it, and proclaim to you
the eternal life which was with the Father and was made
manifest to us—
that which we have seen and heard
we proclaim also to you,
so that you may have fellowship with us;
and our fellowship is with the Father
and with His Son Jesus Christ.
And we are writing this that our joy may be complete (1
Jn 1:1-4).

The Believing Community Around the Glorified Lord

According to Scripture the young Church as "eyewitnesses" (Lke 1:2) of the human life of Jesus Christ,
professed the profound salvific meaning-for-us of that
human encounter with the Son of the Father. The first
encounter of the Apostles with Jesus took place in nor-
mal interhuman associations. Jesus fascinated them as a
man. They followed Him because a profound human
power of attraction went out from Him. In an increasingly intimate association with them Jesus Himself gave
them faith in His Person, by which their living with Him
became more and more clearly a human translation of
His living-together-with-the Father. By their human encounter with Christ they discovered more and more in
Him a divine Self-communication, a coming of God in
their concrete human world.

It was only after the resurrection and the ascension
that the Holy Spirit showed them the glorified human
existence of Christ with the Father as the completion of
creation, as the perfect human experience of the divine
Love that communicates itself in the continuous creation
of man. Only then did it become perfectly clear to them

that "in him the whole fulness of deity dwells bodily" (Col. 2:9).

From the day of Pentecost, the Spirit of the glorified Lord—He will "bring to your remembrance all that I have said to you," and "will guide you in all truth" (Jn 14:26; 16:13)—inspired the Apostles to give an ever more complete testimony to the salvific mystery of their encounter with the Son of the Father in their association with the man Jesus Christ.

The whole apostolic preaching is concentrated around the salvific reality that the human life of Jesus, His acts and His words were a constant self-communication of the Son of the Father to all who gave Him a personal surrender in a radical act of faith. The inspiration of the Holy Spirit opened to the minds of the Apostles the two-fold dimension of His existence, namely, He lives completely in the world of the Father and, at the same time, lives completely in our human world.

Hence the apostolic testimony is not an account of the historical human actions of Christ: together with the human experience of His fascinating nearness, there appeared ever more clearly on the horizon of their faith the divine dimension of His human existence. And in their testimony about Jesus they also translated the salvific significance for all of that encounter with God in the man Jesus Christ.

For in that man the Apostles discovered the divine intention of creation. By their faith in Him they rose in that human encounter to a being-with-His-Father. That human life, as the creatural expression of divine Love in which He as the Son lives together with the Father, revealed to them the interior orientation and destiny of their own human existence.

And the Apostles learned to understand this perfect human fellowship of the Son of the Father in its full salvific dimensions: instead of and for the benefit of all men He completely responded to the divine plan of creation with respect to all men, and in His all-embracing resurrection to a glorified human existence with the Father He gives to all who believe in Him, through the sending of His Spirit "the power to become children of God" (Jn 1:12).

The Church lives by the dynamic presence of Him who for the benefit of all men experienced His being-the-Son-of-the-Father in the abandonment by God of our sinful human existence, and who now experiences His divine life with the Father in a glorified human life with us.

2. THE CHURCH IN BIBLICAL PERSPECTIVE

The word *ekklesia*, as used in the New Testament, can have the purely profane meaning of "a gathering of the people" (Acts 19:30, 40). But most of the time it signifies a religious-theological idea. And as such it goes back to the Old Testament word *kahal* or *kehâl*, the awareness of the people of Israel, that it is the community of the Covenant with Yahweh. The *ekklesia* (from *ek-kalein*, to call forth, to call up) is the people of the Covenant that was called out of Egypt and is constantly called to experience its existence as being-together with Yahweh as a people through obedience to the Law of Yahweh.

The young apostolic community calls itself the *ekklesia*, because it knows it is the fulfillment of the people of the Covenant. It is the New Covenant, the salvific community of men who are saved in Christ.[1] For its glorified Lord is the Emmanuel, the God-with-us, who in and through His human fellowship with us has passed, as saving and fulfilling, through the whole earthly reality.

1. Cf. W. G. Kümmel, *Kirchebegriff und Geschichtsbewustsein in der Urkirche und bei Jesu,* Uppsala, 1943.

This community's glorified Lord is the high point of the Father's creative plan. From its very beginning He has propelled creation to that perfect being-with His Father. That is why "He (the Word) was in the beginning with God" (Jn 1:2). And it is for that reason that the Word manifests Itself in the permanently actual deed of the Father's creation, until creation attains its fulfillment in the Incarnate Word:

> Blessed be the God and Father of our Lord Jesus Christ, who has blessed us in Christ with every spiritual blessing in the heavenly places, even as he chose us in him before the foundation of the world, that we should be holy and blameless before him.
>
> He destined us in love to be his sons through Jesus Christ, according to the purpose of his will, to the praise of his glorious grace which he freely bestowed on us in the Beloved.
>
> In him we have redemption through his blood, the forgiveness of our trespasses, according to the riches of his grace which he lavished upon us. For he has made known to us in all wisdom and insight the mystery of his will, according to the purpose which he set forth in Christ as a plan for the fulness of time, to unite all things in him, things in heaven and things on earth.
>
> In him, according to the purpose of him who accomplishes all things according to the counsel of his will, we who first hoped in Christ have been destined and appointed to live for the praise of his glory. In him you also, who have heard the word of truth, the gospel of your salvation, and have believed in him, were sealed with the promised Holy Spirit, which is the guarantee of our inheritance until we acquire possession of it, to the praise of his glory.
>
> For this reason, because I have heard of your faith in the Lord Jesus and your love toward all the saints, I

do not cease to give thanks for you, remembering you in my prayers, that the God of our Lord Jesus Christ, the Father of glory, may give you a spirit of wisdom and of revelation in the knowledge of him, having the eyes of your hearts enlightened, that you may know what is the hope to which he has called you, what are the riches of his glorious inheritance in the saints, and what is the immeasurable greatness of his power in us who believe, according to the working of his great might which he accomplished in Christ when he raised him from the dead and made him sit at his right hand in the heavenly places, far above all rule and authority and power and dominion, and above every name that is named, not only in this age but also in that which is to come; and he has put all things under his feet and has made him the head over all things for the church, which is his body, the fulness of him who fills all in all (Eph. 1:3-23).

The young apostolic Church knows that it is the community of faith and worship of the glorified Lord, in virtue of the Spirit who is active in the sacramental proclamation of the word.[2] She experiences human existence in Christ as the salvific reality of the God-with-us, as the fulfillment of the creation that is orientated to that Covenant.

But various texts of the New Testament also show us that the apostolic Church underwent a development in its self-consciousness, and we must analyze these writings if we wish to understand the concept of the Church in the New Testament. This analysis will clearly show that it is impossible to reduce all approaches to the mystery of the Church to a common denominator. If we wish to discover the full salvific reality of the Church, we must pay attention to the variegated aspects of it that are presented in the books of the New Testament.

2. J. M. Nielen, "Zur Grundlegung einer neutestamentlichen Ekklesiologie," *Festschrift F. Tilleman,* Düsseldorf, 1950.

a. The Church as the Intermediary Time

If we wish to understand Luke's idea of the Church in his twofold work of Gospel and Acts, it is important to study Christ's conversation with His disciples during the Last Supper.[3]

A dispute arose among them which of them was to be regarded as the greatest. And he said to them, "The kings of the Gentiles exercise lordship over them; and those in authority over them are called benefactors. But no so with you, rather let the greatest among you become as the youngest, and the leader as one who serves. For which is the greater, one who sits at table, or one who serves? Is it not the one who sits at table? But I am among you as one who serves.

You are those who have continued with me in my trials; as my Father appointed a kingdom for me, so did I appoint for you that you may eat and drink at my table in my kingdom, and sit on thrones judging the twelve tribes of Israel.

Simon, Simon, behold, Satan demanded to have you, that he might sift you like wheat, but I have prayed for you that your faith may not fail; and when you have turned again, strengthen your brethren" (Lke 22:24-32).

According to Conzelmann,[4] Luke distinguishes three phases in salvation history: the time of Israel, the time "in between" of Jesus and the time of the Church. The Church lives from that which constitutes the center of salvation history, namely, the Incarnation, that is the fulfillment of the Messianic reality of the Old Covenant:

3. H. Schürmann, *Der Abendmahlbericht Lukas 22, 7-38 als Gottesdienstordnung, Gemeindeordnung, Lebensordnung*, Leipzig, 1960.
4. H. Conzelman, *Die Mitte der Zeit, Studien zur Theologie des Lukas 3*, Tübingen, 1960.

"And there was given to him the book of the prophet Isaiah. He opened the book and found the place where it was written, 'The Spirit of the lord is upon me, because he has anointed me' . . . And he began to say to them, 'Today this scripture has been fulfilled in your hearing.' " (Lke 4:17-21).

The Church stands as a prolongation of the Old Testament People of God: "I grant you . . . that you will sit on thrones ruling over the twelve tribes of Israel." Salvation for Israel is found in the Church of Jesus Christ: "I bring you good news of great joy which will come to all the people" (Lke 2:10). That is why St. Luke stresses the fact that Jesus must finish His work of salvation in Jerusalem, the holy city of the Jewish people: "When the days drew near for him to be received up, he set his face to go to Jerusalem . . . I must go on my way . . . for it cannot be that a prophet should perish away from Jerusalem" (Lke 9:51; 13:33).

And after the bloody ordeal and His rejection by representatives of His people Jesus appears to His apostles in Jerusalem and gives them the commission to proclaim salvation "beginning from Jerusalem . . . Stay in the city, until you are clothed with power from on high" (Lke 24:47-49). The sending of the Spirit is the fulfillment of the Old Testament prophecy of Joel: "You shall receive the gift of the Holy Spirit. For the promise is to you and to your children and to all that are far off, every one of whom the Lord our God calls to him" (Acts 2:38-39). Although the universality of the message of salvation is present in St. Luke from the beginning of his gospel (Lke 2:32), he sees the Church so much in continuity with Israel that it is only at the end of Acts that he is ready to accept the guilty rejection of the chosen people (Acts 28:17-30).

The Church is rooted in the universal salvific power of

the total obedience of Christ to His Father: You have been faithful to me in my trials. And as my Father has given to me the kingdom because of my obedience, so do I give you a place in my Kingdom. The time of Jesus passes over into the time of the Church and is concretely realized in the sending of the Holy Spirit, which for the Apostles means sharing in the fullness of the Spirit whom Jesus acquired for Himself through surrender to His Father.

By the power of the Spirit who is active in the Church in the preaching of the word, the Kingdom of God that is fulfilled in Christ breaks through into the world: "And once converted, confirm your brethren." The Church is the community and, at the same time, the organ in which the glorified Lord brings about the Kingdom of God through the sending of His Spirit, until this Kingdom reaches its fulfillment in the Lord's return.

Thus the third phase of salvation history, the time of the Church, according to Luke, is the actualization of the Old Testament salvific reality which in Christ finds its fulfillment in time and space, for all men, countries and ages. The time of the Church is bounded by the ascension and Christ's return: "This Jesus, who was taken up from you into heaven, will come in the same way as you saw him go into heaven" (Acts 1:11). And as to content, this Church-historical phase of salvation history is defined in the commission: "You shall receive power when the Holy Spirit has come upon you; and you shall be my witnesses in Jerusalem and in all Judea and Samaria and to the end of the earth" (Acts 1:8).

The distinguishing characteristic of Luke's view of the Church is his salvation history approach to that mystery:[5] the Church's existence and activity is seen in the

5. E. Lohse, "Lukas als Theologe der Heilsgeschichte," *Evangelische Theologie*, vol. 14(1954), pp. 256 ff.

light of the eschatological presence of the absent Lord
during the tense intermediary period between the ascension and Christ's return, between His personal fulfillment, and the fulfillment of the whole of creation.

It is from the eschatological point of view that St. Luke
characterizes the preaching of the word, the administration of the sacraments, the apostolic structure and the
function of the Church. In the proclamation of the word
it is necessary to bring out the certainty of salvation: in
spite of the sinfulness and powerlessness that characterizes the "intermediary time," our salvation is anchored in
Christ. "Satan has wanted to sift you like wheat. But I
have prayed for you that your faith may not fail."

In the sacramental life of the community the Eucharist as the eschatological banquet occupies a central position: "As my Father has given me a Kingdom, so do I
(already now) grant you a place in my Kingdom, to eat
and drink at my table." The Eucharist continually is a
bridge connecting the community with the salvific actions of the earthly Jesus, which reached their high point
in the Last Supper: "This is my Body that is delivered for
you." The Eucharist provides also the definitive connection with the glorified Lord in the Kingdom of God: "I
shall not eat it until it is fulfilled in the kingdom of God"
(Lke 22:19; 16).

This shows also why Luke stresses so much the apostolic foundation of the Church. For it is precisely on the
basis of their being faithful in Christ's trials that the
Apostles are given a place in the Kingdom of God
through the Eucharist, and authority over the twelve
tribes of Israel. Because they are involved in the earthly
salvific work of Jesus, they receive, at the Last Supper
the commission to make that salvific work present in all
countries and times during the Lord's absence: "Do this
in remembrance of me" (Lke 22:19).

It is only through connection with the apostolic community that the believers of the future centuries can encounter the Lord in His salvific activity during the time between the ascension and the return: "After this the Lord appointed seventy others, and sent them on ahead of him, two by two, into every town and place where he himself was about to come. . . . 'He who hears you hears me, and he who rejects you rejects me, and he who rejects me rejects him who sent me.' The seventy returned with joy, saying, 'Lord, even the demons are subject to us in your name!' " (Lke 10:1-20).[6]

The same thought appears when a successor has to be chosen to replace Judas: "So one of the men who have accompanied us during all the time that the Lord Jesus went in and out among us, beginning from the baptism of John until the day when he was taken up from us— one of these men must become with us a witness to his resurrection" (Acts 1:21-22). Typical is the special attention given to Peter amidst the other Apostles: "Simon, Simon." While a clear reference is made to Peter's denial as an evidence of his own sinfulness, he is given the task of guiding the community of believers, as representing Christ: "I have prayed that your faith may not fail . . . Confirm your brethren in turn."

Finally the conversation of Jesus with His disciples during the Last Supper illustrates Luke's idea of the office in the Church. While the commission: "Do this in remembrance of Me" is still sounding in the room of the Last Supper, the Apostles begin a discussion about "who is the greatest among them." Because they will take His place, Jesus puts Himself forward as their example: "I am among you as one who serves." This task of serving that must characterize the office is continually recalled in the Acts, both on the occasion of the appointment of the seven for "daily distribution of food" (Acts 6:1-6) and

6. J. M. Gerritsen, *Het apostolisch ambt,* Amsterdam, 1953, pp. 40-48.

when the commissions are given to *presbyteroi* and *episkopoi* in the community. "Take heed to yourselves and to all the flock, in which the Holy Spirit has made you guardians, to feed the Church of the Lord which he obtained with his own blood" (Acts 20:28).

Although St. Luke gives no clear picture of the hierarchical order of the office of the Twelve and the Elders, he shows in full relief the nature of the office as a service of the community in virtue of a commission by Christ.

b. The Church as Salvific Community and as Instrument of Salvation

The dualism of Matthew's idea of the Church is perhaps most clearly expressed in two of Our Lord's words: "Where two or three are gathered in my name, there am I in the midst of them" (Mt. 18:20), and the text in which, on the occasion of the Apostles' mission to preach the word and administer the sacraments, He gives this guarantee to them: "and lo, I am with you always, to the close of the age" (Mt. 28:20).

In the Church as a believing community as well as in the official actions of the Church what matters is the presence of Christ who ascended to Heaven.

On the one hand the Church is the new People of God, that has taken the place of the nationally limited Israel: "The kingdom of God will be taken away from you and given to a nation producing the fruits of it" (Mt. 21:43). And its universality will be an invitation to all men: "And this gospel of the kingdom will be preached throughout the whole world, as a testimony to all nations; and then the end will come" (Mt. 24:14).

The Church is the true Israel[7] that Jesus has won with

7. W. Trilling, *Das wahre Israël, Studien zur Theologie des Matthäusevangelium*, Leipzig, 1959.

the Father in His self-surrender for the benefit of all: "This is my blood of the new covenant, which is poured out for many (i.e., all) for the forgiveness of sins" (Mt. 26:28).

The realization that that conformity of Jesus with the will of the Father through the absolute dominion of God over heart and mind (Sermon on the Mount) is the vital power of that community that believes in Him, leads to the identification of the love for God and the love of one's neighbor (Mt. 22:36-40) and to the deeply-felt encounter with Christ in one's compassion with suffering men: "As you did it to one of the least of these my brethren, you did it to me" (Mt. 25:40). The Church lives by the Kingdom of God that is actualized in Christ, and in all her vital expressions she experiences the presence and the saving action of Christ.

Hence the Church, as a believing community united to Christ, is a permanent gratuitous gift, and an ever new offer of love: "The Kingdom of heaven may be compared to a king who gave a marriage feast for his son, and sent his servants to call those who were invited to the marriage feast; . . . Tell those who are invited, Behold, I have made ready my dinner . . . go therefore to the thoroughfare, and invite to the marriage feast as many as you find" (Mt. 22:1-9). But she experiences at the same time this Kingdom of God that is active in her at present, as a task that is still to be fulfilled. She knows that in her field the good seed and the weeds still "grow together until the harvest" (Mt. 13:24-30) and that in her as in "a net . . . are gathered fish of every kind" (Mt. 13:47).

The Church lives by the grace which the now absent Lord has merited for her with the Father: "It will be as when a man going on a journey called his servants and entrusted to them his property." But because of her con-

stant failings she trembles at the same time, being aware
of her responsibility and knowing for certain that "after a
long time the master of those servants came and settled
account with them" (Mt. 25:14-30).

The Church is the people of God which is on its way
and looks forward to the return of Christ as the Church's
complete salvation: "For the Son of men is to come with
his angels in the glory of his Father, and then he will
repay every man for what he has done" (Mt. 16:27).

On the other hand, the Church takes on Christ's pastoral care of His flock: "What do you think? If a man has a
hundred sheep, and one of them has gone astray, does he
not leave the ninety-nine on the hills and go in search of
the one that went astray? And if he finds it, truly, I say to
you, he rejoices over it more than over the ninety-nine
that never went astray. So it is not the will of my Father
who is in heaven that one of these little ones should
perish" (Mt. 18:12-14).

Here the Church is called to assume the responsibility
of representing Christ in His all-embracing love, and in
virtue of His authority she has the office of actualizing
and applying the saving power of the Kingdom of God
that was realized by Christ; this is her function toward
all who "do the will of my Father in heaven" (Mt.
12:50).

Not only does the Church live through Christ's obedience to the Father, but she also enjoys the authority
given by Christ, in her proclamation of the word and the
administration of the sacraments: "And I tell you, you
are Peter, and on this rock I will build my church, and
the powers of death shall not prevail against it. I will give
you the keys of the kingdom of heaven, and whatever you
bind on earth shall be bound in heaven, and whatever
you loose on earth shall be loosed in heaven" (Mt.

16:18-19). For "all things have been delivered to me by my Father; and no one knows the Son except the Father, and no one knows the Father except the Son and any one to whom the Son chooses to reveal him" (Mt. 11:27).

Hence the order: "Go therefore and make disciples of all nations, baptizing them in the name of the Father and of the Son and of the Holy Spirit, teaching them to observe all that I have commanded you: and lo, I am with you always, to the close of the age" (Mt. 28:20).

Those two aspects are characteristic of Matthew's idea of the Church: the Church as believing community lives by being-together-with the absent Lord, and she can experience that togetherness because the Church, in her official actions of proclaiming the word and administering the sacraments, stands as salvific instrument empowered by Christ.

That we are in the presence of two inseparable aspects of one reality is evident from the following passage: "If your brother sins against you, go and tell him his fault, between you and him alone. If he listens to you, you have gained your brother. But if he does not listen, take one or two others along with you, that every word may be confirmed by the evidence of two or three witnesses (the Church as community of salvation). If he refuses to listen to them, tell it to the church (the Church as instrument of salvation); and if he refuses to listen even to the church, let him be to you as a Gentile and a tax collector (as no longer belonging to the Church as a community of faith). Truly, I say to you, whatever you bind on earth shall be bound in heaven, and whatever you loose on earth shall be loosed in heaven (the Church as empowered by Christ)" (Mt. 18:15-18).[8]

---

8. W. Trilling, *Hausordnung Gottes, Eine Auslegung von Matthäus 18*, Düsseldorf, 1960.

c. The Church as Bond-of-Life with the Glorified Lord through the Dynamic Presence of His Spirit

St. Paul approaches the mystery of the Church in many images. To discover the reality designated by those images, it is important that we not only mark the boundaries between image and reality, but we must also analyze the proper character of the diverse aspects of the one reality hidden under those images.

In accord with the two principal aspects of the Church, we must clearly distinguish two catagories of images:

On the one hand, the Church is
> the People of God
> the City of God, the New Jerusalem
> the House of God, the Temple of the Holy Spirit
> the Body of Christ.

On the other hand, the Church is considered under the aspect of
> partners in a Covenant
> bridegroom and bride
> head and body.

In the first series of images, it is a matter of the Church as the community of faith that gives stature to her bond-of-life with the glorified Lord. In the second, what is expressed is the pneumatic origin and the actualization of that community of faith. Both catagories are intended to illustrate the same reality of the Church, but from a different standpoint.

1. BOND-OF-LIFE WITH THE LORD

People of God

The Pauline idea of the Church as the people of God, comes from the view of faith that creation is a salvific event. Man's creative task to be fruitful in marriage, mentioned in Genesis, is the realization of God's salvific plan for creation. But the fact that this creative fruitfulness of the community of husband and wife is oriented to the realization of the people of God, is fully revealed only in the relation of Christ to His Church: "Therefore a man leaves his father and his mother and cleaves to his wife, and they become one flesh" (Gen. 2:24). "This is a great mystery, and I take it to mean Christ and the church" (Eph. 5:31-32).

The long history of this people of God is the story of God's redeeming and completing salvific activity. God's salvific plan regarding the earthly reality in and through "the First-born of all creation" (Col. 1:15) becomes manifest in mankind's slow self-realization. The various salvation-historical phases of the Old Testament people of God are prefigurations and pre-actualizations of the believing community that lives through Christ. The time of the Church is the final phase of that orientated salvation history.

This final phase finds its clearest *typoi* or prefigured reality (1 Cor. 10:6) in the salvific acts of Moses: the liberation of the chosen people from the slavery of Egypt, his passage with the people through the Red Sea, his pilgrimage through the desert toward the promised land, his role in making the covenant between Yahweh and the people on Mt. Sinai through the sprinkling with the blood of animals offered in sacrifice. These salvific acts are the beginnings of the revelation of the Christ-mystery of creation: "All were baptized into Moses in the cloud and in the sea, and all ate the same supernatural food and all drank the same supernatural drink. For they drank from the supernatural Rock which followed them, and the Rock was Christ" (1 Cor. 10:2-4).

The Church is the true "Israel of God" (Gal. 6:16), the

people of God that lives by the fullness of His salvific actions.[9] Through baptism, through this "washing of water with the word" (Eph. 5:26), this people is in Christ the sanctified mankind that through the blood of His total self-surrender to the Father is saved from the deadly slavery of sin and, on its way to the house of the Father, lives by the food and drink of His self-sacrifice for the benefit of all.

St. Paul struggled with the troublesome question whether the rejection of Christ by His own people was not a failure of God's promise; was this not an injustice and even a faulty shortcoming on the part of God? (Rom. 9:1-11, 12).[10] But he knew that in the Church as the new people, God had shown His fidelity to the salvific plan with respect to the chosen people: "In that day the remnant of Israel and the survivors of the house of Jacob . . . will lean upon the Lord, the Holy One of Israel, in truth. . . ." And Isaiah cries out concerning Israel: "Though the number of the sons of Israel be as the sand of the sea, only a remnant of them will be saved; for the Lord will execute his sentence upon the earth with vigor and dispatch" (Is. 10:20-22).

It is only in the Church that the promise connected with the call of Abraham to be the patriarch of the chosen people became a complete reality: "By you all the families of the earth shall bless themselves" (Gen. 12:3). God's salvific activity is universal from the very beginning. From the very beginning that salvific activity was ultimately directed to the experience of the Christ-mystery of creation in the Church of Jesus Christ that embraces all men. From this universality of salvation in

9. N. A. Dahl, *Das Volk Gottes,* Oslo, 1951; A. Oephe, *Das neue Gottesvolk,* Gütersloh, 1950.

10. K. L. Schmidt, *Die Judenfrage im Lichte der Kapittel 9-11 des Römerbriefes,* Zollikon-Zürich, 1951.

God's act of creation, God's activity concentrated itself in salvific Israel, in His holy "remnant," and finally in Christ; and from Him that salvation fanned out over all peoples. In Christ Israel's national frontiers of salvation were transcended. Resting on this certain fact, St. Paul was able to announce that "you" (the pagans) who "were at that time separated from Christ, alienated from the commonwealth of Israel, and strangers to the covenants of promise, having no hope and without God in the world . . . now in Christ Jesus you who once were far off have been brought near in the blood of Christ . . . fellow heirs, members of the same body, and partakers of the promise in Christ Jesus through the gospel" (Eph. 2: 19; 3:6).

But this salvific activity for the benefit of all peoples is already latent in Israel: "Even us whom he has called, not from the Jews only but also from the Gentiles. As indeed he says in Hosea, 'Those who were not my people I will call "my people" and her who was not beloved I will call "my beloved" ' " (Rm. 9:24-25).

The Church lives by the salvation of Israel fulfilled in Christ: "That in Christ Jesus the blessing of Abraham might come upon the Gentiles . . . for in Christ Jesus you are all sons of God, through faith. For as many of you as were baptized into Christ have put on Christ. There is neither slave nor free, there is neither male nor female; for you are all one in Christ Jesus. And if you are Christ's, then you are Abraham's offspring, heirs according to promise" (Gal. 3:14; 26-29).

Israel has not been rejected but the latent universality of the salvation that is present in that people has become manifest in Christ: "For he is our peace, who has made us both one, and has broken down the dividing wall of hostility, by abolishing in his flesh the law of commandments and ordinances, that he might create in himself one new man in place of the two, so making peace, and might reconcile us both to God in one body through the cross, thereby bringing the hostility to an end" (Eph. 2:14-16).

The New Jerusalem

St. Paul develops that image when he calls the people of God, that Christ has acquired before His Father from among the Jews and the pagans, "the New Jerusalem." The Church stands in the hereditary line of Isaac, the son "in virtue of the promise," while the Jewish people has become the disinherited child of the slave woman to the extent that it consciously has rejected Christ as the foundation of its existence as a people and of its salvation history (Gal. 4:21-31).

House of God and Temple of the Holy Spirit

St. Paul has more fully defined the idea of people of God by the images of "house of God" and "temple of the Holy Spirit." Here he reveals the moment of discontinuity in the continuity between the old and the new people of God. The prophet Joel had already seen the sending of the Spirit as the power that was to renew and fulfill all things during the final eschatological age: "And in the last days it shall be, God declares, that I will pour out my Spirit upon all flesh" (Joel 3:1-5; Acts 2:17-21). This eschatological gift of God is given to all in the solidarity of the creative Word of God with sinful mankind.

Christ is the "life-giving spirit" (1 Cor. 15:45) for all men, who offers to all the real power to experience creation fully as the Covenant, as being-together-with His Father: He "has qualified us to be ministers of a new covenant, not in a written code but in the Spirit; for the written code (that is, appealing to a code which refers to

Christ while rejecting Christ) kills, but the Spirit gives life. . . . The Lord is the Spirit, and where the Spirit of the Lord is, there is freedom. And we all, with unveiled face, beholding the glory of the Lord, are being changed into his likeness from one degree of glory to another; for this comes from the Lord who is the Spirit" (2 Cor. 3:6-18).

It is only here that we see clearly what makes the Church be the people of God. The foundation and formative principle of the ecclesial community is to be sought in the bond-of-life of all with Christ. This bond comes from the same Spirit who inspired our Lord's earthly life, so that it was in complete agreement with the will of the Father, and who now directs our life toward a complete likeness with Him. It is the Spirit of the Lord who effects all that makes that believing community the Church of Jesus Christ: "So then you are no longer strangers and sojourners, but you are fellow citizens with the saints and members of the household of God, built upon the foundation of the apostles and prophets, Christ Jesus himself being the cornerstone, in whom the whole structure is joined together and grows into a holy temple in the Lord; in whom you also are built into it for a dwelling place of God in the Spirit" (Eph. 2:19-22).

The Spirit is the dynamic and perpetually active principle of life of the Church who makes Christ's salvific work fruitful in all. He is the Spirit who develops the salvific fullness of the crucified and risen body of Christ into His ecclesial body: "one body and one Spirit" (Eph. 4:4). For through Christ we have "access in one Spirit to the Father" (Eph. 2:18). "We are the temple of the living God; as God said, 'I will live in them and I will be their God, and they shall be my people. . . . I will be a father to you, and you shall be my sons and daughters" (2 Cor. 6:16; Ez. 37:27).

The Body of Christ

Here the Pauline vision of the Church reaches its high point.[11] The idea of people of God, "you are all one in Christ Jesus" (Gal. 3:28) passes over, through the experience of the community-forming power of the Holy Spirit, to a new image: "For as in one body we have many members, and all the members do not have the same function, so we, though many, are one body in Christ, and individually members one of another" (Rom. 12:4-5). When St. Paul calls "body of Christ" the believing community that lives by the Spirit of the glorified Lord, he is in line with the old Semitic idea of solidarity. The Semite did not experience the body in its communicative, but in its society-building function: "Then (after the death of Saul) all Israel gathered together to David at Hebron, and said, 'Behold, we are your bone and flesh. . . .' And they anointed David king over Israel" (1 Chr. 11:1-3).

This Old Testament concept of corporate personality has three aspects:

First, the corporate personality is the personified unity of the community that embraces also all the members of the past and the future in a real bond of destiny.

Secondly, that personality is not a fictitious ideal or a literary projection, but it is a real entity and manifests itself in very concrete activity.

Thirdly, there is great fluidity between the corporate personality and the individual. The community is represented by, and acts in the individual, especially in the

11. H. Hegermann, "Zur Ableitung der Leib-Christi-Vorstellung," *Theol. Literaturzeitung*, vol. 85 (1960), pp. 839 ff.; T. Soiron, *Die Kirche als der Leib Christi, nach der Lehre des hl. Paulus exegetisch, systematisch und in der theologischen wie praktischen Bedeutung dargestellt*, Düsseldorf, 1951.

patriarch. The whole people is identical with its ancestral patriarch.[12]

Against this background St. Paul sees the "body of Christ" growing as a corporate personality through the action of the same Spirit in all who in baptism "have put on Christ" (Gal. 3:27). The individual and social aspects of that salvific reality in Christ can no longer be separated. The personal union with Christ, on the one hand, blossoms out through the active presence of the Spirit of Christ in the believing community; on the other hand, it prompts all to live in true togetherness animated by the Spirit of the glorified Lord.

This essential compenetration of the individual and the social aspects of the believing community gives the Church a unity of life and work. The personal diversity of those who are "members one of another" makes the Church a living organism. As such, the Church leaves much room for what is proper to individual members, but at the same time experiences all schisms and individual-istic-charismatic fanaticisms as so many deadly amputations:

> For just as the body is one and has many members, and all the members of the body, though many, are one body, so it is with Christ. For by one Spirit we were all baptized into one body—Jews or Greeks, slaves or free —and all were made to drink of one Spirit.

> For the body does not consist of one member but of many. If the foot should say, "Because I am not a hand, I do not belong to the body," that would not make it any

12. H. Robinson Wheeler, "The Hebrew Conception of Corporate Personality," *Zeitschrift f. Alttest. Wissenschaft,* Beiheft 66 (1936), pp. 49-61; *The Religious Ideas of the Old Testament,* London, 1949; *The Christian Doctrine of Man,* Edinburgh, 1931; E. Best, *One Body in Christ,* London, 1955; J. A. Robinson, *The Body. A Study in Pauline Theology,* London, 1952.

less a part of the body. And if the ear should say, "Because I am not an eye, I do not belong to the body," that would not make it any less a part of the body. If the whole body were an eye, where would be the hearing? If the whole body were an ear, where would be the sense of smell? But as it is, God arranged the organs of the body, each one of them, as he chose. If all were a single organ, where would the body be?

As it is, there are many parts, yet one body. The eye cannot say to the hand, "I have no need of you," nor again the head to the feet, "I have no need of you." On the contrary, the parts of the body which seem to be weaker are indispensable, and those parts of the body which we think less honorable we invest with the greater honor, and our unpresentable parts are treated with greater modesty, which our more presentable parts do nor require.

But God has so adjusted the body, giving the greater honor to the inferior part, that there may be no discord in the body, but that members may have the same care for one another. If one member suffers, all suffer together; if one member is honored, all rejoice together.

Now you are the body of Christ and individually members of it. (1 Cor. 12:12-27).

It is difficult to distinguish the boundaries between image and reality in St. Paul's vision of the Church as the body of Christ. For instance, in the following passage of the Epistle to the Corinthians he evidently interweaves image and reality: "The cup of blessing which we bless, is it not a participation in the blood of Christ? The bread which we break, is it not a participation in the body of Christ? Because there is one bread, we who are many are one body, for we all partake of the one bread" (1 Cor. 10:16-17).

There is more here than a mere image. "Must the same

word 'body' (*soma*) used in verse 16 and in verse 17 be understood in the same sense? It seems difficult to accept that Paul would, without further explanation, use that fundamental word in two different senses within one continuous course of thought. The following seems to us the proper meaning of the text before us: the 'one body' that the many of us are, because we all participate in one bread (verse 17), is the same 'body of Christ' that is received by us sacramentally in the Holy Eucharist. By the fact that we receive in our body, through the sacramental rite, the sacrificied personal body of the Lord (cf. 1 Cor. 11:23-29), we are altogether this same body of the Lord: this same personal body of Christ (that is Christ Himself, considered from the standpoint of his corporal being) which our bodies (that is, we human beings, considered from the standpoint of our bodily being) receive in themselves and that unites us."[13]

It is certain that Paul greatly stresses the ecclesial dimensions of the eucharistic presence of Christ and that from it flows a bond-of-life between the glorified Lord and His believing community. Nevertheless, it seems to us that the conclusion that Malberg draws from that passage—that it "gives the key for Paul's *identification* of the Church with the personal, sacrificed and glorified 'body of Christ' "[14]—is not convincing. We believe that it would lead to a mystification in the Catholic's Church-consciousness as well as to much misunderstanding on the part of Reformed Christians.

The Church is the body of Christ (Eph. 1:23, 4:12), "we are members of his body" (Eph. 5:30). "That you may belong to another, to him who has been raised from

---

13. F. Malmberg, *Een lichaam en een geest. Nieuwe gezichts-punten in de Ecclesiologie*, Utrecht, 1948, p. 54.

14. Malmberg, *op. cit.*, p. 53. Cf. Lucien Cerfaux, *La Théologie de l'Eglise suivant Saint-Paul*, Paris, 1948, p. 258.

the dead" (Rom. 7:4). And yet the Church may not be
identified with the physical body of Jesus on earth or
with that of the glorified Lord who is with the Father.
Just as in the Eucharist we may not view the real presence as an identification of the "bread that is blest" with
the physical body of Christ, but as a presence-in-a-sign of
the glorified man Jesus Christ, so in the Church it is not a
matter of the physical body of Christ, but of the permanently living and active presence of Christ in the form of
a community that believes in Him.

In the creation mystery of the Incarnation of God's
Son we can distinguish several modes of existence or
forms of manifestation that must not be identified with
one another, for they are analogous modes of existence
of the same Christ:

> the veiled pre-revelation in the Old Testament people
> of God
>
> His historical-earthly mode of existence
>
> His glorified existence with the Father
>
> His sacramental-eucharistic presence
>
> His socio-ecclesial form
>
> the new creation in which through Christ "God may be
> everything to every one" (1 Cor. 15:28).

The Church is the socio-ecclesial mode of existence on
earth of the glorified Lord who is with the Father, because the same Spirit binds the baptized to Christ and
also binds the baptized to one another.

2. THE SALVIFIC ACTIVITY OF THE LORD

St. Paul uses the figures of people of God, New Jerusalem, house of God, temple of the Holy Spirit, body of
Christ to shed light on the Church in terms of the community of those who believe in Christ and in terms of the
creation in which the mystery of Christ occurs, which in
Jesus' life, suffering, death and resurrection has reached
the fullness of time.

In a second series of images—those of partners in a Covenant and in marriage, of bridegroom and bride, of head and body—St. Paul looks at the Church from the standpoint of Christ, particularly as the one who initiates and actualizes salvific activity. The Church then is seen as the believing community of the Lord.

Head and Body

At the foundation of that view of the Church lies St. Paul's experience on the road to Damascus when the persecutor of the Church was literally struck down by the word of the glorified Lord: " 'Saul, Saul, why do you persecute me?' And he said: 'Who are you, Lord?' And he said, 'I am Jesus, whom you are persecuting' " (Acts 9:4-5).

This mystery of Christ's presence in the Church that completes creation and saves mankind, runs like a golden salvific thread through all the letters of St. Paul. In the Church the Father exercises "the working of his great might which he accomplished in Christ when he raised him from the dead and made him sit at his right hand in the heavenly places, far above all rule and authority and power and dominion (the spiritual powers that govern the social, political, cultural and religious life of mankind[15]) and above every name that is named, not only in this age but also in that which is to come; and he has put all things under his feet and has made him the head over all things for the church, which is his body, the fullness of him who fills all in all" (Eph. 1:19-23).

The Church is the full measure (*plērōma*) of Christ, the believing community that is filled with Christ and through Him fills all.[16] She participates in the cosmic dimensions of the Christ mystery, in which the Father

15. H. Schlier, *Mächte und Gewalten in neuen Testament,* Freiburg, 1959.
16. H. Schlier and V. Warnach, *Die Kirche im Ephesenbrief,* Münster, 1949, pp. 12-14.

unfolds His eternal salvific plan for creation: "To me, though I am the very least of all the saints, this grace was given, to preach to the Gentiles the unsearchable riches of Christ, and to make all men see what is the plan of the mystery hidden for ages in God who created all things; that through the church the manifold wisdom of God might now be made known to the principalities and powers in the heavenly places. This was according to the eternal purpose which he has realized in Christ Jesus our Lord" (Eph. 3:8-11).

Christ is the Church's source and purpose of life, of her entire existence and all her activity. He is "the Head, from whom the whole body, nourished and knit together . . . grows with a growth that is from God" (Col. 2:19). "In him the whole fullness of deity dwells bodily" (Col. 2:9), and He draws all who believe in Him into the orientation toward the Father of His human existence. The grace of being-the-Church of Jesus Christ is a sharing in the grace of the Head, in the grace of His suffering and resurrection: "He is before all things, and in him all things hold together. He is the head of the body, the church; he is the beginning, the first-born from the dead, that in everything he might be preeminent. For in him all the fullness of God was pleased to dwell, and through him to reconcile to himself all things, whether on earth or in heaven, making peace by the blood of his cross" (Col. 1:17-20).

Bridegroom and Bride

We find the most perfect expression of Yahweh's devoted love for His people of the Old Covenant in the image of bridegroom and bride particularly in the Song of Solomon, Ezechiel and Hosea. St. Paul likewise approached the relation between Christ and His Church in the New Covenant from the standpoint of the relation-

ship between husband and wife. Being the Head of
the Church is a constant, permanent, loving care of the
Church. "Husbands, love your wives, as Christ loved the
church and gave himself up for her, that he might sanctify her having cleansed her by the washing of water with
the word, that he might present the church to himself in
splendor, without spot or wrinkle or any such thing, that
she might be holy and without blemish. . . . No man
ever hates his own flesh, but nourishes and cherishes it,
as Christ does the church, because we are members of his
body" (Eph. 5:25-30). In those words there is a clear
reference to baptism and the Eucharist as instruments of
His continued loving care and presence.[17]

Included in that image of bridegroom and bride is the
Old Testament principle of solidarity. Over against the
un-salutary community of the first Adam, there stands
the salvific community of the last Adam who "became a
life-giving spirit" (1 Cor. 15:45). As members of His
body, the believers are connected with His destiny and
predestination and are co-workers for the fulfillment of
His salvific work. In baptism they have "been united with
him in a resurrection like his," have been "crucified with
him," "died with him," "buried with him," "raised with
him," and "glorified with him" (Rom. 4:3-6; Col. 2:12;
Phil. 3:21; Eph. 2:5-6). The celebration of the Eucharist
is "communication with the body of Christ" (1 Cor
10:16) and a sharing in the death of the Lord until he
returns (1 Cor. 11:26). Being the Church of Christ is a
"sharing in his passion in order to share also in this
glory" (Rom. 8:17) and a being led with Him to the
Father (1 Thes. 4:14). For "when one member suffers,
all members share in the suffering. And when one member is honored, all share in the honor" (1 Cor. 12:26).

17. H. Schlier, *Der Brief an die Epheser*, Düsseldorf, 1947, p.
260.

3. THE OFFICE

To help the members in their self-realization and exercise of their proper functions within the body, there is the office which operates as an instrument of the glorified Lord. In it He actualizes the grace-filled activity of His Spirit throughout countries and ages: "Now there are varieties of gifts, but the same Spirit; and there are varieties of service, but the same Lord; and there are varieties of working, but it is the same God who inspires them all in every one. To each is given the manifestation of the Spirit for the common good. To one is given through the Spirit the utterance of wisdom, and to another the utterance of knowledge according to the same Spirit, to another gifts of healing by the one Spirit, to another the working of miracles, to another prophecy, to another the ability to distinguish between spirits, to another various kinds of tongues. All these are inspired by one and the same Spirit, who apportions to each one individually as he wills" (1 Cor. 12:26).

This passage does not yet clearly trace the boundaries between office and charism, but it stresses the fact that in those services rendered to the believing community the activity is exercised "in the person of Christ" as an active presence of His Spirit, as making concrete the bond-of-life between the Head and the body.[18] The office acts always "by the grace that has been given" to each (Rom. 12:3). It stands as a commission and hence as having received authority and power from Christ: "Paul an Apostle—not from men nor through man, but through Jesus Christ and God the Father, who raised him

18. E. Lohse, *Die Ordination im Spätjudentum und im neuen Testament*, Göttingen, 1951; F. Wötscher, "Vorchristliche Typen urchristlicher Aemter?" *Festgabe für Kardinal Frings, Die Kirche und ihere Aemter und Stände*, Köln, 1960.

from the dead" (Gal. 1:1). The absent Lord remains present in His Church by the office. And He makes all share in His human participation in the divine life, a participation He acquired before the Father through His salvific actions accomplished for all in the human fellowship He has in common with us: "And his gifts (to the Church) were that some should be apostles, some prophets, some evangelists, some pastors and teachers, for the equipment of the saints, for the work of ministry (universal priesthood), for building up the body of Christ, until we all attain to the unity of the faith and of the knowledge of the Son of God, to mature manhood, to the measure of the stature of the Son of God . . . from whom the whole body, joined and knit together by every joint with which it is supplied, when each part is working properly (through the dialogue between the particular and the universal priesthood) makes bodily growth and upbuilds itself in love" (Eph. 4:11-16).

This apostolic commission to build, by preaching the word and administering the sacraments, "the house of God, that is the church of the living God, pillar and foundation of truth," requires a permanent authority and regulation in that believing community: "This is why I left you (Titus) in Crete, that you might amend what was defective (in the Church) and appoint elders in every town as I directed you" (Tit. 1:5).

Whereas the office has vague contours in Paul's first letters, in his pastoral letters he becomes more explicit in describing the functioning of the apostolic succession: "Paul, an apostle of Christ Jesus by command of God our Savior and of Christ Jesus our hope, to Timothy, my true child in the faith"; and he gives Timothy power of office: "What you have heard from me before many witnesses entrust to faithful men who will be able to teach others also" (1 Tim. 1:1-2). "Our Savior Christ Jesus abolished death and brought life and immortality to light through the gospel. For this gospel I was appointed a preacher and apostle and teacher. . . . Follow the pattern of the sound words which you have heard from me, in the faith and love which are in Christ Jesus; guard the truth that has been entrusted to you by the Holy Spirit who dwells within us" (2 Tim. 1:10-14).[19]

The guarantee of anyone standing in the apostolic succession lies, according to St. Paul, in the imposition of hands whereby the commission and power of Christ for building the Church are imparted: "I remind you (Timothy) to rekindle the gift of God that is within you through the laying on of my hands" (2 Tim. 1:6). And he gives expression to the awareness of that imparting of the office, and of the continuous reception of the power of Christ, in the consciousness of the bond with the apostolic Mother Church of Jerusalem: "Then after fourteen years I went up again to Jerusalem with Barnabas . . . and I laid before them (but privately before those who were of repute) the gospel which I preach among the Gentiles, lest somehow I should be running or had run in vain" (Gal. 2:1-2).

In St. Paul also does the tension of the duality within the office become manifest. On the one hand, the office is pure service for the self-realization of the glorified Lord (*sola scriptura, sola gratia, sola fide*). But, on the other hand, God's salvific action is incarnate in Christ and it is permanently mediated through the activities of those who have received power and who therefore have authority. It is only through the apostolic succession; which finds its structure in the permanent bond of the local Churches with the universal Church, that the office is legitimized as a commission given by Christ.

19. H. Schlier, "Die Ordnung der Kirche nach den Pastoralbriefen," *Die Zeit der Kirche*, Freiburg, 1956, pp. 129-147.

d. The Church as Diaspora

Whereas the captivating power of the Pauline vision of the Church lies in the multitude of aspects which he brings to light from that rich reality of salvation, the First Epistle of St. Peter and the Epistle to the Hebrews seek a synthesis of the mystery that is accomplished in the believing community. All the Pauline images of the Church return, but they now function in an attempt to show the Church as a *diaspora*.

Paroikia

If we wish to discover the biblical-theological content of the concept of *diaspora* in its religious dimensions, it is necessary to take into account the cognate concept of *paroikia*, especially because the New Testament increasingly avoids using the term *diaspora* on account of its technically Jewish meaning.

The idea of *paroikia* governs the whole Old Testament. Israel is a Covenant people, always conscious of the fact that in God's salvific plan it is raised above the factual situation of its existence as a people. This plan Yahweh, ever faithful to the Covenant, fulfills with His people even when that people proves unfaithful.

On the one hand, this chosen people is made to experience even its most profound humiliation during a hopeless exile, as a tense expectation of the Messiah's coming Kingdom. On the other hand, this longing for the Messiah may not be permitted to disappear even during the peaceful and rich possession of the Promised Land during the times of David and Solomon. This double dimension of its existence makes both the exile and the Promised Land appear as phases of the true happiness that is still to come.

Hence Israel is not a citizen (*katoikos*) in this world in

which he has a fixed abode. Neither is he a stranger
(*xenos, parepidēmos*) who has no rights and nowhere
feels at home in this world. Israel is a people of *paroikoi,
metoikoi;* their final destiny forbids them to strive for the
possession of citizens' rights and for a permanent abode;
and on the other hand, they are obliged to claim some
definite rights, for they know, because of their vocation,
that Yahweh by His Covenant constantly and decisively
intervenes in the history of the peoples among whom
they live. Wherever they dwell, they live with the firm
conviction that their own history as a people—even at
times when their very existence is in danger—is ultimately Yahweh's salvation offered to all peoples.

This situation that is unique to the Jewish people, is
determined by its faith in Yahweh who, beginning with
the patriarch Abraham, leads this people in fidelity to the
Covenant, along His own divine but often obscure ways,
toward the salvation of all men in the Messiah who is to
come. Believing in Yahweh, Abraham leaves his own
country in order to dwell as a *paroikos*, a sojourner in
foreign lands. But through this *paroikos* all those peoples
become involved in the salvific plan that Yahweh will
accomplish henceforth in the history of Abraham's descendants: "Then the Lord said to Abram, 'Know of a
surety that your descendants will be sojourners in a land
that is not theirs. . . . Go from your country and your
kindred and your father's house to the land that I will
show you. And I will make of you a great nation, and I
will bless you, and make your name great, so that you
will be a blessing . . . and by you all the families of the
earth shall bless themselves' " (Gen. 15:13; 12:1-4). The
patriarch of the Jewish people is a *typos*, in which Israel
must see the proper meaning of its own existence as a
people.

The stay of the chosen people in Egypt as well as their

possession of the promised land, the Babylonian-Assyrian exile, and the return to Palestine, must all be seen in the same religious perspective: Israel is a chosen people in and through which God is already establishing His future Kingdom in this world. They are permitted to think that the promise of that Kingdom is a reality that is already being achieved in the promised land of Canaan. But the exile must free them from a too human expectation of that Kingdom and from every form of self-satisfaction that makes them pride themselves on being privileged possessors of that Kingdom. It is precisely as *paroikoi* that they must always preserve an openness and readiness with respect to God's salvific plan for the benefit of all mankind.

This eschatological duality of the Old Testament reality of salvation becomes most manifest in the extreme situations in which the chosen people finds itself. On the one hand, amidst the full possession of the promised land and at the high point of his kingship, David prays thus in the presence of the whole people: "Blessed art thou, O Lord, the God of Israel our father, for ever and ever. Thine, O Lord, is the greatness, and the power, and the glory, . . . for all that is in the heavens and in the earth is thine; . . . thou art exalted as head above all. . . . O Lord, the God of Abraham, Isaac, and Israel, our fathers, keep for ever such purposes and thoughts in the hearts of thy people, and direct their hearts toward thee" (1 Chron. 29:10,19). But, on the other hand, the prophets Ezechiel, Jeremiah and Isaiah continually announce during the exile that Yahweh, even in that seeming annihilation of His chosen people, is simply going on with the realization of His salvific plan.

The Psalmist has expressed that fundamental religious attitude in prayer: "I am thy passing guest, a sojourner, like all my fathers" (Ps. 39:12). That we are here truly in the presence of the most profound dimensions of all true faith in God and that this human attitude of faith is the necessary condition, given by God Himself, of the realization of His salvific plan, is clearly shown in the New Testament where Abraham is portrayed as an example of justification through faith for all Christians: "By faith he sojourned in the land of promise, as in a foreign land, living in tents with Isaac and Jacob, heirs with him of the same promise. For he looked forward to the city which has foundations, whose builder and maker is God. By faith Sarah herself received power to conceive, even when she was past the age, since she considered him faithful who had promised. Therefore from one man, and him as good as dead, were born descendants as many as the stars of heaven and as the innumerable grains of sand by the seashore. These all died in faith, not having received what was promised, but having seen it and greeted it from afar, and having acknowledged that they were strangers and exiles on the earth" (Heb. 11:9-13).

"No distrust made him waver concerning the promise of God, but he grew strong in his faith as he gave glory to God, fully convinced that God was able to do what he has promised. That is why his faith was 'reckoned to him as righteousness.' But the words, 'it was reckoned to him,' were written not for his sake alone, but for ours also. It will be reckoned to us who believe in him that raised from the dead Jesus our Lord" (Rom. 4:20-24). It is only in the New Covenant that this attitude of faith, that propelled the Old Covenant with dynamic power toward its fulfillment in Christ, attains its full development. The believing community of the New Testament lives by the salvific reality that the Incarnate Son of the Father has brought about through His salvific actions of total fidelity to the divine plan of creation, for the benefit of all men, in all human relationships and all earthly values.

To be a Christian is, on the one hand, a knowing for certain that our human existence in Christ is a saved existence, that our work in the earthly reality is, through the constant actual encounter with Christ, a contribution to the realization of the Kingdom of God that is fulfilled in Him, of God's salvific plan for His creation: "Come to him, to that living stone, rejected by men but in God's sight chosen and precious; and like living stones be yourselves built into a spiritual house, to be a holy priesthood, to offer spiritual sacrifices acceptable to God through Jesus Christ. . . . But you are a chosen race, a royal priesthood, a holy nation, God's own people, that you may declare the wonderful deeds of him who called you out of darkness into his marvelous light. Once you were no people but now you are God's people; once you had not received mercy but now you have received mercy" (1 Pet. 2:4-10).

On the other hand, though it is true that the Christian and the Church have the task to fulfill God's plan of creation, this believing community in Christ, at the same time, transcends this world so as to enjoy a personal encounter with His Father. For the Son, as one of us, experienced His divine relation to the Father in a human existence and thereby gave us the power to transcend our human existence in a conscious encounter with His Father. Although the Christian must fully engage in the possibilities offered by human existence and human values, his power to transcend the world in Christ also makes him realize that we are "aliens and exiles" (1 Peter 2:11) in this world. Moreover, so long as Christ has not placed the powers of this world under His complete dominion in the *eschaton*—that is, as long as this creation has not reached its fulfillment in Christ—sin continues to exercise great power over man and the world rebels against God's Kingdom. Hence creation during the "intermediary" time retains a kind of unruliness, a radical ambiguity: the Kingdom of God is advancing toward its fulfillment but is still far from God. Because of that dividedness in creation, the Christian, while aware of his earthly mission, also feels it necessary to keep in mind and act according to these words: "Beloved, I beseech you as aliens and exiles to abstain from the passions of the flesh that wage war against your soul. Maintain good conduct among the Gentiles, so that in case they speak against you as wrongdoers, they may see your good deeds and glorify God on the day of visitation" (1 Pet. 2:11-12). But this deep sense of being an exile, should not tempt the Christian to a flight from the world, for, in virtue of the encounter with Christ in word and sacrament, he must live in the earthly reality as being a son of the Father.

This apostolic consciousness of already now establishing God's Kingdom on earth dominated the young Church so much that Peter, in his Epistle, addresses himself to "the exiles of the Dispersion in Pontus, Galatia, Cappadocia, Asia, and Bithynia" (1 Peter 1:1), and Clement in his letter to the Corinthians begins with the words: "The Church of God which sojourns in Rome as *paroikia*, to the Church of God which sojourns as *paroikia* in Corinth."[20] And the story of the martyrdom of Bishop Polycarp names the local communities simply the "*paroikiai* of the holy and catholic Church."[21]

Diaspora

Starting from the biblical idea of *paroikia*, the concept of *dispora* that was originally geographical, received

20. *Clementis ad Corinthios* in F. X. Funk, *Opera Patrum Apostolicorum*, vol. I, Tübingen, 1887, pp. 60-61.
21. *Martyrium sancti Policarpi episcopi Smyrnae*, in Funk, *op. cit.*, pp. 282-283.

slowly, in the Old Testament, a religious content and this trend is continued in the New Testament.

The term *diaspora* arose in the Jewish commercial colonies of Syria, Phoenicia, Asia Minor and Egypt, and was used as a technical term to designate the Jewish communities that lived outside Palestine.[22] But during the Assyrian and Babylonian captivity that term acquired a religious dimension with respect to those who dwelt in a foreign land. The captivity was looked upon by the Jewish people as a punishment for their constant infidelity to the Covenant: "For they disobeyed thy commandments, and thou gavest us over to plunder, captivity, and death; thou madest us a byword of reproach in all the nations among which we have been dispersed" (Tob. 3:4).

However, when many Jews, after the Exile, did not make use of their freedom to return to Palestine, there arose a freely-willed diaspora, in which the sense of punishment was to give way entirely to an apostolic consciousness: "He has scattered us among them. Make his greatness known there, and exalt him in the presence of all the living, because he is our Lord and God, he is our Father for ever" (Tob. 13:4). As a consequence of that missionary impetus a great many proselytes, in the diaspora, went over to Judaism.

After the destruction of Jerusalem in the year 70, the Jewish diaspora became a people without a country, and on that account Israel lost its center and, with it, its dynamic power and even its existence as a people. How-

---

22. E. L. Rapp, "Jüdische Diaspora," *RGG* II[3], pp. 174-177; H. Kruska, "Zum neuen Verständnis der Diaspora. Einer Ueberblick über Versuche einer neuen Klärung de Diasporabegriffes," *Theologia viatorum*, 1959, pp. 299-321; G. Niemeijer, "Diaspora als Gestalt kirchlichen Seins und kirchlicher Sendung," *Evangelische Theologie*, 1948, Heft 7/8, pp. 226 ff.; Th. Heckel, *Kirche jenseits der Grenzen*, Göttingen, 1949.

ever, at that time, this apostolic consciousness had already passed over to Christianity. The young Church knows that it is the new Israel that, as a diaspora, must proclaim and realize the great salvific deeds of God in Christ amidst the pagan peoples. "And he commanded us to preach to the people, and to testify that he is the one ordained by God to be judge of the living and the dead" (Acts 10:42). Both James and Peter direct their letters to the Christians "of the Dispersion" (Jm. 1:1; Pet. 1:1).

Even if those Apostles had addressed themselves to communities of Jewish Christians—but this is not at all evident, for they may have been Gentile-Christians—the word *diaspora* does not have here exclusively a technical sense. It contains the biblical *paroikia* idea: as Christians they are, in this world, sojourners who must fulfill a missionary task with respect to the peoples among whom they live as a minority.

For, in the meantime, an essential change had taken place in the consciousness of the diaspora. In the Old Testament what was predominant was the being-away from the only center of worship of Israel, namely, the Temple of Jerusalem. The synagogue that arose in the diaspora and later spread also in Palestine, had no independent function, but it always had to refer to the Temple of Jerusalem. The diaspora idea of Israel has always a local dimension.

The New Testament does not know any exclusive center of worship that has a local connection; hence it has no diaspora in the true sense. The word, at first, was still retained as a remembrance of the Jewish diaspora, but then disappeared to be replaced by the idea of *paroikia*. For the center of the new people of God is the glorified Lord who has gone to the Father in His fulfillment, but who is, at the same time, present everywhere as fulfilling, wherever the word is proclaimed and the sacramental salvation mysteries are celebrated. The prophecy of Malachi is accomplished: "I have no pleasure in you, says the Lord of hosts, and I will not accept an offering from your hand. For from the rising of the sun to its setting my name is great among the nations, and in every place incense is offered to my name, and a pure offering; for my name is great among the nations, says the Lord of hosts" (Mal. 1:10-11).

The Church is still an *ekklesia paroikousa,* a sojourning community, because "as long as it is called 'today'" (Heb. 3:13) her fulfillment has not yet been accomplished. The time of the Church is "the time of your exile" (1 Pet. 1:17). "So then, there remains a sabbath rest for the people of God" (Heb. 4:9). But at the same time a real beginning of that fulfillment is already at work in the Church: "But you have come to Mount Zion and to the city of the living God, the heavenly Jerusalem, and to innumerable angels in festal gathering, and to the assembly of the first-born who are enrolled in heaven" (Heb. 12:22-23). Let us then with confidence draw near to the throne of grace, that we may receive mercy and find grace to help in time of need" (Heb. 4:16).

The "Leitmotiv" of the Epistle to the Hebrews is the firm belief that Jesus, as the First-born of creation (Heb. 1:1-14), as one of ours (Heb. 4:14-5:10), in the total fidelity of His suffering and death has gone away through the "curtain" of earthly reality, and has entered into the glory of His Father. From there He functions as Mediator for us (Heb. 2:5-18). The community of those who believe in Him is on a pilgrimage as sojourners in this world and still far from Him and "exposed to abuse and affliction" (Heb. 10:33), but it knows it is safe: "Since you knew that you yourselves had a better possession and an abiding one. Therefore do not throw away your confidence, which has a great reward. For you have need of endurance, so that you may do the will of God and receive what is promised. 'For yet a little while, and the coming one shall come and shall not tarry; but my righteous one shall live by faith, and if he shrinks back, my soul has no pleasure in him' " (Heb. 10:34-38).

This message of consolation amidst suffering undergone for the faith is also the central theme of the Epistles of St. Peter. "More than any other writings of the New Testament, those Epistles (and the Apocalypse) are full of eschatological expectations by which the Church lives."[23]

In this eschatological situation, the question whether the Church is a quantitative or qualitative minority is devoid of importance with respect to one who consciously lives the idea of *paroikia*. The Church must everywhere live with the awareness that she is a community that sojourns in exile. "For here we have no lasting city, but we seek the city which is to come" (Heb. 13:14). Thus, the words *diaspora* and *paroikia* as used in the New Testament express one same idea. The young Church prefers the term *paroikia* because she remembers the technical meaning of the Jewish concept of *diaspora*. But *paroikia*-consciousness borrowed its apostolic zeal from the realization that the Church was a *disaspora*. The Church that lives as *diaspora* is a missionary Church.

e. The Church as the Bride of the Lamb

The tension contained in the consciousness of that eschatological orientation of the Church mystery finds its apotheosis in the last book of the New Testament, the

23. Th. Spörri, *Der Gemeindegedanke im I Petrusbrief*, Gütersloh, 1925; E. Käsermann, *Das wandernde Gottesvolk*, Göttingen, 1957.

Apocalypse or Revelation.[24] The dominant idea throughout this "document of religious resistance" is this: the
Church of martyrs is God's salvific plan for His creation
that is fulfilled in Christ. The Kingdom of God is already
begun in this believing community subject to so much
persecution, and God's judgment is already passed upon
the religious decision for or against Christ.

The Woman and Her Child

And a great portent appeared in heaven, a woman
clothed with the sun, with the moon under her feet, and
on her head a crown of twelve stars; she was with child
and she cried out in her pangs of birth, in anguish for
delivery. And another portent appeared in heaven; behold a great red dragon. . . . And the dragon stood
before the woman who was about to bear a child, that he
might devour her child when she brought it forth; she
brought forth a male child, one who is to rule all the
nations with a rod of iron, but her child was caught up
to God and his throne. And the woman fled to the desert,
in which to be nourished for one thousand two hundred
and sixty days. . . .
And I heard a loud voice in heaven, saying
"Now the salvation and the power and the kingdom
of our God and the authority of his Christ
has come, for the accuser of our brethren
has been thrown down,
who accuses them day and night before our God.
And they have conquered him by the blood of the
Lamb
and by the word of their testimony,
for they loved not their lives even unto death."
And when the dragon saw that he had been thrown to
the earth, he pursued the woman who had borne the
male child. But the woman was given the two wings of

24. W. Thüssing, *Die Erhöhung und Verherrlichung Jesu im Johannesevangelium,* Münster, 1960.

the great eagle that she might fly from the serpent into the wilderness, to the place where she is to be nourished (Rev. 12:1-18).

In this pericope we hear a resonance of the story of creation in Genesis and the prologue of St. John's Gospel. The Woman is the chosen people of God of the Old Covenant; she is the whole creation blessed in Israel which from its very beginning is orientated to the Incarnation of her First-born. The whole creation is "pregnant, in her pangs of birth and in anguish for delivery" for its fulfillment in Christ. In His resurrection and ascension, creation has attained the full accomplishment of the divine plan of salvation. Creation is, in Christ, already with the Father.

But together with the fullness of salvation, evil has also reached its fullness and it is personified by the dragon. The definitive crisis has begun. Although creation that has attained fulfillment in the Church knows it is hidden in Christ with the Father, and hence is beyond Satan's reach, that crisis must still become manifest in the decisive battle between the Woman and the dragon, between the persecuted Church and the powers of this world that are enemies of Christ. This is not a war whose outcome is uncertain, for the matter is already decided, although it must still become manifest in individual men. The Church has already found an inviolable asylum in the desert, where she overcomes Satan because she is nourished "by the blood of the Lamb and the word of their testimony."

The Bride of the Lamb

By slightly shifting the image of Christ's relationship with the Church we get a much clearer view of that relationship:

Let us rejoice and exult and give
him the glory,
for the marriage of the Lamb has
come,
and his Bride has made herself
ready;
it was granted her to be clothed with
fine linen, bright and pure—
for the fine linen is the righteous deeds
of the saints.
And the angel said to me, "Write this:
Blessed are those who are invited to the
supper of the Lamb" (Rev. 19:7-9).

Creation as gathered in the Church has not only attained its fulfillment in Christ, but it experiences that fulfillment as something that is constantly actualized through its bond-of-life with Him. Christ is not only the perfect fruit of creation (Lke 1:42); He is above all the Head of creation who, as the "First-born of creation" constantly gives existence to creation: "All things were made through him" (Jn 1:3). The man Jesus Christ who reached perfection, who, as the Lamb of God, constantly stands as a mediator before the Father, also constantly desires to experience the youthful newness of the wedding banquet with His Bride. He continuously gives her everything from the fullness of His own perfect humanity. The Church lives her own life in Him and already shares in His glory with the Father.

The New Creation

This intimate connection of life with Christ reaches its climax as pictured in the book of Revelation, in the Church seen as the new creation:

Then I saw a new heaven and a new earth; for the first heaven and the first earth had passed away, and the

sea was no more. And I saw the holy city, new Jerusalem, coming down out of heaven from God, prepared as
a bride adorned for her husband; and I heard a great
voice from the throne saying, "Behold, the dwelling of
God is with men. He will dwell with them, and they
shall be his people, and God himself will be with them,
he will wipe away every tear from their eyes, and death
shall be no more, neither shall there be mourning nor
crying nor pain any more, for the former things have
passed away."

And he who sat upon the throne said, "Behold, I make
all things new." Also he said, "Write this, for these
words are trustworthy and true" (Rev. 21:1-5).

Creation is oriented to the Covenant, to being-together-with-God. Being-man, as a *personal* existence, is a
"being-toward." Man, in virtue of his being a person, is
essentially related to others, and finally to The Other, to
God who constantly calls him into existence. In Christ, as
the Emmanuel, the God-with-us, being-man has attained
its most intimate union of existence and of life with God.
That is why creation has reached its ultimate goal in
Him; and all men, in their encounter with that perfect
Man, can become conscious of their own existence as a
being-together-with His Father. For the same reason the
Church as a human believing community is, in Christ,
the living House of God in this creation. The God-with-
them in Christ will be their God.

*f. The Church As Humanly Involved in the Divine Unity of
Life That Exists Between Father and Son Through the
Spirit*

This apocalyptic vision of the Church finds its theological foundation in the Christological explanation of creation given in the Gospel of St. John:

I came from the Father and have come into the world.
. . . This is eternal life, that they know thee the only

true God, and Jesus Christ whom thou hast sent. I
glorified thee on earth, having accomplished the work
which thou gavest me to do; and now, Father, glorify
thou me in thy own presence with the glory which I had
with thee before the world was made. . . .

All that the Father has is mine; . . . all mine are
thine, and I am glorified *in them* . . . The glory which
thou hast given me I have given to them, that they may
be one even as we are one. I in them and thou in me,
that they may become perfectly one, so that the world
may know (in them) that thou hast sent me and hast
loved them even as thou hast loved me.
Father, I desire that they also, whom thou hast given
me, may be with me where I am, to behold my glory
which thou hast given me in thy love for me before the
foundation of the world. . . . (Hence) When the Spirit
of truth comes, he will guide you into all the truth; for
he will not speak on his own authority, but whatever he
hears he will speak, and he will declare to you the things
that are to come. He will glorify me, for he will take
what is mine and declare it to you. All that the Father
has is mine (Jn 16:28; 17:3-10; 17:22-24; 16:13-15).

The ecclesiological dimensions of that mystery of creation revealed in the Incarnation of the Word of God,
through whom all things are created and who came Himself in this world in order to give "to all who received
him, who believed in his name, . . . power to become
children of God" (Jn 1:1-18), become manifest in the
figure of the vine, recalled by St. John, which has its
counterpart in Paul's vision of the Church as the body of
Christ:

I am the true vine, and my Father is the vinedresser.
Every branch of mine that bears no fruit, he takes away,
and every branch that does bear fruit he prunes, that it
may bear more fruit. You are already made clean by the
word which I have spoken to you. Abide in me, and I in
you. As the branch cannot bear fruit by itself, unless it

abides in the vine, neither can you, unless you abide in
me. I am the vine, you are the branches. He who abides
in me, and I in him, he it is that bears much fruit, for
apart from me you can do nothing.

By this my Father is glorified, that you bear much
fruit, and so prove to be my disciples. As the Father has
loved me, so have I loved you; abide in my love. If you
keep my commandments, you will abide in my love, just
as I have kept my Father's commandments and abide in
his love (Jn 15:1-12).

Here the Church's bond-of-life with the Father through
Christ is expressed with even greater intimacy than in St.
Paul. In virtue of the Holy Spirit, Christ has lived in a
human way His divine unity with the Father, in order
that, from His glorified existence with the Father, He
might be able to send that same salvific Spirit to all who
believe in Him.[25] By the power of the Spirit of Christ we
too can experience that divine unity with the Father in a
human way: "He who believes in me as the scripture has
said, 'Out of his heart shall flow rivers of living water.'
Now this he said about the Spirit, which those who believed in him were to receive" (Jn 7:38-39).[26]

The act of faith is a constantly-lived personal act of
surrender to the Father: "whoever believes in him . . .
shall have eternal life" (Jn 3:16). But it is never an
individualistic act; it is always an action in the midst of
the community, marked with the sign of the community,
as is evident from baptism as the sacrament of reception
into the Church of Jesus Christ: "Truly, truly, I say to
you, unless one is born of water and the Spirit, he cannot
enter the kingdom of God" (Jn 3:5; cf. Mk 16:16). And
this ecclesial act of faith finds its highest living expres-

25. M. E. Boismard, "De son ventre couleront des fleuves
d'eau," *Rev. Biblique,* vol. 65 (1958), pp. 522 ff.
26. R. Schnackenburg, *Die Sakramente im Johannesevangelium,* Paris, 1959.

sion in being involved in the Eucharistic surrender of Christ to His Father:

> Who is it that overcomes the world
> but he who believes that Jesus is the Son of God?
> This is he who came by water and blood, Jesus Christ,
> not with the water only but
> with water and the blood.
> And the Spirit is the witness,
> because the Spirit is the truth.
> There are three witnesses,
> the *Spirit, the water, and the blood,*
> and these three agree (1 Jn 5:5-9).

The Spirit of the glorified Lord cultivates faith through the sacraments of baptism and the Eucharist. Through the sacrament of penance also, as the ever-relived baptism, is applied to the penitent what Christ said: "Receive the Holy Spirit. If you forgive the sins of any, they are forgiven; if you retain the sins of any, they are retained" (Jn 20:22). The life, passion, death and resurrection of Jesus for the benefit of men become for us a personal event of salvation through the faith-inspiring Spirit in the sacraments of the Church.

This human involvement in the divine unity that exists between the Father and the Son through the power of the Spirit, is the foundation of the unity in the Church and of the constant care to preserve that unity: "For the Father himself loves you, because you have loved me (and the man Jesus Christ) and have believed that I came from the Father" (Jn 16:27). Practical love of neighbor is the concretely exercised love of God: "He who does not love his brother whom he has seen, cannot love God whom he has not seen" (1 Jn 4:20).

In the Church of Jesus Christ the love for the Father is translated into mutual love that forms a community: "I am the good shepherd. The good Shepherd lays down his

life for his sheep. . . . I know my own and my own know
me, *as* the Father knows me and I know the Father; and I
lay down my life for the sheep. And I have other sheep,
that are not of this fold: I must bring them also, and they
will heed my voice. So there shall be one flock, one
shepherd" (Jn 10:14-16).

It is precisely in this unity of love of the Church, as
salvific community of the glorified Lord, that lies the
power of grace of the Church as a salvific instrument of
the glorified Lord: "That they may all be one; even as
thou, Father, art in me, and I in thee, that they also may
be in us, so that the world may believe that thou hast
sent me. The glory which thou hast given me I have
given to them, that they may be one even as we are one. I
in them and thou in me, that they may become perfectly
one, so that the world may know thou hast sent me and
hast loved them even as thou hast loved me" (Jn 17:21-
23). The loving union of all mankind is the salvific sign,
the sacrament of God's effective love for each man personally.

For the edification of that human community in love
there is the function of the office which is exercised in
the devoted consecration of the one and only Shepherd of
the flock: " 'Simon, son of John, do you love me more
than these?' He said, 'Yes, Lord, you know that I love
you.' He said to him, 'Feed my lambs' " (Jn 21:15). The
office is a sharing in Christ's mission which He received
from His Father: "Sanctify them in truth; thy word is
truth. As thou didst send me into the world, so I have
sent them into the world. And for their sake I consecrate
myself, that they also may be consecrated in truth" (Jn
17:17-19). By that function of the office that serves to
build up the community, the Lord "makes true" His all-
embracing love in all ages and countries: "I do not pray
for these only, but also for those who believe in me
through their word" (Jn 17:20).

g. *Principal Aspects of the Biblical Church-Consciousness*

Our analysis of the principal aspects of the Bible's way of looking at the Church mystery shows clearly that Scripture sees the Church first of all as the human community which, in loving mutual union and in her work for human values, already experiences and lives in a *kenotic way* her being-together with the glorified Lord.

The Church is an eschatological reality. On the one hand, the Church is:

> the fulfilled Israel as people of the Covenant
> the final phase of God's salvific plan for creation
> the new creation
> the *pleroma,* the fullness of Christ
> the body of Christ
> the bride of the Lamb
> the temple of the Holy Spirit
> the house of God.

For in the Church is achieved the human involvement in the divine living unity that exists between Father and Son through the Holy Spirit, through the encounter with Christ. All men are crucified, have died, were buried, rose and were glorified *together with* Christ.

On the other hand, the Church is:

> the "intermediary time"
> God's People on-the-way
> *paroikē,* sojourner
> diaspora.

For she is still far from the Lord and still undergoes and experiences her fulfillment in Christ in the ministry of word and sacrament as a "sharing in the death of Christ, until He returns." She is already filled with Christ, but it is still a veiled presence by which she has still to fulfill everything in Christ. The personal glorification of Christ must still become the glorification of all mankind through the experience of the gift of God transmitted through the office, the gift of the vivifying Spirit.

Through the power of that encounter with Christ in word and sacrament, that believing community must live the being-the-son-of-the-Father in Christ, *in* this reality: "The glory which thou hast given me I have given to them, *that* they may be one even *as* we are one" (Jn 17:22). And it is precisely in this loving unity of the Church, as salvific community of the glorified Lord, that is found the power of the Church that fulfills all creation, as the salvific instrument of the glorified Lord.

3. THE CHURCH AS PILGRIM PEOPLE OF GOD THAT LIVES BY A DIALOGUE AROUND THE SACRAMENTAL WORD

a. Discovery of the Church

We have lived as members of the Church of Jesus Christ for twenty centuries. In spite of that, our reflection on being God's people saved in Christ has not yet advanced to the stage that permits us to present a balanced integral vision of the mystery of salvation that is being accomplished in the Church. In the long and rich history of Catholic theology we look in vain for ecclesiology. And the many theologians who have noted that strange absence find it difficult to give a satisfactory explanation of that fact.

On the one hand, the Christians of our own time have come to realize that there has been a one-sided speculative reflection upon matters of faith; the distinct aspects of the reality of Revelation have not been approached enough from the standpoint of the all-illuminating central mystery of Christ. A theology that does not start from the biblical testimony about Christ inevitably bogs down into isolated treatises that lose sight of the one supreme salvific event. And then the Church does not clearly appear as the personally lived reality of salvation in which the diverse aspects of the mystery of Christ attain their synthesis.

On the other hand, the Church has not been seen as constituting the whole mystery of Christ which is being achieved during the period "in between," that begins with the ascension and ends with the return of Christ. On that account theological reflection during the many centuries of the Church's defensive struggle against threatening heresies became mixed in the reflection upon the outward, socially-organized structure of that salvific event.

Hierarchism

"The Church is the association of people who are bound together by the profession of the same Christian faith and participation in the same sacraments, under the guidance of lawful pastors, particularly the Pope of Rome as Vicar of Christ upon earth."[27] This is Bellarmine's "definition" of the Church that has governed the Catholic proclamation of the faith even in the twentieth century. In it we find echoes of the attacks made upon the faith by the Reformation, Gallicanism, Conciliarism and humanism.

The concept of the Church suffered another impoverishment in the defense against the rationalistic and deistic ideas of the eighteenth century, and she was not able to escape from their influence. J. A. Möhler sharply characterized that narrowing of the concept of Church when he wrote: "God (in the beginning) created the Hierarchy, and the Church is more than well provided for until the end of the world."[28]

We find the culmination of that development in the

27. *De conciliis*, 1.3, c.2, Cf. J. Beumer, "Die kirchliche Gliedschaft in der Lehre des heiligen Robert Bellarminus," *Theologie und Glaube*, 1947-48, p. 243.

28. J. A. Möhler, *Theologisches Quartalschrift,* vol. 104 (1923), p. 497.

declaration of the dogma of the primacy and infallibility of the Pope during the First Vatican Council. It is true that doctrinal declaration was the eleventh chapter of the Schema on the Church and that events prevented further discussion of this subject. In the first chapter the Church is spoken of as the Mystical Body of Christ, on the basis of Ephesians 4; and there are clear signs of the presence of a new concept of the Church.[29] It is nevertheless characteristic of the still predominant apologetic and defensive Church-consciousness, that the Council arrived at the isolated and hence one-sided dogma of the primacy and papal infalibility, without feeling it necessary to relate it to the whole mystery of the Church. On that account the sudden and fatal ending of the Council occasioned an extreme emphasis upon the juridical-hierarchical aspect of the Church; and later on this would be echoed by the New Code of Canon Law of 1917.[30]

The Second Vatican Council stigmatized that apologetic ecclesiology as clericalism, hierarchism, papalism and triumphalism.[31] The concept of the Church in Catholic thought and life had become so narrow that she was almost exclusively thought of as an organ of salvation that was endowed with divine guarantees, an organ enjoying a certain amount of autonomy which distributes the truth and grace imparted by Christ to individual believers on their way to heaven.

29. *Acta et decreta sacrorum conciliorum recentiorum, Collectio lacensis, 1870-1890*, vol. 7, p. 567; J. D. Mansi, *Sacrorum conciliorum nova et amplissima collectio*, Paris, 1901-27, vol. 51, p. 529.

30. Yves Congar, "Bulletin d'Ecclésiologie," *Recherches Sc. Phil. et Théol.*, vol. 31(1947), pp. 272 ff. Cf. M. Pribella, "Vom Ringen um die Kirche," *Stimmen der Zeit*, vol. 124 (1933), pp. 289 ff.

31. F. X. Arnold, "Das gott-menschliche Prinzip der Seelsorge in pastoral-geschichtlicher Entfaltung," *Theol. Quartalschrift*, vol. 124 (1943), pp. 99 ff.; vol. 125 (1944), pp. 57 ff.; Congar, *Jalons pour une théologie du laicat*, Paris, 1953, p. 24.

"What is the idea that the average modern Catholic has of the Church? It must be admitted that there has been a change in the thoughts of Catholics during the last ten years, but it remains true that the generality of Catholics are still viewing the Church principally from the standpoint of her external appearance rather than according to her inner nature. A long historical development of theological and religious thought, of which the controversies with the Reformation constitute one important phase, drew an increasingly exclusive attention to the organic externals of the Church. It was primarily a matter of proving that the Church, according to her own concept of herself, is a "perfect society"; that she is truly the Church that was founded by Jesus Christ, who gave her a visible head in Peter and his successors; that in the Church there is a distinction between priests and lay people, between the authority that gives orders and a docile flock. Finally, theology was concerned with proving that the Church is the great Institute of salvation proclaiming the truth of Christ and administering the sacraments. In this way the whole activity of the Church both within and without the liturgical worship, became an affair of the clergy alone. Thus more and more Catholics came to look upon the Church as an external and demanding power which, like the State, promulgates laws and regulations, controls and punishes, and whose principal task is to contribute a kind of public moral police force."[32]

When the Catholic spoke about the Church, he saw her almost exclusively as the salvation instrument of the glorified Lord. Christ's fidelity to His Church was so cen-

32. F. Hofmann, "Geloofsgrondslag van de liturgische vernieuwing," *Theologisch Perspectief*, vol. 3, Hilversum, 1960, p. 78. Cf. St. Jaki, *Les tendances nouvelles de l'ecclésiologie*, vol. 3, Rome, 1957, p. 189.

tral in his thought that he paid almost no attention to the human community of believers, in which Christ's words and action receive a human form. He was so strongly conscious of the gift of salvation in the word and sacrament of the Church, that, in his heated controversy with the Reformed Christians, he scarcely ever became aware of the fact that the task of the Church is never fulfilled.

Because he did not sufficiently see the Church as the eschatologically orientated community of salvation, as the people of God that was still on the way, he saw the Church as the historical prolongation of the Incarnation; he spoke about the identity of Christ and the Church and raised the Church's words and actions to the height of the words and actions of Christ.

When he confessed the infallibility of the Pope "of himself" there always sounded a triumphant self-assurance, as if the Church were the possessor of truth. And in the salvific actions of the Church a too exclusive attention was paid to the aspect that the sacraments work salvation *ex opere operato*, that is, they give grace by the power of the salvific action itself. That is why he attributed to the proclamations by the Church, a purity which because of her involvement in the situation of man and the world in her own time she cannot possibly possess. That is why the Church's administration of the sacraments was in danger of acquiring a too automatic and magical character; and in sacramental theology too little attention was paid to the essential interaction between Christ's act of salvation and man's act of faith.

"God and One's Own Soul"

The Reformers were driven to an ever more radical opposition to the Catholic Church in the reaction of their faith against that one-sided Catholic idea of the Church. The Reformed Christian stressed ever more the sinfulness of human life and the sinful incompleteness of the Church.

And because he lived according to this overstressed concept of the eschatological situation of the Church as a community of faith, he was unable to accept the Church as a salvific instrument of Christ. In this view of the Church of Jesus Christ there was no room for the divine guarantee that Christ would never abandon His Church until the end of the world. In the mind of the Reformed Christian, the Church was so much the people of God, far away from the Lord, that is his reaction against the Catholic over-insistance on the other side, he was unable to resist to the temptation to lower Christ's fidelity to the Church to the level of the sinful Church's fidelity to Christ.

That is why he felt unable to speak of the infallibility of the Church, in spite of the guarantee given by Christ. The truth of the Church's proclamation and the salvific power of the Churches' sacramental actions were measured by the genuineness of personal faith.

This excessive attention to the genuineness of the act of faith inevitably led to a religious individualism that was expressed in the words "God and one's own soul," in which Church-consciousness was in danger of becoming wholly atrophied. B. R. Rother voiced the attitude-of-faith of many Reformed Christians in the words: "According to the Lord's intention, the form in which the Kingdom of God . . . must be outwardly expressed is not the Christian Church." And E. Troeltsch went so far as to propose that the term "church" be dropped and left to Catholics.[33]

"The Church Awakens in Souls"

The period of transition in which we are living seems to be a collision between the extreme of an old world view

33. A. de Quervain, *Gesetz und Freiheit*, Stuttgart, 1930, p. 210.

and a radically new Christian view of the world. Both Reformed Catholics and Christians are now experiencing a complete revaluation of what it means to be a Christian through a "rediscovery of the Church." Both are aware of the salvation-historical significance of being thrown back together upon the fundamental question of what it means to be a Christian. In all Churches there are many who are afraid that Christians might tragically fail to make use of the opportunities that are offered them because they are unable to find one another during this time of mutual renewal. Never during the centuries of separation have Christian Churches come so close to one another as in our own day. If we fail now, we shall, perhaps, grow definitively apart.

"This awakening of the question concerning the Church, "says Thurneysen, "seems to me precisely characteristic of the hour of history in which we are living. I believe that this question will continue to greatly occupy our minds and move us during the coming years and decades."[34] And Guardini adds: "An event of inconceivable scope and consequences has taken place: the Church awakens in souls."[35] The ecumenical dimension of this rediscovery of the Church comes increasingly to the fore: "If we could only become one here, all doctrinal difference would either be easily put aside, or be neutralized, or at least they would be more bearable."[36]

It was for the fulfillment of an ecumenical task that Pope John expected so much from the Church renewal that was to be initiated by the Second Vatican Council, to

34. E. Thurneysen, "Die Frage nach der Kirche," *Zwischen den Zeiten,* vol. 4 (1926), pp. 470 ff.

35. Romano Guardini, "Von Sinn der Kirche," *Hochland,* 1921-22, p. 257.

36. K. G. Steck, "Was der Papst über seine Kirche lehrt," *Stimmen der Gemeinde,* vol. 2 (1950), pp. 5, 8. Cf. W. von Loewenich "Das bevorstehende Konzil der römischen Kirche," *Una Sancta,* vol. 14(1959), pp. 172 ff.

which he invited representatives of the other Churches as active collaborators: "With the help of God's grace we shall call the Council together. And we desire to prepare it by considering everything that needs to be strengthened and made alive within the Catholic Communion of faith, in accordance with our Lord's intentions. And when we have completed that enormous task, avoiding everything that might impede its rapid progress, we shall then present to the world the Church in her full splendor without spot or wrinkle. And we shall say to our separated brethren, Orthodox and Protestant: Behold, brethren, this is the Church of Christ. We have tried to be faithful to her and ask the Lord to give us the grace that she may so remain as He has desired her to be."[37]

b. The Mystery of the Church

The renewal of religious reflection upon the mystery of the Church began with the three greatest theologians of the nineteenth century: J. A. Möhler, M. J. Scheeben and Cardinal John Henry Newman.

According to J. Geiselman,[38] the development of ecclesiology passed through three phases in Möhler's thought.

a. In the first works of Möhler there is still a predominance of the juridical concept of the Church that belonged to post-Tridentine theology. But a growing attention is paid to the "mystical" reality of the Church; the operation of the Spirit, the invisible community of faith and love. Those two aspects are still juxtaposed and in opposition to each other.

b. In the first edition of *Die Einheit in der Kirche*

---

37. August 9, 1959. *Osservatore Romano*, August 10-11.
38. J. R. Geiselmann, "Einheit und Liebe, Ihr Gestaltwandel in Möhlers Theologie der Kirche," *Die eine Kirche*, ed. by H. Tüchte, Paderborn, 1938, p. 137; Y. M. J. Congar, "La signification oecuménique de l'oeuvre de Möhler," *Irenikon*, 5 (1938). pp. 133 ff.

(1825), Möhler tries to unite those two aspects. He attempts this by looking upon the Church as an organism in which the dynamic power of the Holy Spirit as the interior principle of her life unites the many members into one community which becomes visible as a hierarchical organization.

c. In his later works he turns increasingly away from an organic and pneumacentric concept of the Church in order to shed light on her incarnational structure. He sees Christ as central in the Church and, in analogy with the unity of Person of the God-man, he emphasizes the unity of the Church within the distinction of the divine and the human aspects.

Scheeben saw the Church as the "prolongation of the mystery of the Incarnation." She is the Body of Christ, in which all members participate in the divine glory of the Head and through Him live in union with one another. As once took place in Mary, so in the Church, as the Bride of Christ, the Son of God is continually born by the overshadowing of the Holy Spirit. It was in Mary that that marriage of mankind and Christ was begun and in her that the community of life was most perfectly realized. That is why she is "the Mother of the Mystical Body of Christ."[39]

According to Newman, the Church is the living organism of the reality of the Revelation which is the Incarnation of God's Son. This organism unfolds in time and by it Christ Himself accomplishes His work of salvation in the sending of His Spirit. The Church's development through history is a germinating, growing and maturing

39. Scheeben, *Mysterien des Christentums.* Cf. K. Algermissen, *Konfessionskunde,* Paderborn, 1950, p. 180; A. Kerkvoorde, "Le mystère de l'Eglise d'après Scheeben," *La Vie spirituelle,* 58 6 (1939), pp. 133 ff. 167 ff.

of the original seed that was already placed in her from the beginning through the Incarnation.[40]

These efforts to revaluate biblical and especially patristic thought made possible the rediscovery of the Church, because they opened up the full perspective on the Church as a *mystery:* the visible organizational structure of the Church is the sacramental sign of the human community of life with the glorified Lord.

The First Vatican Council

The renewal of the concept of the Church after World War I clearly sought to make a connection with the tendencies that were already present in the unfinished Schema "De Ecclesia" of Vatican Council I, under the influence of Möhler and Scheeben. "This project has remotely become the foundation for the dogmatic treatment of the doctrine concerning the Church."[41]

This dogmatic Constitution sees the Church as the Mystical Body of Christ: "The only-begotten Son of God, who enlightens every man who comes into this world, and never denies His help to the unfortunate children of Adam, in the fullness of time, as determined by eternal decree, became like to men. He appeared visibly in the figure of our body, in order that earthly and corporal men might 'put on the new nature, created after the likeness of God in true righteousness and holiness' (Eph. 4:24). It is in this way that they must form the Mystical Body of which He himself is the Head.". . .

40. M. Laros, "Newman als ökumenische Gestalt," *Die neue Ordnung*, 1946-47, p. 71. Cf. W. H. van de Pol, *De Kerk in het leven en denken van Newman*, Nijkerk, 1936.
41. J. Neuner and H. Roos, *Der Glaube der Kirche in der Urkunden der Lehrverkundigung*, Regensburg, 1961, p. 217 Cf. J. Leder, "L'oeuvre ecclésiologique du Concile du Vatican," *Etudes*, 1960, pp. 289 ff.

"The Church has all the properties of a true society. Christ did not leave this society completely undetermined and without any fixed forms. Rather, He Himself gave it existence and His will also determined what her form of life was to be and He gave her the constitution. . . ."

It is from this source that comes "the visible office of teaching which proclaims openly what must be interiorly believed and must be confessed outwardly. Hence also the visible priestly office that in virtue of an official commission directs and cares for the interior sanctification of men and the glorification due to God. Hence also the visible office of leadership that administers and directs the whole outward and public life of the faithful in the Church and establishes order and unity among the members."[42]

Through the influence of powerful writers like Romano Guardini[43] and Karl Adam[44] this idea of the Mystical Body of Christ has penetrated deeply into Catholic religious thought. E. Mersch was able to speak about "the mystical Christ, center of theology as a science."[45] C. Feckes, basing himself on that Vatican vision of the Church, tried to construct a new ecclesiology in which, at the same time, the elements of the traditional organizational idea of the Church could be incorporated: "The great significance of all that is visible in the Church consists in this that it is useful for the 'extensive' work of mediation of the divine Head and the incarnate Mediator, and that it does give a permanent testimony to the Christocentric character of our salvation. The structure of an institute of salvation is the fundamental form of the

42. Neuner and Roos, *op. cit.* pp. 228-230.
43. Romano Guardini, *Vom Sinn der Kirche*, Mainz, 1923.
44. Karl Adam, *Das Wesen des Katholizismus*, Düsseldorf, 1924.
45. *Nouv. Rev. Théol.*, 5 (1934) pp. 449 ff. cf. E. Mersch, *La Théologie du Corps mystique*, 2 vols., Brussels, 1944.

Church because the incorporation into it constitutes the foundation for an actualized Mystical Body. . . . Here indeed we find the connection between the two concepts of the Church. . . . The organizational means of the institute of salvation are nothing but the operative organs of the Mystical Body."[46]

Crisis

While this vision of the Church as the Mystical Body of Christ enjoyed a monopoly, there was no lack of criticism of its one-sidedness. There was little chance for the critics to be listened to at first, for it provoked astonishment and even anger,[47] but since 1940 that criticism has brought about an increasingly evident tension in the Catholic Church.

The dissatisfaction with the one-sided approach to the Church as the Mystical Body of Christ developed chiefly for the following reasons:

The Church was looked at only from the standpoint of one of the many biblical images, and this image was speculatively developed in one direction only: the relation between Christ and the Church was described on the basis of the functioning of the human body.

The defenders of the "Mystical Body" theory finally and naively crossed the boundaries that separate image and reality.

What content can one give to the term "mystical" which, moreover, is not of Pauline origin? Devout imagination is liable to misuse it as a cover for a false mysticism.

46. C. Feckes, *Het mysterie der heilige Kerk*, Averbode, 1939, pp. 175-182.
47. E. Przywara, "Corpus Christi mysticum, Eine Bilanz," *Zeitschrift für Aszese und Mystik*, 15 (1940), pp. 197 ff; K. Adam, "Ekklesiologie im Werden," *Theol. Quartalschr.*, 122 (1941), pp. 145 ff.

Is it possible to avoid the danger of viewing the Church as the pronlongation of the Incarnation and even of identification of Christ and the Church?

Church-consciousness is threatened by a biologism that makes lawful every development as being merely an organic growth and by a juridicism that constantly over-emphasizes the office by placing authority in opposition to the community of faith.

In this vision of the Church there is an exclusive stress on "being-already" in Christ; there is no room for the "not yet" of her eschatological incompleteness and her sinful dividedness.

The most serious objection, however, is the fact that the Church is isolated from salvation history and from the whole of God's salvific action with His creation in His First-born, from which follows of necessity an exclusive identification of the Church of Jesus Christ with the Roman-Catholic Church.

Especially Koster and Cerfaux have endeavored to bring theological reflection back to the perspective of the salvation history in God's Covenantal activity. In this way they re-oriented theology to the idea of the "People of God":

"The 'People of God' constitutes the presupposition, the point of departure, the foundation, the frame, the norm for the understanding of the other designations of the Church. None of these designations should be explained and understood as contrary to what is expressed in the term 'People of God.' Each one of the other designations can express only a side or a viewpoint that is not at once seen in the term 'People of God' alone. . . . The meaning contained in 'People of God' is everywhere decisive for the meaning of images and metaphors, for these stand in the service of the understanding of 'People of God,' and they cannot have any value of their own that could set a standard for the interpretation of 'People of God.' Consequently, they must always be interpreted in relation to 'People of God' and not *sociologically, politically, 'familiarly' or even biologically, as has unfortunately become* the custom."[48]

"The Church, then, continues the ancient People and fulfills the idea God conceived of His chosen People: she is the Israel of God. She, is, from another standpoint, a new People, because of the great newness established by the Spirit in contrast with the 'flesh,' namely, the ancient People. She is a point of departure, a creation in the spiritual order. The new People was present in God's mind when He granted Abraham heavenly goods through a testament. Hence the Christian Church is, in Christ, the true legatee of God."[49]

The work of Koster met with strong opposition in Germany. The idea of the "People of God" would reduce the Church to an invisible communion; individual decisions of conscience would be played off against the Church's teaching authority, the general priesthood against the specific office, a semi-quietism would diminish man's share in the work of salvation, irrational thinking would seek an outlet in an exaggerated "liturgism."[50] Under the heavy pressure of political persecution, the inner tension in the Church of Germany increased very rapidly and caused a profound confusion. In that crisis Archbishop Gröber of Feiburg made an appeal to his fellow-bishops

48. M. D. Koster, *Ekklesiologie im Werden*, Paderborn, 1940, pp. 147-148.

49. L. Cerfaux, *La Théologie de l'Eglise suivant Saint Paul*, Paris, 1942, p. 299.

50. E. Przywara, "Theologie der Kirche, Ekklesiologie," *Scholastik*, 16 (1941), pp. 321 ff. Cf. M. Kassiepe, *Irrwege und Umwege im Frömmigkeitsleben der Gegenwart*, Wurzburg, 1940.

and to Pope Pius XII. This appeal formed the background of the Encyclical "Mystici Corporis Christi" of June 29, 1943.[51]

The Encyclical "Mystici Corporis Christi"

The encyclical, on the one hand, turns against every sort of apologetic rationalism which "sees and wants to see in the Church nothing but a juridical and social union." On the other hand it opposes every attack of those who "through empty fear look upon so profound a doctrine (of the Mystical Body of Christ) as something dangerous."[52]

For just as "the Word of God willed to make use of our nature, when in excruciating agony He would redeem mankind; in much the same way, throughout the centuries, He makes use of the Church that the work begun might endure." Hence "we shall find no expression more noble, more sublime or more divine than the phrase which calls it 'the Mystical Body of Jesus Christ.' "[53] The Encyclical also refers to the Schema "De Ecclesia" of Vatican Council I.

Amidst the great debate regarding the relations between the visibility and the invisibility of the Church, the Encyclical is intent on finding a synthesis of the two alternatives. On the one hand every attempt to reduce being-a-Christian to being a member of an invisible Church is repudiated: "If the Church is a 'body' (Col. 1:18) it. . . . is not enough that the Body of the Church be an unbroken unity; it must also be something definite and perceptible to the senses. . . . Hence they err in a

51. El. Lialine, "Une étappe en ecclésiologie, Réflexions sur l'Encyclique Mystici Corporis," *Irenikon,* 19 (1946) pp. 129 ff., 283 ff. (1947) pp. 34 ff.

52. *The Mystical Body of Christ, Encyclical of Pope Pius XII,* America Press, 1943, nos. 12-13, p. 7.

53. *Ibid.,* no. 16-18.

matter of divine truth, who imagine the Church to be invisible, intangible, a something merely 'pneumatological,' as they say, by which many Christian communities, though they differ from each other in their profession of faith, are united by a bond that eludes the senses."[54]

"For this reason above all the Church is called a body, that it is constituted by the coalescence of structurally united parts, and that it has a variety of members reciprocally dependent. . . . One must not think, however, that this ordered or 'organic' structure of the Body of the Church contains only hierarchical elements and with them is complete. . . . When the Fathers of the Church sing the praises of the Mystical Body of Christ with its ministries, its variety of ranks, its offices, its order, its duties, they are thinking not only of those who have received sacred orders, but all those, too, who, (are) following the evangelical counsels. . . . they were thinking of those (also) who, though living in the world, consecrate themselves wholeheartedly to spiritual or corporal works of mercy; as well as those who live in the state of holy matrimony."[55]

Although the Church is a society with a visible structure, her nature lies, nevertheless, is an invisible reality of salvation: "To this Spirit of Christ, too, as to an invisible principle, is to be ascribed the fact that all the parts of the Body are joined one with the other and with their exalted Head; for He is entire in the Head, entire in the Body and entire in each of the members. To the members He is present and assists them in proportion to their various tasks and offices."[56]

On the other hand, the encyclical wishes to remove

54. No. 18.
55. Nos. 20-22.
56. No. 69.

every threat of juridical or biological one-sidedness regarding the manner of conceiving the mystery of the Church: "There are several reasons why it (the expression 'Mystical Body') should be used; for by it we may distinguish the Body of the Church, which is a society whose Head and Ruler is Christ, from His physical Body, . . . as well as from any ordinary body in the natural order, whether physical or moral."[57]

"In a natural body the principle of unity so unites the parts that each lacks its own individual subsistence; on the contrary in the Mystical Body that mutual union, though intrinsic, links the members by a bond which leaves to each intact his own personality. Besides, if we examine the relation existing between the several members and between the members and the head, in every physical, living body, all the different members are ultimately destined to the good of the whole alone; while every moral association of men, if we look to its ultimate usefulness, is in the end directed to the advancement of all and of every single member. For they are persons."[58]

"But if we compare a Mystical Body to a moral body, here again we must notice that the difference between them is not slight, rather it is very considerable and very important. In the moral body, the principle of union is nothing more than the common end, and the common cooperation of all under authority for the attainment of that end. Whereas in the Mystical Body, of which We are speaking, this collaboration is supplemented by a distinct internal principle, which exists effectively in the whole and in each of its parts, and whose excellence is such, that of itself it is vastly superior to whatever bonds of union may be found in a physical or moral body. This is something, as We said above, not of the natural but of

57. No. 73.
58. No. 74.

the supernatural order. Essentially it is something infinite, uncreated: the Spirit of God."[59]

"From what We have thus far written and explained, Venerable Brothers, it is clear, We think, how grievously they err who arbitrarily picture the Church as something hidden and invisible, as do they also who look upon it as a mere human institution with a certain disciplinary code and external ritual, but lacking power to communicate supernatural life."[60]

"For this reason We deplore and condemn the pernicious error of those who conjure up from their fancies an imaginary Church, a kind of Society that finds its origin and growth in charity, to which they somewhat contemptuously oppose another, which they call juridical. . . . There can, then, be no real opposition or conflict between the invisible mission of the Holy Spirit and the juridical commission of Ruler and Teacher received from Christ."[61]

Persistent Dissatisfaction

This Christocentric and well-balanced Encyclical was not able to remove the existing dissatisfaction because its speculative-theological consideration was based too much on one biblical image, whereas the many other biblical images were scarcely and certainly not fully taken into consideration. And from an ecumenical standpoint, that view was unsatisfactory because it exclusively connected the sending of the Holy Spirit with the specific office and left no room for the recognition of the Christian and ecclesial status of the separated communions of believers. This dissatisfaction culminates in the question:

Is the Church an institute of salvation, given to all

59. No. 75.
60. No. 78.
61. No. 79.

centuries, through which the individual believer passes onward to the Father, and in which he receives the revelation of the eternal divine truths, the eternal divine laws and the sacramental means of salvation? *Or* is the Church herself on her way as the People of God, a People already saved in Christ, but that tries, in an ever present encounter with Christ, to give a contemporary response to its being-saved in Christ, even though it is profoundly aware of its own incompleteness and sinful infidelity?

We should avoid over-emphasizing the opposition between that static dogmatic view of the Church and the dynamic salvation-historical concept; on the other hand, the monopoly of speculative thinking did result in a petrifaction of Catholic reflection on the faith.

Logical reasoning threatened to push aside the ever-actual loving initiative of the Father in Christ. In its reflection upon the nature of God and the divine attributes, scholastic manuals of theology congealed the Father's salvific activity that is accomplished in Christ and His Church, making it a static reality from which truths that are valid for all times could be logically deduced.

That scholastic theology has constantly failed to do justice to the actuality of God's salvific activity and to the eschatologically oriented historicity of human life. The history-making entrance of God into His creation through Christ cannot be fixed rationally; but it constantly crucifies the anti-Christian possibilities of human thought. Man is constantly led, in his totality, through Christ, by way of Golgotha, to the morning of the resurrection.

Religious reflection must, therefore, be always at the service of the contemporary response of our being-a-Christian. In it, an absolute priority must be given to God's salvific action in this time, in this culture and these present concrete social circumstances. God's loving activ-

ity in Christ cannot be precalculated with logical necessity; we can be aware of it only in our constant readiness
to listen to the word of God, as it is being proclaimed.

It is on the basis of that consciousness of the mystery
of the Church in terms of salvation history that we must
explain the dissatisfaction that remains even after the
Encyclical *Mystici Corporis Christi*.

The Second Vatican Council

This council sanctioned the renewal of Catholic reflection on faith by considering the Church primarily from
the salvation-historical perspective as the People of God.
It thereby opened the way for an internal Church renewal and an ecumenical rapprochement to the other
Churches:

" 'But in every nation any one who fears him and does
what is right is acceptable to Him' (Acts. 10:35). God,
however, does not make men holy and save them merely
as individuals, without bond or link between one another.
Rather has it pleased Him to bring men together as one
people, a people which acknowledges Him in truth and
serves Him in holiness. He therefore chose the race of
Israel as a people unto Himself. With it He set up a
covenant. Step by step He taught and prepared this people, making known in its history both Himself and the
decree of His will and making it holy unto Himself."

"All these things, however, were done by way of preparation and as a figure of that new and perfect covenant,
which was to be ratified in Christ, and of that fuller
revelation which was to be given through the Word of
God Himself made flesh. 'Behold the days are coming,
says the Lord, when I will make a new covenant with the
house of Israel, and with the house of Judah. . . . I will
give my law within them, and I will write it upon their
hearts; and I will be their God, and they shall be my

people. . . . For they shall all know Me, from the least of them even to the greatest, says the Lord' " (Jer. 31:31-34).

"Christ instituted this new covenant, the new testament, that is to say in His Blood (1 Cor. 11:25), calling together a people made up of Jew and gentile, making them one, not according to the flesh but in the Spirit. This was to be the new people of God. For those who believe in Christ, who are reborn not from perishable but from an imperishable seed through 'the living. . . . word of God' (1 Pet. 1:23), not from the flesh but from water and the Holy Spirit, are finally established as 'a chosen race, a royal priesthood, a holy nation, God's own people. . . . Once you were no people but now you are God's people' (1 Pet. 2:9-10)."

"Israel according to the flesh, which wandered as an exile in the desert, was already called the assembly (Church) of the Lord (Num. 20:4). So likewise the new Israel which while living in this present age goes in search of a future and lasting city (Heb. 13:44) is called the Church of Christ. . . . Moving forward through trial and tribulation, the Church is strengthened by the power of God's grace, which was promised to her by the Lord, so that in the weakness of the flesh she may not waver from perfect fidelity, but remain a bride worthy of her Lord, and moved by the Holy Spirit may never cease to renew herself, until through the Cross she arrives at the light which knows no setting."[62]

Bipolarity of the Mystery of the Church

An ecumenical rapprochement between the separated Churches must be considered possible in the climate created by the Council. This will have to focus its attention

62. Dogmatic Constitution on the Church, NCWC ed., 1964, no. 9.

before all on the bipolar mystery of the Church. Many, both Reformed and Catholic Christians, have tried to analyze the bipolarity of that mystery, and each time they have put the accent differently and the danger of offensive or defensive one-sidedness has always been present. Thus, the Church has been presented as a complex totality of:

Appearance and reality (R. Grosche, G. Holstein)

Reality and ideal (K. Adam, A. Seitz)

Juridical Church and Church of Love (R. Sohm, K. Neuendorfer)

Organization and Organism (A. Rademacher, K. Steck)

Society and community (F. Tonnis)

Sacramental Church and Church of Grace (F. Hoffmann)

Hierarchical Church and Mystical Body of Christ (M. Scheler)

Institute of Salvation and community of salvation (G. Wehrung)

Institution and event (J. L. Leuba)

Churchdom and Church (Th. Harnack)

The horizontal and the vertical (W. A. Visser 't Hooft)

The objective and the subjective (K. Barth)

The static and the dynamic (K. Rahner)

The divine and the human (J. Bernhart, Th. Sartory)

Gift and task (W. Koster, Y. Congar)

Community and personality (H. Odeberg)

Collectivity and personality (A. Strom)

Law and love (H. Wulf)

Authority and freedom (K. Adam)

Office and pneuma (O. Mauer)[63]

In this groping for the contrasting aspects of the Church, theology aims at making transparent the exter-

63. M. Valeske, *Votum Ecclesiae*, Munich, 1962, pp. 30-33.

nal social way the Church appears to men, in order to
discover in it the salvific reality of the mystery of Christ
that is being accomplished in this creation.

In order to express that bipolarity of the mystery of the
Church we have chosen the words "community of salvation" and "instrument of salvation" in the sense of a
"redeemed and redeeming community," of an ever actual
gift and an ever unfinished task. We realize that this
terminology also expresses incompletely the salvific activity of the Church and invites justifiable criticism. But
we prefer these terms to others, because they express
better the tension that exists in the salvific reality of that
Mystery.

c. The Church as a Field of Tension

Isaiah, in his sublime prophecy about the Messiah as
the *Ebed Yahweh*, not only foretold His life of complete
fidelity to the Father and His glorification by the Father,
but he also announced the real change that His solidarity
with sinful man was to bring about in the whole of man's
life: "It was the will of the Lord to bruise him; he has put
him to grief. . . . he was wounded for our transgres-
sions, he was bruised for our iniquities; . . . the Lord has
laid on him the iniquity of us all, . . . although he had
done no violence, and there was no deceit in his mouth.
. . . By his knowledge shall the righteous one, my servant, make many to be accounted righteous, and he shall
bear their iniquities. Therefore I will divide him a portion
with the great and he shall divide the spoil with the
strong, because he poured out his soul to death" (Is.
53:2-12).

This prophecy of Isaiah opens a perspective on the salvific activity of Christ *and* also on the People of God
which He will acquire by His self-oblation, it opens a
perspective on the Church as a community-of-faith that

knows that it is saved in Christ. The community of all who in their believing self-oblation will die and rise with Him is already an objective reality in His glorified human existence with the Father, that is, the Church is already an objective fact: "And being made perfect, he became the source of eternal salvation to all who obey him being designated by God a high priest after the order of Melchizedek" (Heb. 5:9-10).

Trinitarian Dimensions of the Church

The salvation of all men lies contained in the Incarnation of God's Son:

a. "By the Father you have been raised with Christ. . . . Your life is hidden with Christ in God" (Col. 3:1-3).

b. The glorified Son of the Father continues to be present as saving in the saving signs of word and sacrament, in all ages and countries, as the source of salvation for all men: "He who hears you, hears me" (Lke 10:16). And "he who believes and is baptized, will be saved" (Mk 16:16). for "he who hears my word, and believes him who sent me, has eternal life" (Jn 5:24).

c. In His glorified human existence Christ realizes His mediatorship for us with the Father by sending us His Spirit in the word to which we respond and the sacrament we believingly receive: "I will not leave you desolate; I will come to you" (Jn 14:18). "While Peter was still saying this, the Holy Spirit fell on all who heard the word." For "exalted at the right hand of God and having received from the Father the promise of the Holy Spirit, he has poured out this Spirit which you see and hear" (Acts 10:44; 2:33).

The Church, as the People of God that was acquired by Christ, lives wholly by the divine revelation of the mystery of the Incarnation and has definite Trinitarian dimensions in her personal relation to the self-communicating divine Persons: she is "House of God," "Body of Christ" and "Temple of the Holy Spirit."[64]

The Christocentric approach to the mystery of the Church is, therefore, beyond the Reformational accusation of Christo-monism, which forgets that we are living in the era of the Spirit. For the Church does not live in an immediate relation with the Third Person, but from the dynamic presence of the Holy Spirit sent by the Father in the Incarnation of the Son. "The Lord is the Spirit" (2 Cor. 3:17). The man Jesus Christ was conceived of the Holy Spirit and it was only after His human accomplishment that He was able to send His Spirit" (Jn 7:39). In the Church it is a matter of receiving of the Spirit of Christ. "The presence of the Holy Spirit in the Church must not be thought of as without the real presence of Christ, the Crucified and Exalted."[65]

The Church as Community of Salvation and Instrument of Salvation of the Glorified Lord

The glorified man Jesus Christ is not only the *Head of the Church* (Col. 1:18) as the Savior of mankind, but He is also the First-born of all creation, who himself, for the benefit of all men, responded to the ideal that the Triune God had in view with the creation of every individual man. For this reason in Him is contained also the whole

64. Y. Congar, "Ecclesia de Trinitate," *Irenikon*, 14 (1937), pp. 131 ff. H. Schlier, "Die Einheit der Kirche nach dem neuen Testament," *Catholica* 1960, pp. 161 ff.

65. O. Weber, *Versammelte Gemeinde, Beiträge zum Gespräch über Kirche und Gottesdienst*, Neukirchen, 1949, p. 134. Cf. Y. Congar, "L' Esprit-Saint dans l'Eglise," *Lumière et Vie*, 10 (1953), pp. 51 ff.; K. Rahner, "Das Charismatische in der Kirche," *Stimmen der Zeit*, 82 (1957), pp. 161 ff.; B. Neunhauser, "Die Lehre vom Geist Christi nach der Enzyklika Mystici Corporis," *Liturgie und Mächtum* 4 (1949), pp. 60 ff.; Ingo Hermann, *Kyrios und Pneuma, Studien zur Christologie der paulinischen Hauptbriefe*, Munich, 1961; H. Berkhof, *De leer van de Heilige Geest*, Nijkerk, 1964.

life of the believing community of the Church: "Now you are the body of Christ, and individually members of it" (1 Cor. 12:27).

His glorified human existence is at the same time the visible image of the grace-full love of the three divine Persons toward all men (the fulfilled creation) and the instrument of Their saving entrance into our human existence (the creation that accomplishes itself). That is why He is, in His glorified existence with the Father, the fundamental sacrament for the salvation of all men.[66]

This "sacrament" or visible sign of God's coming to man, however, must still be "unfolded" in time and place, it must still be made present to men of all countries. For every man must still subjectively accept by virtue of the Holy Spirit, in a conscious act of faith (as a response to the proclaimed word of God) and must personally live (in the sacraments as a lived experience of the full salvific power of the word) what Christ has already objectively accomplished in His human life for each man's benefit.

The twofold salvation perspective of the mystery of the Incarnation becomes visible in the Church as the human community of faith that continues to live by the saving presence of the Spirit of Christ in word and sacrament. On the one hand, the Incarnation is an entrance of the three divine Persons through the man Jesus into sinful mankind, in order that we human beings might become sharers through the Spirit in the glorified human life of the Son of the Father. This is the line of salvation. On the other hand, the Incarnation is an ascent of all men in the man Jesus into the glory of the Father, in order that we might live our human existence through the power of the

66. E. Schillebeeckx, *Christ, the Sacrament of the Encounter with God*, New York, 1963, pp. 25-46. Cf. O. Semmelroth, *Die Kirche als Ursakrament*, Frankfurt, 1953, pp. 35-44.

Spirit as dying-with and being-glorified-with Christ. This is the line of worship.

The salvific meaning of the Church's complex reality is fully revealed in those two dimensions of the mystery of Christ: *the Church is not merely the community of salvation of the glorified Lord, but also His salvific instrument.*

The Church is the ever-actual resultant of two personal acts:

1. The salvific act of Christ, who in word and sacrament constantly and savingly intervenes in the estrangement from God of our sinful human existence: "And he has put all things under his feet and has made him the head over all things for the church, which is his body, the fullness of him who fills all in all" (Eph. 1:22-23).

2. The believing act of this human community that tries to live by that all-fulfilling nearness of Christ through the Spirit, who is sent in the word and the sacrament "until we all attain to the unity of the faith and of the knowledge of the Son of God, to mature manhood, to the measure of the stature of the fullness of Christ" (Eph. 4:13).

The Church is the field of tension between two poles: on the one hand, Christ's fidelity to the community that believes in Him, from which, on the other hand, there constantly arises anew the fidelity to Christ of that community of faith. The Church is "a redeemed and redeeming community" (Newton Flew): she is a community of faith redeemed in Christ, which as such accomplishes redemption in this world.

A Redeeming Community

On the one hand, the Church which came and still continues to come forth *from the divine initiative of love of the Father,* who through the Spirit has sent and continues to send His Son into our sinful human existence.

To be a Christian is to live by a continuously personal encounter with the man Jesus Christ, in virtue of which the Christian becomes ever more like to the glorified human life of the First-born of the whole creation, in thought, will and activity: "Have this mind among yourselves which you have in Christ Jesus" (Phil. 2:5). Christ desired that all men in the successive generations and in all parts of the world should share in that salvific act and event and for this purpose He gave His Church the task of proclaiming the word and administering His sacrament. In function of that power of authoritative preaching and bringing salvation to men He gave that human community of faith a visible and hierarchically organized structure.

In this community men are enabled to enter into Christ's universal mandate that was given Him by the Father: "All authority in heaven and on earth has been given to me. Go, therefore, and make disciples of all nations, baptizing them." "As the Father has sent me, even so I send you." And the fact that Christ concludes that mission with the guarantee: "And lo I am with you always, to the close of the age" (Mt. 28:18-19; Jn 20:21), shows that Christ is present in His Church not only as its protector, but especially in a dynamic way as glorified Lord.

It is the "life-giving Spirit" of the glorified Lord who, beginning with Pentecost, is Himself forming the Church in this world through the authoritative proclamation and the administration of the sacraments. "All this is from God, who through Christ reconciled us to himself and gave us the ministry of reconciliation. . . . So we are ambassadors of Christ, God making his appeal through us" (2 Cor. 5:17-20).

The word and the sacrament are the personal acts of the glorified Lord in the audible and visible structure of the functional acts, that is, the delegated and hence authoritative acts of the Church. In the proclamation of the Church he personally announces to each one of us the unsuspected good news that we are already chosen in Him, that we are saved and sanctified. And in the sacraments of the Church, as the complete salvific activity of the proclamation of the word, He personally accomplishes that salvation in us and gives us the fully conscious living of our redemption.

If the Church is thus considered from the standpoint of the salvific activity of Christ, she is in that respect the glorified Lord's instrument of salvation. She is the projection on earth of the continous mediation before the throne of the Father of "the lamb as if slain": the Lamb alone is worthy to open the book of God's salvific plan, that is, to fully reveal it in one's own human life and realize it in all men (Rev. 5:8 ff.).

From this standpoint the Church is the visible image of the fidelity of Christ, the perpetually actual gift of His saving presence in this earthly reality, the mystery of Christ that is being accomplished in time and space. *And under this aspect the Church is the one, holy, catholic and apostolic Church.*

A Redeemed Community

On the other hand, the Church acquires a form in this world *by the faith* of this human community that is saved in Christ. The Church becomes visible in this world by the life of faith and the believing reflection, as the human response to the proclaimed word and the sacrament that has been administered.

St. Paul, in his Epistle to the Ephesians, has described the salvific event of the Church as a dialogue that is held between the proclamation of the faith and the response of faith. "He himself gave some men as apostles, and some as prophets, others again as evangelists, and others as pastors and teachers" (the Church as instrument of salvation) for this purpose: "for the equipment of the saints, for the work of ministry, for building up the body of Christ, until we all attain to the unity of the faith and of the knowledge of the Son of God, to mature manhood, to the measure of the stature of the fulness of Christ. . . . Rather, speaking the truth in love, we are to grow up in every way into him who is the head, into Christ, from whom the whole body, joined and knit together by every joint with which it is supplied, when each part is working properly, makes bodily growth and upbuilds itself in love," that is, the Church as community of salvation (Eph. 4:11-17).

Hence the constant actual gift of the saving work of the Lord in word and sacrament remains a never finished task for that community of faith. The final fulfillment is still a mere expectation. The Church is still the People of God on its way to the Lord. She must still grow into a holy temple in the Lord, in whom "you are built into it for a dwelling place of God in the Spirit" (Eph. 2:21-22).

This thought has already led to ecumenical consequences within divided Christianity. First of all, within the religious reflection of Reformed Christians there is a growing attention to the ecclesial dimensions of the fact of salvation, namely, that all men are drawn together into the human solidarity of the Son of the Father, that all men are already saved in Christ:

> When Christ was crucified, died, was buried, rose and was glorified, what took place in Him was a new start of mankind, as the "second Adam," as the representative of the coming new humanity. That is why those realities affect us directly: we are crucified with Him, have died, were buried, rose, were glorified with Him, as we are constantly told in Ephesians and Colossians. That is

why we must say 'you have received fullness in Him;
that is, through baptism and faith you have been transferred to that new and grace-full dominion of Christ
. . . The Church is the dominion of Him who rules over
all. That means: Christ's dominion over everything is
still hidden, but somewhere in the cosmos there is room
within which it is already revealed. Somewhere in the
cosmos, the Head of all things, representative of all
things, is already recognized and obeyed . . . Here then
Paul sees the Church in a cosmic-eschatological light. In
her is anticipated the praise which the universe some
day will give to the Lord. . . . The gifts and functions
which Christ entrusts to the Church, are there (Eph.
4:7 ff.) placed against the background of His exaltation
and acceptance of power over the whole cosmos. They
are the signs and the proof that the exercise of that
power has already begun. . . . What Paul wants to do in
proclaiming the Church as being the dominion of Christ
is to characterize her as the *prophetical-eschatological
new reality* in which Israel and the peoples have found
their common Lord and destiny and thus also have
found one another.[67]

Secondly, an opportunity is now offered to Catholic
reflection on the faith to draw conclusions from the
growing realization that the Church as a community of
faith is a never completed salvific event: "always carry-
ing in the body the death of Jesus, so that the life of
Jesus may also be manifested in our bodies. For while we
live we are always being given up to death for Jesus' sake,
so that the life of Jesus may be manifested in our mortal
flesh" (2 Cor. 4:10-11). God's ever actual gift in Christ is
accomplished as an always unfinished task of self-unfolding in Christ: by a life of faith and the experience of

67. H. Berkhof, *De Katholiciteit der Kerk*, Nijkerk, 1962, pp.
63, 59-60: cf. *One Lord, One Baptism, Studies in Ministry and
Worship*, World Council of Churches, Commission on Faith and
Order, London, 1960, pp. 12-42.

word and sacrament, all mankind must still become what it already is in virtue of its being created and being saved, so as to be conformed to Christ.

Hence the words of St. Paul "my power is made perfect in weakness" (2 Cor. 12:9) are still applicable to individual believers and to the Church as a community of faith. Christ continues to occupy himself with His Church, "that he might sanctify her, having cleansed her by washing of water with the word; in order *that he might present* the Church to himself in splendor, without spot or wrinkle or any such thing, but that she might be holy and without blemish (Eph. 5:26-27). The Church then, as the believing People of God, is not yet the glorious Bride of Christ. As a community of faith the Church "knows only in part," she sees now only as "in a mirror dimly" (1 Cor. 13:12). For, "while we are at home in the body we are away from the Lord" (2 Cor. 5:6), and the Church must constantly keep in mind that she deserves to hear Christ's reproof: "I have a few things against you" (Rev. 2:14).

Although the Church is the holy Church in Christ, and in virtue of Christ's Spirit is always able to overcome the sin that is in her midst, she may never forget, at any time of her earthly existence, that sin is her inseparable companion during her exile. She must complete her temporal pilgrimage as a community of faith, confessing that she repeatedly forsakes her fullness of Christ and falls back into sin. God's kingdom is actively present in her, but it is still only in the eschatologically broken way that is proper to this time "in between." Only in the completed mystery of Christ will the glory of the children of God shine forth in her. *Hence, considered as a community of faith, the Church is not yet fully the one, holy, catholic and apostolic Church.*

d. No Identification

Being-the-Church is actually achieved within a tension between two poles, viz., on the one hand, the salvific act of Christ in word and sacrament, on the other, the act of faith as the personal living response of this human society that is saved in Christ. These two poles do not and cannot coincide during the present eschatological time "in between" while we are still "exiled from God."

In our life of faith we may attempt either to reduce Christ's fidelity to the measure of His Church's fidelity to Christ (and here lies the danger of the Reformed Christians' approach) or to exaggerate the Church's fidelity to her task, by raising it to the level of Christ's fidelity, and thus identify being-the-Church with Christ's salvific activity (the danger of the Catholic approach). Either of these attempts inevitably leads to the removal of the essential tension between those two poles. In each case one-sided attention is given to one aspect of the mystery of the Church. Not only is this mystery thus misunderstood, but that one-sidedness inevitably also brought about an opposition that has been fatally active in divided Christianity.

History reveals how the Reformation and the Catholic Church have lived during four centuries in hopeless struggle and controversy because both approached the mystery of the Church in a one-sided way. The opposition can perhaps be briefly summed up and characterized as follows:

The view of the Reformation: where the word is proclaimed in its purity and the sacraments are administered in all their purity, there the Church is.

The Catholic view: where the Church is, there the word is proclaimed in its purity and the sacraments are administered in all their purity.

Members of both camps, thanks to their ecumenical encounters, have come to realize that in the heat of the battle they have permitted an erroneous opposition to become part of their Christian view of faith. Both views represent legitimate aspects of the mystery of the Church, but they have become one-sidedly limited as used in the apologetic battle.

a. *The Catholic Christian* is beginning to realize that he is causing misunderstanding in the minds of Reformed Christians and that he endangers the purity of his own living experience of the Church mystery when he proclaims that the Church is the prolongation of the Incarnation, that she is even "the Word's prolonged becoming-a-Savior."[68]

Such ideas and propositions inevitably affect the way one lives his faith and the Catholic creates the impression that he believes that the Church has come to take the place of the Lord after His Ascension. He thus makes it appear that the mystery of the Ascension must not be taken seriously, that he looks upon the Church as the "successor" of the saving presence of Christ in the horizontal line of human history.

Are we not unlawfully exaggerating the Church's eschatological reality and raising it to the level of Christ's salvific activity when we continually speak of the identity between Christ and the Church? The Catholic thus gives the impression that the Church is *in itself* a reality of salvation and that her salvific activities have salvific power *in themselves*, as if the Catholic Church possesses the truth and is able to impart it to the individual man from her own fullness of grace.[69]

68. F. Malmberg, "De Kerk des Heren," *Genade en Kerk*, Utrecht, 1953, p. 271.

69. L. Köster, *Die Kirche unseres Glaubens, Eine theologische Grundlegung der katholischen Weltanschauung*, Fribourg, 1935.

Reformed and Catholic Christians agree in confessing the unique fact of the Incarnation, which is bound to historical data in the history of salvation. Those salvific acts cannot be repeated; they cannot be continued. The Incarnation is continued, not in the Church, but in the glorified existence of the man Jesus Christ who is with the Father. There is likewise no difference of opinion among the Christians about Christ's salvific work: Christ has once and for all (*ephapax*) accomplished that work of salvation (Rom. 6:10; Heb. 7:27; 9:28; 1 Pet. 3:18). To this nothing can nor must be added. But the ways of believing have become steadily more divergent with respect to the Church's salvific function of making present, in various ages and countries, the all-sufficient salvific action of Christ.

Should not the Catholic who reflects upon the salvific function of the Church have to make a correction by accepting the consequences of the fact that actions are inalienably proper to persons, hence cannot be attributed to any other person? The Church's activities of proclaiming the word and administering the sacraments can, therefore, never be identified with the salvific actions of Christ.

The ecclesial action is a complex symbolic action; Christ is actively present in a human action. In the Church's proclamation and action there is effected a meeting with her glorified Lord. St. Paul brings out clearly that more profound dimension of the ecclesial action when he begins his important testimony concerning the Last Supper with the words: "For I received from the Lord what I also delivered to you" (1 Cor. 11:23), namely, the tradition of the Church.

In and through this human action of the Church, which is an action of another person and keeps its own human and imperfect character, Christ realizes what He has accomplished for our benefit in His human life.

The Church, then, is a salvific reality in this world. There is power of salvation in her sacramental activity. But it is *solely through Christ,* because the Church is the earthly image of His presence and the instrument of His salvific activity. The Church does not "possess" the truth; she is not the fullness of grace. But she is in Christ, in the inexhaustible source of all truth and grace.

In stressing this distinction between the action of Christ and the action of the Church's proclamation of the word and the administration of the sacraments, it is necessary to give full attention to the *Church's obedience* to her glorified Lord. The necessary condition for the salvific effect of those ecclesial actions is that the word be proclaimed truthfully by mandate of Christ and that the sacraments be administered in all purity through His power. Because we are dealing here with human actions, any kind of automatic truth and every sort of sacramental magic are unacceptable.

It is true that the proclamation of the word and the administration of the sacraments always shares in the salvific instrumentality of the glorified Lord (*ex opere operato Christi*), though "God is greater than our hearts" (1 Jn 3:20) and He is "able to do far more abundantly than all that we ask or think" (Eph. 3:20). But this does not mean that the Church is not obliged to constantly put her own present vision of faith and life of faith to the test by comparing it with the Gospel.

b. *The Reformed Christians,* too, have discovered the one-sidedness of their own view of the Church. Typical of this growing awareness of their narrowmindedness with respect to their idea of the Church is the fact that the struggle between divergent trends within the Dutch Reformed Church has been dominated for years by sterile semantical discussions over the words "because" and "to the extent that": is the Dutch Reformed Church a "revelation of the one, holy, catholic or universal Christian Church" *because* word and sacraments are administered in her in all their purity or *to the extent that* word and sacrament are administered in all their purity?

The Dutch Reformed Church felt caught between the devil and the deep sea: to accept the "because" would drive her in the direction of the Catholic concept of the Church and this would mean a divisive struggle for the preservation of her unity. On the other hand, to accept the "to the extent that" would inevitably lead to the complete undermining of her own confession; it would degrade the Church to a home of religious individualists.

This hopeless struggle could lead only to irreconcilable ecclesial trends and to major divisions within the Church by reason of conscience. And the Reformed Christians came to the painful realization that they were faced with an insoluble dilemma within the one-sided confines of their own Church-consciousness.

Nor was the new Church Order of 1951 able to reach a satisfactory solution. To make it possible for all trends to stay in the Church, that Order was unable to do more than declare that the Church "in communion with the confession of the Fathers. . . . makes a profession of the self-revelation of the Triune God."[70]

Ecumenical Discoveries

Thanks to the ecumenical reflection that has engulfed all Churches, the separated Christians are increasingly realizing that the forced opposition is something that

70. Kerkorde der Nederlandse Hervormde Kerk, 's Gravenhage, 1959, art. X.

Christians must reject. In reality it is necessary to stress both aspects equally, the salvific act of Christ *and* man's act of faith in our consciousness of the mystery of the Church.

The Perfect Fidelity of Christ

The Church, as instrument of salvation, is the Church of Jesus Christ *because* in her the sacramental word is proclaimed in all its purity. The testimony of Himself that God gave in the Old Covenant has become a full human reality in the Incarnation of the Son: "So shall my word be that goes forth from my mouth; it shall not return to me empty, but it shall accomplish that which I purpose, and prosper in the thing for which I sent it" (Is. 55:11). The Word of God—by whom all things were created and who has revealed Himself in the divine act of creation as the life and the light of all men (Jn 1:1-14)—participates in human existence with a saving and sanctifying power. He is, in His complete existence as man, our Mediator with the Father by the fact that He finally sends His Church to proclaim His salvific word: "The Gospel is the power of God unto salvation to everyone who believes" (Rom. 1:16). "When you heard and received from us the word of God, you welcomed it not as the word of men, but, as it truly is, the word of God, who works in you who have believed" (1 Thess. 2:13).

The Church lives by the salvific power of the word that is proclaimed in virtue of Christ's commission, for in that word the glorified Lord speaks to every man who personally accepts it in faith and He is present to that human community as one who saves. "The Lord gave the word. Great is the company of the preachers."[71]

In virtue of the divine power of the word, to which

71. Händel, *The Messiah.*

Christ has attached His guarantee of permanent presence, the Church can never be unfaithful to Christ. For, in the first instance, the Church does not hold on to Christ by a fallible human effort. But in virtue of His proclaimed word Christ continues to hold His Church in the grasp of the saving plan which the Father completes in the mystery of the Son's human fellowship with us.

[God, by the Incarnation took] the world fundamentally and once and for all into his mercy. . . . But now in the Word of God, God's last word is uttered into the visible public history of mankind, a word of grace, reconciliation and eternal life: Jesus Christ. The grace of God no longer comes (when it does come) steeply down from on high, from a God absolutely transcending the world, and in a manner that is without history, purely episodic; it is permanently in the world, in tangible historical form, established in the flesh of Christ as a part of the world, of humanity and of its very history. . . . God did not simply set up a fully equipped stage, for men to act out the drama of history on their own. God himself has taken part, acted, given the drama the denouement he himself wanted—salvation, grace and eternal life.

The Church is the abiding presence of the primal sacramental word of definitive grace, which Christ is in the world. . . . The Church is the official presence of the grace of Christ in the public history of the one human race. In its socially organized form the people of God as in fact redeemed by Christ, receives his permanent presence through history. And when we examine what this one reality implies, it means a presence, as it were an incarnation, of the truth of Christ in the Church through Scripture, tradition and magisterium. . . .

Through [Christ's] Incarnation the people of God exist. This has socially organized form in the Church, which is consequently the abiding and historically manifest presence of this saving grace in Christ, the fundamental sacred sign of this grace. From this the necessity of the Church for salvation—at root it is the necessity of

Christ himself—directly follows. . . . To deny the ecclesial character of all grace and redemption would either imply that grace is not always related to the incarnation, to history and so to the Church, or else it would imply that one can attain salvation without the grace of Christ.

The Church (is) the fundamental sacrament. . . . the grace of God in the "flesh" of a historical and tangible ecclesiastical embodiment, which therefore cannot be emptied of what it signifies and renders present, because otherwise the grace of Christ (who always remains man) would also be something merely transitory and replaceable.[72]

The self-consciousness of every Christian Church, then, is nourished by this certainty of faith: *because,* through the commission received from Christ, the word is proclaimed and the sacrament is administered in virtue of His authority. The Church is abidingly the Church of Jesus Christ.

Here then we have a fundamental ecumenical discovery whose future consequences are still in calculable. Today, the separated Christians feel more deeply than ever that, for the sake of the *Ecumene,* they must not lightheartedly play down the dividedness of the Church of Jesus Christ. Nevertheless, after centuries during which they accused one another of radical infidelity, they now feel obliged to testify for one another, on the basis of their common belief that the Lord Jesus Christ is always faithful: a Church that conscientiously tries to live by faith in His word cannot utterly abandon Christ because He continues to hold fast to her. He "upholds the universe by his word of power" (Heb. 1:3). The Church cannot err; she cannot speak falsehood. By the power of the Spirit of Christ, who becomes embodied in the act of

72. K. Rahner, *The Church and the Sacraments, Quaestiones Disputatae* 9 Herder and Herder: New York, 1963, pp. 13-24.

faith of that human community, she has always spoken the truth.

The Imperfect Fidelity of the Church

The Church as a community of faith is the Church of Jesus Christ *to the extent* that the sacramental word is proclaimed in all its purity in her.

In our ecumenical era we have rediscovered the fact that the others also are Christians. The Catholic Church has learned to listen to the testimony of faith of the Reformed Christians as a legitimate protest. And the Churches of the Reformation have accepted the Catholic self-examination that has taken place in the Council as an invitation for their own renewal. A favorable climate has thus been created for the mutual recognition that Christ's fidelity to His Church has always been achieved historically amidst the failing in fidelity of that community of faith.

Both Churches have dared to confess their guilt and to recognize that the conversations about the faith were those of Christians who felt obliged in conscience to oppose one another. Thus, there was no chance for the development of a genuine dialogue of men who in their common condition of being seized by Christ could never abandon one another. Those Churches committed the historical fault of letting their conversations degenerate from the start and develop into juxtaposed monologues containing the germ of separation. These monologues had no other object than the condemnation of the opponent, and no attention was paid to shades of meaning that can be known only when there is patient listening to, and questioning of the other in a true dialogue. Such monologues and religious disputes inevitably led to a one-sided overemphasis of one aspect and to an equally undifferentiated under-estimation of the other aspect of the reality of Revelation in Christ.

If we, separated Christians, have the courage to look with an open mind at the past centuries, we will realize with shame that we have been objectively unfaithful while imagining to be faithful to Christ, with respect to both the proclamation and the living of the faith. Personal contact and common religious reflection and dialogue have been impossible for centuries. The Churches, on that account, became increasingly hostile to one another in a diversity of defensive schools of theology. They forced one another to adopt atrophied forms of Christian life because of the mutual antagonism. Fear of error became the inspiration of each one's proclamation of the faith. And on both sides of the ever widening abyss that kept them separated the full reality and content of Revelation was no longer proclaimed nor fully lived.

Fortunately in our day these isolated monologues of the Churches are disappearing. And the liberating experience of meeting others as fellow-believers has made us realize that the redeeming reality of being-a-Christian is broader than any system of theology, and that Christ's grace-giving activity transcends visible ecclesial boundaries. Many have made the wonderful discovery that there exists a much larger and more profound unity in Christ than had hitherto been supposed.

In the presence of all that still divides the separated Christians, they will now reflect together upon the redeeming reality which is at work in their lives in virtue of their common faith in Jesus Christ, which transcends all frontiers. What do Christians who belong to separated Churches experience when they jointly profess their faith in the words of Christ: "If a man loves me, he will keep my word, and my Father will love him, and we will come

to him and make our home with him?" (Jn 14:23)? The
Churches are now placed in an entirely new situation
which only a few years ago was not considered possible.

On the one hand, no ecumenically-minded Christian
will dare to maintain that the dogma and the theology of
his Church is the complete expression of God's self-com-
munication-to-us in the historical redemptive actions of
the man Jesus Christ. On the other hand, he has learned
in his ecumenical encounters with others to be modest
and to acknowledge that he—despite his dogmatic
knowledge of the other Churches' confessions of faith—
has not been able in the past to attain an emphatic
understanding of the other Christians.

In this situation the Catholic has found room for this
question of conscience: what is it that the Reformation
rejected in its protest against the Catholic Church: Was
it some aspect of Revelation, so that those Churches
became heretical? Or was it because of the caricatural
way in which that aspect of Revelation was lived in the
Catholic Church? And the Reformed Christian discovers
unsuspected scriptural dimensions behind the Catholic
dogmas so strongly contested.

Hence, Christians from all the Churches must now
continually take account of the astonishing fact that
underneath a formal opposition of dogmatic formulae
there is an increasingly more evident—though legitimately distinct—unity of believing insight and of living
the faith.

These ecumenical experiences of our profound unity
in Christ cannot, yet, at this stage of re-acquaintance, be
expressed in a profession that is acceptable to all Christians. We have lived too long as strangers to be able now
to express such a formulation. But if we learn to discard
our controversial style of thinking and are ready to strip
our own profession of faith down to its evangelical core,

we shall stand in the midst of the religious miracle that there is a growing integration of the Catholic and the Reformed ways of being-a-Christian.

Hence the dominant question at this ecumenical moment of salvation is this: will the separated Christians be able to testify to one another without any reservation, that each one's own being-a-Church *as* a community of faith is the Church of Jesus Christ only *to the extent* that word and sacrament are administered by that community in all their purity?

For, although Christian self-consciousness lives by the certainty of faith that the Church as the Lord's instrument of salvation has always spoken the truth in virtue of the Lord's power, there is still room for the question whether the Church as a community of faith has always spoken the full truth in its apologetic self-defense. If the legitimacy of that question is accepted and lived by, an ecumenical renewal of one's own way of being-a-Christian and of one's own being-the-Church will become possible.

e. No Autarchy

This ecumenical liberating view of the Church has developed from the rediscovered awareness that the Church is still *Ecclesia paroikousa,* a sojourning church, which as long as the present lasts (Heb. 3:13), is still waiting for her completion. She is the pilgrim people of God which is already on its way to its Lord; but she, nevertheless, knows at the same time that "while we are at home in the body we are away from the Lord" (2 Cor. 5:6).

The Church's time "in between" is "the time of your exile" (1 Pet. 1:17) but it is also a fact that the saving presence of the Spirit of Christ through word and sacrament has already begun and constitutes a real beginning of the Church's final achievement: "You have come to Mount Zion and to the city of the living God, the heavenly Jerusalem." The Church, while in the diaspora, knows that she is already "the festal gathering, and. . . . the assembly of the first-born who are enrolled in heaven" (Heb. 12:22-23).

In that diaspora consciousness, so full of eschatological expectations, it is now becoming possible to have a pure idea of the relationship between the Church as an *instrument* of salvation and the Church as a *community* of salvation of the glorified Lord. Being aware of that eschatological tension of the as yet unfulfilled Kingdom of God, we can now see clearly that those two aspects of the Church, as we have already established, cannot yet coincide: there are *two* aspects. On the other hand we see at the same time that these two aspects may not be made autarchic.

Any attempt to assign autarchy to one of those aspects will necessarily falsify the Church. It can make us conceive the Church in a too juridical way; it will then make us look upon the Church of Jesus Christ as the instrument of divine truth and ignore the fractured state of that believing community. Or, on the contrary, we can have too static an idea of Christ's Church-establishing presence, permitting it to be overshadowed by the profound awareness of the sinful incompleteness of the community that confesses Christ.

Our Church-consciousness must be nourished by the dynamic tension existing between those two aspects. For here we do not have two realities that can be separated: the salvific act of Christ *and* the act of faith of men. But we have two legitimate aspects of *one* reality that must always function simultaneously in the life of faith. The Church is not *either* the instrument of salvation *or* the community of salvation; similarly, she is not the instrument of salvation *and* the community of salvation; rather she is the instrument of salvation *in* the community of salvation.

If we wish to see the far-reaching ecumenical consequences of that view of the Church, we must look at her in the light of the mystery of Christ as seen in a renewed reflection of faith.

The Self-Emptying Man Jesus Christ is Personally the Son of the Father

The Triune God, the Father, the Son and the Holy Spirit, is our Savior, but the three divine Persons accomplish that salvific event in all men *in* and *by* the Incarnation of the Son. There is no access to the Father, and no life by the Holy Spirit is possible except through the encounter with the man Jesus Christ who, in virtue of the Holy Spirit, lives His being with the Father in the self-realization of His human existence as the Son: "No one comes to the Father, but by me. If you had known me, you would have known my Father also. . . . He who has seen me has seen the Father. . . . Do you not believe that I am in the Father and the Father in me? The words that I say to you I do not speak on my own authority; but *the Father who dwells in me does his works*" (Jn 14:6-10).

Reflection on faith can speak about God only on the basis of the self-testimony of the man Jesus Christ. The Christian knows who the Father is and what intentions the Father has with respect to his own human life only to the extent that the Father shows Himself also as our Father in the life-history of that Man. The Christian can live by the Holy Spirit, only insofar as he lets himself be inspired by the mentality[73] and the ideals of life of that Man who was ceaselessly moved by the Spirit.

73. Denziger, no. 302.

Hence the Church's profession of the Triune God always takes place within the limits of the salvation history of the Christ mystery that begins in the Old Covenant, and is fulfilled in the New. The scriptural testimony about the human life of the Son of the Father remains the source of inspiration for all contemporary reflection.

For centuries it was thought that the Council of Chalcedon terminated the religious reflection upon the mystery of Christ. In the declaration of that council the Church made the following profession:

On the one hand, the divine and the human modes of existence of Christ cannot be divided nor separated because of the unity of His Person. The same Person lives in the divine world of His Father *and* in our human world. On the other hand, those modes of existence cannot change or blend because of the qualitatively infinite distance between God and man. Christ shares fully in the divine life of His Father, but He shares just as much in our human life (Jn 14:11). Hence, to do justice to our integral salvation consciousness, every profession of faith that diminishes the truly human existence of Jesus must be rejected, just as much as a profession that attacks His true divinity. The Council of Chalcedon, however, did not thereby make any positive statement regarding the mutual relations between the two modes of existence in Christ.

In our own time religious reflection strongly concentrates its attention upon the salvific consequences of the scriptural testimony to the fact that Christ, in obediently living His human existence, has given form *in a human way* to His existence as God, to His divine life with the Father. This important shift in our present Christology has brought about a renewal of our whole religious thinking and of our whole way of living and experiencing the faith; it also strongly affects our way of experiencing the mystery of the Church.

On the basis of the total otherness of God and man the Church professes a clear distinction between the divine mode of the Son's being with the Father and the mode of His existence with us, but this does not permit us to accept a division in the one Person of Christ in any shape or form.

But how can our human way of conceiving things give a real content to the notion of "two modes of being" without *either* secretly thinking of *two* persons, or without seriously neglecting one of those two ways of existence?

Faith, however, puts us before the historical fact that in Christ there appear two forms of *one* Person. The "I" who is in the Father (Jn 14:11) and the "I" who is hungry in the wilderness (Lke 4:1-4) are not two persons, but it is one and the same Person who experiences His life with the Father in resisting Satan during that experience of hunger. Christ never experiences His being-man as separated from His realization that He is the Son of the Father.

The contemporary proclamation of the faith must be completely orientated to the saving meaning-for-us of the mystery that the Son of the Father has truly become man for the benefit of all men. And in that proclamation every separation between the Son of the Father *and* the man Jesus must be wholly discarded.

The "I" that Jesus experiences in all His human actions, is the divine Person of the Son of the Father, who realizes Himself in a human way in a meeting with His fellow-men and in His constant confrontation with earthly reality. Hence the mystery of Christ is concerned with His truly human consciousness of Himself as the

Son of the Father. And it is by this human self-consciousness that He has experienced Himself as a human person. Although in Christ there is no opposition between a divine and a human person, He is man in a personal way. For the Son of God is personally the man Jesus Christ.

Here lies the point of renewal in present Christological thought: Jesus Christ is the Son of God, but He has experienced His being-together with the Father in a human way, that is, personally as a man. Jesus did not experience his relation as a divine person to the Father *directly* but in His human self-consciousness. Although it is contrary to the Church's profession to say that Jesus is a human person, the life of faith will have to concentrate finally on the encounter with the man Jesus Christ who is personally the Son of the Father.

Because of the defensive struggle against Arianism, that aspect of the mystery of Christ has had no opportunity to penetrate fully into the Church's reflection. Arius' claim that "there was a time when the Son did not exist" and hence that Christ became only later the Son of God must be discarded as heretical.[74]

And yet, the salvific event that is finally being accomplished in our encounter with Jesus Christ lies precisely in the mystery that this Man has experienced His being-the-Son-of-the-Father in His radical human self-"emptying" and in His being totally available for others. He became conscious as man of what He already was in virtue of His being born of the Father and in virtue of His living with the Father.

Our Salvation Does Not Lie in the Pre-existent Christ but in the "Pro-existent" Christ

The separated Christians, in their renewed reflection upon what the Church of Christ is must find their com-

74. Denziger, no. 125.

mon starting point in the salvific-meaning-for-us of the mystery of the Incarnation of God's Son: this man has become the Son of the Father in the self-realization of His human existence. When John professes in the prologue of his Gospel: "In the beginning was the Word, and the Word was with God" (Jn 1:1), it is not his intention to testify about the Son as He was with the Father before creation (pre-existence), but about the Son as He reveals Himself in His salvific work for the benefit of all men from the beginning of creation (pro-existence): "All things were made through him, and without him was not anything made that was made. . . . in him was life, and the life was the light of men" (Jn 1:3-4).

The Son of the Father has realized Himself as man in the *kenosis* (Phil. 2:6-8). This human "emptying of himself" refers not only to His being-man but especially to human existence as it has become through sin. *He is precisely the Son of the Father in that "he made himself to be sin"* (2 Cor. 5:21). For the benefit of all men He has experienced being-sinful-man as His own mode of existence: "My God, why hast thou forsaken Me?" (Mt. 27:46).

Our salvation lies not in Christ's pre-existence but in His pro-existence. Only in the *kenosis* of His pro-existent love, only in His self-denying suffering for others has the Father accepted us as His children: "God (the Father) was in Christ reconciling the world to himself" (2 Cor. 5:19). It is only from the pro-existent glorified humanity of Jesus with the Father that we receive the Holy Spirit: "For as yet the Spirit had not been given, because Jesus was not yet glorified (i.e., had not completed His human existence for our benefit). . . . he will take what is mine and declare it to you" (Jn 7:39).

The dogmatic declaration of Chalcedon proclaims that in Christ there is no change nor merger of His humanity and divinity. Hence we must reject every attempt to produce a sort of metaphysical merger that would degrade Christ by making Him a demiurge who stands between God and man, as Greek philosophy conceived such a being. But the Council, at the same time, greatly stressed the perfect unity of those two modes of existence of Christ; hence when the encounter with Christ is experienced by us as the human revelation of the Son's divine life with His Father through the power of the Holy Spirit, this must be considered to be in accord with the Council's profession of faith.

Christ is not God *and* man. This way of stating things runs the risk of leading to a misunderstanding and the idea that there are two personalities in Christ. Also in Him there is no merger of a divine and a human life, for otherwise He would be neither truly God nor truly man. The salvation mystery of the Incarnation lies in this that the Holy Spirit inspires the man Jesus in His human existence and in making Him always experience in all His human deeds that He is the Son of the Father.

We must attribute to Christ everything that makes God God and makes man man. But it must be done in such a way that He lives His divine life in a human way and that He raises His human life to a divine height, that is, that He has perfectly responded in His human existence to the plan of salvation the Father had when creating man: "Although he was a Son, he (the man Jesus Christ) learned obedience through what he suffered; and being made perfect he became the source of salvation" (Heb. 4:8-9). That is why Christ is fully the Son of the Father only in His glorified human existence that began after His resurrection: "Designated Son of God in power according to the Spirit of holiness by his resurrection from the dead" (Rom. 1:4).

Christ experiences His unity as a divine Person with

the Father in His human existence, but the frontier between God and man is never crossed in Him; still less is
that creatural boundary taken away. The more intensely
human His human actions are, the more they are revela-
tions of the divine Son. In the measure that His actions
were a more profound and total consecration to God—as
was the case in His preaching and prayer, His suffering
and death—He experienced more intensely His existence
with the Father: "Believe me that I am in the Father and
the Father in me. Or else believe me for the sake of the
works themselves" (Jn 14:11). Christ knew how to transcend His whole human existence as a personal encounter with the Father: the "you" of fellowmen was for Him
a reference to the "Thou" of His Father; for Him the
experience of earthly reality became transparent as a
personal being together with His Father.

In our religious reflection upon the salvation mystery
that the Son of the Father is our fellowman, we must
purify our concepts and remove any idea that behind the
man Jesus, behind the child in the crib and the man on
the Cross who struggles with the Father's will, the di-
vinely-perfect Person is hiding.

In the loving interplay between the Father and the
man Jesus we should avoid making the Son a sort of
"third" spectator who knew everything beforehand and
can do all things by His divine power and holiness. Otherwise His human life becomes a make-believe and the
salvific meaning for us of the Incarnation of God's Son is
completely devaluated.

Jesus manifests Himself as the Son of the Father in His
human existence, but He does it in a human way. When
Jesus says: "I and the Father are one," it is the Son of
God who is speaking, but it springs from a human self-
consciousness. His orientation toward the Father is a
human orientation. And the dynamic power of the Holy

Spirit in His life is a being-moved in a human way. The Son continually experiences His connection with the Father by virtue of the Holy Spirit, in a human love, in human longings and ideals, in human obedience and struggle: "For we have not a high priest who is unable to sympathize with our weaknesses, but one who in every re-pect has been tempted as we are, yet without sinning. . . . Therefore he had to be made like his brethren in every respect, so that he might become a merciful and faithful high priest in the service of God, to make expiation for the sins of the people" (Heb. 4:15; 2:17).

At the Incarnation no new person was born but there was a new way in which the Son began to stand before the Father, namely, in a human relationship. Because being-man is a task that is fulfilled to the extent that man comes to self-consciousness, the Incarnation implies that Jesus knew God in a human way; His knowledge was subject to a human development (Lke 2:52); He con-stantly arrived at a higher religious perfection (*ibid.*); and in the struggle against the constant temptation, proper to our human existence, of being abandoned by God, He had to battle with himself in order to do the will of the Father and become obedient for the benfit of all men. (Mt. 4:1-11; 26:39; Heb. 5:7-10).

Christ fully experienced on the Cross what it means to be human, a sinner before God. His cry upon the Cross: "My God, my God, why hast thou forsaken me" (Mt. 27:46) was the cry of our humanness which He made His own. It was the unveiling of our sinful situation before God, into which He had descended. Although "in him there is no sin" (1 Jn 3:5) as a personal action, He was personally involved in the intimate guilt of man with respect to God.

But although He had experienced the reality of our constant temptations—"not as I will, but as thou wilt"

(Mt. 26:39)—He did not fall in with them, and He could not have yielded to them. For while experiencing the inviting power of sin He experienced His being-with the Father, and heard the invitation of the Father. In being truly man He desired to be the Son of the Father. *In being-like-to-us He experience being-like-the-Father: "I always do what is pleasing to him"* (Jn 8:29).

Jesus experiences His divine unity with the Father and the Holy Spirit for us in human actions and not outside nor above those actions. It is true that the man Jesus, because of His personal unity with the Son of God, has a divine mode of existence. Nevertheless, we would introduce two persons in Him and thereby devaluate the universal salvific dimension of His human actions if we were to accept that He experiences that divine life *also* outside His human consciousness, outside His human activity and human prayer.

Our Human Existence Becomes Transparent as an Encounter with the Father in the Encounter with Christ

The salvific significance of the mystery of the Incarnation lies precisely in this that Christ was able to live His whole human life, His human love and struggle, His human prayer at all times, as an encounter with His Father. In our still-veiled togetherness with the man Jesus Christ in the sacramental proclamation of His word we have a perspective upon the most profound reality of our human existence.

For, as John testifies in the prologue of his Gospel: "All things were made through him, and without him was not anything made that was made. In him was life, and the life was the light of men" (Jn 1:3-4). John speaks here of the man Jesus Christ who is the Son of the Father. This Man is the lasting foundation of the existence of every man and of the whole creation. And as the Emman-

uel, the God-with-us, He has passed—saving and fulfilling us a fellowman—through our whole sinful and God-
forsaken human existence.

By Him, our whole earthly reality is continually created and redeemed from its sinfulness for companion-
ship with His Father: "For God so loved the world that he
gave his only Son, that whoever believes in him should
not perish but have eternal life" (Jn 3:16). He in whom
"the whole fullness of deity dwells bodily" (Col. 2:9)
draws all who believe in Him into the orientation of His
human existence toward the Father.

We discover in the encounter with Christ through the
sacramental word that we cannot love God independently
of the earthly reality, but that in Him we can make our
human life, our human relations and our task of realizing earthly values transparent as a life lived with His
Father. This messianic reality is announced in the Old
Covenant with the words: "This is the covenant which I
will make with the house of Israel after those days, says
the Lord: I will put my law within them, and I will write
it upon their hearts; and I will be their God, and they
shall be my people" (Jer. 31:33).

When we consider the earthly reality in the light of
that Christology we can appreciate the radical pastoral
appeal of Bishop John A. Robinson. It is only in meeting
the man Jesus Christ that man becomes conscious of the
ultimate reality of his human existence; it is only then
that he sees clearly the meaning of human togetherness
as availability for others and of his daily work as the
self-realization of mankind in creation. It is in this
human existence which he can experience transparently
as such only in Christ, that he meets God, not outside nor
above it. To that extent a Christian of today must agree
with Robinson. But then he does not experience God as
"the ultimate depth of all our being, the (impersonal)

creative ground and meaning of all our existence."[75] For in his meeting with Christ he discovers that his being-man is not a neutral "being" but a continual being together with the Father.

When Robinson seeks for a new way of being a Christian and tells us that if we wish to meet God we must go to the world, apply ourselves to an earthly holiness and service of our fellowmen, this way of being a Christian lies precisely in this that we learn to experience and live the social and cosmic dimensions of the mystery of the Incarnation of the Son of the Father: the "you" of the other man refers us to the "Thou" of His Father, and the world is the space within which the self-realization of our manhood in conformity with Christ must take place.

This ideal St. Paul expresses in the startling words: "Put on the Lord Jesus Christ" (Rom. 13:14). "When I read those words, my thoughts go always to a painting by Rembrandt preserved in a museum of Leningrad: a Christ only half revealed, in dark colors from which blossoms forth a most lovely face, that is both deeply human and unearthly, with a look that is both mild and profound, that expresses peace, strength, tenderness, purity and above all goodness, a truly infinite goodness (for as much as it is given to men to be able to picture such things). *He* is the one we are asked to resemble."[76]

It is only in that Christological context that a Christian can accept as authentic the contemporary appeal of Robinson and Bonhoeffer:

It is in this ultimate surrender of self, in love "to the uttermost," that Jesus is so completely united to the Ground of his being that he can say: "I and the Father

75. John A. Robinson, *Honest to God,* Philadelphia, 1963, p. 47.
76. W. Grossouw, *Innerlijk leven,* Utrecht, 1957, pp. 15-16.

are one. . . . the Father is in Me and I am in the
Father." It is in Jesus and Jesus alone, that there is
nothing of self to be seen, but solely the ultimate, unconditional love of God. . . . For it is in making himself
nothing, in his utter self-surrender to others in love, that
he discloses the Ground of man's being as Love.[77]

Jesus does not call us to a new religion, but to life
itself. . . . And I call a full earthly life: to live in the
variegated multitude of tasks, questions, success and
failure, experiences and desperation. Then you give
yourself completely to God; then your own suffering is
no longer your principal concern, but it is the suffering
of God in the world; you, then, are watching with Christ
in Gethesemane. This, in my opinion, is faith, this is
"conversion" and thus you become man, you become
Christ.[78]

Faith means: to share in that existence of Jesus (Incarnation, Cross, and Resurrection). Our relation to God
is not a religious attitude toward the highest, most powerful and best Being that we can conceive—this is not true
transcendence—; but a new life "solely for others" means
that we are participating in the life of Jesus. Transcendence does not mean transcending the utmost boundaries
of finiteness, but rather taking the step toward our near-
est Neighbor who is constantly placed on our way.[79]

To be a Christian means to constantly discover Christ
as the ground and foundation of our existence, of our
ideals and actions and, through the power of the Holy
Spirit, to transparently experience the concreteness of

77. Robinson, *Honest to God,* pp. 74-75.

78. This was written by Bonhoeffer when in prison, July 21,
1944, after he had heard about the unsuccessful attempt on the
life of Hitler, in which he was so closely involved. That evening
he had fully accepted the ultimate consequences of his religious
rebellion.

79. D. Bonhoeffer, *Wer ist und wer war Jesus Christus?* Hamburg, 1963, pp. 35-39.

our daily life by our love for others, as an encounter with the Father: "Beloved, let us love one another, for love is of God, and he who loves is born of God and knows God. . . . No man has ever seen God; if we love another, God abides in us and his love is perfected in us. . . . for he who does not love his brother whom he has seen, cannot love God whom he has not seen" (1 Jn 4:7-20).

The Church of Jesus Christ in the State of Kenosis

This endeavor to shed new light on the universal salvific event that God's Son is a fellowman of ours will perhaps offer the separated Christians a means of getting out of the blind alley in which they have been trapped for several centuries. On the one hand, the Catholic identifies his Church as the salvific instrument of the glorified Lord exclusively with the Church of Jesus Christ, because she alone proclaims the word with authority and administers the sacrament with full power. On the other hand, the Reformed Christian must constantly put the glorified Lord's ever unfaithful community of faith under scrutiny by the light of Holy Scripture; and he can recognize other Christian Communions as being the Church of Christ only in so far as the word and sacrament are administered in conformity with that absolute standard.

In the hopeless situation of these irreconcilable views, the Catholic Church was unable to respect the other Communions as the Church of Jesus Christ and the only thing she could do was to appeal to the separated Christians and urge them to return to that one true Church. On the other hand, the Churches of the Reformation had to cling unswervingly to the testimony of their conscience that no dialogue with the Catholic Church was possible, if this Church was not ready to submit unconditionally to the critical test of Scripture.

Is it not possible to break through those rigid positions and meet in the apologetic no-man's-land where we listen to the testimony of Scripture that tells us that the Son of the Father is the First-born of all creation, who also became the First-born from among the dead? For just as we may not violently introduce a duality and opposition between Christ's divine being with the Father and His solidarity with sinful men, so there can be no dilemma of choice for the separated Christians between the Church as an instrument of salvation and the Church as the salvific community of the glorified Lord.

Together they must reflect upon the ecclesial dimensions of the mystery that the Son experienced His self-realizing human life as a *kenosis*, as a self-emptying. This human self-emptying refers not only to the fact that Christ became man but also to human existence as affected by sin. *It is precisely in His "having been made sin" that He is the Son of the Father.* He experienced human sinfulness as His own way of existence.

In the mystery of our being the Church of Christ we experience that Christ as the First-born from among the dead draws after Him in His glorified human existence with the Father the whole sinful creation. He already fulfilled His human existence; He now desires to be present, saving and completing. This He does by sending us the Spirit, making the sinful community of faith experience the word sacramentally, so that He might lead all men to the height of His glorified human life with the Father.

It is true that we must make a distinction between Christ's salvific presence in word and sacrament and the believing experience of that sinful human community; nevertheless, this distinction may never make us separate the two realities. For in the mystery of our being Christ's Church there is question of the Lord's dynamic presence in the struggle of faith of that sinful human community.

Christ cannot be encountered outside the proclamation of faith of one's own time and outside one's culture-conditioned life of faith. And it is in this human structure and situation that the operation of His Spirit meets with the limitations of God's Kingdom that is not yet eschatologically achieved. Scripture is always read through glasses one-sidedly colored by the actual problems of faith of individuals and communities. The Church's proclamations are an ever human and imperfect effort to translate God's word in a concrete believing community; and in the administration of the sacraments, the efficacy of the full salvific power of God's word is weakened by an ever present refusal to radically surrender oneself in faith.

The Spirit sent by Christ is active as saving and completing in the word that is authoritatively proclaimed and in our personal believing response. This believing community of our time is the salvific instrument of the glorified Lord in our contemporary dialogue of word and response. But the Lord's salvific presence is continually tempered by the sinful incompleteness of that community of faith.

That is why Christ's Church is always in a state of "emptiness" while she exists in this eschatological time "in between." She still faces the as yet unfulfilled task of being always on the way to the glorified Lord, by virtue of this presence. She lives in the eschatological tension by which she remains *the still incomplete Church on earth.*

Christ, as First-born, is the creative pattern of all creation. The salvific dimensions of His self-emptying, *kenotic* humanness cast a new light upon the mystery of the Church for our joint reflection. Just as Christ experienced His existence with the Father in His self-emptying human life, so the Church is the salvific instrument of the glorified Lord in the incompleteness of that believing community. But there is an important difference between the *kenosis* of Christ and the *kenosis* of the Church, and this difference will have to be taken into account in our further religious reflection.

The Son of the Father experienced the self-realization of His human existence in a freedom of choice that necessarily accompanies the unfinished human condition and that also implies the experience of the attractive power of sin: "Not as I will, but as thou wilt" (Mt. 26:39). Because of His personal union with the Son of the Father, the man Jesus was unable to sin; and He experienced that invitation to sin as an invitation of His Father to overcome human sinfulness by complete surrender to the Father. Though His whole historical human existence bore the marks of mankind's disobedience, He himself did not fail by disobedience. For the benefit of all, He gave shape to His life of union with the Father in that sinful human existence.

Although the glorified Lord actualizes His salvific word in all ages and countries in the personal actions of the believing community, there exists no personal unity of Christ and the Church. She is not the prolongation of the Incarnation. In the Church there is, therefore, not only an unfinished mankind on its way to its self-unfolding in Christ, but she is also always incapable of offering a definitive resistance to the inciting power of sin that as a real possibility always accompanies the freedom of choice. Here we are in the presence of the "scandal" of the mystery of the Church, namely, that Christ's all-conquering salvific activity is exercised in the sinful experience of our as yet unfinished human existence. *Here we have the dynamic presence of Christ's Spirit in the kenotic structure of a still disobedient community of faith.*

*f. The Community of Salvation as an Eschatologically In-
   complete Instrument of Salvation*

Is it possible for the separated Christians, when things
are seen in that Christological view of the Church, to
come to an integration of their one-sided oppositions?
The Church is both a community of salvation and an
instrument of salvation. These two antithetically emphasized aspects of the Church may be made neither identical nor independent from one another.

The Church as the community of salvation *is* the glorified Lord's instrument of salvation. Reformed Christians
will have to revaluate that aspect, stressed by Catholics,
through a renewed reflection upon the mystery of the
divine Son's human fellowship with us. Then every appeal to a Scripture that stands outside and above that
sinful community will no longer be tolerable.

The Church as the community of salvation, however,
is still an eschatologically incomplete instrument of salvation that continues to struggle with its own sinfulness.
The attention that the Reformed Christians have given to
this aspect in their reflection must prompt Catholics to
return once more to an encounter with Christ in the
Scripture which by His full authority is proclaimed and
experienced in the Church as the immanent norm and
the permanent source of every ecclesial renewal. In that
community of faith, Christ's Spirit is always active as
overcoming sin and as sanctifying men in the authoritative proclamation of the Scripture.

1. *Unity in Diversity*

Today the Catholic Church faces the task, in her own
life of faith and in her approach to the other Churches,
of working out the radical consequences of recognizing
the following fact:

The *unity of the Church*, as instrument of the word and of the salvific activity of the glorified Lord, manifests itself *in the ever imperfect diversity of the Church* as the salvific community existing in various countries and cultures.

Because a one-sided emphasis was placed on the fact that the Church is the instrument of salvation, there came about in preaching and life an unacceptable identification between the Church and the Western-Latin type of structure of the community of faith.[80] This narrowness of view regarding the nature of the Church was the product of circumstances of time and place but was not recognized as such; and those who accepted the identification mentioned above were unable to resist the temptation of rejecting as heretical anyone who dared to differ from that Western uniformity.

Scripture, on the contrary, continually testifies to the fact that that diversity is a salvific necessity for an ever more complete realization of the mystery of Christ. Does not the Epistle of James give us a permanent and living testimony to the fact that the Church of Jerusalem conceived and experienced the encounter with Christ in a way that differed from that of the local Church of Ephesus, whose views of faith are expressed in St. John's Gospel, his Letters and the Apocalypse? And if the tradition is right in telling us that Mark founded the Church of Alexandria, we must admit that the proclamation and life of faith in that local Church differed greatly in character from the preaching in the Churches of Corinth, Galatia and Philippi, which finds expression in St. Paul's Epistles.

And yet all those local Churches considered themselves to be one, amidst their rich diversity, through the

80. See the speech of Maximos IV, Melchite Patriarch of Antioch, August 9, 1960, at Düsseldorf in P. Lenz, *Unbehagen an der Kirche*, Essen, 1960; *Het Schild* 47 (1960), pp. 268-273.

salvific operation of the same Spirit in word and sacrament. And this profoundly realized unity found a visible and tangible expression in the common collection taken up by all those Churches for the mother Church of Jerusalem to which St. Paul makes reference in almost all his Epistles.

The rediscovery of that legitimate diversity of our unity in Christ has become an ecumenical blessing for the Catholic Church. It has made this Church revalue the ecclesial reality of these separated communities of faith.

The Dilemma in the Catholic Ecumenical Attitude of Faith

The Catholic Church has listened with great religious earnestness to the question put to her by the Reformation on the occasion of the Schema "On the Church" of Vatican Council II, which was expressed in the following words by Professor E. Schlink, an observer who belongs to the Lutheran World Union:

> Here then [in the Schema] the Church of God is identified with the Church of Rome. Now, it is not necessary to interpret an ecclesiological identification (as such) in an "exclusive" way. In principle, it is certainly possible for a Church to profess that she is identical with the one holy Church, while on the other hand, she at the same time takes account of the possibility that the one Holy Church may also be realized in other Churches. But the Schema evidently conceives the identification of the one holy Church with the Church of Rome in an "exclusive" way. For in this Schema [the term] "Churches" is not used for any other than the Roman Catholic Church. The Schema speaks only of non-Catholic Christians, hence of non-Catholic individuals, but not of non-Catholic Churches. Hence when it is admitted that those individual, non-Catholic Christians are connected with the Church, it does not mean that they, as members of their own non-Roman Church, be-

long to the one, holy, catholic, and apostolic Church. It means rather that those Christians are connected with the Church of Rome, which claims to be the one, holy, catholic and apostolic Church.[81]

Never has the Catholic Church been so unambiguously confronted with the following dilemma in her ecumenical attitude:

On the one hand, if the Catholic Church continues to recognize that individual believers outside the Catholic Church are Christians but refuses to accept that the separated communities of faith are Churches, she cannot escape the traditional view regarding the *Una Sancta,* namely, that the unity of the Church of Jesus Christ can be achieved only by the return to the Catholic Church of all separated Christians. For, if the Catholic Church maintains that she alone is the Church of Jesus Christ and thus refuses to recognize the ecclesial status of the other Churches, it follows that other Christians are Christian only because they belong to the *Catholic* Church; and they can fully live their Christianity only by a return to that Church.

On the other hand, the Catholic Church, in her ecumenical encounter with other Christians, has come to the profound realization that the separated religious communities are truly the Church of Jesus Christ and that those Christians experience their bond with Christ because they belong to those *separated* religious communions. The basis of this assertion lies in this:

1. The separated communities have a biblical *faith* in God's self-communication in the historical-human life of Christ.

81. E. Schlink, *Die Diskussion des Schemas De Ecclesia in evangelischer Sicht,* Deutsche Konzilpresszentrum, October 1963. G. C. Berkouwer, *Vaticaans Concilie en nieuwe theologie,* Kampen 1964, pp. 217-273.

2. They have entered into the salvific reality of His death and resurrection through *the proclamation of the word* and *the administration of the sacraments*.

3. They transmit that salvific reality (*paradosis*) in the functioning of the *office*.

In the Decree on Ecumenism, Vatican Council II has recognized this: "The Spirit of Christ has not refrained from using them [the separated Churches] as means of salvation."[82]

It is easy to detect the tension of that dilemma in the present Catholic reflection concerning faith. Many Catholics, seeing the increasing consciousness of their own ecclesial sinfulness and the growing appreciation of the Reformed Churches, fear more and more that within their own Church there might come about a levelling of the faith for ecumenical purposes. And they withdraw to one pole of the Church as the Lord's instrument of salvation: "We may not leave those who differ from us under the impression, nor especially make them believe, that we expect reunion as the result of a sort of give-and-take. We understand it as a return to the *one* Church under the *one* Supreme Shepherd, *one* Church which can be radically changed in her structure and in the entire form in which she appears on earth, but not in her doctrine and her teaching authority. I feel it is our dire obligation, based on Christian love and a genuine ecumenical sense, not to leave our separated Christian brethren in the dark concerning that point."[83]

But must a Catholic not take most earnestly the religious scancal of the self-emptying of the Son of God? Must he not dare to become familiar with the thought

82. *Decree on Ecumenism*, no. 3, p. 197, *The Sixteen Documents of Vatican II*, St. Paul Editions, Boston, 1965.

83. L. J. Rogier, *Rede op the Lustrumviering van de Katholieke Universiteit te Nijmegen*, May 30, 1964.

that the unity, the holiness, the catholicity and apostolicity of the Church during this time "in between" on earth are still appearing in the kenotic structure of a human community that in a sinful way experiences the subjective incompleteness of being-objectively-saved in Christ?

Ecumenicity is not an accidental characteristic of the Church that is added to her as a task now because she has actually become divided as a matter of history. Ecumenicity is the Church's essential task: as People of God that is not yet completed, she must live and realize with ever greater intensity her fullness of Christ, in complete unity, holiness, catholicity and apostolicity, through the power of the Spirit.

The Church Continues to Experience Her Unity in Christ in the Sinful Dividedness of the Believing Community

The Church is one, holy, catholic and apostolic in Christ and yet at the same time has still to become one, holy, catholic and apostolic. *For this reason she still experiences her unity in Christ in the sinful dividedness of that community of faith. And it is precisely in the measure of the power with which she overcomes that sin of division through the Spirit, that she is the Church of Jesus Christ.*

She is Christ's Church in fulfilling her ecumenical mandate to overcome her own dividedness, just as Christ experienced his togetherness, as Son, with the Father, in overcoming the sinfulness of human existence. The Catholic must, therefore, do away with the familiar image of the one true Church of Christ facing many Christians who have separated themselves from her and to whom the Church can address herself only by inviting their return. By the fact that the other Reformed communities have been recognized as Churches, the Catholic Church has come to stand in an entirely new position toward them, for such a recognition directly implies that the Catholic who faces the Reformed Christian will be led to confess that *the Church of Christ is divided because she has sinfully renounced her ecumenical mandate.*

Such a common profession of guilt by all would be an expression of a disarming tendency if it implied the recognition that all Churches have the same qualitative value. This would mean that one seeks peace at all cost and does not take the tragedy of division seriously enough. The ecumenical movement would then become an anesthetic for the pain caused by that dividedness and it would lose all its religious dynamism. But in their mutual confession of guilt the Christians profess that the division of the Church *results from the degree of difference by which the local Churches function as instruments of salvation of the glorified Lord.*

It is precisely the honest readiness to surrender to Christ that has brought those separated communities together in the ecumenical movement, because they desire to take a serious account of the fact that other local Churches function with greater fullness as instruments of salvation. They know they need one another in order that in this eschatologically tense time "in between" they may become more fully the Church of Jesus Christ, and they know also that their sinful division prevents them from fulfilling their ecumenical task.

Because of the difference in intensity in being-the-Church-of-Jesus-Christ, the contribution of the diverse Churches to the full ecumenical stature of the Church will likewise be diverse.

The Catholic Ecumenical Task of Faith

The Catholic Church at the present time must seek a solution of the above-mentioned dilemma in view of the separated Churches. These Churches have a right to demand that she radically discard every kind of ambiguity in her view regarding the *Ecumene*.

On the one hand, the Catholic Church expresses her religious awareness of the fact that she is the salvific instrument of the glorified Lord. The local communities of the Catholic Church, by their bond in the salvific reality of tradition and by the functioning of the collegial office of the bishops throughout the world around the primacy of the Bishop of Rome, live, always in their sacramental experience of God's word, in virtue of the mission of Christ sent by the Father: "As the Father has sent me, even so I send you . . . All authority in heaven and on earth has been given to me. Go therefore and make disciples of all nations, baptizing them, . . . and lo, I am with you always, to the close of the age" (Jn 20:21; Mt. 28:18-20).

On the other hand, the Catholic Church does not function in her fullness as instrument of salvation of the glorified Lord in those local communities because these communities have failed to take account of the ecclesial reality of the separated communities in their life of faith.

The Catholic Church has come to realize that the Holy Spirit's unfailing assistance, promised and guaranteed to her by Christ, cannot be fully revealed when she claims exclusive possession of that assistance. Because of her age-long rejection of the separated Churches, the Catholic Church cannot fully proclaim and experience Christ's Gospel because those Churches also function as the instrument of salvation of the glorified Lord in virtue of faith, baptism, and office. The ecclesial reality has been atrophied in the Catholic Church because she thought that she alone was Christ's Church, and because she was thus unable to constantly enrich herself in Christ by a living dialogue between the lawfully diverse communities of faith.

The Catholic Church, in her defensive attitude *vis-à-vis* the separated Churches, let certain aspects of the unfolding mystery of Christ be cut off from the Catholic life of faith. Because of the controversial approach, the seriousness of that impoverishment with respect to her ecclesial reality was constantly underestimated. Whenever the recognition of that impoverishment threatened to disclose itself in the religious dialogues with other Christians, it was immediately side-tracked with the remark that the Catholic Church never denied those aspects; hence they had never been wholly absent from the Catholic life of faith. But if this community of faith is the Lord's instrument of salvation, then the mist that has for centuries been hanging over certain aspects of the faith in the Catholic Church implies a constantly weakening of her salvific function of proclaiming the Gospel and living the sacraments. But now through the dialogue that at long last has been opened with the separated Churches, the Catholic Church has once more the opportunity to become fully Church of Jesus Christ in our time.

The following aspects of the Christ mystery that is being accomplished in the Church are particularly involved in that integration:

1. A profound consciousness of sinfulness as the situation of our human existence which has abandoned God. The Catholic experiences sin too exclusively as an action, a transgression of God's law. He does not consider himself sinful as long as he is not conscious of any concrete fault.

2. The realization that we are totally dependent on Christ for our condition of grace. Because the Counterreformation greatly stressed good works, the Catholic, in

his religious life, puts much emphasis on the moralistic fulfillment of clearly defined obligations and on the part man's effort plays in obtaining salvation.

3. The idea that good works are signs of our election in Christ. Because so much stress has been placed on our cooperation with grace, the Catholic sees the working of God's grace through Christ too much as a strengthening of his own powers. He knows that without grace he cannot do anything; yet he constantly seems to think that grace is necessary only because his good works cannot lead to eternal life without that additional help of God. Typical of that distorted preaching of the faith is the following answer that used to be given in the Catechism: "To reach heaven grace alone (the Reformed "by grace alone") is insufficient. We must also co-operate with grace."

4. A proclamation that is constantly inspired by God's word. Because the sacramental character of the proclamation of the word was devaluated, the preaching in the Catholic Church has always been strongly moralistic. The administration of the sacraments has been too isolated from the proclamation of the word and has acquired an automatic and magical character. The sacrament is not experienced as the word, in the fullness of its dialogical power of salvation.

5. Familiarity with God's word in daily Scripture reading. Because the Counter-reformation looked upon tradition as an independent source of revelation, ecclesiastical preaching functioned as the practical norm of faith in the Catholic Church, and Scripture was left too much in the vague background; as a result it disappeared from the perspective of the Catholic. A believing attention to the Church's preaching made a personal contact with Scripture superfluous. This degradation of scriptural reading and its removal to the fringe of Christian life was fos-

tered by the official catechesis which expressed itself in
propositions such as: "The reading of Holy Scripture is
not necessary, though it must be called useful."

6. Personal responsibility in decisions of the faith and
the prophetical testimony of the general priesthood. The
Catholic views fidelity to Christ too one-sidedly as an
unconditional obedience to ecclesiastical authority, so
that there is little room in the Church for the proper task
of the general priesthood and for personal responsibility
in decisions of faith.

7. The function of the special priesthood in the believing community of the Church. The general priesthood is
underestimated and there is a one-sided juridical concept
of the Church as being Christ's salvific instrument. This
makes the Catholic experience the Church as a hierarchy
that stands above him. This gives the special office of the
clerical priesthood a strong monological character and it
does not function in organic connection with the faith of
the whole Church. Being-the-Church is not experienced
as a dialogue between the authoritatively proclaimed
word and the ever new response given to it in a personal
decision.

8. The effective recognition of the proper value and
the particular character of the local Church as the
Church of this people. The primacy can function only in
a collegial context. Following the declaration of papal
infallibility in Vatican Council I, the primacy of the
Bishop of Rome was viewed in the Catholic Church in a
way that is too one-sided. On account of the constant
tendency toward uniformity and centralization, too little
room is left for the collegial functioning of the primacy
and for the proper responsibility of the local Church. The
Bishop of Rome can exercise the primacy only in communion with the episcopate of the whole world, as *liturgoi*, teachers and shepherds of the universal Church

and of the local Churches that are entrusted to them.

9. The Christological re-orientation of all Marian dogmas. There was an underestimation of the salvific function of the Incarnation of the Son and of the absolute uniqueness of His salvific action; this brought about a Marian obscuration of the mystery of Christ. The Catholic Church has now gained a twofold insight occasioned by the legitimate protests of the Reformed Churches. First, she has seen that the Marian dogmas may not primarily concern the person of Mary, but that they must aim at the concrete aspects of the salvation that Christ has wrought in the life of every man. Secondly, she should not base her Marian declarations on isolated scriptural words about Mary, but on the whole biblical testimony of the salvific mystery of Christ. The Catholic Church must re-examine her Marian dogmas from the standpoint of that new understanding that Mary is the eminent believer; because of her perfect readiness to surrender herself, she became the Mother of God's Son; and as such, she is the personification of the whole Church considered as the receptive community of faith with respect to Christ.

In this renewal of the ecclesial profession of faith we are not dealing with some harmless matter, as if nothing more is required than that individual Christians in their personal life of faith pay more attention to a number of neglected aspects. In this ecumenical task the *whole* ecclesial reality of the Catholic Church is at stake. When those aspects mentioned above do not appear in the proclamation of the faith and in the life of faith, Christ cannot actualize the fullness of His salvific work by word and sacrament in this community of men: "But how are men to call upon him in whom they have not believed? And how are they to believe in him of whom they have never heard? And how are they to hear without a

preacher? . . . So faith comes from what is heard, and
what is heard comes by the preaching of Christ" (Rom.
10:14-17).

Only if the Catholic Church knows how to correct
those one-sided ways in her encounter with the Reformed
Churches, will all these Churches together be able to
fully become the salvific instrument of the glorified Lord
by overcoming their sinful dividedness, just as Christ has
fully lived His divine being together with the Father
while He overcame the sinfulness of our human existence.

2. *Diversity in Unity*

In the intensive religious encounter with the Reformed
Churches the ecclesial reality of the Catholic Church is
presently being ecumenically renewed. But, at the same
time, the separated Christians have, together, acquired a
new vision, against that background, of their own contribution as Reformed Churches to the unification of the
Church of Jesus Christ.

The Catholic Church, we saw, has been able to express
the ecclesial reality of those separated religious communities on the basis of the recognition that the unity of the
Church as Christ's instrument of salvation must manifest itself in the rich diversity of local Churches as eschatologically incomplete communities of faith. The Reformed Churches have similarly discovered that the
imperfection in the proclamation and the life of the faith
in local Churches, which is necessarily connected with
that incompleteness, can be corrected only through a
strong functional unity of the Church as the salvific
instrument of the glorified Lord's preaching and saving
action. In the interests of the coming *Ecumene*, the separated Christians must keenly make one another feel the
pain of dividedness. The separated Churches are not

qualitatively equivalent parts of Christ's Church that are only waiting for a merger.

The separated Churches stand opposite one another and they must stand protesting against one another because they are the Church in diverse ways. In being-the-Church in a different way, they are all still incomplete, but it is a question of *another* incompleteness. The Catholic Church is incomplete in another way than the Reformed Churches. And that is why both have something proper to bring into the *Ecumene*.

The Catholic Church *is* the Church of Jesus Christ because her local believing communities experience their unity by standing together in the salvific reality of the apostolic tradition and by the functional bond of those Churches with the Church of Rome. But that salvific activity of Christ in her proclamation of the word and the administration of the sacraments *does not function fully*, because, by rejecting as heretical the Reformed life of faith, she has not let herself be enriched by the ecclesial reality of those local Churches.

The Churches of the Reformation *are* the Church of Jesus Christ because the Spirit of Christ, through faith and baptism, is present as forming-the-Church and because they function as Church of Jesus Christ through the office. But because—as a consequence of their separation and mutual dividedness—they cannot stand fully in the reality of tradition and because the office does not function in unity with the other Churches, *they cannot be fully the Church of Jesus Christ*.

The roads to the *Ecumene* to be taken by the Catholic Church and the Reformed Churches, then, are different and in a certain sense opposite: The Catholic Church will have to actually recognize the diversity of the local Churches as being the authentic ecclesial reality, on the basis of the one salvific reality in which all believers in Christ are situated.

The Reformed Churches will be obliged to correct the necessary imperfection of that diversity by an effective functioning of the oneness in Christ of the local Churches. *The ecumenical task of the Reformed Churches must be inspired by the religious insight that the eschatological incompleteness of the local believing communities will inevitably become a sinful dividedness if they do not have a strongly experienced unity.*

The Incompleteness Becomes a Sinful Division if There Is No Unity

Men are subject to the cultural pattern of their own time and the character of the people to which they belong. They are also limited in their mental powers. On that account the proclamation of the word and the administration of the sacraments by the Church must necessarily result in a great diversity of local Churches, and particular aspects of Revelation are either overestimated or underestimated. The ecclesial reality of the local Churches is determined by the character and the abilities of the leaders in the historical development, by the spirituality of the particular period, by the cultural progress and the social structure of the particular people.

The inevitable one-sidedness of local Churches will ultimately be overcome if they maintain the necessary bond with all the believing communities of the universal Church, so that, through united reflection on revelation, mutual and unimpeded correction is made possible.

In times of religious tension, however, that lawful pluriformity is in danger of becoming a fixed one-sidedness. Then the *hairesis* makes its appearance as a divisive choice: constrained religious conviction drives people to absolutize their own view of the mystery of Christ in the Church in opposition to other Christians and other religious communities and to risk even a secession. Even the early Christian Communities were acquainted with the danger of *hairesis*, of absolutely preferring a particular aspect of the faith and so leading to a schism in the Church. St. Paul wrote to the Church of Corinth: "It has been reported to me by Chloe's people that there is quarreling among you, my brethren. What I mean is that each one of you says, 'I belong to Paul,' or 'I belong to Apollos,' or 'I belong to Cephas,' or 'I belong to Christ.' Is Christ divided? . . . Or were you baptized in the name of Paul? . . . No other foundation can any one lay than that which is laid, which is Jesus Christ. . . . you are Christ's; and Christ is God's" (1 Cor. 1:11; 3:11; 3:23). In the Church of Corinth which generally lived according to the Pauline vision of the Christ mystery, there was a danger of division, because some appealed to the Greek-oriented preaching of Apollos, as opposed to Paul, to the original Palestinian proclamation of Peter or directly to Christ, to the exclusion of all human mediation and all apostolic authority.

The inevitable diversity of the local Church as an indigenous manifestation of the Church of Jesus Christ necessarily becomes atrophied into a schism when that Church, precisely because of its bond with the universal Church, cannot function fully as the salvific instrument of the glorified Lord. But there is no fullness in the proclamation of the word and in the administration of the sacraments when there is a schism, a severance of *the bond with the corrective and enriching influence* of the whole believing community. For when a local community absolutizes its own imperfect condition and claims that it is the only authentic structure of the Church of Jesus Christ, the way to interior renewal is thereby cut off.

It was not an insignificant confession of guilt on the part of the separated Churches within the World Council of Churches when, at Evanston, they endorsed, in all sincerity, the following declaration: "There is a diversity that is not sinful but good because it reflects both the diversity of the gifts of the Spirit in the one body and diversities of creation by the one Creator. *But when diversity disrupts the manifest unity of the body, then it changes its quality and becomes sinful division.*"[84]

The Unsalutary and Salutary Functions of the Schism

It will be necessary to re-examine the schism from the standpoint of the cosmic range of the mystery of the Incarnation of God's Son. Creation is not the neutral hunting ground of God's grace, it is not the sinful space within which God constantly and from without intervenes in order to save individual men or groups of men.

Jesus Christ is the First-born of the whole creation (Col. 1:15). And in this creation that is predestined for that purpose (Rom. 8:28-30) He has attained glory because, by the power of the Holy Spirit, He has experienced His divine being together with the Father in perfect human fellowship with us. Precisely as the perfect Man, in whom the whole creation has already achieved objective fulfillment, He is our Mediator with the Father: "There is one mediator between God and men, *the man Christ Jesus*, who gave himself as a ransom *for all*" (1 Tim. 2:5).

The whole creation is involved and functions relative to God's coming with grace in Jesus Christ: "in order that life might be restored through the very instrument that brought death."[85] For just as Christ has lived and experienced His divine love for the Father in this earthly sinful reality and in sin-laden human situations, we must actualize our being-in-Christ in inter-human relations and in the development of earthly values. No encounter with

84. *The Evanston Report*, London, 1965, p. 87.
85. The Preface of Passiontime.

Christ is possible outside the human community and outside the earthly reality. "In virtue of the work Christ has accomplished once and for all, and into which we are drawn through baptism and faith, the Church is the space within which Christ builds up His dominion of grace in a prophetic and exemplary way."[86]

By the destruction of visible unity through a schism, the Church is essentially affected as a human salvation-society in her function of being a salvific instrument of Christ. St. Paul unmasks the unsalutary power of schism: "Is Christ divided?" (1 Cor. 1:11).

If in the Church of Jesus Christ one pulpit stands against another, one altar is opposed to another, her proclamation and sacramental action will inevitably lose the fullness and the sacred power of Christ. The visible unity of the Church is based on the fact that Christ has taken on human nature.[87] This religious insight of the separated Churches at Evanstown implies the recognition that, because of the rupture of the visible unity, the local Church can no longer be called the Church of Jesus Christ in the full sense of the word, but only in an analogous sense.

It is in the light of that truth that we, separated Christians, only now see clearly the full extent of the Luther tragedy. The renewed study of Luther has convinced Catholics also how important and significant the man of Wittenberg was in salvation history for the renewal of the late medieval Church. Luther was moved with prophetic compassion when he desired to stand protestingly in a Church which for many had become uninhabitable, and he strove to call her back to evangelical authenticity.

86. H. Berkhof, *De Katholiciteit van de Kerk*, Nijkerk, 1962, p. 66.
87. *The Evanston Report*, p. 83.

The Catholic Church has re-discovered the Churchly character of the Reformed communities on the occasion of her Council, and she has also come under the spell of evangelical renewal. On that account a climate for a mutual liberating confession of guilt has been created that once more open the way for reunion of the Churches after many centuries of separation.

It will be necessary, on the one hand, for the Catholic Church to rehabilitate Luther, because she made it impossible for him to fulfill his prophetic vocation in the Church and refused him the opportunity of an honest dialogue. On the other hand, the Reformed Churches must be willing to admit that Luther should never have broken his bond with all local communities of faith, in spite of the humanly unbearable resistance which he encountered, for this made him become unfaithful to his vocation to the whole Church. He should have had the courage, inspired by faith, to remain in the visibly lived communion with all local Churches while continuing his protests.

We know the unsalutary effect of dividedness on all religious communities, preventing them from being fully the Church of Jesus Christ. But today we are also discovering and admitting with decreasing shyness that the evil of schism has at the same time ecumenical dimensions and salutary results.

Those religious communities are, though in diverse ways, the Church of Jesus Christ; hence we must abstain from trying to reduce them to a common level, thus paralyzing them, for the sake of increasing unification. We have to admit that they are all within the salutary influence of Christ's work of salvation; we must recognize that the local Churches that no longer function within the visible unity of the Catholic Church around the primacy of the Bishop of Rome are also "the Church of Jesus Christ." Their ecumenical salvific significance lies in the historical fact that they have preserved the native and proper character of the local Church in various countries at a time when an increasing uniformity developed in the unity of the Catholic Church. Those Churches conscientiously thought it was necessary for them to risk going into schism for the sake of preserving what was proper to them and they always felt that they were the Church of Jesus Christ in those countries.

"Present-day competent Catholic historians interpret the great schism [between the Western and Eastern Churches] as the failure to impose the Roman centralization upon the Eastern Churches, which during their ten centuries of union with Rome, were accustomed to combine a legitimate diversity with that unity. . . . Orthodoxy alone at this moment possesses the authentic Eastern tradition. . . . God, who knows how to draw good from evil, has willed that that unfortunate separation should protect the Orthodox Churches against centralization and latinization, for the great benefit of the ecumenical dialogue and the reunited Churches."[88]

Although, according to Catholic thought, the Eastern Orthodox, the Anglican and the Reformed Churches are not on the same level from the standpoint of ecclesial reality, they are alike in their ecumenical function of salvation with respect to the Catholic churches in various countries. For all those separated Churches have preserved authentic native Christian values that have been lost by Catholic Churches because of Roman centralization and the establishment of uniformity.

Practical recognition of that ecumenic salvific func-

88. Intervention of Elias Zoghby, Greek-Melkite Vicar of the Patriarchate in Egypt, at the Second Vatican Council. See Yves Congar, *Concilie toespraken*, Hilversum, 1964, pp. 34-37.

tion must imply that the encounter between the Catholic
Church and the other Churches may never be dominated
by the secret desire to divorce individuals or entire
Churches from their tradition and their history. An ecumenical dialogue should not begin with an endeavor to
make the others pass over and return to the Catholic
Church, but with respect for the native Christian tradition of so many centuries. It is necessary to be profoundly convinced that for centuries Jesus Christ desired
to be actively present through those believing communities in those centuries, and this conviction must make
the Catholic Church sensitive to the unique value of
those traditions: they represent a legitimate contribution
in the pluriformity of the future *Ecumene:*

> While preserving unity in essentials, let all members
> of the Church, according to the office entrusted to each,
> preserve a proper freedom in the various forms of spirit-
> ual life and discipline, in the variety of liturgical rites,
> and even in the theological elaborations of revealed
> truth.[89]
> History, tradition, and numerous ecclesiastical insti-
> tutions manifest luminously how much the universal
> Church is indebted to the Eastern Churches. This sacred
> Synod, therefore, not only honors this ecclesiastical and
> spiritual heritage with merited esteem and rightful
> praise, but also unhesitatingly looks upon it as the heri-
> tage of Christ's universal Church.[90]

The local communities of the Catholic Church must
recognize that revelation is rooted in the particular character of diverse peoples; they must, therefore, correct the
one-sidedness of their own uniform Latin countenance
when they meet other Christians in ecumenical encounters. They must seek to enrich themselves, absorbing the

89. *Decree on Ecumenism,* No. 4, par. 7.
90. *Decree on Eastern Catholic Churches,* No. 5.

native traditions that have been preserved by non-Catholic Churches in their own country.

Today the Churches are called to take a fresh look at the concrete consequences flowing from both the unsalutary and the salutary function of the schism in their own past, in the light of God's fidelity to His Covenant with the People He has acquired in Christ: "When you are in tribulation, and all these things come upon you in the latter days, you will return to the Lord your God and obey his voice, for the Lord your God is a merciful God; he will not fail you or destroy you or forget the covenant with your fathers which he swore to them" (Dt. 4:30).

All Churches have a need to make up for their historical guilt in this matter.

The Lawfulness of Pluriformity

But the separated Churches must not be content with confessing their own guilt. When they have removed the hitherto impossible historical barrier by honestly acknowledging their guilt, they must engage in the ecumenical task of radically erasing all traces of a centuries-long division. Only now that it has become possible for them to fully understand one another, they deeply realize how weak a divided Church is as the Lord's instrument of salvation. They see every day, in their contradictory proclamations of the Gospel, how powerless the divided Church is when she tries to approach modern man in a way appropriate to our time. Because of their dividedness, they have become a historical residue of the Church of Jesus Christ which modern man passes disinterestedly.

It will be necessary, therefore, for every local Church sedulously to let confirmation by the universal Church legitimatize its own proclamation of the word and its own sacramental life. Only a Church that is in dialogue with all the other Churches can in its own time and place be Christ's organ of salvation.

Scripture itself gives a striking testimony of that solicitude that existed in the apostolic Church. The Acts of the Apostles and the Letters of St. Paul reveal the tensions in the young Church, the tensions of a lively dialogue that reaches its high point at the first Council of the Church in Jerusalem (Acts 15:1-29). But attention to the necessary unity of the local communities, which inspired all participants, neutralized every threat of division amidst those strong tensions.

In the same Letter to the Galatians, in which Paul speaks without any reservation about the opposition between himself and Peter—"but when Cephas came to Antioch I opposed him to his face, because he stood condemned" (Gal. 2:11)—that dynamic Apostle testifies to unity: "Then after fourteen years I went up again to Jerusalem with Barnabas, . . . and I laid before them (but privately before those who were of repute) the gospel which I preach among the Gentiles, lest somehow I should be running or had run in vain. . . . But when they saw that I had been entrusted with the gospel to the uncircumcised, just as Peter had been entrusted with the Gospel to the circumcised . . . , and when they perceived the grace that was given to me . . . , James and Cephas and John, who were reputed to be pillars, gave to me and Barnabas the *right hand of fellowship*" (Gal. 2:1-9).

This giving of the right hand of fellowship as a sign of communion is needed by every local Church in order that the fullness of Christ's Church may be able to function. Hence the first and most important ecumenical task of the Reformed Church is to reflect upon what is taught by Scripture, namely, that if Churches wish to legitimatize their own local diversity they must be in *visible unity with the universal Church, a unity brought about around the scriptural world of God.*

This belief of what constitutes their ecumenical task was expressed by the Churches of the World Council at New Delhi in the "Saint Andrew Statement" of the *New Delhi Report* (p. 116):

> We believe that the unity which is both God's will and his gift to his Church is being made visible as all in each place who are baptized into Jesus Christ and confess him as Lord and Saviour, holding the one apostolic faith, preaching the one Gospel, breaking the one bread, joining in common prayer, and having a corporate life reaching out in witness and service to all and who at the same time are united with the whole Christian fellowship in all places and all ages in such wise that ministry and members are accepted by all and that all can act and speak together as occasion requires for the tasks to which God calls his people.
>
> It is for such unity that we believe we must pray and work.

g. *The Church As Dialogue*

In the land of Palestine, the Son of God lived his being together with the Father as the First-born of the whole of creation and as our representative; by constantly overcoming the experience of sin in our human existence. On Easter morn the Father accepted, in the glorification of His Incarnate Son, the whole of mankind as His finished creation, which they together actualize in the sending of the Holy Spirit.

The Church, as the People of God that is already eschatologically saved in Christ, already lives her life of union with the Father through Christ, in the history of mankind in all countries and all centuries, in a human community of love; this community is called together by the Spirit in the proclamation of the word, and is bound together in the administration of the sacraments.

The Spirit, as bond of love between the Son and the Father, effects the unity of love between all men through establishing the Church by His Presence. The Church is the salvific instrument of the Spirit of the glorified Lord by functioning as the community of love of all men gathered around the word and the sacraments.

But the Church is constantly weakened in her saving instrumentality because she has not offered opposition to the temptation of living her eschatological unfulfilment in a state of sinful division. But she can overcome her sinful shortcomings in her task of actualizing salvation in Christ, in virtue of the power of the Spirit that will enable her to exercise an all-embracing love. Just as Christ has exercised His love for the Father in true love toward us, so must love toward the Father be translated in the Church of Jesus Christ, into a love toward all men, in virtue of the inspiration of the Spirit.

Vatican Council II begins its dogmatic *Constitution on the Church* with a striking new approach of that mystery: she is "by her relationship with Christ, a kind of sacrament or sign of intimate union with God, and of the unity of mankind."[91]

The Church is a sign and an instrument, a human sign that functions as an instrument of salvation in the meeting of persons. The Church is permanently the contemporary dialogue between the word that is proclaimed authoritatively through a commission of Christ, and man's response arising from his personal responsibility. In the human community that arises from that probing dialogue between the special and the general priesthood of the People of God, the whole of mankind exercises its dialogue with a personal surrender to the Triune God.

91. *Constitution on the Church*, No. 1.

The Reformational Protest Against a Church That Believes in Monologue

Because dialogue is a necessity of conscience, because God appeals to the person through His word and calls for a personal answer of faith, the Reformation took the risk of divorcing itself from a Church in which the monologue was predominant.

The life of the Church was, they say, no longer experienced as a dialogue in which the proclamation of the word is constantly listened to in function of a search for a contemporary way of being a Christian. On that account the Reformed Christian saw the ministerial proclamation and administration of the sacraments within the Catholic Church as a one-way street permitting movement only to possessors of the truth and distributors of Christ's grace.

The Reformation protests against the concentration of the Church's salvific function in the special office that has made the Catholic Church a hierarchical-clerical Church which places itself before the individual believer as the sole means of salvation. This way of being-the-Church the Reformers want to discard because they consider it a human and arrogant attempt to place itself between Christ and the believer as the proclaimer of His truth and the mediator of His grace. By thus obnubilating Christ, the Catholic Church has led man to a wrong path in which man can only meet human seekers and not the God who reveals Himself in Christ. That Church, they claim, has drawn man's attention away from God's salvific action in Christ and concentrated that attention on her human mediation.

That view of the Church is "contrary to Scripture for she considers the office as a prolongation of Christ's priesthood; she neglects the prophetic element of the office, that occupies the first place; and she places the office in such a way between Christ and the community that the faithful in their communion with the true Shepherd and Bishop of their souls (1 Pet. 2:25), are made totally dependent upon that office, and treated as minors; in this way the great good of the general priesthood of the faithful runs the danger of getting lost."[92]

In opposition to the pretension to authority of the hierarchical-clerical Church, the Reformation found it necessary to say that God speaks authoritatively to each individual believer. That is why the Reformation, leaving aside every form of human mediation, constantly returns to the permanent source of God's word as contained in Holy Scripture. Only this word of God in Scripture (*sola scriptura*) is the means of salvation, by which man knows himself secure in the merits of Jesus Christ, as the only and totally sufficient foundation of his salvation (*sola gratia*). And by faith alone (*sola fide*) that, as a personal act of total surrender to Christ, constitutes the reverse side of God's active word, the believer has the salutary certainty that Christ's merits are also valid for himself personally.

The personal act of faith in Christ, to which only God's word can constantly call man, stands at the center of the ecclesial life of the Reformation. The Church functions within the personal response of faith, that is nourished exclusively by the daily dialogue between God and man in the proclamation of the word and the reading of the Bible. By that act of faith in God's word, the believer enters into immediate relationship with Christ. Every

92. *Herderlijk Schrijven van de Generale Synode der Nederlandse Hervormde Kerk betreffende de Rooms-Katholieke Kerk.* 's Gravenhage, 1950, p. 36.

human intervention that tries to do more than to be helpful and that puts itself up as an authority, is an attack upon the one mediatorship of Christ.

This immediate personal meeting between God and man excludes every kind of ecclesiastical hierarchy, every sort of priestly mediation. "The New Testament knows nothing about a human-priestly mediatorship; it knows only what the Reformers call 'the universal priesthood of the faithful.' "[93]

In the tension that exists between God's salvific activity in Christ, and the office of human intervention in proclaiming the word and administering the sacraments, the Reformation gives radical predominance to God's initiative. There is no room for an ecclesiastical teaching power that can invoke divine authority as a guarantee for its binding pronouncements; for God himself always keeps the initiative in His own hands by speaking in Holy Scripture, and the believer always experiences that God is personally occupied with him.

The Church must always respect that personal dignity of the believer to whom God directly speaks. The special office must always remain conscious that it is subservient to the functioning of the universal priesthood of the faithful in the Church community. For in the Church there must be every opportunity for the individual believer to witness daily in word and deed to his personal election in Christ, that is realized in him by his believing acceptance of the Good News.

Over against a clerical-hierarchical Church that stands with full authority before the individual, we must place the universal priesthood of the Church as the believing community of all whom God calls out of the world to be His children and who, professing their belief in that

93. *Ibid.,* p. 35.

election, unite in Christ. This Church Christ wills as the community of salvation within which the individual Christian can personally live and exercise his gratitude for being called by Christ by "raising the signs of election." She is the auditorium in which the word of God that he has found favor in Christ is continually proclaimed by ministers, but these "are at the same time subordinate to the word and, as being of age, the community can always appeal against them to this word."[94]

The Reformed Christian very deliberately desires to live by "faith alone." But he resolutely dismisses every suggestion of religious individualism or subjectivism, for He experiences that certitude of salvation in Christ as a reality of faith that is constantly given him by the Spirit. And he knows also that he is in communion with all believers through the work of that Spirit. But he must stress the primary aspect of being-a-Christian, namely, that in the act of faith there is question of that immediate relation to God, of a personalistic encounter with God.

Holy Scripture—the Church—Faith

Being the Church of Jesus Christ is a correlative reality in which we must distinguish three aspects:

1. The Father's constantly actual initiative of love in sending His Son into our sinful human existence.

2. The authoritative sending of the Church by Christ to proclaim His word and administer his sacramental actions of salvation.

3. The personal act of faith in which the individual

94. *Ibid.*, p. 37. Cf. E. Wolfe, *Peregrinatio, Studien zur reformatorischen Theologie und zum Kirchenproblem*, München, 1954; L. Newbegin, *The Household of God, Lectures on the Nature of the Church*, London, 1953; F. M. Braun, *Neues Licht auf die Kirche, Die protestantische Kirchendogmatik in ihrer neuesten Entfaltung*, Einsiedeln-Köln, 1946.

Christian expresses in his human existence and the concrete decisions of his daily life that he is saved in Christ.

On the basis of the mystery of the Incarnation of God's Son, the tension between those three aspects is an essential characteristic of being-the-Church-of-Christ. For in the Church it is always a question of an interhuman encounter with the Son of the Father. But the divided Christians ran aground in their religious controversy because on both sides they neutralized that tension:

Does the Church spring forth from the immediate relationship of God speaking to us and of us responding with faith, so that the Church's mission is pushed into the background by a direct appeal to Scripture that ultimately stands high above the Church? Or does the Church draw her constant origin from the authoritative proclamation of the word and the administration of the sacraments which the individual Christian experiences in a believing acceptance, so that the personal meeting of God's word in Scripture is put in the shadow of ecclesiastical pronouncements of faith?

On the one hand, the Reformed Churches are giving increasing attention in their ecumenical self-reflection to the question: do the principles of "Scripture alone" and "faith alone" leave room for the mission of the Church as the Lord's salvific instrument and for the functioning of the special priesthood?

What man experiences in his earthly-eschatological situation is not an immediate encounter but only an interhuman encounter with God. Likewise, the believing individual does not receive in Scripture the word of God as speaking to him directly in isolation from the believing community. The Reformed Christian begins once more to see the full consequence of Luther's emphasis on the *viva vox Evangelii,* the living voice of the Gospel: the act of faith is the personal response of life to the Scripture that is proclaimed in the Church.

Scripture as such is a dead book. It has only the historical value of an account of the faith of the primitive Church. It is only when that testimony of the apostolic Church concerning Christ and His task is proclaimed and experienced in community, that it becomes "the word of God, which. . . . is at work in you believers." The Church lives by "the word of God which you heard from us," through the proclamation of the Scripture (1 Thess. 2:13). "The way we generally handle the expression 'Scripture alone' manifests a one-sidedness for which there is no justification. . . . We can never sufficiently point out that the Reformational principle regarding Scripture rests upon the equation of God's word with Scripture; now this is wholly unreformational."[95]

> The difference that exists between the Roman-Catholic and the pure Reformational concept of the relationship between Scripture and tradition does not consist in the fact that the Roman Catholic Church is relative to Holy Scripture on the basis of, and guided by, Church tradition, whereas we have a so-called unprejudiced and immediate relation to Scripture by simply rejecting all Church tradition. That rejection is, in any case, a fiction. . . . The Bible is not transmitted in a "sterilized" and closed reliquary, but it is transmitted to us precisely by being used in the Church and thus making history. . . . The proper content of Scripture reveals itself only in its living actualization in the Church. The experiences gathered by faith and the Church in this actualization are the "primary commentary" called up by the Bible itself for a proper understanding of it. . . . *That is why the proper content of Scripture is discovered only*

95. H. Rückert, *Schrift, Tradition, Kirche,* Lüneberg, 1951, p. 22.

when it is read and proclaimed in the pneumatic atmos-
phere of the Church.[96]

On the other hand, the Catholic Church is presently
faced with the question: do the Church's dogmas leave
room for personal responsibility in the Church as a community of faith of the Lord, and permit the functioning
of the universal priesthood?

The Church's dogmas are the crystallization of the
Church's profession of faith at a particular time and in a
particular period of culture. Not only is that profession
expressed in the particular language and according to the
world-view that belonged to that community of faith; but
the Church also expressed herself only about those aspects of the reality of salvation that at that time called
forth the attention of believers or that she knew to be
endangered.

If the Church wishes to free herself from an unacceptable identification of the content of faith with the way a
certain culture expressed itself and which way the
Church then adopted in her pronouncements of faith,
and if she wants to leave ample room for the inspiration
of the Spirit in a further reflection of faith upon the word
of God in other times and other cultures, she must realize
that a dogma is never a final point; it can never be a final
decision for all centuries.

Because of her belief in the active presence of the
Spirit who, since the first Pentecost is sent to her by
Christ, the Church can never withdraw a dogma as un-
true. Karl Barth too speaks of the "essential infallibility
and perennial character of the Church" and acknowl-

---

96. E. Kinder, "Schrift und Tradition," in M. Roesle und O.
Cullmann, *Begegnung der Christen*, Stuttgart, 1960, pp. 115-131,
137; Cf. Berkouwer, *Vaticaans Concilie en nieuwe theologie*, pp.
105-133.

edges that the People of God "cannot fail in its goal."[97] If we take seriously the ecclesial reality of the separated Churches, we cannot simply force them to go to Canossa. The Church's profession of faith stands always in the tradition of the Church of all countries and centuries. She lives always on the basis of the salvific reality that God has entered into our human existence.

And yet the Church, in every period and especially when there is a great change in the image of man and the world, must take up her dogmas once more to correct any sort of one-sidedness by placing them in the newly-discovered dimensions of the reality of salvation. As Schillebeeckx says,

When there is a dogmatic definition we must, therefore, make a fine distinction between what constitutes the real core of the dogmatic affirmation—that is, what is required to *in-tend* the inexpressible content of faith in an authentic and truthful manner—and, on the other hand, the accidental *ways of clothing them with words;* but this must be understood to mean that the absolute "moment-of-truth" can never be formulated with a purity that is free from human ways of conceiving things. It can, on the contrary, be intended *only* through conceptualization; and so it is never possible to clearly distinguish what is absolute and what is a relative in a dogma; the reality of salvation is *"in-tended"* in imperfect concepts. It is only when new human experiences or new positive data have been obtained, that the question of the difference between "the content of faith" and the "garb of faith" can be made explicit, and that we are able to see whether the so-called "garb" is merely a way

97. K. Barth, *Die Frage nach der Kirche*, Barmen, 1927, p. 370. Cf. Y. Congar, "Pourquoi le Peuple de Dieu doit-il sans cesse se réformer?" *Irenikon* 21 (1948), pp. 365 ff.; "Wahre und falsche Reform in der Kirche," *Una Sancta* 6 (1951), no. 2; "Heiligkeit und Sünde in der Kirche," *Dokumente* 4 (1948), pp. 531 ff., 610 ff.

of proposing things or belongs precisely to the dogmatic content.[98]

But the consequent recognition of the historicity of human thought and of the whole of human existence is not enough. It is illusory to believe that a new contemporary formulation of the content of faith will bring about an ecumenical liberation from dogmatic oppositions. The decisive element will be the ecumenical willingness of the Churches to free themselves from one-sided, historically crystallized views concerning the reality of salvation and their readiness to enrich themselves by accepting aspects of the reality of the Revelation that until now have been allowed to lie dormant or unknown because of an apologetic defensive attitude. What the *Ecumene* requires is an openness to all Churches and to a wholly new way of encountering Christ in Scripture, as if we have only just now become Christians.

In our time the Biblical re-orientation of the ecclesial profession of faith must direct itself especially to the trinitarian dimensions of the Christ mystery, to the function the earthly reality plays in the salvific plan of divine revelation, to the ecclesial aspects of Christ's grace and the administration of the sacraments, to the normative value of the Scripture proclaimed by the Church, to the Christological explanation of the Marian dogmas, to the service character of the office, even if that office is supreme, to the maturity and personal responsibility of every believer, and to the problem of authority.

In terms of the renewed encounter with the other

98. E. Schillebeeckx, "Het begrip waarheid," *Theologische Peilingen I, Openbaring en theologie*, p. 198. Cf. H. de Lubac, *Catholicism;* "Le problème de développement du dogme," *Recherches de Science Religieuse* 22 (1948), pp. 160 ff.; M. D. Koster, *Volk Gottes im Wachstum des Glaubens*, Heidelberg, 1950; E. Schlink, "Die Struktur der dogmatische Aussage als ökumenisches Problem," *Kerugma und Dogma* 3 (1957), pp. 251 ff.

Churches of Jesus Christ, the Catholic Church will have to tackle that ecumenical task with the deep conviction that *a Church dogma must never be permitted to block the contemporary personal way of experiencing God's word.*

The Community of Salvation in Dialogue as the Salvific Instrument of the Glorified Lord

If the Reformation is willing to put Scripture in the pneumatic frame of the Church, and if the Catholic Church is willing to re-direct her profession of faith toward the contemporary and personal way of experiencing God's word, both will experience being-the-Church of Jesus Christ as a renewed dialogue. *For the Church is the salvific instrument of the glorified Lord by functioning as a community of salvation that is engaged in dialogue.* The being-the-Church of Jesus Christ is accomplished as an engaging dialogue between the divine word sacramentally proclaimed by the special priesthood and the human response in which the universal priesthood translates in society at large that being-spoken-to-by God.

Revelation is not a one-sided monologue spoken by God to man; it is not an immediate speaking of God who directly communicates to man divine truths and commandments as practical directives for his daily life. In revelation God communicates Himself in the Incarnation of the Son of the Father through the overshadowing of the Holy Spirit: "And this is the testimony, that God gave us eternal life, and this life is in his Son. He who has the Son has life; he who has not the Son of God has not life" (1 Jn 5:11-12).

Revelation is a divine salvific event in the shape of human history: in the man Jesus Christ, in the human believing community around Christ, God lets men meet Him. In being spoken to by that Man and on the author-

ity of that Man, all men are invited by God to respond
with their human return of love.

That is why God's salvific plan for all mankind, a plan
already fulfilled by the Son in His human life as the
First-born of all creation for the benefit of all men, calls
for a personal human response. The fact that God became man in Christ demands the total involvement of all
that we are and have as men, a total commitment of all
human powers and talents, of our whole human idealism. The Church is mankind already objectively saved in
Christ, and at the same time mankind, as still subjectively in need of being saved by Him.[99] Christ, as mankind objectively saved in Him, remains active in that
community in which He is present through the sacramental proclamation of His word in Scripture. As mankind still subjectively to be saved, He gives constantly to
that community "the power" (Jn 1:12) to give its personal living response.

If we do not experience divine revelation as a human
dialogue between being-called by the human community
that is saved in Christ and the response of this community that personally discovers and experiences this call to
salvation in Christ, we distort revelation and make of it a
being-spoken to by God from outside, a speaking from
another world, a world of which we know nothing and
from which no voice comes through to us.

Man can then experience revelation as something he
can listen to without obligation or the word of God as
something he can reject without being affected in the
least in his being-man. He has then no idea of the seriousness of sin; he does not see that sin is the negation of

99. Y. Congar, "Der mystische Leib Christi und seine sichtbare
Manifestation," M. D. Iserland, *Die Kirche Christi*, Einsiedeln,
Köln, 1940, pp. 27 ff.; A. Wikenhauser, *Die Kirche als der mystische Leib Christi nach dem Apostel*, Münster, 2nd ed., 1940, p.
37.

likeness to Christ and that it degrades human life in a deadly manner.

This inter-human dialogue that takes place within the Church between her being-saved in Christ and her still needing to be saved by Him must continually be made transparent by faith in order that we may discover the more profound reality of salvation behind it. In this human community engaged in dialogue around the word of Scripture, God speaks and fulfills His salvific plan for this world in His First-born.

It is precisely because the Son has lived His divine being with the Father in the struggle of His human obedience for our sake and because that life-with-the-Father continues to give shape to His glorified human existence as mediation for us, that this community engaged in dialogue is the instrument of God's salvific operation.

We would introduce two persons into Christ and thus degrade the salvific significance of His Incarnation if we held that He could also have lived His divine life outside His human consciousness. Similarly, God always acts and speaks through that human community that is called together around the word of Scripture and never outside that human dialogue or above it, as through a Scripture that falls directly from heaven like a meteor.

The Special and the Universal Priesthood

St. Paul, in his Epistle to the Ephesians, has described that human-dialogical form of Christ's enduring salvific presence in this world:

> But grace was given to each of us according to the measure of Christ's gift . . . (For "He ascended" what does it mean but that he had also descended into the lower parts of the earth? He who descended is he who also ascended far above all the heavens, that he might

fill all things.) And his gifts were that some should be apostles, some prophets, some evangelists, some pastors and teachers, *for the equipment of the saints, for the work of ministry, for building up the body of Christ,* until we all attain to the unity of the faith and of the knowledge of the Son of God, to mature manhood, to the measure of the stature of the fulness of Christ; so that we may no longer be children, tossed to and fro and carried about with every wind of doctrine, by the cunning of men, by their craftiness in deceitful wiles. Rather, speaking the truth in love, we are to grow up in every way into him who is the head, into Christ, from whom the whole body, joined and knit together by every joint with which it is supplied, *when each part is working properly,* makes bodily growth and *upbuilds itself in love*" (Eph. 4:7-16).

Christ has saved mankind objectively ("He who ascended" is "He who also descended") and is still actively present ("His gifts were that some should be . . .") to save all men subjectively ("for the equipment of the saints, for the work of ministry"). The point at issue in that dialogue that is constantly initiated by Christ is the functioning of the special and the universal priesthood. But this should not be understood to mean that it is a dialogue between two groups of persons in that community.

For the special office does not stand over against or above the rest of the community of faith, but stands in the middle of the Church. The special office is not a personal quality, but a function of the whole community in which this community gives shape to its being already saved in Christ and thereby savingly stands in this world. At the same time, however, the office is more than a function of the community of faith, because it represents Christ before the community in the proclamation of the word and the administration of the sacraments through the help of the Spirit: "God . . . through Christ recon-

ciled us to himself and gave us the ministry of reconciliation" (2 Cor. 5:18). But the person who is placed in the
function of the special office by the community stands
himself as a member of the community in the universal
priesthood.

It is necessary, therefore, that we clearly distinguish in
the one who is invested with the special office, between
the Christ-representing function of the whole community
as already saved in Christ, and the person who amidst
the community lives his being-saved by Christ. For in the
Church our sole mediator Jesus Christ accomplishes the
mystery of his obedient human fellowship with us for the
benefit of all. The whole community of faith must cooperate in realizing that self-giving to the Father through
the power of the Spirit of the glorified Lord in obedient
self-surrender of one's own life to the Father. The Church
accomplishes a true sacrifice in that co-offering with
Christ and she is a priestly people of God: He "made us a
kingdom, priests to his God and Father" (Rev. 1:6).

In God's creative plan "in His First-born" it is a matter
of forming a people that is sanctified in Christ: "If you
will obey my voice and keep my covenant, you shall be
my own possession among all peoples; for all the earth is
mine, and you shall be to me a kingdom of priests and a
holy nation" (Ex. 19:5).

The special priesthood is in function of that priestly
exercise of our human existence through our togetherness with the glorified man Jesus Christ who, as Lamb of
God, constantly and in our name, presents to the Father
His complete surrender as a sacrifice of praise and adoration. Those special priests are "ministers of the priestly
people."[100] Whereas, then, the universal priesthood is an
everlasting quality of the whole community of faith, the

100. H. R. Weber, "Ministers of the Priestly People," *Laity* 9,
(1960), pp. 5 ff.

special priesthood is a referential and transitory function of that community, because it represents the Lord who is absent during the time "in between" the Ascension and His final return.

The special priesthood points to "the inalienable priesthood" of the Lord who is established in power, and who makes all men be His sanctified people through His word that is proclaimed through His mission and through the sacrament that is administered in virtue of His authority. The special priesthood is a transitory function because this sanctified people, once the fulfilled mystery of Christ is fulfilled, will—without the sacramental mediation of the hierarchy—perpetually offer itself to the Father through the glorified Lord, as the perfect response to God's creative word.[101] It is only by fully stressing the fact that the special priesthood is a function of the whole Church insofar as she is already saved by Christ that the ministerial and dialogical mission of the priestly office is placed in full relief.

The office has the serving task of making the Church, as God's People, be herself in Christ in fulfilling her royal, priestly and prophetic mission, to consecrate the human community to the coming Kingdom of God, to make us live together with the Son of the Father who was crucified and raised for us. The special office can fulfill its task of service only through a constant dialogue with the People of God that is still in pilgrimage, so that it can proclaim the word of Scripture according to the stage of development and culture attained by that people. And the special office will have to keep in mind that every sort of

101. J. Fr. Görris, *Die leibhaftige Kirche, Gespräch unter Laie,* 3rd ed. Frankfurt, 1950, p. 36; H. de Lubac, *Méditations sur l'Eglise,* Paris, 1953, pp. 39-64; O. Semmelroth, *Ich glaube an die Kirche, Erwägungen über das göttmenschlich Geheimnis der Kirche,* Düsseldorf, 1959, p. 30; O. Cullmann, *La royauté de Jesus Christ et l'Eglise dans le Nouveau Testament,* Paris, 1941, p. 22.

fundamentalism in appealing to the testimony of Scripture and to tradition will inevitably lead to a paralyzing petrifaction of the salvific instrumentality of that community of faith.

The Form of the Office

A renewed reflection upon the special office must begin with the scriptural view that the sacramental proclamation of the word is always in function of the self-realization of the People of God that is saved through the Spirit of the glorified Lord.[102] The essence of the office consists in that serving task with respect to God's People. And the divided Christians are faced with the startling question: what could be the ecumenical consequences of the insight that this essence of the office must be clearly distinguished from the concrete form which the office has taken in its historical development within the believing community?

Continuity

On the one hand, basing ourselves on Scripture, it is impossible to draw either historically or theologically, a direct conclusion concerning the form of the office in later Church life.

The Apostles have, as eye-and-ear witnesses of Christ's salvific work, a wholly unique position in the early Church: "So one of the men who have accompanied us during all the time that the Lord Jesus went in and out among us, beginning from the baptism of John until the day when he was taken up from us—one of these men must become with us a witness to his resurrection" (Acts 1:21-22). The Apostles belong to the constitutive phase

102. J. Gewiesz, "Die neutestamentlichen Grundlagen der kirchlichen Hierarchie," *Hist. Jahrbuch der Görresgesellschaft,* 72 1953, pp. 1 ff.

of the Church, during which the Father's self-communication in the human fellowship of the Son with us has been accomplished through the Spirit: "He will glorify me (among men), for he will take what is mine and declare it to you (to the Apostles). All that the Father has is mine; therefore I said that he will take what is mine and declare it to you" (Jn 16:14-15).

That apostolic office, by which that fullness of the divine revelation in Christ has been fulfilled in earthly reality, is unique and cannot be repeated because of its essential relationship to the historical facts of the Incarnation and Redemption. By the apostolic office the Church was established as the earthly-eschatological reality of the Christ mystery that is being fulfilled in the development of the Kingdom of God.

The ecclesial office in the post-apostolic times has an essentially different value because it does not function for the foundation of the Church but serves to actualize the apostolic Church in time and space, in passing on and making present the salvific work that was accomplished once, through the Spirit of the glorified Lord.

Although Scripture, as the permanent living fixation of the apostolic proclamation, is the only and absolute norm of what the Church truly is in all ages, we cannot simply borrow from Scripture a pattern for the office in the Church of post-apostolic times, even if we leave out of consideration the vagueness of the ecclesial arrangement in the first Christian communities.[103]

The concept of the office in the Catholic Church, that has paid exclusive attention to the continuity between the apostolic and the post-apostolic office, is, on that account, presently confronted with the scriptural testi-

103. W. Mauck, "Probleme des frühchristlichen Amtsverständnisses," *ZNW* 48 1957, pp. 200 ff.; L. Cerfaux, *L'Eglise primitive de Jerusalem*, Paris, 1943.

mony to the effect that there is a precise moment of discontinuity in that continuity: Apostles are not followed by Apostles, Peter is not followed by Peter.[104]

Discontinuity

On the other hand, Scripture offers no foundation for the Reformational view which tries to impose, in the historical development of the ecclesial office, an opposition between the charismatic presbyterate of the young Pauline churches, and the monarchical episcopate in the local churches that were founded at a later time.

This opposition has received its strongest expression in the opposition between "the Church of the Spirit and love" (*Geist- und Liebeskirche*) and "the juridical Church" (*Rechtskirche*).[105] And though they do not formulate it as strongly, many Protestant Churches stress the point that the discontinuity existing between the apostolic and the post-apostolic office is not recognized in the historical development. Because they pay no attention to the continuity, they consider that development as scriptually illegitimate.

Jesus appointed the twelve Apostles as the foundation of the Church. They borrowed their very special authority from the fact that they were eye-witnesses of Salvation. The transmission of their authority to later officeholders is not clear in the New Testament. We can, in any case, distinguish three types of concepts of office:

104. O. Cullmann, *Petrus, Junger-Apostel-Martyrer, Das historische und das theologische Petrusproblem*, Zürich 1960; J. Ringger und J. Schmid, "Petrus der Fels"; E. Stauffer und K. Hoffstetter, "Das Petrusamt in der Urkirche," in M. Roesle und O. Cullmann, *Begegnung der Christen*, pp. 271-390; O. Karrer, *Um die Einheit der Christen, Die Petrusfrage*, Frankfurt, 1953; P. Gaechter, *Petrus und seine Zeit*, Innsbrück, 1958.

105. R. Sohm, *Kirchenrecht I, Die geschichtlichen Grundlagen*, Leipzig, 1892; H. Camphausen, *Kirchliches Amt und geistliche Vollmacht in der ersten Jahrhunderten*, Tübingen, 1953.

a. The view which is especially prominent in 1 Corinthians, where the office is a charism among many others, and is hardly conspicuous among the many (1 Cor. 12:19).

b. The kind that is spoken of in the Acts, where we meet with an evident authority, certainly at the time when it was established. There is a college of elders or "supervisors" who "teach" and "shepherd" the local community.

c. In the so-called Pastoral Letters (Tim., Tit.) we meet with three distinct offices, namely, those of "supervisor," "elder," and "deacon." The "supervisor" now stands independently from, and more or less higher than the college of elders.

A further stage of development is seen in the Letters of St. Ignatius: here every place has its office headed by one man, the bishop, who is above the presbyterium. Protestants consider this phase post-canonical and hence without normative value.

While the Roman Catholic Church continues type c according to the direction of Ignatius and speaks of growth and lawful development, Protestantism prefers the older types. The so-called Free Churches consider the office as just one of the many functions in the local community and appeal to type a. The properly Reformational Churches combine types b and c (especially Calvin). As to laypeople, emphasis is placed on the fact that Paul was accustomed to address his letters to the whole community, from which the conclusion is drawn that there was an authority over the community besides that of the officeholders.[106]

Continuity in Discontinuity

The problem of continuity and discontinuity between the apostolic and the post-apostolic office is one of the most troublesome issues with which the divided Christians of our time are confronted. In all Churches there

106. H. Berkhof, *Kerk, ambt en gemeentelid naar reformatorische opvatting,* DO-C papers, 68, 1.

exists a crisis with respect to the office, but this crisis has clearly ecumenical perspectives and contains the promise of a mutual rapprochement.

Reflection upon the legitimate character of the form which the office has in our time must start from the Scriptural tension between the mission of sacramentally proclaiming the word given by Christ and the charism of experiencing the word given by His Spirit. That tension is what determines the concrete form of the special office throughout the centuries. Underneath the hesitating and diverse forms of the Church order in the first Christian communities and the increasingly clearer uniformity of the ecclesiastical structure in the post-apostolic hierarchy of later centuries, there lies hidden the same essential task of the office, namely, *serving, in Christ's name, the self-realization of the People of God.*

Christ who went away from his followers in His visible form in His Ascension (1 Jn 1:1-4) remains the Lord of His Church. He continues to send His Spirit in the authoritative proclamation of the word and the authoritative administration of the sacraments; by this He makes the People of God, that He has acquired in solidarity with sinful mankind (Is. 53:12; Phil. 2:9-11), share in His glorified existence with the Father: "And they devoted themselves to the apostles' teaching and fellowship, to the breaking of bread and the prayers . . . and *the Lord* added to their number day by day those who were being saved. . . . So the church throughout all Judea and Galilee and Samaria had peace and was built up; and walking in the fear of the Lord and in the comfort of the Holy Spirit it was multiplied" (Acts 2:42-47; 9:31).

The Church aims at the self-realization of the People of God through the Spirit who is sent, the Kingdom of God, the breakthrough of the creation that is completed in Christ. With respect to that eschatological salvific event the office is secondary and temporary. The actual structuring of the office is secondary with respect to the salvific reality that is accomplished by it, provided two elements that belong to the form of the office continue to stand at its center, namely, the mandate of Christ and the service of the People of God. These two essential aspects of the office are inseparably connected:

> Every one who calls upon the name of the Lord will be saved. But how are men to call upon him in whom they have not believed? And how are they to believe in him whom they have never heard? And how are they to hear without a preacher? And how can men preach unless they are sent? . . . *So faith comes from what is heard, and what is heard comes by the preaching of Christ* (Rom. 10:13-17).

The whole Church, as a community of faith, stands before the task of actualizing the salvific reality of the Christ mystery in the various sectors of the earthly reality, under the charismatic inspiration of the Holy Spirit. But she can realize that function of the universal priesthood only by being connected with the proclamation and the administration of the sacraments of the apostolic office by which the Church is established once for all as a reality of salvation: "God was in Christ reconciling the world to himself, not counting their trespasses against them, and entrusting to us the message of reconciliation. So we are ambassadors for Christ, God making his appeal through us. We beseech you on behalf of Christ, be reconciled to God" (2 Cor. 5:19-20).

Only the proclamation based on things "as they were delivered to us by those who from the beginning were eyewitnesses and ministers of the word" (Lke 1:2) takes place in virtue of a mandate by Christ. The relation of the ecclesiastical office to the apostolic office in its function of establishing the Church is essentially this: "the Church, of which I became a minister according to the divine office which was given to me for you, to make the word of God fully known, the mystery hidden for ages and generations but now made manifest to his saints" (Col. 1:25-26).

It is in this essential relation to the apostolic foundation that we find the point of continuity between the apostolic office and the ecclesiastical office. It is with fervent apostolic care and concern that Paul watches over that continuity:

> But even if we, or an angel from heaven, should preach to you a gospel contrary to that which we preached to you, let him be accursed. As we have said before, so now I say again, if any one is preaching to you a gospel contrary to that which you received, let him be accursed. Am I now seeking the favor of men, or of God? Or am I trying to please men? If I were still pleasing men, I should not be a servant of Christ. For I would have you know, brethren, that the gospel which was preached by me is not man's gospel. For I did not receive it from man, nor was I taught it, but it came through a revelation of Jesus Christ (Gal. 1:8-12).

Particularly the first words of St. Paul "but even if we" show how firmly convinced he was of the divine origin and the permanent continuity of the preaching of the word.

In the Incarnation the Father has realized His Kingdom through His Son's fellowship with us men in the community of His disciples. For the light of this salvific mystery the Christ-empowered mission given for the sacramental preaching of the word, concretely comes about by the fact that this community of faith calls, from its midst, definite persons to the service of the office. To be called by the community is to be sent by Christ. That is

why the Church grants that power and authority of
Christ through prayer and sacrament.

But that call to an office by the Church can be an
entering into the power of Christ only when it is done in
visible bond with the universal community of all local
Churches. The office in a local Church must be made
legitimate by the universal Church, if it wishes to stand
within the continuity of the reality of salvation. This
visible bond is necessary because all the local Churches
must be rooted in the apostolic office that establishes the
Church-communion:

> Hence I remind you (Timothy) to rekindle the gift of
> God that is within you through the laying on of my
> hands; for God did not give us a spirit of timidity but a
> spirit of power and love and self-control. . . . Follow the
> pattern of the sound words which you have heard from
> me, in the faith and love which are in Christ Jesus;
> guard the truth that has been entrusted to you by the
> Holy Spirit who dwells within us. . . . What you have
> heard from me before many witnesses entrust to faith-
> ful men who will be able to teach others also (2 Tim.
> 1:6-14; 2:2).

Hence the continuity of the apostolic and the ecclesiastical office has its foundation in the salvific reality
which Christ has performed in human existence and
which He continues to actualize throughout the centuries
and in various lands in a human community that is
united in love. Where the mandate to love the neighbor
no longer takes the shape of truly living together, there
Christ's response of love for His Father is no longer fully
"translated" by the local believing communities and the
latter are no longer fully the salvific instrument of the
glorified Lord.

But the discontinuity between the apostolic and the

post-apostolic office must be clearly taken into account in that continuity. Every attempt to place the apostolic succession exclusively in the ecclesiastical hierarchy and every attempt to monopolize the mission by Christ in the special priesthood detracts from the proper mission of the universal priesthood to realize on its own responsibility the dominion of God over the whole of creation in Christ, on the basis of baptism, confirmation and Eucharist: "There are varieties of gifts, but the same Spirit; and there are varieties of service, but the one Lord" (1 Cor. 12:4-5).

It follows from the nature of the special office, as serving the self-realization of the People in Christ's name, that being the Church of Jesus is a permanent dialogue between the sacramental preaching of the word by the special priesthood, and the creative living of the word by the universal priesthood. It is in this eschatological tension between the official and the charismatic activities of the Church that every local Church seeks a manner of existence that is adapted to its own time and native character.

This task of the office to serve the local self-realization of the believing community, necessarily has its repercussion on the form of the office. It is one-sided clericalism and illegitimate fundamentalism to accept only the monarchical-episcopal development as genuinely scriptural. The discontinuity does not permit us to appeal to Scripture because that development resulted from the unique situation of the apostolic office. Moreover, Scripture also shows a rich variety in the various local churches, with respect to the form of the office. In this matter also the unity in Christ was experienced in a plurality of forms.

Our present time, which wishes to give every opportunity for the charismatic and prophetic abilities of the

People of God,[107] is looking for new forms of the office: primacy within a collegial context, collegiality of the world episcopate, apostolic council, episcopal conferences, the participation of laypeople in a council, episcopal and parochial councils. *A Church that has a more synodal structure is now beginning to temper the one-sidedness of the primacy and of the monarchical episcopate.*

This development in the Catholic Church that is going on with great difficulty but can no longer be stopped, is important from the ecumenical standpoint. On the one hand, it brings within the Catholic horizon the recognition of the office that exists in other Christian Churches. On the other hand, the growing togetherness of all local Churches presents the possibility of legitimizing the office.

Experiments on the Basis of Our Redemption in Christ

This view of the special priesthood is the foundation for the revaluation of the universal priesthood of all the faithful. The Church, as community of salvation, is the People of God (*laos tou Theou*), the layman who has the divine vocation of consciously living his redemption in Christ in all fields of social life and making visible the nearness of the Kingdom of God and of that creation:[108]

107. Y. Congar, *Lay People in the Church*, Westminster, 1965; H. Küng, *Structures of the Church*, New York, 1965.

108. E. Kinder, *"Allgemeines Priestertum" im Neuen Testament*. Berlin, 1953; K. Rahner, *Die Kirche der Sünder*, Freiburg, 1948; L. Bouyer, "Où en est la théologie du Corps Mystique," *Rech. Sc. Rel.* 22 (1948), pp. 313 ff.; H. Küng, *Council and Renewal, Renewal as a Call to Unity*, New York, 1962; H. Kraemer, *Het vergeten ambt in de Kerk, Een theologische fundering*, 's Gravenhage, 1960; H. Rückert, "Kirche und Amt in der Diskussion der evangelische Theologie," in L. Reinisch, *Theologie heute*, Munich, 1959, pp. 103-144; H. Asmussen, *Katholische Reformation*, Stuttgart, 1958, pp. 202-203; Y. Congar, *Priest and Laymen in the Church*, New York, 19.

Come to him, to that living stone, rejected by men but in God's sight chosen and precious; and like living stones be yourselves built into a spiritual house, to be a holy priesthood, to offer spiritual sacrifices acceptable to God through Jesus Christ. . . . But you are a chosen race, a royal priesthood, a holy nation, God's own people, that you may declare the wonderful deeds of him who called you out of darkness into his marvelous light. Once you were no people but now you are God's people; once you had not received mercy but now you have received mercy (1 Pet. 2:4-5; 9-10).

By living his being-the-Church-of-Jesus-Christ, in accord with his own time, amidst the world and in his social and cultural milieu, the layman must give shape to that creation that is saved in Christ, in a manner that appeals to all. His act of personal surrender in faith to Christ must clearly determine the pattern of his own life and that of his family. He must put his powers of mind and heart at the service of the sphere of social life for which he bears responsibility together with others. This, precisely is his contribution so that creation may become ever more what God wants according to His salvific plan in Christ, namely, the Kingdom of God, the area within which the love of God, and love for the sake of God, acquires human shape.[109]

With respect to this life task the layman receives no ready-made guide lines from the proclaimed word of God for his decisions in the various situations of life, for these are always proper to himself personally and variable.

109. E. Schillebeeckx, "Het apostolische ambt van de kerkelijke hierarchie," *Stud. Cath.* 32 (1957), pp. 258 ff. *Christ, the Sacrament of the Encounter with God;* A. Suster, *De leek in der Kerk, Theologisch Perspektief III,* pp. 97-125; K. Rahner, *Das freie Wort in der Kirche,* Einsiedeln, 1953; *Freiheit in der Kirche, Schriften zur Theologie II,* pp. 95-114.

Here he must take a personal initiative. He must try things out and experiment on the basis of his redemption in Christ. That is why in thus personally living his being-the-Church-of-Jesus-Christ, he is called to make his own contribution, in the particular place he occupies in social life, to the formation of a constantly more precise and definite public opinion of faith in the Church.

This vocation of the layman is an ecclesial task in society. This does not mean that he must, as an extension of the hierarchy, make the world more ecclesiastical, or that he tries to make sacred what is profane. But he must make his contribution so that all the spheres of human life—science, culture, society, the economy, technology and politics—fulfill their function in the realization of the Kingdom of God, while they retain their own particular norms and their proper task.

The hierarchy, the special office, that must sacramentally proclaim to God's people its being-saved in Christ, has no specific earthly task, no social or political mission. Although the layman accepts the proclaimed Scripture as the lasting norm of his conduct, he must with personal responsibility "translate" God's word in the personal decisions of conscience he makes in his daily life. He must make this preached word of God concrete here and now, so as to be able to fulfill his task of cooperating in achieving the salvation of this world.

The Church cannot manifest the full riches of the Christ mystery in this world if the layman does not live his redemption in Christ according to his personal responsibility. If the Church is deprived of the daring initiative of faith of the layman, she is in the midst of society like an organ that is foreign to the world, and she sterilizes her salvific message within Church walls. She is then, in all spheres of social life, an absentee who is not even missed by any one. Everyday life passes by her doors without arousing her interest. Only the layman can give to the word of God a content that is concretely livable and that attracts others.

The layman *is* the Church and he must, independently and with personal responsibility give shape to that his being-the-Church in this world. "The bearers of office may be the prompters of the laypeople, the *laikoi,* but it is these members of the People of God who are the real actors on the stage of life."[110] If the bearers of office know how to make distinctions and avoid confusion, they may realize that they too are laypeople in their daily lives.

Being-the-Church is, therefore, an absorbing dialogue between the scriptural word that is preached, and the personal response of man, a wonderful dynamic interplay of divine grace and human freedom, though not as two mutually complementary powers. This means that the Christian must live in his personal and proper life situation according to what he can and must be through God's revelation in Christ.

For God does not wield His salvific plan-in-Christ like a cliché according to which He makes all men live their being-the-Church in a uniform way. God respects us as persons; He respects our character, our native milieu, our formation and our particular place in society. Every man can and must live his being-saved-in-Christ in a way that is wholly his own and personal.

The hand has a wholly proper, though not independent, function in the human body, and a man cannot fully do his work if he does not have all his members at his disposal. So also the Christ mystery cannot manifest itself in its full salvific power in this world without the total personal commitment of every individual Christian.

110. J. C. Hoekendijk, quoted by H. van der Linde, *De komende oecumenische Kerk,* Utrecht, 1956, p. 55. Cf. J. C. Hoekendijk, *De Kerk binnenste buiten,* Amsterdam, 1964, *passim.*

> For just as the body is one and has many members, and all the members of the body, though many, are one body, so it is with Christ. For by one Spirit we were all baptized into one body—Jews or Greeks, slaves or free —and all were made to drink of one Spirit. For the body does not consist of one member but of many . . . if the whole body were an eye, where would be the hearing? If the whole body were an ear, where would be the sense of smell? But as it it, God arranged the organs in the body, each one of them, as he chose (1 Cor. 12:12-18).

If individual Christians lived their being-saved-in-Christ in a uniform way in this world, it would mean an impoverishment of the full salvific work of Christ. It is precisely in the rich variety of their living personal response that Christians make their wholly personal contribution to the full manifestation of the Christ mystery in the Church. This is done not independently, not by their own powers, but as living through Christ.

Every Christian is conscious at the same time that he manifests only particular aspects when he personally "translates" that salvific reality. No individual, no people, no particular time can manifest the fullness of Christ. It is only together with the local churches of all times and places that the Church can become an ever more complete expression of the "unsearchable riches of Christ" (Eph. 3:8).

The Collegiate Character of the Church Office as Legitimation of Authentic Pluriformity

That believing response to the word that is proclaimed is, from one standpoint, authentic because individual believers and local believing communities live their salvation, as already accomplished in Christ, in that response. The divided Christians, therefore, should realize that the foundation of the Church's infallibility lies in the universal priesthood.

On the other hand, the Christian experiences that he is saved in Christ within the eschatological fractured condition of this earthly situation in which he still needs to be saved by Christ. His whole human existence, his thought and activity, his desires and ideals are still completely dominated by the deeply felt tension between the completeness of his human existence in Christ and the sinfulness of the Adam who is still living in him. His daily life is the painful combination of those conflicting powers and influences. Even if he tries to judge himself honestly, he cannot discern where the inspiration for a concrete decision came from, from the Spirit of Christ or from the spirit of his own sinful desires that are so deceptively camouflaged. Similarly, the public opinion, the collective sense of faith existing in local communities of faith, is still groping for their concrete answer amidst the ever-changing and bewildering situations of human society.

For God has no uniform salvific plan for all centuries and cultures with respect to man. That is why separate Christians and local churches can arrive at conflicting convictions and decisions on the basis of diverse situations of life. Since in a living Church, every Christian and every community must make their own personal contribution to the response of their time to God's word and the activity of Christ, it is necessary that tensions should arise as signs that there exists a truly personal ecclesial life. Unity is not dead uniformity. It is precisely in the fierceness of the dialogue that the fullness of Christ's revelation breaks through as a light. But this lively dialogue must always be accompanied by the readiness of the individual Christian to test his judgment of faith through comparison with the discernment of others; similarly one local Church should permit itself to be enriched and corrected by another.

The primacy of the Bishop of Rome stands in function of that dialogical self-actualization of the Church. In the dialogue between Christians within distinct communities and between various local Churches there takes place a process of purification with respect to extreme views and a consolidation of opinions. This process by which the public religious opinion is formed often lasts many years, especially during a time of transition and of growing Church-consciousness. It goes hand in hand with a vigorous feeling of being truly seized by Christ, a personal dilemma of conscience and conflicting opinions.

But it is precisely then that Christians and Churches will come to realize the dangerous threat of division. They live by Christ's appeal to them and it is only by staying together around His word that they will be able to live the fullness of the Christ mystery within their pluriformity. No Christian can say at a decisive moment in a dilemma of conscience: "Here I stand; I cannot do otherwise," without becoming petrified in a one-sided monologue. Conscience demands that he remain in dialogue, if necessary that he keep protesting for many years within the Church, thus allowing the Spirit to make use of his testimony of faith as an instrument of His salvific work.

Church unity is a salvific necessity for fully being-the-Church. Just as the individual Christians, in the tension of their dialogue, continually express their unity by their fidelity to the special office of the local bishop, so do local churches, as pluriform patterns of the Church, constantly live the gift of their collegial unity in Christ and the task of their collegial fidelity to Christ in the recognition of the primacy of the Bishop of Rome. This primacy is the visible sign and the instrument of the pluriform unity of the many local Churches.

The primacy, too, as the highest form of the special office, is not a personal quality; it is a function of the whole community of faith, in which it gives shape to its being already saved in Christ, and thereby occupies a saving role in this world. The Church in all countries and ages, in her believing fidelity to the primacy, experiences that Christ has passed through this creation completing and saving it, and this glorified Lord remains actively present in the world-wide dialogue of His People that is still on its pilgrimage. The whole Church, as living through Christ, is infallible and lies permanently in the grip of the salvific plan of the Father in His First-born of the whole creation. But this infallibility of the Church, this abiding in Christ, while remaining sinfully incomplete, functions in the primacy of the Bishop of Rome. On that account this primacy stands, as representing Christ, also over against the believing community through the assistance of the Spirit.

Hence within the believing community of the Church, *the Pope alone is personally infallible, but he is not the only one who is infallible:* he has a collegial primacy that he can exercise only in structural connection with the whole world episcopate as teachers, shepherds, and official *liturgoi* of the universal Church and of their own local Churches. Hence the collegial functioning of the primacy has its foundation in the recognition that the primacy is a function of the whole community of believers which, in being concentrated around the Bishop of Rome, seeks to give a contemporary answer to her redemption in Christ. Through the recognition of the primacy that activity of the Spirit in the universal Church is present in its fullness in the local Church.[111]

For, through the functioning of the collegial primacy of the world episcopate gathered around the Bishop of Rome, the authentic pluriformity of the local Church is

111. K. Rahner, *Episkopat und Primat,* Freiburg, 1961, pp. 28 ff.

legitimized. Local diversities, in spite of their incompleteness, are authentic forms of the divine revelation in Christ *only if* they let themselves become legitimized through communion with the Bishop of Rome in a corrective and enriching dialogue with the world-wide Church.

This collegial functioning of the primacy inevitably produces tensions in the Church:

> The mutual compenetration of a vicariate that is at the same time a personal and a collegial vicariate, has no counterpart in any secular form of administration and government. It cannot simply be called a monarchy nor an aristocracy. That is why it is so difficult to form a concrete idea of the simultaneous functioning of both forms of government. Considered from a purely organizational standpoint, that form would inevitably seem to lead to rivalries. Thus it is not surprising that this very human—all too human—weakness is not absent from the way the vicariate pattern established by Christ has been exercised in history.

> That is also why it is impossible to determine in the smallest details how the two forms of vicariate should work together. One thing is certain: they must function together, not only as an ever present presupposition but also as a visible fact; this is required by obedience to a divine commission.

> But if we wish to understand somewhat the profound meaning of the two forms of vicariate and their joint functioning, we must realize that we are involved here in a mystery that ultimately points to the common dominion of the Father and the Incarnate Son in the unity of the Spirit. For in accord with the mystery of the sending of the Son by the Father there took place also the sending of the Apostles, for Christ said: "As the Father has sent me, I also send you." This is the mystery of the presence of the One who sends in the one who is sent, a mystery that Christ actualized by the mission of the Spirit, in and through whom He himself, as One who sends, is present in those who are sent, until the

end of time. In this one Spirit, with whom all who are
sent are anointed, there cannot be, nor may there be,
any rivalry about the first place, nor can there be any
competition of competency, but there is only a care for
unanimity in the one Lord: He desires to rule all who
are His own for their salvation, as the one Lord of all
times and places, by means of a collegial vicariate.[112]

A Break Through the Impasse?

Does this view of the Church as a community of faith
engaged in dialogue, and which experiences her unity in
Christ and her fidelity to Christ in the interconnection of
the local Churches around the collegially functioning
primacy, not offer to the divided Christians the possibility to break through the hardened impasse of their mon-
ologizing division?

By means of the liberating experience of being-the-
Church of Jesus Christ as an open dialogue:

1. tradition can be appreciated once more as the bond
of faith between the preaching of the Gospel in the local
Churches and the universal Church of all countries and
ages;

2. the special office can function once more as a commission legitimized by the universal Church for an
authoritative preaching within a local Church;

3. the primacy can become the instrument of the *Ecumene*, of the Church becoming one. For in her ecumenical task no Church may sacrifice that which according to
her firm conviction belongs to the inalienable evangelical
content of faith and Church order; but, at the same time,
no Church can determine what precisely belongs to the
unchangeable nature of the Gospel, except in collegial

---

112. J. G. Groot, "Vragen rond het primaat," *Oecumene*, 1
(1962), p. 135.

unity with all the local Churches, which becomes visible and functions in the primacy.

The Churches of the Reformation are in the process of rediscovering that ecumenical function of tradition, the office and the primacy. This can be seen by the fact that the divided Churches assemble and are getting closer to one another in the World Council of Churches. Here the Churches seek to legitimize the diversity of the way they preach the word and administer the sacraments in a search for unity in a common testimony of faith and increasing intercommunion. In this, the function of the primacy is again coming into sight.

Under this aspect, the World Council of Churches mirrors the Catholic Church when it is gathered in Council. Here the local Churches of five continents seek to experience the collegial unity of the world episcopate around the primacy of the Bishop of Rome in a legitimate diversity, by which the authentic testimony of faith of the separate Churches is finally honored.

CHAPTER FOUR

WORD AND SACRAMENT

1. THE SACRAMENT AS SIGN AND INSTRUMENT OF THE GLORIFIED LORD

The Sign in the Interpersonal Sphere

Every sacrament is performed in the Church in accordance with the commission of Christ: "Do this . . . in remembrance of me" (1 Cor. 11:25; cf. Lke 22:19). This action is not merely accompanied by a subjective, mental remembrance of His historical salvific acts, it is not merely an occasion on which we think of all that Christ has done for us in the distant past.

But the essence of the sacrament consists in this that here in virtue of His commission, a sign is posited that has salvific power, because the eternally actual value of His historical salvific actions is made present to this human being. It is an objective memorial celebration in which the same Lord, though now glorified, is present and accomplishes in us in a participated way, what He has undergone for us in His human nature.[1]

1. "In the scriptures both of the Old and New Testament, *anamnesis* and the cognate verb have the sense of 'recalling' or 're-presenting' before God an event in the past, so that it becomes here and now operative by its effects." Gregory Dix, *The Shape of the Liturgy*, Westminster, 1954, p. 161.

Because that sign is posited by mandate of Christ, it belongs to the interpersonal sphere. It is through signs that persons manifest their interior life to one another. The more profound the love that persons have for each other, the richer is also the content of the most simple sign. They exteriorize to each other their ineffable subjectivity. In the sign they express to each other their most cherished and therefore most secret thoughts, desires and strivings. Love reads the language of the signs, but also experiences the irresistible power of that outwardly powerless gesture.

The sign of Christ in the sacrament has salvific power where it encounters believing love. For this sign generates faith and imparts love, because it is the self-manifestation of the glorified Lord to this or that man. In this simple gesture the Lord expresses the intensity of His salvific will to the human being who believes in Him. In and through that sign's interpersonal contact He enters into this person's thought and striving, into his whole existence as a man, in order to make it ever more similar to His own glorified human existence.

"The sacraments sanctify efficaciously, because they are the signs, that is, the bearers by which God's love enters into human life, not only as inviting love but also as inspiring the Yes of a loving response. The sacraments are signs by which God's love creates the salvific situation of man with respect to Him and in it re-creates man."[2]

The Instrument of Prolongation of Personality

The sacrament is a sign in the interpersonal sphere that is freighted with the power of the glorified Lord, for

2. P. Smulders, "Verlossingsdaad en sacrament," *Jaarb. Kath. Theol. in Ned.*, 1957, p. 50. Cf. E. Schillebeeckx, *De sacramentele heilseconomie,* pp. 152-183.

it works out in us that whole reality of salvation which is hidden behind that short word and behind that simple gesture, according to Christ's intentions. Christ thereby makes this sacramental action a "prolongation of His personality," in which He visibly remains active in our midst throughout the ages and in the various countries of the world.

Christ has saved us by becoming man. His human nature was the "conjoined and animated instrument" of our salvation.[3] The divine Person of the Word has used our human nature in order that He might experience His solidarity with us even to the utmost consequences of being abandoned by God, and thereby might be able to transform His being-like-to-us into our being-like-to-Him. Just as His human nature was the instrument by which He has saved us, so does the glorified Lord use human signs as efficacious instruments of salvation and make salvation present to men in every age.

Man lives in this world by constantly entering into relations with his fellow-men and with a variety of objects. Only by making use of instruments can he make his person be with his fellow men and with things. Man handles a chisel to express his personal experiences in stone; he uses the pen to communicate his thoughts to other human beings. Man thus "subjectivizes" those instruments, making them a "prolongation of his person." Through them he himself is present with his fellowmen and he is present to his world.

Christ desires to live His glorified human fellowship with us through the instrumentality of ecclesial actions performed in virtue of the commission received from Christ; and by them He is able to be constantly present in our midst. "Hence we are permitted to say that in the

3. "La seigneurie du Christ sur l'Eglise et sur le monde" *Istina,* vol. 6 (1959), pp. 133, 134.

sacraments that which is visible and tangible, that which can be reached by the senses—what the theologians call the 'form' and the 'matter' of the sacraments—is seized by the glorified corporality of Christ, and is subjectivized; and it is thus capable of producing effects that can be produced only by the Lord."[4]

The Gift as the Giving of Oneself to the Other

A gift is a particular instrument by which a person can be with the other. In and through a material object he wishes to give himself, to leave himself, as it were, behind even when he has gone away. The other person's love recognizes in this powerless gesture the profound meaning it has and sees in it that the giver wishes to give himself in person.

Precisely because we are bodily human beings, we can give ourselves only in a material and corporeal way; that is why the highest form of mutual self-giving and personal surrender is expressed in the bodily union of marriage. The more this bodily act is subjectivized by both partners, the more intensely they become spiritually identified with each other through that bodily surrender. And yet human beings can never make the gift so subjective, even in marriage, that they actually give their whole person to the other. Though they may express in the act of marriage that they are for each other in perfect loyalty, they remain two.

This, in a certain sense, is also applicable to the sacraments. They are ecclesial acts, in and by which the glorified Lord is present to us and gives Himself to us. In the sacraments He subjectivizes the salvific acts of His divine-human life, but never in such a way that He gives

4. J. B. W. M. Möller, "De transsubstantiatie," *Ned. Kath. St.,* vol. 61 (1960), p. 9.

His whole Person in those acts. Only in the Eucharist does He give Himself completely to us.

a. The Activity of the Spirit of the Glorified Lord in Establishing the Church

The Apostles knew that they were personally involved in the salvific mystery of the Incarnation of the Son of the Father, which reached its highest point in their togetherness at the table with the suffering Lord on the last evening of His life and in the reception of the Spirit of the glorified Lord on the day of Pentecost. They also knew they were eye-and-ear witnesses of that salvific event, and that to them had been entrusted the commission of the glorified Lord: "All authority in heaven and on earth has been given to me. Go therefore and make disciples of all nations, baptizing them in the name of the Father and of the Son and of the Holy Spirit, teaching them to observe all that I have commanded you; and lo, I am with you always, to the close of the age" (Mt. 28:18-20).

This task and authority to preach His word and administer His sacramental salvific activity is implicitly contained in the words of Christ: "Do this in remembrance of me" (Lke 22:19). By the preaching of the word and the administration of the sacraments Christ Himself makes present-for-all His glorified human existence with the Father, in all countries and in all ages, and actualizes in the believers the salvific actions of His historically-lived human life so that it becomes a personally lived salvific event: "He holds his priesthood permanently, because he continues for ever. Consequently he is able for all time to save those who draw near to God through him, since he always lives to make intercession for them" (Heb. 7:24-25).

The Apostles have lived by that commission in order to

make present the glorified human fellowship of their
risen Lord through their preaching of the word and the
administration of the sacraments, by which presence the
risen Lord, through the power of the Holy Spirit, involves
all men in His being-together with the Father: "And
while staying with them he charged them not to depart
from Jerusalem but to wait for the *promise of the Father,*
which, he said, *'you heard for me,* for John baptized with
water, but before many days you *shall be baptized with
the Holy Spirit.'* . . . 'You shall receive power when the
Holy Spirit has come upon you; and you shall be my
witnesses in Jerusalem and in all Judea and Samaria and
to the end of the earth' (Acts 1:4-8).

The Apostles were to be baptized with the Holy Spirit;
the indwelling Spirit of Christ was to impart to their life
the mentality and attitude (Phil. 2:5) that had governed
Christ's own life of complete surrender to the Father. On
the other hand, through this sending of the Spirit, they
would receive the power to be witnesses of Christ for all
men, "until Christ be formed in you" (Gal. 4:19).

One characteristic of the sending of the Spirit on the
first Pentecost is the fact that the Spirit of the glorified
Lord is given to individual Christians as an eschatological gift, as a guarantee and pledge of a full participation
in the glorified human existence of Christ: "This is what
was spoken by the prophet Joel. 'And in the last days it
shall be, God declares, that I will pour out my Spirit upon
all flesh' . . . This Jesus God raised up, and of that we all
are witnesses. Being therefore exalted at the right hand
of God, and having received from the Father the promise
of the Holy Spirit, he has poured out this which you see
and hear" (Acts 2:14-41).

On the other hand, that Pentecostal event is characterized by the activity of the Spirit of the glorified Lord in
forming the Church. The Apostles know that, through

the power of the Spirit given to them, they are the community of the Lord who was raised to the right hand of the Father and who is His salvific instrument for the world. Hence communion of life with Christ is not possible except in and through the ecclesial bond: "An individual Christianity that should or would like to form itself far away from and outside the 'community,' is something that was unthinkable for the primitive Church. Faith in Christ, bond with Christ, life through Christ exist only in the bosom of the faithful community bound together with its Lord. The 'Church' is constitutive for Christian existence."[5]

God's salvific activity toward individual men is a Covenant activity that finds its fulfillment around the glorified Lord as being-together-with-the-Father through the power of the Spirit who has been received:

> You know the word which he sent to Israel, preaching good news of peace by Jesus Christ (he is Lord of all), the word which was proclaimed throughout all Judea, beginning from Galilee after the baptism which John preached: how God anointed Jesus of Nazareth with the Holy Spirit and with power; how he went about doing good and healing all that were oppressed by the devil, for God was with him.
>
> And we are witnesses to all that he did both in the country of the Jews and in Jerusalem. They put him to death by hanging him on a tree; but God raised him on the third day and made him manifest; not to all the people but to us who were chosen by God as witnesses, who ate and drank with him after he rose from the dead.
>
> And he commanded us to preach to the people, and to testify that he is the one ordained by God to be judge of the living and the dead. To him all the prophets bear

5. R. Schnackenburg, *Die Kirche im neuen Testament, Quaestiones Disputatae,* 14, Freiburg, 1961, p. 14.

witness that every one who believes in him receives
forgiveness of sins through his name (Acts 10:36-43).

In these words we hear the whole self-consciousness of
the young Church: through the Spirit she continues to
live in a permanent living bond with her glorified Lord in
whom the salvation of all men is contained, and, through
the power of the Holy Spirit, her testimony effects that
salvation in all who come to believe in Christ.

St. Luke makes that self-consciousness stand out concretely in three aspects: "They devoted themselves to the
apostles' teaching and fellowship, to the breaking of
bread and the prayers" (Acts 2:42).

a. Preaching the word: "With great power the apostles
gave their testimony to the resurrection of the Lord
Jesus, and great grace was upon them all . . . And more
than ever believers were added to the Lord, multitudes
both of men and women. . . . And day by day . . . the
Lord added to their number those who were being saved"
(Acts 4:33; 5:14; 2:47).

b. Administration of the sacraments: "And day by
day, attending the temple together and breaking bread in
their homes, they partook of food with glad and generous
hearts, praising God" (Acts 2:46).

c. Community life: "Now the company of those who
believed were of one heart and soul, and no one said that
any of the things which he possessed was his own, but
they had everything in common" (Acts 4:32).

At the heart of that community stood the preaching of
the word and the administration of the sacraments as
commissioned and empowered by Christ.

A. Preaching the Word

The apostolic preaching lives by the self-testimony of
Jesus: "The time is fulfilled, and the kingdom of God is

at hand, repent, and believe in the Gospel" (Mk 1:14). This testimony about Jesus is itself a salvific word: "And we also thank God constantly for this, that when you received the word of God which you heard from us, you accept it not as the word of men but as what it really is, the word of God, which is at work in you believers" (1 Thes. 2:13).

But His salvific power can be effective through that word only in those who believe: "For the word of the cross is folly to those who are perishing, but to us who are being saved it is the power of God. . . . It pleased God through the folly of what we preach to save those who believe. . . . We preach Christ crucified, a stumbling block to Jews and folly to Gentiles, but to those who are called, both Jews and Greeks, Christ the power of God and the wisdom to Gentiles" (1 Cor. 1:18-22). ". . . provided that you continue in the faith, stable and steadfast, not shifting from the hope of the gospel which you heard, which has been preached to every creature under heaven, and of which I, Paul, became a minister" (Col. 1:23).

Believing is already entering into God's Kingdom. The Spirit effects faith in the word of God that is offered to man, and by this man already has a share in the glorified human existence of Christ:

> And even if our gospel is veiled, it is veiled only to those who are perishing. In their case the god of this world has blinded the minds of the unbelievers, to keep them from seeing the light of the gospel of the glory of Christ, who is the likeness of God. For what we preach is not ourselves, but Jesus Christ as Lord, with ourselves as your servants for Jesus' sake. For it is the God who said, 'Let light shine out of darkness, who has shone in our hearts to give the light of the knowledge of the glory of God in the face of Christ (2 Cor. 4:3-6).

The enthusiasm of faith of that profoundly experienced salvific power of God's word resounds in the prayer of the young Church:

> "And now, Lord, look upon their threats, and grant to thy servants to speak they word with all boldness, while thou stretchest out thy hand to heal, and signs and wonders are performed through the name of thy holy servant, Jesus." And when they had prayed, the place in which they were gathered together was shaken; and they were all filled with the Holy Spirit and spoke the word of God with boldness (Acts 4:29-31).

The charismatic gifts in the young Christian communities blossomed forth from that activity of God's word that renewed all human relations:

> Let the word of Christ dwell in you richly, as you teach and admonish one another in all wisdom, and as you sing psalms and hymns and spiritual songs with thankfulness in your hearts to God. And whatever you do, in word or deed, do everything in the name of the Lord Jesus, giving thanks to God the Father through him (Col. 3:16-17).

Although St. Paul knows the danger of "speaking by the Spirit," he acknowledges the ecstatic rapture as an authentic gift of the Spirit: "in such a state my spirit prays." And he is particularly concerned with leaving all possible room in his community for the bold proclamation of the word of God: "I want you all to speak in tongues, but even more to prophesy" (1 Cor. 14:5; 12:3-12).[6]

6. H. Schlier, *Wort Gottes, Eine neutestamentliche Besinnung,* Würzburg, 1958; P. Schoonenberg, "De analogie tussen sacrament en prediking," *Jaarb. Kath. theol. in Ned.,* 1954, pp. 44-47; J. A. M. Weterman, "De Verkondiging van Gods Woord," *Levende Zielzorg,* Utrecht, 1954, pp. 174-205.

To personally live the word of God remains the dynamic power of being a Christian and of the edification of the community of faith around the glorified Lord: "Do not extinguish the Spirit, do not belittle prophetic gifts, approve everything, keep what is good." For no one can say 'Jesus is Lord' except by the Holy Spirit" (1 Cor. 12:3).

The rule of the glorified Lord acquires shape in this world through the dialogue between the apostolic preaching of the word of God that is exercised through the power given by the Spirit, and the charismatic experience of that word that is inspired by the Spirit: you are "built upon the foundation of the apostles and prophets, Christ Jesus himself being the cornerstone, in whom the whole structure is joined together and grows into a holy temple in the Lord; in whom you also are built into it for a dwelling place of God in the Spirit" (Eph. 2:20-22). For "there are varieties of gifts, but the same Spirit; and there are varieties of service, but the same Lord; and there are varieties of working, but it is the same God who inspires them all in every one. To each is given the manifestation of the Spirit of the common good" (1 Cor. 12:4-7).[7]

B. *The Administration of the Sacraments*

It was only after the reception of the Holy Spirit at Pentecost that the Apostles fully experienced the salvific reality of the question they had hastily answered: " 'Are you able to drink the cup that I drink, or to be baptized with the baptism with which I am baptized?' And they said to him, 'We are able.' And Jesus said to them, 'The cup that I drink you will drink; and with the baptism

7. J. Brosch, *Charismen und Amter in der Urkirche,* Bonn, 1951; K. Rahner, *Das Dynamische in der Kirche,* Freiburg, 1958.

with which I am baptized, you will be baptized' " (Eph.
5:26).

Baptism, in the young Church, was seen as the "washing of water with the word" (Eph. 5:26), as the sign,
filled with the Holy Spirit, of the salvific power of God's
word that in the human life of Jesus became a full
reality of salvation in fellowship with Christ:

> Repent, and be baptized every one of you in the name
> of Jesus Christ for the forgiveness of your sins; and you
> shall receive the gift of the Holy Spirit. . . . Those who
> received his word were baptized, and there were added
> that day about three thousand souls (Acts 2:38-41).

In baptism in the name of Jesus, the washing with
water symbolizes and effects the full salvific power of
God's word in the believer:

> Then Philip opened his mouth, and beginning with
> this scripture (Is. 53: the suffering servant of Yahweh)
> he told him the good news of Jesus. And as they went
> along the road they came to some water, and the eunuch
> said, "See, here is water! What is to prevent my being
> baptized?" And he commanded the chariot to stop, and
> they both went down into the water, Philip and the eu-
> nuch, and he baptized him (Acts 8:35-38).[8]

The reception of this sign of baptism in the name of
Jesus signifies at the same time being-received in the
salvation community that lives by the encounter with the
glorified Lord, as is clear from the controversy about the
entry of pagans into the young Church of Jerusalem:

8. O. Cullmann, *Die Tauflehre des Neuen Testaments,* Zürich,
1948; F. J. Leenhardt, *Le baptême chrétien, son origine, sa signification,* Paris, 1946; M. Adler, *Taufe und Handauflegung,* Münster, 1951.

While Peter was still saying this, the Holy Spirit fell
on all who heard the word. And the believers from
among the circumcised who came with Peter were
amazed, because the gift of the Holy Spirit had been
poured out even on the Gentiles. For they heard them
speaking in tongues and extolling God. Then Peter declared: "Can any one forbid water for baptizing these
people who have received the Holy Spirit just as we
have?" And he commanded them to be baptized in the
name of Jesus Christ (Acts 10:44-48).

By baptism they were taken up into the new chosen
People of God, in Jesus Christ, without circumcision
(Acts 15:6-29).

The "washing of water with the word" in the Church
effects that the believer experiences his own existence as
a participation in the total orientation of the human life
of Jesus to His Father, as a being-sanctified in the encounter with the glorified Lord: "but you were washed,
you were sanctified, you were justified in the name of the
Lord Jesus Christ and in the Spirit of our God" (1 Cor.
6:11; cf. 1 Pet. 3:18-22).

To be baptized in the name of Jesus means to be
personally involved in the great salvific events, in which
He has lived His utter obedience to the Father in the
place of and for the benefit of all men:

How can we who died to sin still live in it? Do you not
know that all of us who have been baptized into Christ
Jesus were baptized into his death? We were buried
therefore with him by baptism into death, so that as
Christ was raised from the dead by the glory of the
Father, we too might walk in newness of life.

For if we have been united with him in a death like
his, we shall certainly be united with him in a resurrection like his. We know that our old self was crucified
with him so that the sinful body might be destroyed, and
we might no longer be enslaved to sin. For he who has

died is freed from sin. But if we have died with Christ,
we believe that we shall also live with him. For we know
that Christ being raised from the dead will never die
again; death no longer has dominion over him. The
death he died he died to sin, once for all, but the life he
lives he lives to God. So you also must consider yourselves dead to sin and alive to God in Christ Jesus
(Rom. 6:2-11).[9]

According to St. Paul it is in this "mystique" of baptism, in which being-a-Christian is experienced as a
dying, being buried, rising and being glorified *with*
Christ, that we find the basis for the vital necessity of the
Church to constantly give a visible ecclesial shape to her
unity in Christ: "There is one body and one Spirit, just as
you were called to the one hope that belongs to your call,
one Lord, one faith, one baptism, one God and Father of
us all, who is above all and through all and in all" (Eph.
4:4-6). There is a necessary interaction between the salvific effect of the sacramental preaching of the word and
the encounter of Christ experienced in the visible
Church-community: be "eager to *maintain* the unity of
the Spirit in the bond of peace" (Eph. 4:3). The division
of Christians in the visible Church frustrates the Christ
mystery that is at work in word and sacrament: "Is
Christ divided?" (1 Cor. 1:13).

The Eucharistic Supper. In baptism the salvific word
of God initiates in the believing man the Kingdom of God
that is already fulfilled in Christ:

Repent and be baptized every one of you (Acts
2:38), that your sins may be blotted out, that times of
refreshing may come from the presence of the Lord, and
that he may send the Christ appointed for you, Jesus,

9. R. Schnackenburg, *Das Heilgeschehen bei der Taufe nach
dem Apostel Paulus,* Munich, 1950; "Le baptême dans le Nouveau
Testament," *Lumière et Vie,* nos. 26 and 27, 1956.

whom heaven must receive until the time for establishing all that God spoke by the mouth of his holy prophets
from of old (Acts 3:19-21).[10]

The young Church experienced in the eucharistic meal
the high point of that eschatologically orientated salvation in the time between the Ascension and Christ's return: "And day by day, attending the temple together and
breaking bread in their homes, they partook of food with
glad and generous hearts, praising God and having favor
with all the people" (Acts 2:46).

The Eucharist as a memorial celebration of the death
of Jesus for all, and as the eschatological joyful banquet
of the fulfillment of creation in the revelation of the
glorified Lord, bridges that time "in between," by His
presence under the veil of sacramental signs: "For as
often as you eat this bread and drink the cup, you proclaim the Lord's death until he comes" (1 Cor. 11:26).
The eucharistic expression *Maranatha* means both "Let
the Lord come" and "The Lord has come."

In imitation of the symbolic banquet of Jesus on the
last evening of His life, by which He involved His Apostles in the salvific acts of His death and resurrection for
the benefit of all men, the bread and the wine in the
eucharistic meal represent the personal surrender of the
whole of his human existence and of the whole earthly
reality in which the Christian must experience his being-
saved by Christ. In Christ's command: "Do this in remembrance of me" His own words are spoken over the
bread and the wine: "Take, eat; this is my body which is
for you"; "Drink of it, all of you; for this is my blood of
the covenant, which is poured out for many for the forgiveness of sins" (Mt. 26:26-29; cf. Mk 14:22-25; Lke

10. R. Schnackenburg, *Gottes Herrschaft und Reich,* Freiburg,
1961.

22:15-23; 1 Cor. 11:23-25). Those words are the synthesis of the Gospel in which the whole salvific-meaning-
for-us of the Christ mystery is expressed: in the eating of
that bread and the drinking of that wine the salvation of
Jesus' self-surrender to the Father is accomplished in the
believer as a personally lived salvific event.

In the eucharistic meal, therefore, the complete fullness of the salvific power of God's word is expressed, in
an eschatological *prolepsis*, over the whole of human
existence and over the whole earthly reality. Here and
now the Christ mystery is achieved as the "consecration
of the world" (Martyrology for Christmas):

> "The bread which I shall give for the life of the world
> is my flesh." The Jews then disputed among themselves,
> saying, "How can this man give us his flesh to eat?" So
> Jesus said to them, "Truly, truly, I say to you, unless you
> eat the flesh of the Son of man and drink his blood, you
> have no life in you; he who eats my flesh and drinks my
> blood has eternal life, and I will raise him up at the last
> day. For my flesh is food indeed, and my blood is drink
> indeed. He who eats my flesh and drinks my blood
> abides in me, and I in him. As the living Father sent me,
> and I live because of the Father, so he who eats me will
> live because of me." (Jn 6:51-57).

In the eucharistic meal-community, the People of God
on its pilgrimage already experiences here on earth a true
being-together-with its glorified Lord. In this encounter
with the First-born of all creation, who by His obedience
to the Father has become the cause of eternal salvation
for all who believe in him (Heb. 5:7-10), the glorified
Lord effects through His Spirit the likeness with His own
thoughts and desires in the personal decisions of that
believer, in which he experiences his being created after
the image and likeness of God. "The cup of blessing

which we bless, is it not a participation in the blood of
Christ? The bread which we break, is it not a participation in the body of Christ" (1 Cor. 10:16), that is, participation in Christ's self-surrender to the Father?

And yet, in spite of the rich diversity of living the
Christ mystery in personal responsibility, the unity of
being-the-Church of Jesus Christ is a fundamental aspect
of being-a-Christian. Compelling for St. Paul are the ecclesial dimensions of the eucharistic celebration: "Because
there is one bread, we who are many are one body, for we
all partake of the one bread" (1 Cor. 10:17). By the fact
that the one eucharistic Body of Christ is divided among
many, the one ecclesial Body of Christ is built up. Ecclesial division among those who partake of the Lord's Supper is for St. Paul equivalent to despising the community
of God (1 Cor. 11:17-22).[11]

b. Reformational Theology of the Sacraments

The relationship between Christ and man, as seen
from the Reformed Christians' point of view, is always
determined by the "sola fide" principle: God speaks His
all-powerful word to men through Christ, and on the part
of man only faith responds to that salvific word. Here we
have a true personal encounter, a dialogue, in which God
proclaims ever anew to man the Good News of his election in Christ despite all sin; and man can react only as a
recipient who does not understand but is grateful. Man
always stands before God with an outstretched hand. In
this personalistic view of the revelation there is really
only one means of salvation, one sacrament, viz., the
word of God. But this word of God becomes for us an

11. J. Betz, *Die Eucharistie in der Zeit der griechischen Väter,*
Bd. II, 1; *Die Realpräsenz des Leibes und Blutes Jesu im Abend-
mahl nach dem neuen Testament,* Freiburg, 1961; Max Thurian,
*L'Eucharistie Mémorial du Seigneur, sacrifice d'action de grâce et
d'intercession,* Paris, 1959.

audible, visible and tangible reality in a threefold way, namely, through preaching, baptism and the Lord's Supper.

Preaching is a sacramental event, in which God's word powerfully intervenes in man's sinful situation and, if man accepts this word with faith, he knows for sure, and accepts as a reality, that God's salvific work has also taken place for him personally, in Christ.

The two other sacraments, baptism and the Last Supper add nothing new to that reality; they *cannot* add anything to it. They are only a seal, a confirmation and assurance of the salvation that was proclaimed and accomplished.

Hence, according to the Reformational view, the sacraments of baptism and the Lord's Supper are in reality nothing more than "the word of God made visible and tangible."[12] The proclaimed salvation, which has already taken place for us in Christ, is brought home to us by the sacraments in a most concrete and tangible way. In the sacraments, God encounters the believer, who in perpetual wonder and uncertainty learns about his unearned election, by visible confirmations of that election; and, by the particular gestures used in the administration of the sacraments, it is stressed that God's salvation has a perfectly gratuitous character.

The sacraments are, therefore, the visible signs that man's justification has already been proclaimed and effected by the word of God. "It is of fundamental importance in this matter that the proclamation of justification by faith leads to a priority of the word over the sacrament."[13] Calvin taught that a sacrament is never without

12. G. Oorthuys, *De sacramenten*, Nijkerk, 1948, p. 27. **Cf.** *Heidelberg Cathechism*, 66, Bakhuizen van den Brink, 178-179.
13. A. F. N. Lekkerkerker, *Kanttekeningen bij het hervormde dienstboek*, III, 's Gravenhage, 1956, p. 9.

a preceding promise, but the sacrament is added to the promise rather as a sort of appendix.[14]

These sacramental signs and actions do not, therefore, contain salvation: according to the Calvinistic view, our sacramental actions accompany the proclamation of redemption; according to the Lutheran view, redemption is received in, with and through them.

It would, however, be a distorted explanation of the Reformational concept of the sacraments if we said that for the Reformed Christian the sacraments are nothing but a visual instruction about the message of salvation. For, according to them, the sacraments are not only signs and symbols of our being possessed by Christ, but they are also a seal and a confirmation. In baptism and the Last Supper, the recipient is given a divine guarantee that Christ's grace really applies to him also."[15]

It is true that Zwingli attached only psychological value to the sacraments, but this is certainly not the Reformational view. Calvin declared explicitly that the sacraments "are filled with much power."[16] For the Christian can respond to God's word with a total surrender of his whole person, only when the Holy Spirit gives him a divine guarantee through the sacramental sign.

Hence the sacraments are necessary for salvation, also in the opinion of Reformed Christians. Not, however, on the part of God's grace, as if they were bearers of grace, or amplifiers of His word, but on the part of men, because they are a divine guarantee of the genuineness of the recipient's faith. "Through the sacraments, the subjectivity of a man's faith rests on the [objective] word of God."[17] In order to understand the Reformational view of

14. *Institutes*, IV, 14, 3, Sizoo, III, 316.
15. G. C. van Niftrik, *Kleine Dogmatiek*, 2, Nijkerk, 1946, pp. 220-221.
16. *Institutes*, IV, 18, 2.
17. G. C. Berkouwer, *De Sacramenten*, Kampen, 1954, p. 91.

baptism against that background, we do well to compare two statements of the Heidelberg Catechism. One statement says that in baptism "I am as surely washed with His blood and Spirit, of the uncleanliness of my soul, that is, of all my sins, as I am outwardly washed with water that takes away the uncleanliness of the body." But, on the other hand, to the question, "Is the outward bath itself the cleansing from sin?" the answer reads, categorically: "No, for only the Blood of Jesus Christ and the Holy Spirit cleanses us of all sin."[18]

We find the same trend of thought in the concept of the Lord's Supper. On the one hand, the sign of my election in Christ is established because "His body is as surely offered and broken for me on the cross, and His blood as surely shed for me, as I can see with my eyes that the bread of the Lord is broken for me and the drinking cup is communicated to me." On the other hand, bread and wine do not become the body and the blood of Christ, for "just as the water of baptism is not changed into the blood of Christ, nor itself is the cleansing from sin, but is only a divine sign and assurance, so the bread in the Lord's Supper does not become the body of Christ Himself."[19]

c. An Anachronism?

The Reformational protest against the Catholic view on the Eucharist is formulated on the basis of that theology of the sacraments.

The principal aspects of that traditional protest can be briefly summarized and defined as follows:

1. The sacrificial character of the Eucharist is in conflict with the all-sufficiency of Christ's sacrifice on the Cross and the impossibility of repeating it.

---

18. *Heidelberg Catechism,* q.q. 69, 72; Bakhuizen van den Brink, *op. cit.,* pp. 180-183.

19. *Ibid.,* q.q. 75, 78; Bakhuizen van den Brink, *loc. cit.*

2. The Catholic view of the real presence of Christ under the appearances of bread and wine should be rejected because it contains a negation of the mystery of the Ascension.

3. The Catholic conception of Christ's coming and presence in the celebration of the Eucharist is seen as a continuation of the Incarnation, or even a continually repeated Incarnation.

4. Christ's presence under the appearances of bread and wine is manipulated in Catholic life as a holy object, that is present on the altar, and is adored and preserved in the churches.

Ground has been gained in the ecumenical dialogue by the fact that Catholics are able to recognize a justified reaction against their own one-sided concept and practice of faith, in the radicalism with which the Reformational protest rejects the whole Catholic view on the sacramental action of the Church. Because Catholics have isolated the sacrament too much from the word, they experience the sacramental act too much as a means of grace, while paying too little attention to the redemptive power of the word. Making the sacrament independent has led, according to the Reformed Christian, to making grace an independent entity, and distorting the sacramental act so that it becomes a magical occupation with a holy object. It is against this that the Reformed Christians protested by putting an exclusive stress on the word element in the sacrament and on the personal encounter with Christ through that sign. "For the significance of the Reformation on that point is not so much that it reduced the number of sacraments from seven to two, but that it once more discovered and honored the sacramental character of preaching."[20]

Here, too, a justified stand against one-sidedness has

20. *Fundamenten en perspectieven van belijden,* 's Gravenhage, 1949, p. 8.

misled the Reformed Christians and made them choose
one particular item out of the fullness of Revelation. The
undervaluation of God's word and excessive isolation of
the sacrament in the Catholic Church has led to the
Reformational exclusivism of the word in their estima-
tion of the sacrament.

That protest is backed by so much earnestness of faith,
that Catholics feel obliged to consider that question and
admit that they have thought of the eucharistic presence
too much as a visit from God, as if "in the Eucharist,
Christ leaves heaven to descend upon the altar." The
Catholic knows that, especially in sermons and religious
literature, he does not get off scot-free in unwittingly
provoking such a protest.

The joint reflection upon the salvific meaning of carry-
ing out Christ's command "Do this in remembrance of
me" will, if it is to be fruitful, have to be based on a
renewed view of the mystery of the Incarnation. In this
discussion, we Catholics ask Reformed Christians at least
to admit the possibility that their traditional protest can
become an anachronism.

If a Catholic says glibly that he receives God in the
Eucharist, he does not express precisely what constitutes
the heart of the matter in this mystery. The inscrutable
mystery of the Eucharist lies precisely in the fact that
Christ is present *in His glorified humanity under the
signs of bread and wine.* As God, the Son is omnipresent:
but precisely insofar as He desires to live His Sonship of
the Father in a human manner, in solidarity with us, He
is fully present with us on earth—though veiled in signs
—only in the eucharist. This eucharistic presence is a
characteristic of His glorified manhood with the Father,
and it may not be identified with His divine omnipres-
ence, with His divine way of existence that He shares
with the Father and the Holy Spirit.

Inclusive and Exclusive One-sidedness

A new dialogue about the eucharistic Last Supper should begin with the question whether placing a one-sided stress on the "how" of Christ's presence in that Sacrament still corresponds to our present experience of, and reflection upon the faith. In that dialogue the separated Christians must try to meet one another in approaching the eucharist as a salvific event.

This approach we can certainly consider legitimate if we base ourselves on the biblical message of salvation concerning Christ's apparitions to His Apostles after the Resurrection: "Though the doors where the disciples gathered had been closed . . . Jesus came and stood in the midst and said to them, 'Peace be to you!' And . . . he showed them his hands and his side." And "as they . . . marveled for joy, he said, 'Have you anything here to eat?' And they offered him a piece of broiled fish. . . . When he had eaten in their presence, he took what remained and gave it to them" (Jn 20:19 ff; Lke 24:41-44).

If we wish to be able to experience the salvific event of the eucharistic Last Supper we must understand Christ's presence in the context of the salvific message connected with that apparition of the Lord. The question regarding the manner of Christ's presence to the Apostles does not even arise. It is an absolutely unique kind of presence and it is impossible for us to compare it with anything we know or to say a sensible word about it.

Scripture is not primarily interested in giving an apologetic proof of the fact of Christ's Resurrection. All the attention of faith is drawn to the salvific significance for us of the fact that Christ remains a man and that He is the glorified Lord. When we encounter Him with faith through the proclamation of the word and in the administration of the sacraments, we must try to experience what is the significance for our human existence of the fact that Christ has already, in our place, responded perfectly to God's salvific plan for all men.

The celebration of the eucharistic Last Supper occupies the central place in living the Christian belief in the salvific mystery of the Incarnation of God's Son. The proclamation of the word and the administration of the sacrament are directed to that meeting of the pilgrim People of God with its Lord. Full salvation is already offered us in this sacrament under the veils of signs functioning in the interim that separates us from Christ's second coming.

This orientation to Christ in whom the salvific reality is already complete our faith can approach from all sides. All that is given in faith must find a place in that celebration. But, at the same time, no Christian is able to plumb the breadth, the depth and the height of that mystery. While we are on our pilgrimage to the Lord, we are not capable of being fully with Him. This tension between the all-embracing offer of salvation and faith that is still groping in the dark, necessarily includes the danger of one-sidedness in the way this salvific event is lived by the believer.

This one-sidedness is legitimate so long as it is inclusive. Individual Christians will bring this or that aspect of the rich salvific event to the forefront in their religious experience during the celebration, according to their varying situations in life. But this is also true of the distinct believing communities, for these too are determined by the character of the people and the image of the world at a certain time. In every period and in every people there may be shifts in the perspectives and the horizons; they may broaden or become more narrow.

That sort of one-sidedness will, however, tend to divide

the Church, when it seems to adopt exclusiveness, when it leads to a uniformity that excludes all other aspects and leaves no room for pluriform experiences. The Church of Jesus Christ has a long history and she knows the tragic consequences of exclusive one-sidedness. It has caused individual Christians and entire religious communities to oppose one another for conscience sake. They have made it impossible for one another to look upon the Church as "the house of the Father that has many mansions," and they have made her uninhabitable for one another.

The Catholic view of the Eucharist has been characterized by two sorts of one-sidedness during the centuries that lie behind us. Dominant in the life of faith was the "real presence" of the Lord. This making-the-Lord-present was so greatly isolated from the ensemble of the salvific event and made so autonomous an event in the signs of bread and wine that the eucharistic celebration became a sort of audience with the Lord; here He received adoration and thanksgiving, was ready to forgive and to hear the petitions of individuals in their needs. Religious reflection paid exclusive attention to the way Our Lord was present ("transsubstantiation") and to the sacrificial character of the Eucharist. Catholic theology cut off many lawful aspects and distorted the Catholic life of faith, by exclusively paying attention to the Lord's presence and to our involvement in His offering to the Father and making this approach normative. The Catholic Church thereby forced other Christians to leave her.

The celebration of the Last Supper in the Churches that belong to the Calvinistic Reformation have for centuries been threatened with an individualistic and pietistic religious experience that concentrated on the experience of being justified by Christ, and it constantly asked itself whether the believer was worthy to sit at the Table of the Lord. Many, under the inspiration of Zwingli's concept of Christ's presence, experienced it primarily as a subjective remembrance of an event of the past, and this was combined with the Calvinistic idea of a spiritual encounter with Christ in heaven, who "once and for all time" has accomplished His sacrifice for us. Through a reaction against the unacceptable realism of the Catholic view, the coming of the Lord in the Supper was in danger of being reduced to a spiritual presence.

In our own day the Churches have discovered their impoverishment as a result of living in a ghetto isolation for so many centuries. They have opened the doors to one another and learned to respect the religious experience of others as a means of correcting and enriching themselves. Besides that, they have discovered in their conversations with one another that underneath a formal contradiction that appears in one-sided dogmatic formulae of the faith there may lie sometimes a unity of believing understanding and experience that is legitimately expressed in various ways. For it is not possible to approach and formulate in words the deepest core of the life of faith on the basis of rational consideration.

That is why it is inevitable that distinct believing communities and individuals will stress diverse aspects in the way they express their belief, while not differing fundamentally in their life of the faith. The lack of communication for centuries has played an important role in that differentiation. The fact that one comes from this particular Church can be the reason why one stresses certain aspects to which others will not give prime consideration, but which they will certainly not deny when they engage in an honest and open conversation with one another.

"Do This in Remembrance of Me"

When the Church, following the commission of her Lord, celebrates the eucharistic Supper, she does it in

memory of Him who through His historical salvific deeds
has redeemed all humanity and who already represents
the fulfilled creation with the Father in His glorification.
He is the First-born of all creation who, for our sake, has
become the First-born from among the dead (Col. 1).

Our present celebration is the active presence both of
His past death and resurrection and of His future return
when He will hand over all creation to the Father (1 Cor.
15:20-28). Christ is present in His achieved sacrificial
ascent to the Father and in His return in the future He
will fulfill creation.

The Christian who with faith takes part in that celebration is taken up into communion with the glorified
Lord; here Christ brings him to His cross and resurrection by which the Christian can live once and for all and
which make him live toward the future of Christ's kingdom. The eucharistic banquet is time already fulfilled
because present, past, and future coincide in one event.

a. The eucharist is an objective memorial celebration
through which we are drawn into Christ's historical salvific deeds. All the Synoptics tell us that Jesus instituted
the Last Supper in the context of the Israelitic paschal
celebration: "prepare for us the passover that we may eat
it" (Mt. 26:19; Mk 14:14; Lke 22:11). The Bible very
realistically describes the Pasch as a personal presence at
the historical works of God when He wonderfully saved
the People from Egypt and made a Covenant with them
on Sinai: "On this day you shall explain to your son, 'This
is because of what the Lord did for *me* when *I* came out
of Egypt'" (Ex. 13:8). Salvation and making a Covenant
become an actual event here and now with this community, with this person.

This context of the Covenant determines the whole
experience of the community assembled around the eucharistic table as concluding a new Covenant in Christ in
whose salvific deeds the fullness of salvation of all men is

contained. When, following Christ's orders, we are invited to the Table, we can say to ourselves: today there is accomplished in us what Christ has done for us (that is in our stead and for our benefit) in the salvific deeds of His human life, when He suffered, died, rose from the dead and was glorified.

The participating community is confirmed in the definite Covenant that is valid for all time, and which the Father has concluded with all mankind in the death and resurrection of the Lord.

b. The eucharistic banquet is a living communion with the glorified Lord in whom the prophecy of the *Ebed Yahweh* was fulfilled:

> Here is my servant whom I uphold, my chosen one with whom I am pleased, upon whom I have put my spirit. . . . I set you as a covenant of the people, a light for the nations. . . . He was pierced for our offenses. . . . The Lord laid upon him the guilt of us all. . . . Through his sufferings my servant shall justify many (all) and their guilt he shall bear. Therefore will I give him his portion among the great, and he shall take away the sins of many (all) and win pardon for their offenses (Is. 42:1, 6; 53:5-6, 11-12).

The Son of God became one with us human beings by living His life with the Father in this sinful humanness; and this He did in order to draw us into His glorified human existence with the Father. When Christ was baptized by John the Baptist, He accepted the commission as *Ebed Yahweh:* "Thou art my beloved Son, in thee I am well pleased" (Mk 1:11). This vocation He followed to its culmination in the celebration of the Supper on the last evening of His life. All the aspects of the mission of the *Ebed Yahweh* are actively present in the testimony Scripture gives us about the institution of the eucharist: His vicarious suffering and resurrection for the benefit of all, by which God's Covenant with His People was brought to completion.

At that supreme moment of the Last Supper Jesus summed up in *one* sacrificial offering made in our name, the whole obedient experience of His human life in our behalf:

> Father, the hour has come! Glorify thy Son, that thy Son may glorify thee, even as thou hast given him power over all flesh, in order that to all thou has given him he may give everlasting life. Now this is everlasting life, that they may know thee, the only true God, and him whom thou hast sent, Jesus Christ. I have glorified thee on earth; I have accomplished the work that thou hast given me to do (Jn 17:1-4).

He gave His apostles His Body to eat and His Blood to drink under the signs of bread and wine and thereby drew them into that solitary sacrifice offered in our name on Golgotha, and made them sharers in the salvific event of His resurrection on Easter morning: "As the living Father has sent me, and as I live because of the Father, so he who eats me, he also shall live because of me" (Jn 6:58).

c. The Eucharist is a sharing in the glorification of Christ as a future that is already fulfilled. Crystallized in the eucharistic "Maranatha' (Didache) is the whole life of faith of the young Church: "And continuing daily with one accord in the temple, and breaking bread in their houses, they took their food with gladness and simplicity of heart" (Acts 2:46).

Here is the joy born of the knowledge that the Lord is present. The "Maranatha," as we saw, means as much the prayer "Lord, come" as the confession of faith "The Lord has come." The eucharistic assembly is present at an eschatological banquet of joy. In it the young Church had a concentrated experience of her longing for the return of Christ, but she knew at the same time that in this assembly, gathered at the banquet of bread and wine, the final gathering of the elect around the glorified Lord was already taking place. The *parousia* is already anticipated under the signs of eating the bread and drinking the wine together. Those who believing came to Christ and knew that they had died with Him and been glorified with Him in baptism (Rom. 6) experienced in the eucharistic banquet that they were already involved together in that eschatological event of His glorification: "For as often as you eat this bread and drink the cup, you proclaim the death of the Lord, until he comes" (1 Cor. 11:26). This "until" expresses not only a "longing for" but is also an actual event in union with the Lord: "I will not drink henceforth of this fruit of the vine, until that day when I shall drink it new *with you* in the kingdom of my Father" (Mt. 26:29).

The Presence of the Lord

The *anamnesis* command: "Do this in remembrance of me" implies an identity between the Last Supper and the eucharist. The Table at which the Lord sat with His apostles is extended through His power to all countries and centuries. And we are invited to sit at that Table. We are thus drawn into the salvific event which the Lord accomplished that night in His apostles.

The eucharistic Supper is an objective memorial celebration in which the faithful receive a share in the salvific event of the human life of the divine Son. As Firstborn of creation, He has contracted the New Covenant with God for the benefit of all men by living in a new manner His human life as a perfect coexistence with the Father: "But he, because he continues forever, has an everlasting priesthood. Therefore he is able at all times to save those who come to God through him, since he lives always to make intercession for them" (Heb. 7:24).

In this Banquet assembly we experience our dying and rising with Him, our being already glorified with Christ. When we eat the Bread that is given us, we are told in virtue of Christ's power: "This is my body that is delivered for you." This I am in My Self-surrender for you; and when we drink of the cup He tells us: "Drink ye all of this, for this is my Blood of the New Covenant that is shed for many (for all) for the forgiveness of sins." Here and now I die and rise in You.

This objectivity of the eucharistic Banquet stands at the center of our present experience of faith. It is the continuation of the meals the Lord has had with publicans and sinners: "I must stay in your house today" (Lke 19:5). In the midst of His Church, amidst people who are weighed down by guilt, He sets up His Table. He invites the believer who comes to Him with empty hands to sit at that Table and receive from the Lord all that will nourish him. It is an event that comes unilaterally from the Lord to the people who sit at the Table. Here is accomplished the justification of the sinner.

This event is not only an affair between Christ and an individual man. The Church and in her all mankind and all creation are taken up and drawn here in a communion with the Lord. It is the celebration of the community at the Table with the Lord and hence with one another. When we are *one* in Him, we are *one* with one another. The obstacles that prevent true Christian fellowship in society are thereby removed. We sit at the Lord's Table with people with whom we do not otherwise dine, not because of racial or social discrimination but because we are selective in our daily associations. The eucharistic celebration is the removal of individualistic barriers be-

cause Christ's salvific grace breaks open our sinful existence to disclose the inmost scope of God's active plan of
salvation for us.

The Lord is present in the Supper in His mercy. His
coming to us is continuous in His timelessness. The
believer is wrapped up in that salvific-historical actuality
of God's coming into our sinful human existence. What
is fundamental here is His coming from "outside us": it
is a salvific event that comes from outside in the tangible
signs of gifts of bread and wine that are handed to us. It
comes as a relief when at a certain moment the always
subjectively colored words of the proclamation cease and
nothing remains but the invitation: "Take and eat."
There is nothing we, as believers, can more deeply live by
than the objectivity of that salvific event; we are taken up
in it, we are received by it; we just now become men
actualized by the fact that Christ, the glorified Lord who
was crucified for us, comes to us in this way.

Only when the separated Christians are able to return
to the experience of that objective salvific event will they
be able to overcome the endless discussions about the
real presence of the Lord. This question has been ob-
scured for centuries because it was isolated from its
salvific context and because there was a fixation of that
presence in the elements of bread and wine.

The Lord's presence extends over the whole salvific
event that is spoken, heard, experienced and seen in the
context of that celebration. The sign character of the
eucharist lies in that whole Banquet assembly, in the
involvement of that whole community in the partaking of
bread and wine, in getting involved in the world as
human beings who, having been favored by God's grace,
now go out to meet man, experiencing and proclaiming
the coming of the Lord, while occupied in daily tasks.

Hence Christ is not present in the way He was among

men in Palestine; neither is He present through our subjective remembrance of the Lord who is now with the Father, but He is present after the manner of His glorified human existence that is filled with the Spirit. This Spirit He merited for us by His obedient life as a human being because He desired to take us up into that way of living human existence.

We have attained a faith that is a surrendering to Him through that pneumatic presence of the Lord in the proclamation of the word, and in that faith we are constantly strengthened. The Lord is present in the sign of baptism by which we are constituted and made to be the Church as a believing community with Him. In the eucharist the Lord gives Himself as a vivifying Spirit in the totality of His salvific deeds. The whole life of a Christian is one continuous salvific event that the Spirit of the glorified Lord accomplishes in us.

The eucharist is pre-eminently the communion with the glorified Lord who through His resurrection has received dominion over this world, over all creation. So profound is the penetration of that dominion that bread and wine as symbols of human existence and human labor become the signs of the active presence of His Spirit in human life.

On the one hand, the eucharistic Banquet is the breakthrough of the humanization which creation has already received from the glorified Lord. In the glorified man Jesus Christ creation comes already into its proper status, attains that which it can and must be in Him and to which it is destined by the Father. On the other hand, the bread that is broken and the wine that is poured out, as signs of suffering and death, refer so strongly to the sinfulness and brokenness of creation that faith finds it hard to see in those signs the return of the Christ who already takes up creation in His glory with the Father.

These signs of His dominion are so poor that they at the same time manifest the long way the Lord has still to go with His sinful creation.

The Sacrificial Character of the Eucharistic Banquet

Christ's presence should not be made an autonomous entity in the signs of bread and wine. But if we place the salvific action of the Lord who is present at the center of the celebration of the eucharistic Banquet, the right climate arises in which we can view our participation in Christ's sacrifice to the Father.

This celebration is an action performed according to the Lord's commission. He does not come simply as present but as acting, for when He invites us to share in the community gathered around the Table with Him, He desires to involve our salvation in that Sacrifice which, as *Ebed Yahweh*, He once and for all time has accomplished in the name of all men. We can now glorify God with Him, because the same Spirit who has constantly inspired His perfect obedience, now acts effectively in our life. Our predestination in Christ becomes an actual event, for that celebration by His commission is the actualization of God's salvific plan in Christ in our behalf: "For those whom he has predestined, them he has also called; and those whom he has called, them he has also justified, and those whom he has justified, them he has also glorified" (Rom. 8:29-30).

This celebration means knowing for certain and experiencing that our human existence is justified and sanctified in Christ. The Lord who is already glorified in His human existence, as the First-born of all men, confirms His salvific work in us. He makes us be children of God and able, in virtue of that encounter with Him, to conduct ourselves more as children of God in our daily lives. For we are born again through the Spirit (Jn 3:5).

The Churches of the Reformation have always been deeply opposed to the sacrificial character of the Eucharist because they believe that this places man at the center of that celebration and the Church is made to be the one who offers sacrifice. According to the Reformed conviction, what the celebration is concerned with is not what we can do but what the Lord does: it concerns His coming and His salvific action that descends upon us as justification, pardon of sin, as fellowship with Him and the expectation of salvation. "Not the sacrifice I bring, but Thou alone!" For that celebration puts the whole emphasis on the *ephapax,* that is, once for all, Christ has accomplished the sacrifice for us. To this we neither need nor can add anything.

When we have been able to experience that one-sided action of God, we shall desire to offer ourselves also: "I exhort you, therefore, brethren, by the mercy of God, to present your bodies as a sacrifice, living, holy, pleasing to God—your spiritual service" (Rom. 12:1). But, according to the Reformed view of things, that offering is made outside that Banquet, in the daily struggle of life, so as to "be not conformed to this world" (Rom. 12:2). When we emphasize this offering in the very celebration of the Supper, we obscure the meaning of this salvific event. The Church, the individual believer then becomes a co-actor in man's salvation to such an extent that our reconciliation by Christ is pushed into the background and tends to become invisible.

Today's Reformed theologians, however, demand that attention be paid to the historical fact that the Supper as a sacrifice offered by the sanctified is a purely Calvinist datum, that the Christians from the first century on have known to be involved in the sacrifice of Christ as the full experience of His entrance into our sinful existence. Certainly from the very beginning of the Christian era all sorts of sacrificial terms came into use. Through the Lord's kindness, which antecedes all our initiatives and surrounds us on every side, the Reformed reflection on faith will have to make room for the new existence which we have received through Christ's sacrifice. Through the sharing in the eucharistic Table our life becomes ever more like to His. If the offering of the faithful is kept too much removed from experiencing in the Supper the center of God's salvific activity in Christ, then the offering of the faithful threatens to take on the character of a work that is their own. If the sacrifice of the faithful is not seen as strongly involved in the eucharistic Banquet, then we are well on our way to a new form of synergism.

Catholics, on the other hand, have come to realize that the liturgy has one-sidedly overemphasized the sacrificial character of the eucharistic mystery and has called too much attention to the sacrificial offering of the Church, of the faithful: "Pray, Brethren, that my sacrifice and yours may be acceptable to God, the Father almighty." In this and other liturgical texts the consecreation of the believing community to the Father is too much isolated and made independent with respect to the sacrifice of Christ. But in the most classical text of the Canon, which appears in almost all the liturgies, we have a pure expression of the proper relationship between Christ's sacrifice and the sacrifice of the Church. Immediately after fulfilling the Lord's admonition: "As often as you do this, do it in memory of Me," the Church prays:

So now, Lord, we celebrate the memory of Christ, your Son,
We, your people and your ministers, recall his passion, his resurrection from the dead and his ascension into glory,
And from the many gifts you have given to us
We offer to you, God of glory and majesty

This holy and perfect sacrifice: the bread of life
and the cup of eternal salvation.

We offer by recalling Christ's salvific deeds. It is the
only way we can offer. We offer by the fact that we recall
the whole salvific event. The remembrance is the act of
offering. The Lord offers Himself in the actions we perform according to His mandate. It is not primarily a
matter of what we do, but what His Spirit works out in us
when we recall the salvific deeds of His historic life in the
sign of an assembly gathered around the Table. We truly
come with empty hands. But through fellowship with the
Lord we are placed in communion with Him and hence
are sanctified in Him. This is a favorite text for the
Reformed when they prepare for the Supper: "Eat, for
thou hast yet a great way to go" (1 Kings 19:7). If we eat
we are able to make the journey planned for us by the
Lord.

In the eucharistic Banquet we stand wholly as recipi-
ents before the Lord, but not passively. This distinction is
very important. For in virtue of Christ's sacrifice offered
to His Father we can offer "ourselves as a sacrifice, living, holy, and pleasing to God," because we are "not
conformed to this world," but to the First-born of all
creation, in whom "he chose us in him before the foundation of the world that we should be holy and without
blemish in his sight of love" (Rom. 12:1-2; Eph. 1:4).

The "Reservation" of the Eucharistic Bread

For Reformed Christians the practice of reserving the
eucharistic bread because of their fellow Christians'
Catholic belief in the permanent presence of the Lord in
the elements of the eucharistic Banquet is a matter
which defies understanding and is particularly reprehen-
sible. Is it possible to cast some light upon that practice

when we look at the historical record of the early Church? The history of the primitive Church reveals the following regarding the reservation of the eucharistic bread:

1. During the persecutions the Bread was brought to the martyrs who were in prison. This was an extension of the celebration of the eucharist by which they were involved in that action of the community so as to experience their connection with the whole Church in whose midst they were ready to give the highest kind of witness to the Lord.

2. The local Churches sent the Bread to one another, from the eucharistic celebration, as a sign of unity and bond in the Lord: "The bread that we break, is it not the partaking of the body of the Lord? Because the bread is one, we though many, are one body, all of us who partake of the bread" (1 Cor. 10:16-17). The ecclesial Body of Christ is built up through participation in the one eucharistic Body of Christ.

3. Against that background, in the course of centuries, there grew the practice of reserving part of the eucharistic bread to bring it to the sick. We find the first evidence of that practice already in Justin. It is meaningful to celebrate the Supper in the home of those who are ill. And yet, bringing the Bread of the eucharistic celebration to them stresses the fact that the sick belong to the believing community. They are not individuals who stand outside that community.

In all the forms of that practice the point is to bring the absent into connection with the celebration of the Banquet by the community. The Bread that is reserved is destined for being eaten and it has not any independent meaning. Participation in the eucharistic Banquet by the believer who is absent is the only motive for the reservation. Hence the presence of the Lord may in no way be isolated from His salvific activity in the celebration of the Supper. This isolation has, historically, given occasion for great abuses. The reserved Bread must, nevertheless, be handled with respect. If the bond with the eucharistic celebration is preserved, there can also be adoration. But this adoration is not the primary motive for the reservation of the eucharistic bread.

d. New Trends in the Reformational View of the Sacraments

The dialogue about the sacraments and in particular about the eucharist and the Last Supper must be renewed. This matter is of paramount importance ecumenically speaking and it is not without significance that new trends of thought are observable also in Reformational circles concerning that matter.

In the "Consensus" between the Dutch Reformed and the Evangelical-Lutheran Churches we read the following:

Both Churches consider that the sacrament safeguards preaching from idealistic and spiritualistic dissipation. . . . Also, that the connection between preaching and the administration of the sacraments, whatever can be said about them, cannot be categorized into *one* comprehensive formula. . . . Both Churches are of the opinion that the sacrament with its material elements underlines the Incarnation of the Word. Because God, in the Incarnation of the Word, took on the whole of human existence with the exception of sin, He desires to take possession of, and sanctify our whole human existence in body, soul and spirit, through the sacraments. . . . Both Churches confess that the community is called upon, in and through the Last Supper, to commemorate the Lord's death, and this commemoration implies becoming together-with-Christ, so that the faithful become

one plant with Him in becoming identified with His
death and with His resurrection.[21]

These words are perhaps purposely somewhat vague,
but in them appears a hopeful perspective on the salvific
meaning of Christ's death and resurrection, for these are
felt to be the operative cause of actual communion with
Him; for there is "becoming together-with-Christ," becoming "one plant" with Him, and "becoming identified
with His death and resurrection."

Max Thurian, in his book on the Eucharist—a work
that should be read by all divided Christians—asks Reformed Christians to recognize that their doctrine on the
Last Supper is a one-sided protest against late medieval
abuses within the Catholic Church. The exaggerated emphasis on the sacrificial character of the eucharist, and
the tendency to make the Mass almost an independent
sacrifice alongside the sacrifice of the Cross—which
teaching led to the practice of Mass without communion
of the faithful—caused a reaction in the Reformed
Churches and induced them to preach and practice the
Last Supper solely as a communion service.[22]

The question is whether today conscience still calls for
such a strong and one-sided protest against the Catholic
view and practice of the eucharist.

2. WORD AND SACRAMENT

Danger of a Magical Concept of the Sacraments

The Reformational view on the sacraments contains
authentic aspects of revelation that have remained in the

21. C. W. Monnich and G. C. van Niftrik, *Hervormd-Luthers
gesprek over het Avondmaal*, Nijkerk, 1958, pp. 5-6.
22. M. Thurian, *L'Eucharistie Mémorial du Seigneur, Sacrifice
d'action de grâce et d'intercession*, Paris, 1959, pp. 9-18. Cf. F. J.
Leenhardt, "Ceci est mon Corps," *Cahiers théologiques*, 37, Paris,
1956.

background of Catholic religious thought and practice. When we reflect upon the actions of the Church as the personal actions of the glorified Lord, it is of essential importance to stress that word and sacrament belong together. They are but two *aspects* of the ever actual redemptive mediation of the glorified Lord.

As a result of the typically defensive attitude of the Counter-Reformation against the "word alone" doctrine, the redemptive significance of the proclamation has been undervalued in Catholic thinking. In spite of recent, repeated attempts to make people see the proclamation itself as a means of grace,[23] the Reformed Christians are still justified in declaring in opposition to the Catholic attitude: "It is our contention that Jesus Christ, according to the Roman Catholic idea of revelation that is here under discussion, does not really *come* through the preaching that witnesses to Him, and that a real distinction is made where only a logical distinction is possible."[24]

Hence, on the one hand, if Catholics isolate the sacraments from the word, and regard the sacramental actions of the Church too one-sidedly as means of grace that are efficacious in virtue of the action itself (*ex opere operato*), there is then real danger of looking upon the sacraments as mechanical, automatic and even magical actions, for people will be led to imagine that grace is given provided the sign is valid.

On the other hand, when Catholics isolate preaching from the sacraments and regard it as a mere recalling of

23. H. J. Fortmann, *Geloof en sacrament*, Nijmegen, 1949; J. C. Groot, "De preek als genademiddel," *Het Schild* 29, 1952, pp. 131-137; P. Schoonenberg, "De analogie tussen sacrament en preliking," *Jaarb, kath. theol. in Ned.*, 1954, pp. 44-57; J. A. Weterman, *De verkondiging van Gods woord, Levende zielzorg*, Utrecht, 1954, pp. 174-205; F. Haarsma, "De menselijkheid van Gods spreken," *Het Schild* 37, 1960, pp. 7-13.

24. G. E. Meuleman, *De ontwikkeling van het dogma in de Rooms Katholieke theologie*, Kampen, 1951, p. 129.

Christ's life on earth, a life to be imitated by us, they then reduce God's word to the level of the powerless human word: though it may propose truths, the human word can never have the power to make truth produce its effects in man.

The Redemptive Power of God's Word

God's Revelation to the world, the foundation of the Church and the inspiration of Scripture is a single activity on the part of God, a single reality, namely, God's Self-revelation in Christ to mankind. That is why God's word in Scripture is not merely some information *about* God, nor just a revelation of some divine truth, a more detailed statement about God's activity toward man and the world, nor even exclusively a revelation of His inner, divine life.

God's word is a powerful, salvific word, that always effects what it contains and always realizes what it signifies, when it is accepted with faith: "So shall my word be that goes forth from my mouth; it shall not return to me empty, but it shall accomplish that which I purpose, and prosper in the thing for which I sent it" (Is. 55:11). By the word of the Lord the heavens were made, and all their host by the breath of his mouth . . . For he spoke, and it came to be; he commanded, and it stood forth" (Ps. 33:6-9).

God's word is a Self-communication, a divine Self-giving to man. God's speaking and acting are identical. He speaks through His acts and acts through His speech, because His speech is in fact always a being-occupied with men.

Hence the word that God speaks to man has always a salvific power, because it seizes man in his whole being and forces him to make a decision that he cannot evade:

> For as the rain and the snow come down from heaven, and return not thither but water the earth, making it bring forth and sprout, giving seed to the sower and bread to the eater, so shall my word be that goes forth from my mouth; it shall not return to me empty, but it shall accomplish that which I purpose, and prosper in the thing for which I sent it (Is. 55:10-11).

Because the salvific power of God's word always effects in man what it contains, it has always a personal message. It speaks to and contacts this concrete man in his whole personal situation. For it is always a message that is an answer to his doubts and desires. This word is an encounter with God who comes into man's existence, re-creating and opening new perspectives for him: "For the word of God is living and active, sharper than any two-edged sword, piercing to the division of soul and spirit, of joints and marrow, and discerning the thoughts and intentions of the heart" (Heb. 4:12).

It is true that meditation on God's word can lead to a theology, to a theoretical and systematic reflection upon the content of the divine message of salvation for all men. But God's word primarily brings each individual person to existing-together-with-Him and to mutual self-revelation.

When a Christian accepts God's word with faith, it is not primarily his mind that becomes enriched, but his whole human existence, and as a result, his knowledge also benefits by it. When he listens to God who speaks to Him, he is caught up in an event that is filled with divine power: "My speech and my message were not in plausible words of wisdom, but in demonstration of the Spirit and power, that your faith might not rest in the wisdom of men but in the power of God" (1 Cor. 2:4-5).

Because God's word actually effects what it says and

communicates what it signifies, God's speech is sacramental. The very preaching of salvation has power to forgive sins and santify men. This is why revelation, God's Self-revelation to men, tended by inner necessity to the Incarnation of the Word.

The Incarnate Word of God brought about the proto-sacrament of our salvation through solidarity with our nature that was "abandoned by God." For not only did He take on the shape and substance of God's powerful message of redemption, but He also put into effect the forgiving and sanctifying content of the divine message through His redemptive human actions. His death and resurrection both *proclaim* and *realize* God's redemptive will for all men. Through His glorified humanity redemption is announced to the world and all men have, objectively speaking, already been redeemed and sanctified.

This proto-sacrament of Christ's solidarity with all men is "unfolded" in space and time, that is, made present here and now to the individual men, through word and sacrament. Hence the sacrament is the audible, visible, and tangible word, and the word has sacramental power.

The Bi-unity of Word and Sacrament

It is necessary to emphasize the unity of word and sacrament in our practice of the faith. Redemption is a matter of personal relationship between the living Lord and the human being who surrenders his whole person to God, in faith. God's coming and His redemptive activity in man take place in a dialogue. The divine and human partners in the dialogue necessarily belong together in the realization of salvation. God's word and His activity in man have redemptive power but only for the man who believes.

The Lord Himself approaches the man of faith in the preaching of the word and in the daily reading of Scripture, and He creates a true I-Thou relationship. Divine speech is essentially different from the powerless word of man. Human words may be able to stir us, but if we want to convert them into deeds, we must rely on our own efforts.

On the contrary, God's word accomplishes something in man because, through his speech, the glorified Lord re-enters human life that sin had made alien to God. Where impotence reigned, love blossoms out, and in togetherness with God man realizes what it means to be redeemed in Christ. We may compare his feeling to those of a miner who, after being trapped for many days in a caved-in section of the mine and awaiting death, experiences the unexpected signals of rescuers as the promise of a new life.

Not until man existentially experiences that he is encountering the glorified Lord in a personal way and enters into the intimacy of a mutual self-revelation, can Christ live His glorified humanity in him through the eucharist and activate His redemptive human actions through the other sacraments. Only in the unity of word and sacrament does man subjectively experience the fullness of his redemption in Christ. Hence the *ex opere operato* (on the strength of the sacramental act itself) must be seen as an *ex opere Christi* (on the strength of Christ), who gives Himself to us in the proclamation of the word.

It is evident that the preaching of the word has redemptive power. It was in connection with the eucharist that Christ declared: "the words that I have spoken to you are spirit and life" (Jn 6:63). *A sacrament is a visible and tangible word, the word in the fullness of its power.* This idea has been expressed in the Catholic theology of the sacraments, which teaches that the word is the formal and efficient principle of the sacrament. It is the word that makes the act be a sacrament, empowering it with its proper and real efficacy.

There are ecumenical perspectives in these words of St. Augustine about baptism: "Why does Christ not say, 'You art clean through the baptism that washed you but rather, 'You are clean through the word that I spoke to you?' *Does He not mean by these words that in the water the word cleanses?* Remove the word and what is left but water! The word enters into matter and so originates the sacrament. The sacrament is, therefore, a visible word."[25] May we not recognize in this passage an echo of St. Paul's words: "having cleansed her by the washing of the water with the word" (Eph. 5:26), and "as often as you eat this bread and drink the cup, you proclaim the Lord's death until he comes" (1 Cor. 11:26)?

3. WORD AND CHURCH

The essential unity of word and sacrament as two aspects of the one redemptive event in Christ, which is actualized here and now, stresses the ecclesial character of the preaching of the word and the reading of Scripture. If the word has priority in the sacrament, because in the sacramental event God's speech acts in the fullness of its redemptive power, then preaching deals with the *living* word of God, not only stirring man but seizing him in His whole human existence.

The preaching of the word stands wholly within the Church's functioning as a redemptive community. The Scriptures are God's word insofar as they are preached, listened to and practised, insofar as they are lived in the communion of the church. The divided Christians, mis-

25. *In Joannis Evangelium*, 80, 3. Cf. F. van der Meer, *Augustinus, de zielzorger*, Utrecht, 1947, pp. 270-279.

led by many misunderstandings and prejudices, have travelled long and far before they were able to attain this liberating ecumenical outlook on the relation between the proclamation of the word and the Church, between Scripture and tradition.

The definitive break of the Reformation with the Catholic Church actually was the result of a crisis in authority, emanating directly from the Reformational view of God's word in Scripture. God takes the initiative in salvation because He approaches man in his dismal sinful situation, letting His word reach man through Scripture. The word contains the message of man's salvation and justification in Christ. As such the word of God does not need any protection by man nor the authority of the Church, because it is of itself powerful and unambiguous to every person who is ready to listen. That is why Reformed Christians wish to take Scripture as the *only* basis for their way of life; by faithfully listening to the word, they establish an immediate, personal relationship with God.

They feel obliged to reject ultimately every ecclesiastical tradition and every doctrinal authority, because they consider that these violate and obscure the wealth and the supreme power of God's word. They think they are not permitted to admit any authority besides Scripture because this would imply an intervention in their personal encounter and intimate dialogue with God; and it would lead them away from the only path to salvation.

Where God speaks and man confesses, only through grace, that he is redeemed in Christ, there every human authority and every human protection of God's word in the Church fades away. Reformed Christians, therefore, reject as unfounded the Catholic's reproach that they take Scripture out of the Church and hand it over to each individual's free examination, because they believe in the inner power and clarity of God's word and profoundly respect God's speaking to each man personally.

The Traditional Catholic Reaction

Catholics looked upon this Reformational exclusive reliance on Scripture as a dangerous form of religious subjectivism, irresponsibly delivering Scripture to each individual's arbitrary interpretation. They desired to direct this unstemmed flood of Scriptural license into the channel of the Church by stressing tradition as an independent source of revelation. In fact, they argued, Scripture is not self-sufficient. On the one hand, it has to be complemented by unwritten traditions handed down in the Church through the unbroken succession of apostolic authority. On the other hand, tradition, precisely because it is a living tradition, authoritatively intervenes in the understanding and interpretation of Scripture.

This controversial attitude was bound to lead to a distortion of the relationship between Scripture and tradition, i.e., of the Church's function in preaching the word. Firstly, tradition was regarded in the Catholic Church as a supplement to Scripture both with respect to content and to norms. Backing their argument with John 21:25,[26] Catholics regarded Scripture as a limited portion of the apostolic preaching, which not only needed the supplement of extra-scriptural, traditional truths, but also the constant authoritative norm of the tradition from which it originated. Being a system of truths, part of which was later written down in Scripture, tradition formed an independent source of revelation *alongside* Scripture. Because of its priority in the Church and be-

26. "There are also many other things which Jesus did; were every one of them to be written, I suppose that the world itself could not contain the books that would be written."

cause it encompassed revelation as a whole, tradition was given the role of supervising Scripture.[27]

Secondly, the Church was supposed to derive her preaching of the Gospel partly from Scripture and partly from tradition, these being the two sources of revelation. Thus, these two sources acquired a purely historical significance. Scripture and tradition constituted the Church's archives containing Christ's words, from which the contemporary doctrine of the Church was derived. The contemporary proclamation of the Church functioned as the actual norm of faith, while Scripture and tradition were merely remote norms. The sad result of this rigid, defensive attitude was that the Scriptures disappeared into the background of the Catholic picture. In fact, faithful attention to the Church's preaching made personal contact with Scripture superfluous.[28]

Finally, there was a tendency in Catholic thinking to

27. Characteristic of the manner in which the relation between Scripture and tradition was regarded in Catholic thinking is the following question and its answer in a former Dutch Catechism: Q. What sources has the Church of God's revelation? R. They are Holy Scripture and divine tradition (*Katechismus,* Roermond, 1946, Q. 6). A widely used commentary adds: "There are thus *two* sources containing divine revelation, viz., Holy Scripture and tradition . . . The existence of an extra-scriptural tradition is proved by the insufficiency of Holy Scripture as the only source of faith." (P. Potters, *Verklaring van den Katechismus der Nederlandsche Bisdommen* I, 's Hertogenbosch, 1913, pp. 61, 100)

The Council of Trent in fact did not wish to define either the insufficiency of Scripture or the existence of *two* sources of Revelation. Cf. P. Smulders, "Het traditiedecreet van het concilie van Trente" *Jaarb. Kath. Theol. in Nederland,* 1947-48, pp. 150-167; J. R. Geiselman, "Das Missverständnis über das Verhältnis von Schrift and Tradition und Seine Ueberwindung in der Katholische Theologie," *Una Sancta,* vol. 11 (1956), pp. 131-150.

28. Although preaching and liturgy fostered the Catholic life of faith through the word of God, yet this indirect contact with Scripture inevitably led to a fatal undervaluation of its redemptive function. This situation is illustrated by the answer to Q. 9 of the old Dutch Catechism: "Reading Holy Scripture is not necessary but useful." In the newer Catechism an effort has been made to correct this biased view.

regard the doctrine of the Church as the latest stage of the tradition which is handed down uninterruptedly from the Apostles through the hierarchy. This gave rise to the identification of tradition and the Church's doctrinal authority. Since, moreover, the Church's doctrinal authority was confined to the authority of the pope and the ecumenical council, the concept of tradition functioning in the Catholic life of faith was not only lop-sided, but also too narrow; and this concept was placed with authority over against the Reformation's exclusive reliance on Scripture.[29]

The Fallacy of that Controversy

Renewed reflection upon relevation as a divine Self-communication in the incarnation and resurrection of Christ, and a return to the patristic concept of tradition have convinced Catholics that the controversy between the Reformational "Scripture alone" and the Catholic "Scripture and tradition" somehow misses the point. Catholic theology now proceeds from a new outlook on the functional relationship between Scripture and tradition. Reformed Christians, too, have been ecumenically re-examining this relationship and a new appreciation of tradition is clearly seen in their theology. The following passages clearly show this.

> The *sola scriptura* principle in the way we generally hold it, is a one-sidedness for which there is no justification. Catholicism is simply right when it points out to us that a wrong alternative is given in the dilemma "Scripture" or "Scripture and tradition." In the first place, Scripture itself is tradition and, in the second place,

29. This concept of tradition caused serious embarrassment to the Catholic in his discussion with Reformed fellow-Christians when the need arose to justify, for example, the dogma of the Assumption of Mary, which is not mentioned in Scripture and emerges only at a late date in tradition.

even we live by an unwritten—at least not written in the Bible—tradition. Luther himself lived by this tradition. He would never have arrived at the Trinitarian and Christological dogma from scriptural data alone, but he took it over from the tradition of the Church. . . . We cannot stress too much the fact that the Reformational principle of Scripture is based on equating God's word with Scripture, and this is most unreformational![30]

The difference between the Roman Catholic and the pure Reformational concepts of the relation between Scripture and tradition is not that Catholics approach Scripture on the basis and under the guidance of ecclesiastical tradition, while we have a so-called unbiased and immediate attitude toward it, leaving aside all tradition. The latter idea is, in any case, pure fiction. . . . The Bible is not passed on to us locked in a "germ free" shrine, but is handed down to us by being used in the Church and making history in it. . . . The real content of Scripture reveals itself only in its living actualization on the Church. The experience which faith and the Church gain through this is the "primary commentary" called forth by the Bible itself as an aid to true understanding. . . . Thus one may discover the real content of Scripture in its true sense only if one reads and preaches it in the pneumatic sphere of the Church.[31]

Stating the Problem Ecumenically

It is only in the ecumenical encounters of recent years that the divided Christians have been able to free themselves from the prejudices and misunderstandings that

30. H. Rückert, *Schrift, Tradition, Kirche,* Lüneberg, 1951, p. 22.

31. E. Kinder, *Schrift und Tradition, Begegnung der Christen; Studien evangelischer und katholischer Theologen,* Frankfurt, 1960, 2nd ed., pp. 115-131, 127, 123-124; Cf. O. Cullmann, *Die Tradition als exegetisches, historisches, und theologisches Problem,* Zollikon, Zurich, 1954; H. Asmussen, *Katholische Reformation,* Stuttgart, 1958, pp. 35-37, 77-79, 167-169; G. Gloege, *Offenbarung und Ueberlieferung Ein dogmatischer Entwurf,* Hamburg, 1955; J. L. Leuba, "La division des Eglises est-elle nécessaire?" *Verbum Caro,* 54 (1960), pp. 105-114.

poisoned the centuries' old dispute about Scripture and tradition. They have finally been able to discern what constitutes the problem that has kept them apart.

Both Reformed and Catholic Christians agree that Scripture comes down to us through the transmission by the Church and that it can be understood in its purity only within the frame of the Church. They both hold, on the other hand, that Scripture must always remain the norm and yard-stick legitimizing every Church tradition.

Between these poles there exists a tension that has been consciously fostered by Reformed Christianity. The word of God and man's answer to it cannot, it is true, be separated, since God speaks to us through the preaching of the Church. Nevertheless, God's word always is His supremely powerful deed while man's response always remains a receptive act of faith: "One is never absorbed in the other; rather they remain each other's counterpart."[32]

The dialogue, therefore, is centered on God's word as the norm in the Church's preaching. In the Reformational view, God's word, which comes to us in and through preaching, always acts as a corrective over against this preaching, calling it back time and again to the purity of Scripture. This matter is receiving Catholic consideration.[33]

32. Kinder, *op. cit.*, p. 129.

33. The term *tradition* covers both apostolic and ecclesiastical tradition, though they are qualitatively different. Ecclesiastical tradition can be seen according to its active or its passive aspect. Active tradition is the Church's preaching. Passive tradition is the integral doctrine, implicitly passed on through that preaching. Too much attention to the latter aspect has given rise to serious misunderstanding with respect to the concept of tradition, between Reformed and Catholic Christians. And yet, though the passive aspect should not be neglected, greater weight should be given to active tradition in which Revelation is not passed on through the Church's teaching in a fixed and all-embracing way. This tradition has always been time-bound and is always under

The Word in the Church

St. Paul has expressed what constitutes the core of the functional relation between Scripture and tradition in his testimony about his own apostolic office in the words: "I received from the Lord what I also delivered to you" (1 Cor. 11:23). It is in and through the tradition of the Church that the glorified Lord speaks: "I remind you (Timothy) to rekindle the gift of God that is within you through the laying on of my hands. . . . Follow the pattern of the sound words which you have heard from me, in the faith and love which are in Christ Jesus; guard the truth that has been entrusted to you by the Holy Spirit who dwells within us" (2 Tim. 1:6, 13-14).

The task of the Church with regard to the word is one of *paradosis*, transmission; in her preaching she must transmit the word of God that she received from Christ and she must make real in every age the truth of our salvation in Christ. Christ, as the Son of the Father, could say of Himself: "All things have been delivered to me by my Father; and no one knows the Son except the Father, and no one knows the Father except the Son and any one to whom the Son chooses to reveal him" (Mt. 11:27). Through His becoming man, His humiliation and His exaltation, Christ could transmit to His Church what He had received from the Father: "all that I have heard from my Father I have made known to you" (Jn 15:15). The Church is authorized by Christ to proclaim the word through the ages and throughout the world:

---

the criticism of Scripture. Its various elements differ in value and this should be clearly recognized. Contemporary theological views as well as the various forms of popular devotion, for example, belong to this tradition, and as such they need correction on the basis of Scripture. It is true, that, if they are authorized by the Church, they will never contradict revelation. But they can be expressions of a one-sided approach to revealed truth.

"What you have heard from me before many witnesses entrust to faithful men who will be able to teach others also" (2 Tim. 2:2).

Transmission of the word is not chiefly a matter of handing down a doctrine or the historical account of the redemptive actions which Christ did for us long ago. The Church's proclamation transmits the witness to and assurance of the fact that, in Christ, God has intervened redemptively in human history. And when this divine assurance is accepted with faith, the redemptive event that was enacted in Christ as an example for us all, is then accomplished in the individual believer. Hence the Church's preaching makes actual for us the redemptive deeds Christ performed for our sake.

Fulfilling Christ's command, "Do this in remembrance of Me" (1 Cor. 11: 24), the Church in her teaching at all times ties this living bond with the past and not only with the past but also with the future. For by eating the bread and drinking the wine the death and resurrection of the glorified Lord is heralded, that is, will be made a reality in us, "until he comes" (1 Cor. 11:26).

Through the Church's preaching the glorified Lord fills the time "in between" with a reality charged with eschatological tension. He bridges His ascension and His coming by His redeeming presence in word and sacrament: "And Jesus came and said to them, 'All authority in heaven and on earth has been given to me. Go therefore and make disciples of all nations, baptizing them in the name of the Father and of the Son and of the Holy Spirit, teaching them to observe all that I have commanded you, *and lo, I am with you always, to the close of the age*" (Mt. 28:18-20).

The Church of the Word

The incarnation is God's Self-revelation to man. To this divine revelation in Christ the Apostles bore witness in their preaching. Their preaching was not based on a human, historic testimony to the life of Christ, for the Apostles were witnesses, empowered by Christ and blessed by the Holy Spirit, of the redemptive actions of Christ. They were eye and ear witnesses to the works of Christ: "beginning from the baptism of John until the day when he was taken up from us" (Acts 1:22). They alone had the authority of the glorified Lord: "And he commanded us to preach to the people, and to testify that he is the one . . ." (Acts 10:42). They alone had the mission and guarantee of the Spirit who descended on them in a visible form: "When the Spirit of truth comes, he will guide you into all the truth" (Jn 16:13).

The Apostles were intimately involved in the internally divine mission, for in their witness to the incarnation they preached Christ as the Son who became man, the Father who manifested His Fatherhood in Christ and the Spirit who was sent through Christ. As authorized witnesses of the divine Self-revelation in Christ, their preaching itself contains the power of accomplishment. The apostolic preaching constitutes the Church and forms her "deposit of faith," "what has been entrusted" (1 Tim. 6:20) to the Church. It lays down, once for all, the permanent foundation of the Church: "built upon the foundation of the apostles and prophets, Christ Jesus himself being the cornerstone" (Eph. 2:20).

This unassailable foundation of the Church is, however, made up of the common preaching of the Apostles who passed on to one another what the Spirit "brought to their remembrance" and who in this way complemented one another. Out of the individual diversity of the different Apostles flowers the fullness of the apostolic message. Together they formed the Church's deposit of faith, which showed definite growth during the whole apostolic period. A living tradition was given to the Church and it grew constantly in content and depth.

The preaching of the individual Apostles included both personal recollections and the transmission of an already formulated tradition. "I delivered to you as of first importance what I also received" (1 Cor. 15:3), St. Paul told the Corinthians; and writing to the Romans to whom he had not yet preached the Gospel, St. Paul made an appeal to them stating, "Thanks be to God, that you who were once slaves of sin have become obedient from the heart to the standard of teaching to which you were committed" (Rom. 6:17).

Ecumenically speaking, it is most important to find that at least on one point in the controversy about the relation between Scripture and tradition, a definite agreement has been reached between Reformed and Catholic Christians, namely, that *apostolic preaching was given in the form of tradition.* There now exists a common starting point in the ecumenical dialogue. May we not say then that this opens new perspectives? In fact, the fulfillment of Christ's command to pass on what the Apostles themselves had received is explicitly accompanied by the promise of the assistance of the Holy Spirit. "The guarantee of infallibility of apostolic preaching is in fact given in the tradition, which is a passing on of what is received under the guidance of the Holy Spirit."[34]

Scripture as a Living Dialogue Between Christ and His Church

The divided Christians, reflecting together on the violent attacks made by the liberalistic critique of Scripture, have come to the conclusion that it is wrong to see the inspiration of Scripture as if God's word had dropped into

34. B. van Leeuwen, *Regula credendi, Genade en Kerk,* p. 339. Cf. "Schrift en traditie," *Binnenlands apostolaat* vol. 9, 1958, pp. 130-148.

the Church like a meteor from outer space. The Bible is not a history book, nor a biography of Christ, nor an account of the words and actions of Jesus; but it is the resultant of the living dialogue between God who reveals Himself in Christ and man who responds in faith.

The history that is reported in Scripture is kerygmatic; the facts that are recorded stand in relation to the living faith of the Christian communion: "These are written that you may believe that Jesus is the Christ, the Son of God, and that believing you may have life in his name" (Jn 20:31). Scripture always points beyond the narrated facts, on the one hand, to the suprahistorical reality of God's plan of salvation in Jesus Christ, on the other, to the perfection of this reality in His second coming.

The Bible functions in the preaching of the faith and it originated in the midst of the preaching Church. Historical facts and their religious interpretation can no longer be separated in this book of the living Church. Under the supervision of those who had been eyewitnesses of Christ's redemptive actions, a vision of faith grew up based on Christ's message. Scripture is the deposit, not of these historical facts, but of their religious interpretation. This meditation on the historical life, death and resurrection of Christ, a meditation culminating in Scriptural writings, did not flow from the inspired pen of the authors of the Bible, but it flowered from the preaching of the young Church and from her faithful response.

The Bible, then, is the written and inspired form of the preaching of the apostolic Church, and Scripture has sprung from the life of the Church, *from tradition,* This joint discovery "makes the primacy of *paradosis*—of the preaching through the word—over and above written tradition as evident as the fact that these two poles of Christian life have a very flexible relationship. Yet, for centuries, they had been placed in opposition to each

other as black and white, in theological controversy."[35]
This ecumenical point of view enables us to see the
relationship between Scripture and tradition in a new
perspective.

A Functional Relationship Between Scripture and Tradition

As a result of renewed reflection upon the Christ mystery and on tradition, it is necessary to give a broader
significance to revelation than that of a mere communication and transmission of divine truth. Jesus Christ, as
"the image of God whom we cannot see," is not only the
creative pattern after which all men have been made,
and which spurred on the faithful People of God in the
Old Testament to an increasing awareness of their encounter with God. But because Christ is God sharing our
humanity, He is the supreme realization of human existence as created in God's image. Creation was perfected
when God's Son became *the perfect man.*

In the Old Testament, which is the veiled pre-revelation of the Christ mystery, and in the New Testament,
which is the participation in the glorified human life of
the Son, God's transcendent redemptive activity is actualized ever more fully in the free activity of the faithful
community. Through God's Son becoming *man,* the history of man has become the history of God's redemption.
In the encounter with Christ in the Old and the New
Testament man can recognize his own history as the
story of God's activity of grace in His creation. From it
man can learn to see his living together with his fellow-
men in this world as a "translation" of his being-blessed
in Christ.

Revelation, then, is primarily a *redemptive event,* a
divine activity that accomplishes its work within crea-

35. J. R. Geiselmann, *Schrift-Tradition-Kirche, Ein ökumenisches Problem. Begegnung der Christen,* p. 157.

tion. But because God, in performing this redemptive work, accepts man in Christ as His partner in a Covenant, and because man can come to know the whole redemptive dimension of his existence only by listening to God's word, *revelation in existing reality and revelation in the word are two equally essential and inseparable aspects of the one divine Self-communication to man.*

This redemptive reality is accomplished in a veiled manner in the tragic history of the Jewish people and in the humiliation and exaltation of the man Jesus Christ. Only the prophetic word and the self-witnessing of Jesus Christ in the apostolic proclamation can break through the veil which covers redemptive activity, not only to throw light on the content of God's redemptive activity, but also to actualize this divine activity here and now. God's activity and His speech are in fact two inseparable aspects of His Self-revelation; that is why His word has a redemptive effect. "That which was from the beginning . . . concerning the word of life. . . . that which we have seen and heard we proclaim to you" (1 Jn 1, 1-3).

Hence God's revelation is primarily one of redemption in the history of His People, which reached perfection in the life history of Jesus Christ. However, this redemption can attain to consciousness only through the authorized preaching of God's word by the prophets and through the apostolic proclamation. It is on this preaching by the prophets and the Apostles that tradition is established, in the Old Testament within the chosen people, in the New Testament within the communion of the Church; and this tradition, guaranteed by God, gets its written expression in the sacred books.

The era of apostolic tradition came to an end with the death of the last Apostle. The apostolate, as the authentic preaching of the fullness of God's revelation in Christ's salvific actions through which the Christ mystery is consummated in human history, is unique and unrepeatable because of this essential relationship with the Incarnation. The Church *was* established and, with that, the foundation of all subsequent preaching was laid. After the Ascension, no new eye and ear witnesses of the divine Self-communication in Christ and especially of His resurrection could appear in the Church. The apostolic tradition, as the preaching of qualified witnesses, comprehends the totality and fullness of Christ's redemptive work.

Therefore apostolic tradition has a twofold character. One aspect is the Church tradition as it passes on the reality of our redemption, which Christ accomplished for all mankind in time and space. This reality has taken on shape and substance in the living communion of the Church, in her preaching, in her administration of the sacraments and in her prayer. The second aspect is the deposit of the record of the apostolic contact with the humiliated and exalted Lord, that has found shape and substance in Holy Scripture under the guidance of the Holy Spirit.

This twofold character of the apostolic tradition in the Church does not imply a *distinction in content,* as if there were two sources of revelation, but a *distinction between the two ways* in which this apostolic tradition is present and active in the Church. Scripture and tradition together contain, either explicitly or implicitly, the whole apostolic tradition and are each other's complete complement because they both originate from the same source.[36]

36. Congar, "Traditions apostoliques non écrites et suffisance de l'Ecriture," *Istina,* 6, 1959, pp. 279-306; J. R. Geiselman, *Die lebendige Ueberlieferung als Norm des christlichen Glaubens, Die apostolische Tradition in der Form der Kirchlichen Verkündigung, des formalprinzip des Katholizismus dargestellt im Geiste der Traditionslehre von Joh. Ev.,* Freiburg, 1959.

Tradition Makes the Christ Mystery Present in Time and Space

Tradition is the redemptive reality that makes the glorified Lord Himself present in time and space, throughout all countries and ages. Salvation has been consummated in time and space in the testimony of the Apostles, who were involved in the divine Self-communication through Christ's salvific actions. Although the final, eschatological manifestation of that salvific reality must still wait for its ultimate perfection, mankind is already sacred in Christ. This redemptive reality in Christ takes on shape and substance in the whole of the Church's communion of love, and it is at work even where the encounter with Christ has not yet formally taken place, because creation, being blessed in Christ, is in fact called to the Covenant.

The instruments of redemption that actualize tradition and make it a salvific event in human history, are the word and the sacrament. Wherever, the word is preached at Christ's command and on His authority ("Go out and make disciples of all nations"), and the sacraments are administered ("baptizing them"), there the glorified Lord Himself realizes His Church, and she takes her life from His salvation: "and lo, I am with you always, to the close of the age" (Mt. 28:19-20).

The activity of the Church in preaching the word and administering the sacraments is, as such, a *human* activity, but these actions are done at Christ's command, hence they are empowered by His Spirit: "He will take what is mine and declare it to you" (Jn 16:15). This activity of the Church has a divine guarantee because it is authorized by Christ.

The ecclesiastical acts of preaching the faith and administering the sacraments are, therefore, qualitatively

different in content and authority from the apostolic kerygma; in the latter the quite unique event of God's Self-
communication in Christ was accomplished and the
foundation of the Church in which Christ lives was laid
once for all.

And yet, that ecclesiastical activity, through which the
glorified Lord continues to build His Church in human
history, must be seen as the projection of the mission of
the Apostles. Indeed a preaching that is not founded on,
and authorized by the sending of the Apostles cannot
generate true faith nor introduce the Christ mystery into
the present time, through the help of the Holy Spirit:
"How are they to hear without a preacher? And how can
men preach unless they are sent? . . . So faith comes
from what is heard, and what is heard comes by the
preaching of Christ" (Rom. 10:14-17).

If Christ had not authorized the mission and had not
given the fundamental command to the Apostles, the
Church would possess only an historical and hence
human or fallible knowledge of the apostolic tradition,
and her word would be a powerless human word. Hence
it is guaranteed that God's word is contained solely in the
living connection with the authorized mission of the
Apostles.

When seen against that background it is evident that
equating tradition with ecclesiastical preaching is the
result of a biased point of view; it inevitably led to the
assertion by the Counter-Reformation that there are two
sources of revelation. As a first result there came about a
separation of the word and the sacrament. The sacrament as instrument of tradition was devalued, and
preaching the word was reduced to giving information
about divine truths. As a seemingly inevitable consequence, a false rivalry arose between two equally valua-
ble sources of revelation, namely, Scripture and tradi-

tion. In support of this, one could refer to the declaration of the Council of Trent that divine revelation is contained "in the written books and in unwritten tradition" (Denziger, No. 783).

We can get away from this Counter-Reformation interpretation of the Tridentine declaration—that would make unwritten traditions identical with the real tradition—only if the word is always heard in its real relation to the sacrament, and if preaching is always experienced as sacramental redemptive power. Ecclesiastical preaching carries on tradition, not primarily as an oral transmission of truths but rather as a transmission of the redemptive reality which the glorified Lord makes present in this preaching of the word through the administration of the sacraments, since these contain the word in the fullness of its redemptive power.

Secondly, this shows that the subject of ecclesiastical tradition is not identical with and hence may not be confined to "extra-ordinary" teaching (*magisterium extra ordinarium*) that is found in the definitions of general councils and in the infallible pronouncements of the pope as a successor of St. Peter. The primary subject of ecclesiastical tradition is the whole community of the Church that lives through the unity of sacramental preaching and the celebration of the liturgical mysteries. It is in fact the whole faithful Church that transmits the redemptive reality, the tradition. This is so because the glorified Lord actualizes His salvation in the living dialogue between the authorized, preached word and the personal experience of being-the-Church in the actual society to which the word is given.[37]

This dialogue is the source of the "ordinary" Church

37. J. R. Geiselmann, *De traditie* in J. Feiner (ed.), *Theologisch Perspectief, Een overzicht van de huidige situatie in de theologie*, I, Hilversum, 1958, p. 95.

teaching (*magisterium ordinarium*). The Church as a whole becomes conscious of redemptive reality through the subtle relationship between the word that is preached and the response of faith. This relation may cause tensions and even conflicts, for not everything that comes from an honest endeavor to know God's word in a contemporary and personal setting can be accepted as authentic. It must be tested as to its evangelic value by the communion of the Church under the authoritative guidance of the hierarchy.

The ordinary teaching of the Church thus functions in constant agreement with the conviction of life and faith of the whole Church. In a certain respect even more attention should be given to the Church's life of faith with regard to word and sacrament, because the Church is often obliged, in her councils and dogmatic pronouncements, to defend, and to give, negative definitions; she is not often in a position to make a direct, positive and constructive contribution to the authentic, contemporary consciousness of redemptive reality.[38]

The ordinary teaching of the Church is constantly attentive to the pulsating power of the Holy Spirit who gives a special shape to the redemptive work of Christ in each period and in each culture. On the strength of the abiding presence of the Spirit of the glorified Lord, the Church as a whole cannot err, that is, she cannot profess untruth in her generally accepted conviction of faith and in her unanimous preaching. Whenever a certain aspect of revealed truth is recognized and lived in the faith of the whole Church, the confession of this aspect has the same surety of faith as a defined dogma, even when it is not defined in an infallible pronouncement of the Church.

38. Hans Küng, *The Council Reform and Reunion*, London, 1961, pp. 161-8.

It is in this light that we must see the solemn definition of the dogma of Mary's Assumption, which had been long accepted by the whole Church and against which Reformed Christians continue to protest on exclusively Scriptural grounds.[39] This protest would be legitimate if tradition were a transmission of truths not contained in Scripture. Every Christian will defend the fact that the word of God cannot tolerate rivalry. But if tradition is indeed making Christ's salvation present through the word and sacrament, under the guidance of His Spirit, no Christian can rule out the possibility that the Church, in her believing contact with God's word in Scripture, will discover certain aspects that hitherto had remained dormant in the Christian's consciousness.

Scripture as the Immanent Norm and Conscience of the Church

On the one hand, it follows from the dogma of the inspiration of Holy Scripture that the Bible is intended by God to be the permanent norm for all preaching and administration of the sacraments in which the Holy Spirit of the glorified Lord continues, through the ages, the divine Self-communication in the redemptive acts of Christ. Scripture, as the living deposit of apostolic preaching through which the firm foundation of the Church was laid once for all, derives its authority from the Triune God as He reveals Himself. This is why Scripture can never be subservient to, or dependent on any other authority.

On the other hand, the apostolic tradition is actualized

---

39. E. Hendrickx, "Het dogma van Maria's Tenhemelopneming in de ontwikkeling der Kerk," *Ned. Kath. St.*, vol. 47 (1951), pp. 43-53, G. de Gier, "Maria's Tenhemelopneming, Schriftuurlijke fundamenten en dogmatische samenhang," *Ned. Kathol. St.*, vol. 47 (1951), pp. 54-64.

through ecclesiastical tradition, in a redemptive reality which makes its mark here and now.

The starting point of a new insight into the mutual relationship between Scripture and tradition is that both find their origin in the apostolic tradition. Scripture, as the written deposit of apostolic preaching, is the permanent and absolute norm (*norma non normanda*) of all preaching in the Church. The Church's tradition actualizes, on Christ's authority, the apostolic tradition and places in the present that foundation of the Church that was laid by apostolic preaching. Both Scripture and tradition contain the word of God preached by the Apostles, but the glorified Lord speaks in a specific way in each. Thus they need each other; Scripture becomes God's word through tradition, and tradition wholly derives the message of its preaching from Scripture.

The Church's preaching needs Scripture as its divine norm, while Scripture needs the Church's preaching for its authoritative actualization. Scripture cannot replace or eliminate this living word of the Church, nor can Scripture be taken out of the Church and given to the believing individual who, through faithful reading, enters into a personal relationship with God in isolation from the community of the Church.

Scripture, as the permanent norm of the Church's preaching, can function only in the living community of the Church, because only the preached word of God, received with faith, can have redemptive power. Only in the Scripture that is preached by the Church does the glorified Lord speak to the community and to the individual.

Only in the preaching of the Church is Scripture truly the redeeming word of God, that transforms the redemptive acts of Christ into an actual event. This dynamic presence of the glorified Lord in the word of the Church makes it clear that a false dilemma is posed when Scripture is seen as the "opposite" of the Church. A false dilemma, then, is built up when Scripture, as a norm *above* and *outside* the Church, is played off against the tradition of the Church. *Scripture is the exclusive norm of the Church's preaching, but it is an immanent norm.* Only where Scripture is read with faith in the Church and where its preaching is acted upon in the unity of the Church, can it be the revelation of the redemptive Christ mystery.

Divided Christians can come to terms with one another in the view Luther expressed on the function of Scripture in the Church: the word of God is not Scripture in the form of a book, but Scripture lived in the Church (*viva vox Evangelii,* the living voice of the Gospel). The Church is the auditorium for God's word. Moreover, the message of this word, of which the core is the love of God translated into concrete terms of brotherly love, itself builds up the Church. Only in the living actualization of Scripture in the daily life of that community of faith will men feel the redemptive power of the word and discover the content of Scripture in all its fullness.

However, in the ever renewed life of the Church, Scripture is the always inspired and corrective norm. Scripture acts as *the conscience of the Church.* Just as man, in the immanent norm of his own conscience, grows in the knowledge of the will of God that directs his life, so does the life of the Church receive shape through the inner dynamics of the word that is preached in her.

But as soon as the Church threatens to go against this immanent norm, Scripture—in the same way as is done by conscience in the life of man—functions as an "opposite." Scripture then acts as a judgment on the Church, as calling her back and urging her to renew herself. However, just as the life of a man is not brought back to its norm by exterior laws, but by the authority of his conscience, so Scripture does not stand outside the Church but is an immanent independent authority *in* the Church.

CHAPTER FIVE

GRACE AS SOLIDARITY WITH CHRIST

Shaping Our Humanity According to the Divine Exemplar

The Incarnation, in its most profound redemptive sense, is a solidarity of God's Son with sinful man in order that man who was alienated from God might participate in the divine nature of Jesus Christ, through and in the glorification of His humanity. This elevation of man is accomplished within the confines of our human existence. And yet, when Scripture speaks of the Incarnation as the divine pattern of creation—He is the "first-born of all creation" (1 Col. 1:15), the "first fruits of those who have fallen asleep" (1 Cor. 15:20)—it refers to the gift of grace as a participation in the divine nature:

> His divine power has granted to us all things that pertain to life and godliness, through the knowledge of him who called us to his own glory and excellence, by which he has granted to us his precious and very great promises, that through these you may escape from the corruption that is in the world because of passion, and *become partakers of the divine nature* (2 Pet. 1:3-4).

The Incarnation is the mystery of the blessing of all men in this prototype of our humanity: "For those whom he foreknew he also predestined to be conformed to the

377

image of his Son, in order that he might be the first-born among many brethren. And those whom he predestined he also called; and those whom he called he also justified; and those whom he justified he also glorified" (Rom. 8:29-30). This the faithful should know that in Christ "your names are written in heaven" (Lke 10:20).

St. Paul's life was constantly governed by those ideas, this conviction of certainty, and his epistles testify in a rich variety of ways to this central message: "For I through the law died to the law, that I might live to God. I have been crucified with Christ; it is no longer I who live, but Christ who lives in me; and the life I now live in the flesh I live by faith in the Son of God, who loved me and gave himself for me" (Gal. 2:19-20).

In order to illustrate the bond that unites the Christian to the life of Christ, to His crucified and glorified Lord, St. Paul constantly invented new words that were until then unknown in the Greek vocabulary. It is almost impossible to render into our own language the intimacy of the communion with Christ that those words express. He speaks of *sumphutoi* (grown together) through conformity with His death; of being crucified and buried with Him; of living together with Him; of *summorphizesthai* (taking on the same shape as His); of being glorified with Him; of ruling and inheriting with Him; of being built up with Him; even of *susoma* (being one body) with Him.

There is, therefore, a real and mutual fellowship with the life and lot of Christ into which the Christian enters. Thus the Apostle can say that the sufferings, the calamity and the persecutions of the Christians of his time are the sufferings, the calamity and persecutions of Christ. In fact would it be possible to visualize in a more intimate way the bond that unites Christians with Christ? St. Paul describes the situation of the baptized in relation to Christ as "being in Christ," and in his epistles there are no less than one hundred and four instances of the expression "in Christ" or of "Christ being in us." Christ lives in me, Christ is my life (Phil. 1:21). This is the Apostle's most firm conviction.

The fact that we are so securely bound to Christ is possible only because Christ is human as we are human —He shares our nature—while, on the other hand, His very humanity has become a "life-giving Spirit" (1 Cor. 15:45), through His glorification. With His *Pneuma* (Spirit) the Lord fills those who belong to Him. For St. Paul nothing is more certain than this: "He who dies for us on the cross now lives His life in me as the risen Lord."[1]

Explanatory Notes

At this stage it might be useful to add a few notes to certain expressions that are central to these considerations of the Christ mystery in us. Mutual misunderstanding could easily arise between the divided Christians as a result of diverse interpretations of St. Paul's and St. John's view of the way we live our redemption in Christ—a vision that permits us to say that Christ lives in us, that He desires to live His glorified humanity in us, that we can divinely live our human life in Christ.

Although we use those forceful Scriptural expressions to convey Christ's solidarity with us, we do not interpret them as any form of mystical identity that disregards the distinction between the persons concerned. The whole issue in Christianity is a *personal relationship* between the glorified Lord and the person who has faith, through the Holy Spirit. It is certainly wrong to look upon this relationship as merely one between two human persons

1. F. Hoffman, "Geloofsgrondslag van de liturgische vernieuwing," in J. Feiner, ed., *Theologisch perspectief* III, p. 74-75.

who enter into a union and mutually reveal their personalities.

In a human relationship two persons may wish to give
themselves to each other, but in the end each partner has
to actualize in himself what is given by the other. Because of our creation and redemption in the First-born of
all creation, the self-revelation in the union between
Christ and the believer is given only and always by *Him*
and the power to actualize what He imparts similarly
derives from Him alone. However, we must always avoid
seeing this relationship as a causalistic connection in
which the cause automatically produces the effect, for
this would degrade Christianity making it a false mysticism and even a sort of pantheism.

The encounter between God and man, in the testimony
of Scripture, even in the Old Testament, is described in
images that are borrowed from human relationships.
Central in this encounter of God's self-revealing love and
believing man's response is the idea of the Covenant and,
in order to express the intimacy of the Covenant, images
borrowed from the most intimate human relationships
are used, such as relations between father and son,
mother and child, groom and bride, and between brothers.
The relation between God's sovereign power and our
human dependence on Him as creatures must be seen in
the perspective of God's Self-revelation to His partner in
the Covenant. *Creation is secondary to the Covenant.*

Being a Christian is not primarily a matter of being a
creature who can act only in total dependence on his
Creator as sovereign First Cause, but of the completely
new dimension of man who in Christ is loved by the
Father and, through this, is called to give a personal
response of love in return. His experience of dependence
is sublimated by the love that God allows to flourish in
his life, for man sees his creation in the light of his

ultimate destiny, viz., that he is created after God's image and likeness.

The history of mankind is the story of the loving initiative of the Father, who wished to impart Himself to men in the solidarity of His Son, and who, through the Spirit of Him who was brought to perfection for us, wishes to direct all men to the destiny of their creation, to the First-born of all creation.

The community of life with the glorified Lord is thus primarily a personal relationship, a bond of love between two persons, in which the believer is appealed to as a free person. Although the word of Christ contains salvific power and the sacraments effectively realize the content of this word, the actions of the Christian remain his own human and personal response to the Self-revelation of the glorified Lord. The commitment of his faith, the longing of his hope and the inventive power of his love are the personal acts of the man who is saved in Christ, even though these acts owe their origin and continuance to the constant initiative of love of the glorified Lord, who imparts Himself in word and sacrament through His Spirit.

It is indeed the life-giving Spirit who maintains the personal relationship between the Christian and the glorified Lord:

> While Christ alone received this Spirit without measure, to the members of the Mystical Body He is imparted only according to the measure of the giving of Christ, from Christ's own fulness. But after Christ's glorification on the Cross, His Spirit is communicated to the Church in an abundant outpouring, so that she, and her single members, may become daily more and more like to Our Saviour.[2]

2. Encyclical *The Mystical Body of Christ,* America Press, 1943, p. 25.

The Christian is thus given the high task of making his human life ever more like to the life of absolute obedience of Christ to the Father, through his encounter with the glorified Lord, so as to glorify the Father through Him. All his actions must reflect the ideals, thoughts and love that governed Christ's life on earth and now rule His glorified existence with the Father.

Man's Christian existence must be for him an I-Thou relationship with the glorified Lord, who enables him to consciously *become* what he already *is* in Christ and who will teach him to think as Christ thinks and to love that inner driving power which is Christ. Since God loves each one of us in Christ, who fulfills the divine ideal of human surrender in love, the believer is orientated toward the encounter with His Father. Man's whole activity, through which he realizes himself as an individual and as a member of a community, reflects that ultimate destiny in Christ.

The fact that love necessarily concerns *two* persons, who, by placing themselves at each other's disposal, strive for supreme unity, makes us see Christianity as a profound interplay of love between the divine initiative and the human response of faith. In this encounter we learn to see the self-surrendering obedience of Christ toward the Father as an invitation of love that irresistibly prompts us to surrender our own lives.

It is obvious that we shall meet difficulties if we regard this relationship solely from the standpoint of God's sovereign causality and man's consenting co-operation, for such a causal relation does not do justice to the personal character of the encounter. On the one hand, the Incarnation and its subjective experience by each individual man is a continual gratuitous gift of grace, which is God's Self-communication giving rise to creation. The slowly accomplished fulfillment of man's final destiny in Christ is a free gift of God's love that opens the way to an ever closer intimacy.

On the other hand, it is that very speech of God, through Christ, that enables man to give the response of his love, thus realizing himself as a man. For his every activity gives substance to his personal surrender to Christ, in whom God's love is translated for us into fellowship with man.

1. THE CONTROVERSY

Where Our Paths Diverge

In a scriptural perspective, our Christianity is an adaptation of our human life toward conformity with our divine exemplar, the Man Jesus Christ, for it is through the glorification of *His* humanity that we are able to live *our* humanity at a divine level and in a divine manner. This divine life in us is not, however, a static reality that would enable us, once we have become children of God, to act independently, in accordance with this status; it is rather something dynamic, continually present in us through the operative presence of the Spirit of the glorified Lord. Through the working of His Spirit in word and sacrament, the glorified Lord achieves in us the same basic attitude of absolute obedience to the Father which led His human life to the highest perfection.

Misunderstandings on the subject of this gratuitous work of grace that enables man to take full responsibility for his eternal salvation, have alienated Reformed and Catholic Christians ever since the sixteenth century. When the glorified Lord announces to us in His word that He has redeemed and sanctified us through His utmost solidarity with our sinful human existence, and when we come to perform acts of faith and love through His activ-

ity in the sacraments, then we may say that a real change
has been wrought in us.[3]

Because of our encounter with Christ in word and
sacrament, we can do things now we were unable to do
before. Nevertheless, those actions are not being performed in us, but we perform them ourselves, bearing
full responsibility for them. We do not passively undergo
the influence of grace but, through that divine Self-communication, we become actively engaged.

The divided Christians have for centuries walked different roads because they stressed different elements of
the mystery of receiving grace in Christ, and they have
thus been led beyond each other's horizon and become
estranged from one another. The distance that separated
them prevented their meeting but not the vehemence of
their mutual accusations.

The Reformational Thesis of "By Grace Alone"

Reformed Christians live, in a literal sense, by the
word of God. In the light of this salvific message in
Christ, they learn to recognize their sinful situation. In it
sin is revealed to them not as an accidental meanness of
man who could just as well have acted virtuously, nor as
a pardonable human weakness, but as a condition of
existence that necessarily leads to sinful actions.

All human actions are unmasked and are seen in that
light, as manifestations of man's enmity with God. Man
reaches this absolute judgment about himself when he
stands under the cross of Christ. When our Lord died,
everything was accomplished, without man's help. On
the cross all that is human was declared to be non-sus-
ceptible of God. "By the cross man is unmasked in his
most secret motives and revealed as a rebel against God;

3. F. L. Leenhardt, "La présence eucharistique," *Irenikon* vol.
33 (1960), p. 170.

and any foundation for optimism about man's condition is removed."[4]

Man is saved by Christ but this cannot mean that he has been sanctified *as man*. A sinner he remains, his actions remain sinful, because his human nature is essentially sinful. He lives only by God's grace, he literally lives by Christ's grace, who through the merits of His passion and death overcame sin for man. Man resembles one who has been sentenced to death and then reprieved, and who owes his life continuously and solely to the benevolence of society. In response to God's Good News that Christ died also for him, man can merely surrender his whole person to Christ. Through faith he knows that he is saved through Christ's merits which are the sufficient and only ground of his salvation.

That is why Reformed Christians must have constant recourse to Scripture and read the Bible every day. They never tire of listening to God's word in preaching, for they are not personally justified but remain sinners who are in constant need of redemption. Only when God speaks to them and they contact Christ through the word, do His merits become applied also to them individually. Reformed Christians are keenly aware that their entire Christian existence depends on God's speaking to them, that it depends solely on Christ's grace. Again and again they crave the assurance that God has mercy on each of them, for every individual is aware that he is a sinner.

The Catholic Reaction: Man's Cooperation

The Reformational thesis of *sola gratia* as an act of God's absolute sovereignty which frees man and acquits

4. *Herderlijk schrijven van de Generale Synode der Nederlandse Hervormde Kerk betreffende de Rooms-Katholieke Kerk*, 's Gravenhage, 1950, p. 16, Cf. G. C. van Niftrik, *Kleine Dogmatiek*, pp. 116-123; W. J. Kooiman, *Luther, Zijn weg en werk*, Amsterdam, 1954.

him out of sheer gratuitous mercy because of Christ's merits[5] has been regarded by Catholics as a form of false quietism that leads men to pure passivity with respect to God's operation of grace in them. Catholics have reacted by strongly emphasizing man's responsibility. They have repeatedly turned to the idea of reward in Scripture, which keeps asking man to cooperate with grace by doing good works. In this way it was almost impossible for Catholics to avoid the real danger, first, of detracting from God's sovereign majesty and the grace-given character of Christian activity and, secondly, of underestimating the seriousness of sin and human impotence.

In the religious life of Catholics, the attention of the Counter-Reformation to good works led to an excessive emphasis on the moralistic fulfillment of a great number of strictly defined obligations, and on the share of human effort in the gaining of salvation. Catholics, of course, are strongly convinced that they can do nothing without grace, but they seem to look upon grace as a mere strengthening of their efforts. They give the impression that they need grace only because their own good works would not reach eternity without the supplementary support of God.

The Counter-Reformation's distortion of the Catholic idea of grace finds an echo in the old Catechism. To the misleading question, "Is grace alone sufficient for salvation?" there is the following answer that suggests a combination of complementary forces: "To attain heaven grace alone is not sufficient; our cooperation is also nec-

5. W. H. van de Pol, *Karakeristiek van het reformatorisch christendom*, pp. 329-386; M. F. J. Marlet, *Grundlinien der kalvinistischen Philosophie der Gesetzidee als christlicher Transcendentalphilosophie*, München, 1954, pp. 129-134; J. L. Witte, *Het probleem individu-gemeenschap in Calvijns geloofsnorm*, Franeker, 1949, pp. 136-139.

essary."[6] This Catholic reaction is an imbalance between
God's grace and the personal responsibility of human
cooperation. This state of affairs quite naturally provoked a protest.

Is There an Irreconcilable Opposition?

The divided Christians for centuries have faced each
other, forming two camps; they had no sympathy for
each other's convictions and no appreciation for the protests of the other which, of course, became too one-sided.

But now, in the ecumenical encounter, Christians on
both sides have learned to recognize and value the genuine Christian elements in each other's point of view. An
important step forward has been made with respect to
reunion, because this question has been raised: Are our
ideas about the relationship between God's sovereignty
and Christian freedom, between grace and merit, really
so irreconcilably opposed to each other as the struggle of
centuries has led us to believe?

Catholics wish to assure Reformed Christians that
they wholeheartedly agree with them that the man of
faith lives entirely by God's grace. But Catholics have not
been afraid to acknowledge also that they have had a
distorted view of the Reformed witness of faith, as if the
Reformed Christians maintained that man, for God's
greater glory, had been devaluated to a passive receiver
of grace and that the value of human acts had been reduced to impotence.

On the other hand, Reformed Christians have come to
see that, in stressing St. Paul's fierce reaction to the
pharisaical devotion to the Law as an argument against
the Catholic teaching on good works and merit, they have

6. *Katechismus of christelijke leer, ten gebruike van de Nederlandse Bisdommen,* Utrecht, 1948, Qu. 218.

neglected the Scriptural concept of reward. Now there is room for a liberating discussion.

The Reformational Contribution

The contribution of Reformed Christians to this discussion begins with the confession that those who in their preaching fail to appreciate the connection between work and reward do ill service to the Church.

The traditional controversy now loses its sting because we are able, fortunately, to establish the following.

> The present-day Roman Catholic as well as Reformational study of the New Testament demands the greatest attention to this idea of reward. The clear evidence in Scripture makes any reactionary thinking on this point futile. There are no grounds for doubting the biblical emphasis on the need for men to bear fruit, in the passages where Scripture deals with the connection between work and reward, and it is clear that the emphasis is placed in all the earnestness of an eschatological perspective. Those who disavow this connection may, it is true, oppose Rome, but in doing so they are being simplistic and their argument is *a priori* suspect. . . . If serious impoverishment is to be found anywhere, then certainly it exists here. Truly, this matter of reward does not imply any concessions to an egocentric form of Christianity, which is wholly self-centered and, as such, sees God as a means to its own end. . . .
>
> Right through Scripture the meaningfulness of human decision and the significance of human activity stand out. Thus it is wrong to oppose Roman Catholic dogmatists and exegetes who stress this point. Indeed, there is overwhelming evidence that there is an incontestable bond, connection, correlation, congruency—or whatever one might choose to call it—between work and reward. . . . Why should we continue the controversy when we are assured over and again by Roman Catholics that they *only* wish to do justice to the noetic and ontological connection between work and reward?[7]

7. G. C. Berkouwer, *Verdienste of genade?* Kampen, 1958, pp. 25-26.

The Catholic Contribution

Catholics, on their part, can make an important step in the direction of the Reformational witness of faith. The questions that have occupied their minds during the recent years of ecumenical discussion are the following: Was it the intention of the Council of Trent to shut the door once for all to the Reformation? Was the Reformational thought and practice of faith incapable of making a genuine Christian contribution to the Church?

Here the Catholic keeps asking himself whether in fact the Council of Trent was not much more careful in its refutation of the Reformed view of faith than the Counter-Reformation's interpretation of the Council—indiscriminate and rigorous as it was for centuries—was willing or able to admit? One might even ask whether the Reformational concept of grace was in fact condemned by the Council of Trent insofar as it applies to the mystery of the bestowal of grace on man and the relation of grace and human cooperation to salvation.

Are Catholics sufficiently aware, and have they always made it sufficiently clear to their Reformed fellow-Christians, that Catholic dogma does indeed declare that man is predestined, irrespective of his human effort and cooperation, to receive his first grace and everlasting happiness, by the eternal judgment God made in Christ?[8]

Ever since her first reflection on the mystery of grace, in the days of St. Augustine, the Church has considered as crucial to the Christian message the primacy of God's

8. "Deus autem bonus et justus elegit ex eadem massa perditionis secundum praescientiam suam quos per gratiam praedestinavit (Rom. 8, 29 ff.; Eph. 1, 11) ad vitam, et vitam illis praedestinavit aeternam; ceteros autem quos justitiae judicio in massa perditionis reliquit, perituros praescivit, sed non ut perirent praedestinavit; poenam autem illis, quia justus est, praedestinavit aeternam. Ac per hoc unam ei praedestinationem tantummodo dicimus, quae aut ad donum pertinet gratiae aut ad retributionem justitiae." (Denziger, no. 316. Cf. nos. 320-322).

activity and the absolute dependency of man. Objective study of the history of the dogma will show that, though the chief emphasis was on God's sovereign action in grace, it was the mystery of Christian freedom that ran the risk of being neglected, rather than vice versa. All the forms of pelagianism and semi-pelagianism, wishing to clear a place for human freedom *alongside* grace, have been radically condemned by the Church in her eagerness to preserve the unassailable character of predestination.

And yet, while recognizing the absolute priority of God's grace, the Church has had to maintain, on the basis of Scripture, first, that man does not remain passive under God's activity of grace, and secondly, that man is not activated by grace working from outside. On the contrary, grace in Christ lays hold of the whole existence of man and transforms him into God's child; and he is thus empowered to perform acts of true faith and love.

It is against this background that we must understand the Council of Trent when it condemned the following propositions:

First, that man can make the acts of faith, hope, and love and contrition that are necessary in order to enjoy the grace of justification, without the preceding influence and help of the Holy Spirit.[9]

Secondly, that under the influence of grace, the free will of man is like a lifeless instrument and does not act of itself, but passively allows itself to be moved by God,[10] and that God works evil in us in the same way He works

---

9. "Si quis dixerit, *sine praeveniente Spiritus Sancti inspiratione atque ejus adjutorio* hominem credere, sperare et diligere aut poenitere posse, sicut opportet, ut ei justificationis gratia conferatur: A. S." Denziger, no. 813; Cf. no. 797.

10. "Si quis dixerit, liberum hominis arbitrium a Deo motum et excitatum. velut *inanime quoddam nihil omnino* agere *mereque passive* se habere, A. S." Denziger, no. 814; Cf. no. 797.

good, not merely permitting it but actually performing it as His own act.[11]

Thirdly, that the sinner is justified through faith alone, where this is understood to mean that nothing more is required of him, in the way of cooperation, in order to gain the grace of justification and that it is in no way necessary to prepare and dispose himself through an act of free will in order to receive this justification.[12] From the first condemnation it is clear that this preparatory act of the will must be seen as the fruit of the Holy Spirit's grace.

Fourthly, that man is justified only through imputation of the merits of Christ or only through the remission of sins, thus excluding the grace and love that the Spirit pours into our hearts and which inwardly transform us, so that the grace through which we are justified is nothing more than God's favor[13] and that our faith implies no more than an act of confidence.[14]

Do the Reformed Christians who still subscribe to the protest of the Reformation in the sixteenth century feel

11. "Si quis dixerit, non esse in potestate hominis vias suas malas facere, sed mala opera ita ut bona Deum operari, non permissive solu, *sed etiam proprie et per se,* adeo ut sit *proprium* ejus opus non minus proditio Judae quam vocatio Pauli: A. S." Denziger, no. 816.

12. "Si quis dixerit, *sola* fide impium justificari, ita ut intelligat, *nihil aliud* requiri, quo ad justificationis gratiam consequendam cooperetur, et *nulla ex parte* necesse esse eum suae voluntatis motu praeparari atque disponi: A. S." Denziger, no. 819. Cf. nos. 798, 801, 804.

13. "Si quis dixerit, homines justificari vel *sola* imputatione justitiae Christi, vel *sola* peccatorum remissione, *exclusa* gratia et caritate, quae in cordibus eorum per Spiritum Sanctum diffundatur atque illis inhaereat, aut etiam gratiam, qua justificamur esse *tantum* favorem Dei: A. S." Denziger, no. 821. Cf. nos. 799 ff., 809.

14. "Si quis dixerit, fidem justificantem *nihil* aliud esse quam fiduciam divinae misericoridae peccata remittentis propter Christum, vel eam fiduciam *solam* esse, qua justificamur: A. S." Denziger, no. 822. Cf. nos. 798, 902.

that those declarations of the Council of Trent condemn their concept of faith? Are they obliged to hold on to their deeply rooted conviction that after that Council there was no more room within the Catholic Church for their views on grace and justification? Hans Küng's words might well be placed here in the midst of the divided Christians: "Hasn't the time arrived for stopping our arguing at cross purpose?"[15]

The Council of Trent condemned the teaching of the exclusively extrinsic justification through mere imputation of Christ's merits and of the complete passivity of man under the influence of grace. And so, Reformed Christians will happily agree with Catholics that the Council of Trent did not wish to close the door to the further discussions which are taking place in a more serene atmosphere.

The Reformational movements of the sixteenth century were far from being purely Lutheran or Calvinistic. And in the heavy fog that enveloped the Catholic Church during that century it was not always possible to recognize clearly the protesting figures. Moreover, Reformed Christians know too that in the heat of the battle, even within their own camp, positions were defended whose exclusivism and rigorism they now would not wish to answer for.

Amidst that confusion the Council of Trent wished to draw some clear lines to indicate where reflection on the mystery of the gift of grace went beyond scriptural revelation. Objectively speaking, the Council has left ample scope for further discussion between Christians. Hence it is tragic with respect to reunion that those guide lines were seen by Reformed Christians as true barriers that necessitated division and that their Catholic fellow-Christians, in their exaggerated Counter-Reformation in-

15. H. Küng, *Rechtfertigung*, p. 218.

terpretation of the Council's definitions, made it far from
easy to experience them otherwise.

2. A NEW BASIS FOR DISCUSSION

Both Reformed and Catholic Christians, in discussing
the gift of grace to man, will find their common starting
point in the scriptural paradox that leaves them again
and again with unsolved questions. Faith can give an
answer to these questions but not mere human insight.

With respect to man's salvation, Scripture testifies, on
the one hand, that the redemptive initiative proceeds
wholly and continuously from God, from His everlasting
operation of grace in man. Indeed, man is totally incapable of removing himself from his situation of estrangement from God and of maintaining himself against sin.
On the other hand, Scripture does not see that rapprochement of God as a sort of mirage floating above and
beyond the reach of man, nor does it look upon grace as a
power that acts upon him from the outside moving him
to good deeds. It sees God's initiative of love in Christ as a
dynamic renewal of man and penetrating into his whole
being and all his activity.

Hence the theology concerning the operation of God's
grace must constantly strive to give equal and full attention to the primacy of God's grace and transcendent
salvific activity, on the one hand, and to the reality of
man's rebirth, his immanent self-realization, on the
other.

A. God's Sovereign Work of Grace and Christian Freedom

Both God and man take an active part in the process of
man's justification, but in such a way that man's cooperation does not endanger the sovereignty of God's work of
grace, and God's activity does not eliminate human effort
and responsibility. It is most difficult to put that mystery

within the framework of human concepts. And so, when meditating on God's salvific plan, we must avoid the twofold danger of over-emphasizing one aspect to the detriment of the other.

According to Catholic opinion, Reformed Christians lay too great a stress on God's sovereign grace and on the infinite distance between divine holiness and human sinfulness. As a result, a true inpouring of grace into human existence is impossible, and redemption takes place too much beyond man in God's exonerating judgment.

In their turn, Reformed Christians are right in accusing Catholics of thinking of grace as a created supernatural aptitude that enables man to act meritoriously and making grace an objective "thing." Reformed Christians feel that Catholics regard grace as an accumulation of divine energy in man, who then independently can operate the controls.

Both Reformed and Catholic Christians have come to recognize the one-sidedness of those century-old accusations and the dangers to their own vision and practice of faith that lay in that protest. Presently coming together in search of true faith they are ready to consider the relation between God's sovereign work of grace and human freedom. And it is against the background of the central mystery of God's creation in Christ that reflection must proceed.

When man begins to consider God's salvific work in creation, he is faced with the impenetrable mystery of the co-existence of the infinitely perfect God and the finite creature. He who is the fullness of all being and all values has created man; and to man He has given not only individual existence but also freedom of action and thought. Hence the Christian must preserve individual human existence and human freedom in creation in the presence of the divine fullness of all being and God's complete sovereignty. While maintaining God's absolute all-sufficiency of being, he may not deny the reality of the creature. Nor may he negate the activity that is proper to man for the sake of preserving God's almighty sovereignty.

The Mystery of Faith

It is precisely because a Christian fails to understand how human existence and human works can be distinguished in essence from God's being and activity that he encounters humanly insoluble problems throughout the whole field of God's revelation which he makes the subject of his believing reflection. Not through human reasoning but only through faith can he attain to a solution.

If he reasons on the basis of the human idea of independence, he has to admit that God's sovereign grace was in part excluded when man acted on his own and also that man can claim for himself part of the result of his efforts. If, on the contrary, he reasons in a human way about God's complete sovereignty and almighty power, he finds no place for human freedom. And yet faith teaches him that man has an existence of his own and that he is truly free; it teaches him also that this in no way detracts from the absolute primacy of God's grace. *For the existence of the creature lies wholly in God's creative omnipotence and the free acts of man are but the execution of God's sovereign will.*[16]

Thoughts like these cause a short-circuit in human understanding, but the Christian must learn not to con-

16. G. P. Kreling, *De weergave van het katholieke dogma, Antwoord op het Herderlijk Schrijven van de Generale Synode van de Nederlandse Hervormde Kerk betreffende de Rooms-Katholieke Kerk*, Utrecht, 1950, pp. 26-27; G. P. Kreling, "De Kerk, Oecumenica," *Stud. Cath.* vol. 31 (1956), pp. 11-13; G. Bavoud, "Les rapports de la grâce et du libre arbitre," *Verbum Caro* 56 (1960), pp. 328-338.

template God and His works in a too human way. He must come to realize that, when he faces God, all human insight falls short of the mark; he must learn to think in a new order, the order and the level of God.

Basing himself on revelation, the Christian must have the courage to think on so high a level about God's sovereign grace that he dares to speak of the creature's free activity under a God who does everything. The Christian who is aware of his freedom and responsibility does not subtract anything from the recognition of the role of grace in Christian existence; and, on the other hand, he knows that what he does in freedom, is executed only as contained in God's decision about him.

It is essential, therefore, that Christians should believe that God's omnipotence always governs everything in spite of human freedom, and that man is always responsible for his actions in spite of being predestined by God. There is room for Christian freedom and for cooperation with grace in the mystery of predestination.

B. Grace, Yet Also Merits

The tension that exists between God's sovereign activity of grace and the personal responsibility of man is given expression in Scripture in the mystery of predestination, the mystery of man's eternal election in Christ.

Predestination

Scripture leaves no doubt about the fact that man's first desire for God was not the result of human openness and effort but that it came wholly from God's purely gratuitous initative of love:

> Not all who are descended from Israel *belong to* Israel. . . . When Rebecca had conceived children by one man, our forefather Isaac, though they were not yet born and had done nothing either good or bad, in order

that God's purpose of election might continue, not be-
cause of works but because of his call, she was told,
"The elder will serve the younger." As it is written,
"Jacob I loved, but Isaac I hated."

What shall we say then? Is there injustice on God's
part? By no means! For he says to Moses, "I will have
mercy on whom I have mercy, and I will have compassion on whom I have compassion." So it depends not
upon man's will or exertion, but upon God's mercy
(Rom. 9:6-16).

The witness of Scripture shows unmistakably that the
Christian cannot earn God's grace in Christ through his
own efforts or activity. Precisely because he owes his
justification completely to God's loving mercy, the whole
redemption of man—both his Christian life on earth and
his eternal glorification in Christ—is a constant gratuitous grace given him by God through the solidarity of
God's Son with our sinful human existence.

He chose us in him before the foundation of the
world, that we should be holy and blameless before him.
He destined us in love to be his sons through Jesus
Christ, according to the purpose of his will, to the praise
of his glorious grace which he freely bestowed on us in
the Beloved. In him we have redemption through his
blood, the forgiveness of our trespasses, according to the
riches of his grace, which he lavished upon us. For he
has made known to us in all wisdom and insight the
mystery of his will, according to his purposes which he
set forth in Christ as a plan for the fulness of time, to
unite all things in him, things in heaven and things on
earth (Eph. 1:4-10).

The testimony of Scripture cannot be misunderstood:
the first beginnings and thus the whole salvific reality of
God's election in Christ find no basis whatsoever in man,
but only in God, in the free and gratuitous grace of His
redemptive plan in His First-born.

But God, who is rich in mercy, out of the great love with which he loved us, even when we were dead through our trespasses, made us alive together with Christ (by grace you have been saved), and raised us up with him, and made us sit with him in the heavenly places in Christ Jesus, that in the coming ages he might show the immeasurable riches of his grace in kindness toward us in Christ Jesus. For by grace you have been saved through faith; and this is not your own doing, it is the gift of God—not because of works, lest any man should boast (Eph. 2:4-9).

Indeed "when the goodness and loving kindness of God our Saviour appeared, he saved us, not because of deeds done by us in righteousness, but in virtue of his own mercy, by the washing of regeneration and renewal in the Holy Spirit" (Tit. 3:4-5). It is not man who searches for God in this world, but the Father who seeks us in Christ. Our budding love for God "was not in . . . wisdom, but in demonstration of the Spirit and power, that your faith might not rest in the wisdom of men but in the power of God" (1 Cor. 2:5).

Man's Responsibility

Scripture leaves no doubt, either, that God lays responsibility upon man as to the grace given him in Christ and that He gives man His glorification because of man's merits. Good works, *performed in grace,* lend to human existence a likeness to Christ so that his being taken up into the glory of the ascended Lord comes to man as a gift to which he has a "right." "We are children of God, and if children, then heirs, heirs of God and fellow heirs with Christ, provided we suffer with him in order that we may also be glorified with Him" (Rom. 8:17).

The idea that the man who, in Christ, has been given grace, must earn his eternal salvation by works done through grace, is the idea of reward to which Scripture constantly bears witness.[17] Let us give a few examples.

> Blessed are you when men revile you and persecute you and utter all kinds of evil against you falsely on my account. Rejoice and be glad for your reward is great in heaven (Mt. 5:11-12).

> And St. Peter said: "Lo, we have left everything and followed you. What then shall we have?" Jesus said to them, "Truly, I say to you, in the new world, when the Son of man shall sit on his glorious throne, you who have followed me will also sit on twelve thrones, judging the twelve tribes of Israel. And every one who has left houses or brothers or sisters or father or mother or children or lands, for my name's sake, will receive a hundredfold, and inherit eternal life. But many that are first will be last, and the last first" (Mt. 19:27-30).

> Well done, good and faithful servant; you have been faithful over a little, I will set you over much; enter into the joy of your master (Mt. 25:23).

> Each shall receive his wages according to his labor. For we are fellow workers for God (1 Cor. 3:8-9).

> For we must all appear before the judgment seat of Christ, so that each one may receive good or evil, according to what he has done in the body (2 Cor. 5:10).

> He considered abuse suffered for the Christ greater wealth than the treasures of Egypt, for he looked to the reward (Heb. 11:26).

> Behold, I am coming soon, bringing my recompense, to repay every one for what he has done (Rev. 22:12).

Because of the complex teaching of Scripture—that man's actions owe everything to God's power of grace

17. M. F. Berrouard, "Le mérite dans les Evangiles synopti-ques," *Istina*, vol. 3 (1956), pp. 191-209; "Le mérite dans les Epîtres de Saint Paul," *Istina*, vol. 3 (1956), pp. 313-332.

and yet have merit—the Christian must recognize both God's sovereign activity of grace and man's free cooperation and personal responsibility, under God's action, for his glorification in Christ. This he will receive as a reward for the way he has lived his earthly life. God is so exalted above mankind, so totally different from man, that man's efforts cannot possibly lessen His omnipotence.

God Rewards His Own Gifts

Christians accept with faith the humanly inscrutable mystery that God gives man grace to enable him to merit. And thus God rewards His own gift. He rewards what He initially gives to the man whom He makes fully responsible for the gift. This idea contained in Scripture finds an echo in the teaching of the Council of Trent: "It will never occur to a Christian to place his confidence or pride in himself and not in the Lord, whose goodness to men is so great that He desires His own gifts to them to be their merits."[18] But already long before, in 529 A.D., the Council of Orange had defined this Catholic teaching: "As often as we do good, God works in us and with us that we do that good."[19]

Here man faces the spiritual paradox of Christian existence: "Apart from me you can do nothing" and "I can do all things in him who strengthens me" (Jn 15:4; Phil. 4:13). We have the same paradox in these other words of St. Paul: "Work out your own salvation with fear and trembling; for God is at work in you, both to will and to work for his good pleasure" (Phil. 2:12-13).

18. "Absit tamen, ut christianus homo in se ipso vel confidit vel glorietur et non in Domino (1 Cor. 1, 31), cujus tanta est erga omnes homines bonitas, ut eorum velit esse merita, quae sunt ipsius dona." Denziger, no. 810.

19. "Quoties enim bona agimus, Deus in nobis atque nobiscum, ut operemur, operatur." Denziger, no. 182.

Very illustrative of God's sovereign act of predestination coupled with human responsibility are Christ's words on judgment day:

> When the Son of man comes in his glory, and all the angels with him, then he will sit on his glorious throne . . . the King will say to those at his right hand, "Come, O blessed of my Father, inherit the kingdom *prepared for you from the foundation of the world;* for I was hungry and you gave me food." . . . Then the righteous will answer him, "Lord, when did we see thee hungry and feed thee?" . . . And the King will answer them, "Truly, I say to you, as you did it to one of the least of these my brethren, you did it to me." Then he will say to those at his left hand, "Depart from me, you cursed, into the eternal fire *prepared* for the devil and his angels; for I was hungry and you gave me no food." . . . Then they also will answer, "Lord, when did we see thee hungry or thirsty . . . and did not minister to thee?" Then he will answer them, "Truly, I say to you, as you did it not to one of the least of these, you did it not to me." And they will go away into eternal punishment, but the righteous into eternal life (Mt. 25:31-46).

This shows that the decision with respect to man's eternal destiny depends on his concrete actions that translate his personal responsibility for the graces he has received.

New Reflections on Predestination

Of ecumenical importance is what was written by the General Synod and presented to the Dutch Reformed Church as a new reflection upon the Scriptural teaching regarding predestination. On the basis of Scripture, the two aspects of that mystery, namely, God's sovereign act of grace in Christ and human responsibility, are given equal attention, and there is no stress on an antinomy.

On the one hand, this document proposes the following:

If we profess that we live by election, we are saying two things: first, something that is humiliating, namely, that our salvation is not due, even in the slightest degree, to our initiative or power, but depends entirely on God's gratuitous approach to us; secondly, something that is comforting, namely, that our salvation is unshakeably established, since it does not depend on anything in us but only and alone on God's fidelity. Whoever plumbs the depths of the word "grace" will confess our election. For God's grace is in no way a force that supports and supplements our power. Nor is it an act of redemption whose follow-up and working-out is left to us. It is God's free, personal favor that turns toward creatures who, without Him, would be irretrievably lost through their own guilt. Grace is not called up by our desire, sorrow and conversion. Hence whoever gives himself to Christ praises not himself but the Spirit of God alone. To have faith implies indeed that we renounce ourselves and ascribe nothing to ourselves, not even our faith; but we attribute all to Him who works in us to desire and to act.

On the other hand, the Declaration confesses emphatically:

When we thus give man no credit for generating faith this does not mean at all that man is reduced to an instrument in the hands of Almighty God that has no will of its own. The contrary is true. For God and man are not rivals so that the work of one detracts from that of the other. Just as He created us enabling us to live and act beside, with and under Him, so does He recreate us in His grace of election that we might be able to believe and be converted and confirm our election in a life of active love.

And this Declaration also invokes a passage from the *Doctrinal Rules* of Dordrecht that ought to receive more attention and appreciation:

Just as man remained man after the Fall and was still gifted with understanding and will; just as sin, which permeated the whole human race did not take away human nature—though it did corrupt it and kill it in a spiritual sense—so the divine grace of man's rebirth does not work outside of man; it does not destroy his will and attributes, not does it compel these, but it makes him spiritually alive, makes him whole, improves him and changes him both in love and firmness. Where once the rebelliousness and hostility of the flesh reigned supreme, there a new willing and upright obedience begin to rule, and in this lies the real, spiritual recovery of our will.[20]

Contrary to Calvin's doctrine concerning predestination, that was chiefly based on Romans 9:11-23, and in which he taught that God had decreed from eternity to choose a great number of men for eternal rejection, the Declaration of the Synod points out that the Dutch Confession and Doctrine of Dordrecht "has no desire to accept that there is a rejection that precedes guilt but it accepts a rejection only because of guilt."[21]

In this way the Reformational reflection joins hands with the renewed tendency in Catholic theology which strives to free the mystery of predestination from a purely causal relationship and sees it rather as a relationship between persons. In a causal relationship the effect is contained in the cause whereas in a relationship between the persons the response of "yes" or "no" is never contained in the invitation. In fact this invitation presupposes the possibility of either a "yes" or a "no," of a positive or a negative response.

20. *De uitverkiezing, Richtlijnen voor de behandeling van de leer der uitverkiezing, aanvaard door de Generale Synode der Nederlandse Hervormde Kerk,* 's Gravenhage, 1961, pp. 13, 19-20. Cf. *De belijdenisgeschriften van de Nederlandse Hervormde Kerk,* 's Gravenhage, 1957, pp. 140-141.
21. *De uitverkiezing,* pp. 35-41.

God's all-sufficient grace of election does not descend upon man as an overriding act, but as an invitation in a personal meeting. If man accepts the invitation, Christ can live in him His glorified life with the Father. If man refuses the invitation, he shuts himself off in deadly loneliness and God's love in Christ becomes for him truly his ultimate punishment, even a bodily punishment. "Thus this same predestination, this same invitation, this same love of the Father, is heaven for one and hell for another. God's election not only makes heaven a heaven but also makes hell a hell. Even in hell God perseveres in His constancy and fidelity, and clings to His decree."[22]

C. Merit as Sharing in Christ's Glory

Is There Still Room for Self-praise?

At this stage of the discussion, Reformed Christians will be quite ready to endorse the Catholic's appeal to the Scriptures and yet they will be prompted to hold on to their opinion that the Catholic teaching about the merits of human actions distorts the relationship between God's sovereign dispensation of grace and the impotent sinfulness of man. It is true that the Catholic view recognizes that it is only through grace that man can bear responsibility for his actions, and that it defends the priority of grace, but Reformed Christians cannot escape the impression that here the man who receives grace endeavors to maintain himself over against God.

Reformed Christians are keenly aware of the short-circuiting in the Catholic distortion of the mystery of grace. Their objection is directed against the statement that a man who has received grace can claim eternal salvation as a "right" that is due to him. God, in His mercy, pledges Himself to man, giving him the reward of his works; and

22. L. Smits, "De praedestinatie in ruimer perspectief," *Jaarb. Kath. Theologie in Ned.*, 1960, pp. 14, 20-22.

here too much room is left for man to praise himself, to praise his own cooperation with grace:

> The question arises—and it is to the point—whether the emphasis on the glory of God and on the overruling grace is a true answer to the contention of the Reformation, a contention that cannot be silenced. . . . There is only *one* criterion for testing the teaching about merit as to the question whether it is or is not in conformity with Scripture and that is, as the context of the whole Redemption clearly shows, that all that implies self-praise and pretentiousness, everything that resembles the praise St. Paul fought against, is *excluded*. Harnack once spoke very critically and ironically about "the mantle of religion wrapped around a merit that is offensive to religion."[23]

Ecumenical discussion about the relationship between grace and merit, especially since the publication of Hans Küng's *Justification: The Teaching of Karl Barth and a Catholic Reflection* has resulted in drawing divided Christians closer together. And yet, in spite of this better understanding of each other's views, it looks as if the expected agreement of Christians regarding that point has once more been prevented by insurmountable obstacles. This impasse will make the divided Christians believe that the debate about grace and merit will remain pointless, an endlessly repeated antinomy, as long as we go on talking about this mystery in abstract terms.

Would not an entirely new perspective be opened if that problem were placed in the light of the mystery of Christ in whom God's grace appeared to us in concrete human form; and if the relationship of grace to merit were seen as a particular case of the one central redemp-

23. G. C. Berkouwer, *Verdienste of genade?*, p. 37, Cf. P. Kreling, "Verdienste als genade," *Jaarb. kath. theol. in Ned.*, 1959, pp. 110-123.

tive mystery of Christianity, namely, God's redemptive coming and salvific activity with man in the Man Jesus Christ?

The Transcendent Relationship Between the Divine and the Human Modes of Existence in Jesus Christ

Christ is not "both God and man" but He is "God sharing our humanity." This view of the mystery of the incarnation of God's Son clearly illustrates that the distortion of the Christ mystery which lies at the basis of the controversy between grace and merit is the same which underlied the Christological errors in early Christian times, such as Arianism, Nestorianism, Monophysitism, Monotheletism, which put the human person on the same level as the divine Person. This disregard of God's total transcendency with respect to man inevitably leads to inadequacies when one reflects upon the faith, both as regards the Christ and as regards man receiving grace in Christ.

The dilemma seems inevitable: either God forces man or man becomes God's rival. The first horn would mean the end of human freedom and human responsibility for salvation. The second can stem only from a much too human view regarding God's sovereignty and must lead to a distortion of the redemptive significance that the mystery of the incarnation of God's Son has for us, and of the grace given to us in Christ.

Confronted by this dilemma, which in the ancient Church led to opposite heresies, the Council of Chalcedon declared that Christ lives "in two natures" and that those two natures are, on the one hand, "unmixed and unchanged" because of God's transcendence, and, on the other hand are "undivided and inseparable" because of the unity of Person in the Word.

This declaration may sound too technical to our modern

ears but the Council wished to proclaim that Christ is truly God and truly man and yet is a perfect unity because His human existence is wholly contained in His transcendent divine Person. That God and man are not on the same metaphysical plane does not mean that Christ is less man than we are. The mystery that Christ continuously includes His human mode of existence, with its full dignity, in the unity of His divine Person can be explained only on the basis of *God's complete transcendence with respect to man.* On the one hand, He is God in a truly human manner; on the other hand, He is even more *man* than we are, for He is man in a truly divine manner.

This division of faith about the two modes of existence of the Son of the Father, the divine and the human, in their full dignity, the Council of Chalcedon has summed up in the words: "The difference between the natures is in no way cancelled by the unity of the Person; rather the peculiar character of each nature is retained" (Denziger, no. 148).

The same transcendent relationship is present in Christ between His divine and His human will. His human act of the will does not compete with His divine will. His divine will does not determine and force His human will. However, because of the total, divine transcendence, the Son of the Father is able to realize Himself immanently in the human mode of existence. His divine knowledge, His will and love are incarnated and actualized in the man Jesus Christ, so that the acts of the will of His divine and His human modes of existence are "undivided, unchanged, inseparable and unmixed" (Denziger, no. 291). This is why He was able to "increase in wisdom and in stature, and in favor with God and man" (Lke 2:52), and why, "although he was a Son, he learned obedience through what he suffered; and being made perfect he became the source of eternal salvation to all who obey him" (Heb. 5:8-9).

God's Transcendence and Immanence

The mystery of Christ as "God who shares our humanity" is the pattern of God's bestowal of grace upon us in Christ. Hence it is the Incarnation that Christians must regard as the theological norm of the relationship between God and man. In Christ it is made clear to us not only that God's transcendent activity and our human freedom go hand in hand, but more especially that man, through God's activity of grace, can be *more* himself and can reach the highest experience of freedom.

The Son lives His being-together with-the-Father, as man, in accomplishing the Father's will, and in this complete obedience He can develop and perfect His human existence. This goes to show that God does not approach man from outside adding power to man's efforts, for this would mean taking away from man's freedom. But God, working from within enables man to be himself, to fulfill his being that is created for conformity with Christ.

Because God does not "first" create man and "after that" make a Covenant with him, but actualizes the Covenant with man by creating him, God, in His absolute transcendence, enables man to be a person; He enables him to act freely and freely realize himself. Man *is* because God wants him as a partner in a Covenant who freely responds to Him. Man exists in virtue of being continuously created by God and totally influenced by God's transcendent power; he is a conditional being, completely contained in God's creative activity.

God unceasingly gives existence to the world and to man and both constantly hover on the brink of non-existence. God, then, is absolutely transcendent and the absolute sovereign of all that exists outside Him; but His love, at the same time, is the creative power of all reality and of all the activity of His creatures; He is *immanent in all*. And precisely because He transcends *all*, He can also be immanent *in all*. He is the whole ground of all in all.

It follows that God's creative act is transcendent in its causality but immanent in its consummation. God makes His creature, man, exist in accordance with man's nature and activity, that is, in accordance with his being conformed to Christ. God and man are not partners in the Covenant who enjoy *equal dignity*, but God, at the same time, wants man as a partner in the Covenant in man's own *full dignity*. God desires man as a person who can actualize the perpetual bestowal of existence upon him in freedom and with personal responsibility through encountering Christ in word and sacrament.

The Encounter with Christ as a Source of Salvation for All Men

Scripture greatly stresses the fact that Christ, through the Holy Spirit, lived His identity as the Son in loving relationship with the Father in a truly human fashion, because it is here that we see the redemptive significance of the Christ mystery. "Unless a grain of wheat falls into the earth and dies, it remains alone; but if it dies, it bears much fruit" (Jn 12:24). By fulfilling Himself as man in perfectly free obedience, Christ could become the Emmanuel, "God with us," our truly human togetherness with God. "No one has ever seen God; the only Son, who is in the bosom of the Father, he has made him known" (Jn 1:18).

Christ is the Father's countenance turned toward us. Not only is He the manifestation of God's redemptive love for us, but He has also actualized this love for us through His incarnation. "God so loved the world that He gave his only Son, that whoever believes in Him should not perish but have eternal life" (Jn 3:16). The complete redemptive significance of His incarnation is summed up in the words: "It was fitting that he, for whom and by whom all things exist, in bringing many sons to glory, should make the pioneer of their salvation perfect through suffering" (Heb. 2:10). "And being made perfect he became the source of eternal salvation to all who obey him" (Heb. 5:9-10).

Christ's obedience in true fellowship with men is the glorification of the Father for our sake. It is the consecration of His human existence as a universal source of redemption for all men. "It is to your advantage that I go away, for if I do not go away (that is, through His death in perfect obedience), the Counselor will not come to you, but if I go, I will send him to you. . . . He will guide you into all the truth" (Jn 16:7-13). In His glorification by the Father, "designated Son of God in power" (Rom. 1:4), He is the Covenant between God and man brought to perfection, thus representing all men before the Father, encompassing the whole world throughout all ages in His redemption.

The full redemptive significance of the mystery of the incarnation of God's Son can be expressed in these words: Christ became man in order that through living His transcendent divine life in a human life, He might raise up our earthly human existence, enabling us to have a living experience of the divine love which the Father has for us in Christ. His words, "the Son of man ascending where he was before" (Jn 6:62) are charged with redemptive meaning for men of all times. For "the glory which thou hast given me I have given to them" (Jn 17:22).

The Christian Lives by Virtue of Christ's Glory

The biblical reflection upon the mystery of the Incarnation compels divided Christians to ask themselves once more the following question: What exactly do we mean by saying that Christ earned grace for us? Have we not become entangled in juridical and dogmatic terms that touch only the surface of the redemptive event and fail to penetrate into the depths of the existential solidarity of God's Son with our sinful humanity? And hasn't this been the reason for our hopeless confusion whenever, in our debate, we wished to explain to each other the relationship between grace and merit?

In human relations there is only an extrinsic proportion between work and reward, which is based upon right or upon kindness. The nature of the reward is not determined by the work but is arbitrary; one could decide upon any kind of reward. The merits of Christ's work of redemption are not properly valued if we see them only as the outward reward for His sufferings and death, the reward being that the Father lovingly accepts us again as His children. The often heard Catholic statement that Christ, through His obedience to the Father, gave satisfaction for our sins and thus reconciled us with the Father, expresses the relation between His work of redemption and His merits for us in a superficial way. Although this aspect is found in Scripture, the actual biblical vision goes farther.

Reformed Christians, too, remain certainly within the bounds of Scripture when they regard redemption as a state of justification in a juridical sense, namely, that the Father has accepted the obedience of Christ and accredited it also to us: "Blessed are those whose iniquities are forgiven and whose sins are covered; blessed is the man against whom the Lord will not reckon his sin" (Rom. 4:7-8; Ps. 32:1-2). Through faith, the merits of Christ are "reckoned to him as righteousness" and are so reckoned to us (Rom. 4:22). The witness of Scripture, however, does not stop at assuring us of our being ac-

credited with the merits of Christ, and thus being enabled
to live as redeemed. It also reveals the depth and ground
of this state of justification in Christ.

Christ has truly earned grace for us because, in solidarity with sinful mankind, He bent our rebellious wills
back to the Father through his human life of obedience.
Being the representative of sinful man He fulfilled His
Father's will, realized the divine plan of creation with us
human beings, a plan we had frustrated by our sinful
refusal. Taking our place, Christ struggled with our rebellious wills in His passion and death: "Not as I will, but
as thou wilt" (Mt. 26:39). He desired to "partake" (Heb.
2:14) of our sinful human existence in order to guide it
back to obedience towards the Father. For our sake "He
learned obedience through what he suffered; and being
made perfect he became a source of eternal salvation to
all who obey him" (Heb. 5:8-9). Wishing to live our
God-abandoned human existence as His own mode of
existence, He is existentially involved in our redemption
and has indeed taken us up with Him in the glorification
of His humanity.

Divided Christians, when reconsidering the relationship between grace and merit, will be able to meet and
find a common ground in the full message of Scripture
which proclaims that Christ earned grace for us by as-
suming our humanity into His glory through utter
human obedience to the Father. *There exists an internal
relationship between grace and merit because His merit
is precisely the action of grace in our humanity, that is,
our sharing in His glorification.*

Merit is not like an uncashed cheque for an eternal
reward. It must be fully experienced in a personal relationship between the glorified Lord and the man of faith.
Even on this earth, through the work of the grace-giving
Holy Spirit in word and sacrament, the Christian con-

stantly meets the glorified Lord so that he can adjust his daily life ever more perfectly to the ideals, thoughts and desires that governed Christ's human life. This personal relationship with the glorified Lord has, even on earth, a certain continuity through the constant activity of God's Spirit. Merit is, then, the personal aspect of our being-Christian. It makes us who are now on earth grow in likeness to the glorified Lord, though a perfect likeness is clearly an eschatological reality.

Indeed this inner adjustment tends with the dynamic force of faith and hope towards the complete flowering of love and perfect union with the glorified Lord. The encounter with Christ on earth is governed by the certain knowledge that He will re-creatively intervene in our human existence, and that we, by virtue of the resurrection, will be conformed, even in our bodily condition, into His likeness in the glorification by the Father. Thus merit is the raising of our human existence through the Self-communication of the glorified Lord, here on earth; it is still in the darkness of our faith but eventually will attain a full flowering of God's salvific design for us in the First-born.

3. ECUMENICAL CORRECTION ON THE CHRISTIAN'S REFLECTION UPON FAITH

A. *Justitia Aliena* (*Justification by Someone Else*)

The Reformational Teaching of "Alien Justification"

Is there no possibility here for ecumenically integrating that aspect of Christian revelation which the Reformation has rather too strongly emphasized in its teaching of *justitia aliena*? The Christian cannot orient himself to God by his own efforts. Through sin, he has divorced his human thought and will, and especially his love, from a true encounter with God. His human life is imprisoned in his own norms and ideals. Even where God appears on the horizon of his thoughts, man takes God into his service; he wants to use God as a means for his own advancement. In his sinful situation where everything is distorted to fit mans self-centeredness, he makes an idol out of God.

In Christ, God Himself broke into that encapsulated human existence. Christ's sorrowful road to Golgotha has given our human existence an inner orientation and receptivity to the Father. The Christian lives by virtue of our human existence in Christ, by virtue of the justice of someone else, of Christ. He is keenly aware that he cannot put forward his own justification as a work deserving a reward. All he can do is, in wonderment, offer to the Father an "alien justification," the glory of the Man Jesus Christ, who sits at the right hand of the Father and is our only Mediator.

Merit then is not a cheque that holds out a prospect of eternal salvation as a reward for man's works, and so gives a false feeling of security. Even when we stress that God gives us grace to enable us to have merits, and that we experience our merits as grace, the full salvific perspective of merit is not made sufficiently clear. The biblical view of merit is that we can share Christ's glory even here on earth, and that this is possible through His solidarity with our human existence, that is, through grace. Good works are the expression of our being-redeemed in Jesus Christ. These good works provide us with the merit that, already in this life, we are more intimately united with the glorified Man Jesus Christ and conform ever more closely to Him.

Our conformity with Christ, this elevation of our human nature, remains as yet hidden in the eschatological darkness of our faith. "See what love the Father has given us, that we should be called children of God; and so we are. The reason why the world does not know us is that it did not know him. Beloved, we are God's children now; it does not yet appear what we shall be, but we know that when he appears we shall be like him" (1 Jn 3:1-2).

The good works which are the manifest expression of our being blessed with grace in Him, who is the prototype of our humanity, give us, even on earth, the reward of conforming ever more to Him. Our Christian life on earth consists in becoming aware of what we already are in Christ, that is, living as He did, on earth, in complete obedience to His Father. Our eternal happiness will consist in sharing forever, consciously and tangibly, the fullness of the glorification of His humanity, eternally "conforming to Him."

Is it not possible, in that perspective, to interpret the Reformational teaching of "alien justification" in a way that all Christians can accept?

B. Simul Justus et Peccator (Both Just and Sinner)

This view of the relationship between grace and merit removes all possible grounds for a Christian's self-praise and boast on account of his own efforts and actions. In the light of revelation in Scripture he sees so clearly the ideal of humanity that he experiences his Christian mode of existence as a dynamic tension, summed up in Scripture in the words: "where sin increased, grace abounded all the more" (Rom. 5:20).[24]

The very subject of the justification of a sinner has produced a babel of confusion among the divided Christians; it was caused by the never-ending mutual misunderstanding regarding the declarations of the Council of Trent. The Council defined that man can dispose himself for the reception of grace (Denziger, nos. 817, 819), and Catholic theology teaches that man can earn grace as

24. H. Schlier, *Die Zeit der Kirche*, Freiburg, 1958, p. 47.

merited "de congruo" (as something that is fitting and fair); but such declarations in no way negate the permanent and complete impotence of human sinfulness.[25]

The Council of Trent dealt with the grace of man's justification, which comes from the purely gratuitous initiative of the Father who sent His Son into our sinful human situation to restore His creative plan. On the evidence of the actual process of a sinner's conversion, the Council underlines the fact that the gift of complete justification in Christ does not come to a person by surprise, but that he may and can prepare himself to receive this grace.

Catholics have often quoted that declaration in order to support their contention that man must cooperate with grace, whereas Reformed Christians have made use of those words to back up their reproach that the Catholic teaching about good works infringes upon the exclusiveness of grace (the *sola gratia*) in all human activity. It is clear that for the sake of reunion we must ask ourselves why we oppose each other so bitterly.

The Council of Trent, in insisting that we need to prepare ourselves for grace, is referring to the grace of our *complete* justification in Christ. The Council does not deny, however, that the preparatory acts of contrition and desire, which fit us for the complete awareness of our blessing in Christ, are also generated by grace, by the inviting power of the word He unconditionally speaks to us in our desperate sinful situation. On the contrary, the Council explicitly declares: "We say, therefore, that man is justified unconditionally, because nothing that precedes justification, be it faith or good works, can earn this grace of justification. For the Apostle says, 'and if it

25. Berkouwer, *Verdienste of genade?*, Kampen, 1958, pp. 38-49.

is due to grace, then it is not due to good works; if it were, grace would be no grace at all' (Rom. 11:6)."[26]

The Council looks upon the subjective justification of man and his entry into salvation as a developing process. At every stage of this development God's "prevenient" bounty of grace is the fundamental structure, but also at every stage this grace effects man's free cooperation. In fact the Council merely repeats what the Council of Orange had declared: "No merit precedes grace. If we do good works we are rewarded. But unconditional grace must come first before we can accomplish those works."[27]

Faced with this evidently biblical view regarding the justification of the sinner, Catholics must admit that, because of their Counter-Reformation attitude, they have often looked upon grace and human cooperation as two, more or less independent, forces working in juxtaposition. Reformed Christians, on their part, will realize that in their desire to safeguard the thesis of *sola gratia* they have created an untenable contrast.

When man receives grace, the point is that God's inviting grace works *in* our human efforts and these must flower into the consciousness of our co-glorification in Christ.

That is why it is in contradiction with the intention of the Council of Trent to separate its concept of man's capabilities from grace, without which man is caught in the slavery of sin. The Council considers human nature

26. "Gratia autem justificari ideo dicamur, quia nihil eorum quae justificationem praecedunt, sive fides, sive opera, ipsam justificationis gratiam promeretur; si enim gratia est, jam non ex operibus; alioquin (ut idem Apostolus inquit) gratia jam non est gratia." Denziger, no. 801. Cf. no. 797.

27. "Nullis meritis gratiam praeveniri. Debetur merces bonis operibus. si fiant; sed gratia, quae non debetur, praecedit, ut fiant." Denziger, no. 191; cf. no. 200.

only insofar as it is an element of the justified man and
of the man who prepares himself, empowered by grace,
for his justification. In other words, human nature is
distinguished from grace but never separated from it.
The achievements of human nature are, in fact, seen as
belonging not only to the natural order, but as being
completely supported and inspired by grace without
which man is incapable of any good work toward his
salvation.[28]

Both Just and a Sinner

The Reformational thesis "both just and a sinner" may
then be integrated in Catholic thinking. The light God's
word has cast upon man's situation enables Christians to
see that they owe the continuation of their existence
after sin solely to God's saving grace. God has wished to
give man a chance in Christ; He has created man's receptivity to His word. In Christ He has held back the power
of sin that threatens human existence with destruction.
On the brink of his downfall, the necessary consequence
of sin, man is constantly supported by God who still sees
in him the possibility of realizing His redemptive design
in the First-born.

How real is man's sinfulness in spite of his grace
through Christ! Even Catholics will not find it difficult to
discern the idea of "both just and a sinner," in Saint
Paul's words:

Not that I have already obtained this or am already
perfect, but I press on to make it my own, because
Christ Jesus has made me his own. Brethren, I do not
consider that I have made it my own; but one thing I do,
forgetting what lies behind and straining forward to
what lies ahead, I press on toward the goal for the prize

28. J. G. Groot, "Verdiensten of genade?" *Het Schild*, vol. 36
(1959), p. 88; cf. P. Schoonenberg, "De genade en de zedelijk
goede act," *Jaarboek Kath. Theol. in Nederland*, 1950, pp. 203-253.

of the upward call of God in Christ Jesus (Phil. 3:12-14).

C. *Sola Gratia*

Grace and Created Grace

The contemplation of man's blessing in Jesus Christ, the prototype of our humanity, has prompted Catholic theology to formulate the teaching of created grace (*gratia habitualis*).

God cannot work anew in sinful man through Christ without seizing man in the depth of his being and without realizing in him the original design of His salvation. He renews and changes man: "Therefore, if any one is in Christ he is a new creation; the old has passed away, behold the new has come. All this is from God, who through Christ reconciled us to himself and gave us the ministry of reconciliation" (2 Cor. 5:17-18).

Because, in justification, man receives an unearned gift in Christ, Catholic theology speaks of "grace." However, because it is *man* who, through this grace, goes on to perform deeds that he was not able to perform before his meeting with God, Catholic theology speaks of "created grace." This habitual state of grace may not be separated, but should be distinguished, from God's power. This is why God places full responsibility on man for the life he lives by virtue of this gift.

Catholic theology, realizing that it is standing on slippery ground, stresses again and again that created grace may not be regarded as a gift which is at the free disposal of man and by which he would be enabled to act autonomously. Catholics know that their gift of grace in Christ is a continuously operative gift of God and that their attitude toward Him must be one of permanent asking, always prepared to receive.

In spite of this repeated emphatic acknowledgment, Catholic theology has not been able to avoid hearing the equally frequent reproach of the Reformation, namely, that the Catholic view objectifies grace making it a "thing." Reformed Christians can find no grounds in Scripture for man's elevation to the supernatural:

> Neither in the Gospels, nor in the Acts of the Apostles, let alone in the Old Testament, do we find situations or actions in which this boundary (between heaven and earth) is smoothed over, though of course heavenly gifts are poured out. Anyone who has read how St. Paul as it were tempers the use of spiritual gifts and humbles himself, will know that he does not regard grace as a means of raising up nature. The Bible is the book of God's incarnation, not of man's deification.[29]

The Reformed Christians also refuse to accept this habitual state of grace (*gratia habitualis*) as an elevation of human nature because it would endanger the reality of Christ's becoming *Man*, and because it is in contradiction with the Scriptural witness to the Christ who went His way to the Father in uncertainty, struggle, fear and temptation.

Catholics Suspected of Pantheism

At this point we must repeat the question that was raised above: What impression do Reformed Christians get when they hear Catholics speak of the deification of human nature, of the elevation of man to the supernatural order? Do they not accuse Catholics, in thought if not in words, of some form of pantheism? This matter must be brought into the open once more because this unspo-

29. O. Noordmans, *Natuur en genade bij Rome*, The Hague, 1949, p. 3; cf. A. A. Van Ruler, *Achtergronden van het Herderlijk schrijven*, Wageningen, 1955, pp. 21-24.

ken and often half-conscious thought gives rise to an aversion to the Catholic view of man's reception of grace; it poisons the discussion and makes understanding each other extremely difficult, even if both sides make use of the same terms.

The rather flexible language of Catholic theology and especially of Catholic devotion does not make it easy for Reformed Christians to ban this suspicion of pantheism from their thoughts. And yet, for the sake of our ecumenical rapprochement, we Catholics may ask them to reconsider their understanding of the faith witnessed by their Catholic fellow-Christians, on the basis of the unassailable truth that Catholics, too, fully respect the creatural limits of man and the infinite distance between him and God.

Man is raised to the supernatural state by the grace of God, insofar as he receives capabilities and powers that he in no way owes to himself. These divine gifts are chiefly faith, hope, and love, which show him the reality of the world in the light of God's redemptive design in Christ; which teach him to live in a dynamic expectancy of the complete integration of the Kingdom of God into his own life and into all human relationships; which enable him to love his fellow-men and all earthly values that God loves, in the way God loves them.

And yet man remains man! His deification remains within the bounds of his created reality. "Let all agree on this . . . we reject every kind of mystic union by which the faithful would in any way pass beyond the sphere of creatures and rashly enter the Divine, even to the extent of one single attribute of the eternal Godhead being predicated of them as their own."[30] Through grace man transcends all that God has created, and he is raised up by

30. Enc. *Mystici Corporis;* Tr. *The Mystical Body of Christ,* America Press, New York, 1943, p. 35, par. 94.

God above his own human capabilities but still within
creature limits.

Grace Gives Man a New Mode of Human Existence with Christ

Although Christians must respect their infinite
distance from God and His definite "otherness," they
know that by the redemptive event of the Incarnation,
the relationship between God and man is not purely a
relation of the Creator to His creature. "The Word became flesh and dwelt among us" (Jn 1:14). This redemptive fact is concerned with the presence of God's Son in
our human existence, a *human* way of living His divine
life for our sake. "Abide in me, and I in you" (Jn 15:4).

By the Incarnation God's presence is a human presence. No room is left for an abstract presence of God. He
is present in the man of faith and in His Church:

> You are not in the flesh, you are in the Spirit, if the
> Spirit of God really dwells in you. Any one who does not
> have the Spirit of Christ does not belong to him. But if
> Christ is in you, although your bodies are dead because
> of sin, your spirits are alive because of righteousness. If
> the Spirit of him who raised Jesus from the dead dwells
> in you, he who raised Christ Jesus from the dead will
> give life to your mortal bodies also through His Spirit
> which dwells in you (Rom. 8:9-11).

Hence by receiving grace through Christ we receive a
new mode of *human* existence, which consists in living
our human life in the same way He lived as man here on
earth. We live having this mind among ourselves which
we have in Christ Jesus (cf. Phil. 2:5) and let our lives
be directed remembering "we have the mind of Christ" (1
Cor. 2:16). For "their sake I consecrate myself, that they
also may be consecrated in truth" (Jn 17: 19).

Just as a statue is a human expression in stone and as

the artist humanizes lifeless nature by conveying through it the experience of his human existence, so is our human nature deified because Christ has, in this human nature, expressed His being Son of the Father, and because He wishes to express in us His glorified human existence with the Father, albeit in the eschatological distress of our earthly situation. "And we all, with unveiled face, beholding the glory of the Lord, are being changed into his likeness from one degree of glory to another; for this comes from the Lord who is the Spirit" (2 Cor. 3:18).

Clearing the Way for Reunion

Wouldn't Catholics clear the way for reunion if they spoke more distinctly and with greater care about created grace? As a result of the Counter-Reformation attitude, theology has paid excessive and almost exclusive attention to this aspect of God's salvific activity in Christ. In Catholic preaching we are told that in Christ man lives "in a state of grace" as long as he does not turn away from Him through sin. This must give the Reformed Christians the impression that, in Catholic thought, grace once received becomes an autonomous entity in man and that man can live in grace without experiencing it as a continual personal encounter with Christ.

The old Catechism was, no doubt, one-sided when in answer to the question "What do we mean by grace" it said no more than this: "By grace we mean supernatural gifts that are given us to enable us to attain salvation."[31] The Reformed Christians are justified when they look upon that one-sided approach of the created effect of God's salvific acts in Christ as an "objectification" of grace. Indeed, God's *work of our salvation in Christ is*

---

31. *Katechismus of Christelijke Leer ten gebruike van de Nederlandse Bisdommen,* Utrecht, 1948, Q. 205.

concerned not with our possession of grace but with His
bestowal of it.

Christians live only by God's grace in Christ, by the
constant operative presence of the glorified Lord through
the salvific power of His speech to us in the preaching of
the word and of His actions and active presence in the
administration of the sacraments. By virtue of this constant outpouring of grace through word and sacrament
Christians meet Christ in a personal way.

Just as His being loved by the Father meant, for the
Man Jesus Christ, His sanctification by the Spirit, so
man's sanctification is implied in his personal relation to
Christ's Self-communication. Man's sanctification is a
created but not autonomous reality, since it is the created
expression of his being constantly blessed through
Christ's grace.

We should, therefore, do away with any suggestion of
a physical change where man's sanctification is concerned. We can find a feeble image of the real change
that takes place in our lives through the love the Father
bears toward us in Christ, in some human relations, for
instance, in the situation of being loved in marriage. For
truly, in our encounter with Christ, the First-born of
creation reveals and communicates His Person; He
"learned obedience through what he suffered; and being
made perfect he became the source of eternal salvation
to all who obey him" (Heb. 5:8-9).

In that subjective relation, "Christ, the first fruits of
those who have fallen asleep" (1 Cor. 15:20), works out
in us the salvific effect of His obedient life, that He sacrificed for us. The great eucharistic prayer of the Church
sums up the mystery of our personal encounter with the
glorified Lord in these monumental words: "Through
Him, with Him, in Him, to You, God the Father almighty,

in the unity of the Holy Spirit, all honor and glory, forever and ever" (Canon of the Mass).

When the glorified Lord reveals His Person in word and sacrament, an anthropological change is effected. Our humanity becomes a different humanity. We live our human existence in a quite different manner, for our knowledge, our will and effort, and our love assume entirely new dimensions and possibilities which do not belong to our human nature proper. Through Christ, we know that we too are loved by the Father, and this certain knowledge of faith causes a real change in all our human relations. As we meet Christ, we grow in an inner likeness to Him, and we are more and more completely "conformed to the image of his Son, in order that he might be the first-born among many brethren" (Rom. 8:29). Our inner likeness to Him is reflected throughout our lives. In Christ we see and appreciate all earthly values in a totally different way; in Christ our lifework and our contact with our fellow-men is inspired by the dynamic force with which Christ loved man and the world.

However, the real change that comes about in our lives is not itself an entity, but is completely dependent, at each moment, on the presence of the glorified Lord in word and sacrament. If we see grace in this perspective, shall we not rid ourselves of many pseudo-contradictions and thus clear the way for reunion?

CHAPTER SIX

MARY THE EMINENTLY SAVED

The Earnest Questioning of Reformed Christians

Catholics should not find it strange that it is with respect to Mariology that they are most strongly prompted to examine their consciences whenever they meet Reformed Christians.[1] For on those occasions they not only encounter the full power of the one-sided protest and objections of Reformed Christians, but there is also a most keen realization of the one-sidedness which characterized Counter-Reformation Catholics in their religious views.

It so happens that the new Mariological development is itself helpful for clarifying the conflict between Rome and the Reformation. We should not say that the conflict itself has thereby become more vehement. The only result is that a more penetrating light has been focused on that question. For . . . as we fully recognize the variations in theology and the distinction between infallible pronouncements *and* popular devotion, we shall feel obliged to acknowledge that the new Mariological

1. Karl Barth calls the Marian dogma "neither more nor less the critical central dogma of the Roman Catholic Church" (*"nicht mehr und weniger als das kritische Zentraldogma der R. K. Kirche"*). *Kirchliche Dogmatik*, I, 2, p. 157.

development from the fundamental structure of Catholicism is *legitimate*.[2]

It is precisely in Mariology that a Catholic comes to realize that he can no longer brush aside as unimportant the believing earnestness of the questioning that accompanied the rise of the Reformation, has continued to accompany Reformed Christians during four centuries with undiminished vigor, and makes them say:

1. Does giving Mary such a position in the realization of man's salvation not obscure the absolutely unique value of Christ's salvific work for all men?[3]

2. When that role is attributed to Mary do we not make her the exemplar of man in competition with Christ so that man's cooperation in the work of salvation seems to detract from the all-sufficient power of Christ's salvific obedience to the Father?

The Roman Catholic Church sees in Mary the prototype and model of all human cooperation with God's grace. That is why the Church values it so greatly that she stresses the fact that she has no desire to make Mary a goddess or raise her to the rank of a divine being. It is precisely as a *human being* that she deserves that honor. The Church beholds in Mary what man can do through God's grace. Sure enough, salvation comes from God, but by virtue of God's design, Mary is indispensable as co-redemptrix and as servant in that divine plan. So does the Roman Catholic Church honor in Mary that to which God's grace calls man and that of which it

2. G. C. Berkouwer, *Conflict met Rome,* Kampen, 1949, p. 237.

3. "On the Protestant level there is no need of a Mariology, of a doctrine, as such, about Mary. It is the Lord, not Mary we are concerned with! Even though we like to think and speak respectfully about Mary." B. C. van Niftrik, *Kleine Dogmatiek,* p. 105. Cf. H. Bavink, *Gereformeerde Dogmatiek* III, p. 262; B. D. Dupuy, "La mariologie de Calvin," *Istina* 5, 1958, pp. 479-490; J. H. N. Hupperts, "Protestantse bezwaren tegen de Katholieke Marialeer and verering," *De Standaard van Maria,* 40, 1964, pp. 47-81.

makes man capable. Mary is the prototype of the believing man who is called to co-operate with grace.[4]

The Reformed Christian, in his vigorous protest
against that view of revelation, believes that every Christian worthy of the name must express his strongest
objection in the following words: "It is against this deification of man that the Reformation rose in protest."[5]

> This criticism of man's deification does not stand
> alone. It is connected with the other fact that this deifi-
> cation obscures the truth that man's salvation comes
> entirely from Christ. And in the conflict concerning the
> Marian doctrine what is involved again is the signifi-
> cance of God's *grace*. . . . For here, truly, we meet the
> idea that is fundamental in Mariology. Besides the other
> Roman doctrine regarding grace and freedom, the meri-
> toriousness of good works and penance, that Marian
> view is a sign of the Roman doctrine of *grace* in which,
> in spite of all the attempts to put emphasis upon it, the
> sovereignty of grace is *counterbalanced* by the meri-
> torial function of human life.[6]

3. Is that Catholic view of revelation, that sees Mary
as co-redemptrix and mediatrix of all grace, in the light
of her cooperation in the salvific work of Christ, not in
flagrant contradiction with the scriptural testimony that
wholly governs being a Christian: "There is one mediator
between God and men, the man Christ Jesus, who gave
himself as a ransom for all, the testimony of which was
borne at the proper time" (1 Tim. 2:5).

4. For, if we accept that Mary, in virtue of her consent
to become the Mother of the Son of God, had an actual

4. *Herderlijk Schrijven*, pp. 9-10; cf. F. W. A. Korff, *Christologie* II, p. 296. Karl Barth, *Die Kirchliche Dogmatik*, I, 2, pp. 153-
160.

5. H. Bavink, *Gereformeerde Dogmatiek*, III, p. 263.

6. G. C. Berkouwer, *Conflict met Rome*, pp. 217, 221, Cf.
Y. Feenstra, *Geboren uit de Maagd*, Kampen, 1959, pp. 66-67.

part in the work of the *objective* redemption, does she not stand *beside* Christ as she faces the believer?[7]

5. Is Mary, who was assumed into heaven, not credited with having a salvific function of mediatorship in *subjective* salvation, a function that belongs exclusively to the glorified Man Jesus Christ?[8]

6. Finally, when the Catholic too glibly declares that Mary, as the first human being to be saved, has expressed the act of faith of her "Be it done according to thy word" (Lke 1:38) in the name of all mankind,[9] does this not devaluate the Incarnation of the Son of the Father?[10] For it is precisely in our stead and for our benefit that the First-born of all creation has become obedient unto death (Phil. 2:8) in His solidarity with sinful mankind, and that He has brought this to perfection for us through His Resurrection (Heb. 2:10).

We see, then, that the core of the Reformational protest against Catholic Mariology is as follows: It is not Mary but Christ who represents all mankind. The only thing God wishes to reveal to us in the purely scriptural figure of Mary is "that His coming can be expected and received only in *faith*. Mary's faith is the step by which the Word descends into the flesh. She is declared blessed for no other reason than the fact that she has believed."[11] But Mary's act of faith is not a merit on the basis of which she has her own place in Christ's salvific work. "Faith is not by any means an act of reciprocity, but the act of recognition of the one Mediator, beside whom there is no other."[12]

7. G. C. Berkouwer, *Conflict met Rome*, pp. 210-215.

8. M. Thurian, "Le dogme de l'assumption," *Verbum Caro*, 50 (1951), pp. 2-41.

9. Karl Barth, *Die Kirchliche Dogmatik*, I, 2, 157.

10. A. Muller, "Problemen en perspectieven der huidige mariologie," *Theologisch perspectief* II, Hilversum, 1959, pp. 108.

11. J. Koopmans, *De Nederlandse Geloofsbelijdenis*, 3rd ed., Amsterdam, 1949, p. 94.

12. Karl Barth, *Die Kirchliche Dogmatik*, I, 2, 160.

Neither Beside Christ, nor Beside the Believer

The whole of Christian existence is at stake in those acute questions! Our entire approach to the mystery of our salvation in Christ is involved in them. Catholics can no longer dismiss those questions with a smile, as if it were only a question of a tenacious misunderstanding that has to be removed by a mutual and sympathetic understanding.[13] Reformed Christians should not be satisfied with an answer to those earnest questions that is not a genuine ecumenical deed on the part of the Catholic Church. As a matter of conscience, they must reject such excessive veneration of Mary—although the Catholic sees in it a hymn of praise of our redemption in Christ —because in that veneration they find so little that coincides with the scriptural testimony about Mary.[14]

Should the Catholic Church's ecumenical deed not consist in acknowledging that the triumphal veneration of Mary stands in too great a contrast with the humble attitude of faith in which Scripture depicts the Mother of God's profound significance for salvation? Is it not possible for Reformed and Catholic Christians to meet *in a scriptural reflection upon the salvation-dimensions of*

13. "Instead of having a Protestant ask Catholics to give him information about a world of ideas in which he has not been initiated from his childhood he dares in his prejudice to find in it a sign of the divinization of Mary. . . . It is more to the purpose for Catholics who are suspected of collusion, and who can thus serve as witnesses, to come and put Protestants at their ease, regarding that important point. There still remain so *many* imaginations that cause a fundamental separation, that it is a relief when at least this wretched misunderstanding is put out of the way." Gerard Brom, *Gesprek over de eenheid van de Kerk*, Amsterdam, 1956, pp. 233-234.

14. G. C. Berkouwer, *De strijd om het Rooms-Katholiek dogma*, Kampen, 1940, pp. 168-205; J. C. Groot, "Maria in denken en leven der protestanten," *Het Schild*, vol. 31 (1954), pp. 211-216; J. C. Groot, "De Mariologie in oecumenisch perspectief," *Het Schild*, vol. 35 (1958), pp. 157-168.

Mary's act of faith, as the human response to our re-
demption in Christ? For it is precisely in her faith that
she became the mother of God.

If we wish to sketch most purely Mary's unique role in
Christ's salvific work, we must avoid considering it
within the salvation mystery of the Incarnation (the
objective redemption); this, unfortunately, has been the
traditional way in our Catholic theology until now. We
must, on the contrary, reflect upon Mary's role as a prototype of faith, in the scriptural perspective of man receiving the grace of faith (subjective redemption).

By giving the act of faith in Christ a central place in
Mariology, a Catholic's veneration of Mary will acquire a
new depth and it will become more genuinely devout. At
the same time, Reformed Christians are thus given an
opportunity to give their believing attention to the
Mother of our Savior, after centuries in which they, in
their violent protest, have left her out of their life of
faith.

1. THE UNFATHOMABLE RICHES OF THE CHRIST MYSTERY

All Things Have Come About Through Him

A constant meditation on the mystery of the incarnation of God's Son makes the believer discover to his astonishment that there are ever new aspects to his Christian existence. When we reflect upon His word, the
First-born of creation Himself leads us even farther into
the unsuspected depths of our redemption as men in
Him.

The Old Testament is the history of God coming into a
world that of itself is unreceptive to Him. In Christ God's
coming becomes a human possibility. God has communicated Himself to a man. The whole world is redeemed
through the human actions of God's Son who has willed
to experience His being-Son-of-the-Father in our sinful

human nature that was estranged from God. As the high point in creation He will bring this world to its proper destination in His glorification with the Father.

The salvific acts of the Son of God are concretely situated in human history as *human* acts. The historical account of the vicissitudes of the human race is no longer the neutral history of creation but it is salvation history; it is the story of God's coming and His being redeemingly occupied with man in the Man Jesus Christ.

All mankind lives by the historical-salvific fact that God became one with His creation in the incarnation of His Son, and that, entering into human history, He has taken up the world in the mercy of His eternal love.

The last, definitive and all-embracing act of God's salvific plan with man, has already taken place: in the First-born of all creation mankind, far above its own sinful existence, is already brought to its fulfillment in an eschatological anticipation. In spite of the broken character of his existence, man can experience His being-created in God's image and likeness in the glorified Man Jesus Christ.

Man is Really Involved in the Salvific Work of Christ

It follows that since the incarnation of God's Son we can no longer speak about God without speaking about men. "No one has ever seen God, the only Son, who is in the bosom of the Father, he has made (Him) known" in His incarnation (Jn 1:18). Christ has truly drawn us and involved us in His work of salvation, in His historical human deeds by which He has redeemed us. For being the prototype of our human existence for God, He has redeemed us precisely through living His being-the-Son-of-the-Father in utter human obedience. That is why man's salvation can be accomplished only as a dialogue between the divine initiative of love in Christ and the authentic believing response of man.

We cannot proclaim the Gospel of our redemption in Jesus Christ without calling man to surrender himself completely in an act of faith. And in the light of the Incarnation, as the fundamental pattern of being a Christian, we cannot view that act of faith as a mere stretching out of an empty hand, as a passive receiving, but we must view it as an active experience of our being saved in Christ, just as Christ gave to His being-the-Son-of-the-Father the form of a perfect experience of our humanness.

2. MARY'S FAITH AS THE "CONDITION" OF OUR REDEMPTION

When we look at things in the perspective of the Incarnation, human existence and human action acquire an entirely new salvific value as a believing response to God's coming in Christ. And this is true not only of the New Testament, as the believing experience of our human redemption in Christ, but also of the Old Testament as the believing growth toward the definitive redemption of our human existence through the expected Messiah.

It is against that background that divided Christians can make a final effort to come closer together in their hopeless controversy concerning Mary's place in Christ's salvific work.

The Apex of the Old Testament Longing for the Messiah

God spoke to man who sinfully refused to live in likeness to God and who thereby had made his human existence unreceptive of God. God involved man in a salvific plan which assumed the form of an ever more profound dialogue between God's word of election and man's believing response.

This believing reaction, so full of tension, to the divine promise filled the Old Testament with a salvific reality that has effected a profound change in human history. That this response of faith constitutes the real power that has given an ever richer unfolding to salvation history is evident in Abraham, "the father of our faith" who precisely because of his faith was able to hear: "I will make of you a great nation . . . , and by you all the families of the earth shall bless themselves" (Gen. 12:2-3).

> That is why it depends on faith, in order that the promise may rest on grace and be guaranteed to all his descendants—not only to the adherents of the law but also to those who share the faith of Abraham, for he is the father of us all, as it is written, "I have made you the father of many nations"—in the presence of the God in whom he believed, who gives life to the dead and calls into existence the things that do not exist.
>
> In hope he believed against hope, that he should become the father of many nations; as he had been told, "So shall your descendants be." He did not weaken in faith when he considered his own body, which was as good as dead because he was about a hundred years old, or when he considered the barrenness of Sarah's womb (or when God asked him to sacrifice his only son and patriarch Isaac).
>
> No distrust made him waver concerning the promise of God, but he grew strong in his faith as he gave glory to God, fully convinced that God was able to do what he had promised. That is why his faith was "reckoned to him as righteousness" (Rom. 4:16-22).

The people of Israel, from which the Messiah was to be born, *owes its existence to the faith of Abraham in God's freely chosen action*. And the whole history of that people is the story of God's unfolding promise. This promise was faced with a power of unbelief that was at work to destroy the community of faith, and it achieved an increasingly richer reality of grace-laden activity in a group of true believers that became constantly smaller (the holy remnant).

Now, at the height of that whole Old Testament believing expectation, stands the woman whom God had chosen to receive the Messiah and give Him to the world. *Her motherhood with respect to God's Son was the visible manifestation of the salvific reality of Mary's faith.*

Although those two aspects cannot be separated, we must say that it is her faith that is the foundation of her dignity as Mother of God: "Mary is greater by the fact that she received the faith of Christ than because she received the flesh of Christ. Her maternal relationship to Him would not have made her great if she had not born Him more in her heart than in her body."[15] Mary's motherhood of the Son of God is not primarily a personal privilege, but is a personal task of faith for the benefit of all mankind, which God placed at the center of the salvation history of His People in the person of Mary. The divine motherhood is the *sign* showing that God Himself is bringing the salvation history of mankind to a definitive end: "Ask a sign of the Lord, your God. . . . Behold a young woman shall conceive and bear a son, and shall call his name Emmanuel (God with us)" (Is. 7:12).

Her reply to the angel: "Behold I am the handmaid of the Lord" (Lke 1:38) was the synthesis of Old Testament godliness. Her hymn of thanksgiving for her election summed up the expectant faith of many centuries:[16]

Mary said,
   "My soul magnifies the Lord,
and my spirit rejoices in God my Savior,

15. Augustine, *De sancta virginitate*, III, P.L. 40, 398.
16. E. Schillebeeckx, *Maria, Moeder van de verlossing*, 1959, pp. 25-26.

for he has regarded the low estate of his
handmaiden.
For behold, henceforth, all generations
will call me blessed;
for he who is mighty has done great things
for me, and holy is his name.
And his mercy is on those who fear him
from generation to generation.
He has shown strength with his arm,
He has scattered the proud in the
imagination of their hearts,
he has put down the mighty from their
thrones,
and exalted those of low degree;
he has filled the hungry with good things,
and the rich he has sent empty away.
　　He has helped his servant Israel,
in remembrance of his mercy,
as he spoke to our fathers,
to Abraham and to his posterity forever"
(Lke 1:46-55).

The saving love of God and the faith of the whole Old
Testament concentrated in Mary met definitively in "the
fruit of (her) womb" (Lke 1:42). God Himself with
jealous care kept the faith in the Messiah alive in His
chosen people through His word. And He Himself has led
it—in spite of the constant temptation to idolatry—to
the summit of the desire for God, namely, in Mary. In her
"the Word became flesh." *Through her faith she became
the worthy Mother of God.*

Redeemed in View of the Merits of Christ

Just as sin is not an act of passing weakness but the
manifestation of the estrangement from God of our
whole human existence, so is faith not an isolated response to some concrete grace-laden activity of God, but
it blossoms forth from a real change which God has
effected in this human being. Faith, as the surrender of

our whole person to God, can only be the action of a man who, driven by God's mercy, has put his whole life at the disposal of God's salvific work.

In the act of faith expressed in her "be it done to me according to thy word" the whole life of Mary manifests:

a. the realization of our predestination in the First-born of all creation;

b. the culminating point of God's redeeming activity in the Old Testament salvation history;

c. the re-creative power of the incarnation of God's Son.

It is that believing reflection upon God's salvific work in Mary which made her fit, in her act of faith, for the overshadowing reception of the Holy Spirit and for becoming the Mother of God's Son, that has led the Church to proclaim her immaculate conception.

If the incarnation of the Son of the Father is the destiny of the whole of creation and if the salvation history of the Old Covenant is the story of God's redemptive coming in His creation, it follows that the world of men "in view of the merits of Christ,"[17] in spite of the sinful estrangement caused by sin, remains always *His* world: this is the created human existence in which Christ will some day experience His being-the-Son-of-the-Father in utter obedience, and in which He will bring the inner purpose of creation to fulfillment by His self-giving

---

17. " 'Intuitu meritorum Christi Jesu Salvatoris humani generis.' We use, on purpose, those words of the Bull 'Ineffabilis' concerning Mary's immaculate conception; in view of the foreseen merits of Christ, Adam's sin was intrinsically restricted by God's mercy in order that it might fit into the plan of salvation. The immanent tendency of that break with God—which is 'radical' from a twofold standpoint—to hopelessly fix a definitive rupture, was blocked and overcome interiorly by the stronger impetus of grace that prompted the return to God." F. Malmberg, "Enige aspecten van de zonde als christologisch probleem" *Jaarboek Kath. theol. in Ned.*, 1956, p. 13.

surrender to the Father. The "mystery hidden for ages and generations" *now made manifest to his saints* (Col. 1:26) tempered the destructive force of sin during the long centuries of preparation. Doesn't the Reformed Christian recognize in that thought his own vision of the "common grace"?[18]

Mary, in her freedom from original sin at her conception, is the living witness proclaiming that God's love was not diminished because of sin: "where sin increased, grace abounded all the more" (Rom. 5:20). Mary was redeemed by the dynamic power that moved the whole reality of salvation of the Old Testament to its fulfillment: "in view of the merits of Christ."[19]

This dogma wishes to emphasize that *faith is a "condition" of our salvation in Christ, a faith given by God and experienced by man.* Her total surrender was not something that induced nor, especially, that caused God's merciful love in Christ, but it was a condition on God's part. In a purely gratuitous way, God's grace appeared to us as the fruit of Mary's womb. That is why man cannot ask: why was He born of the Virgin? Faith alone knows that God desired and created that human "condition" in his plan of salvation in order to underline the reality of the incarnation of His Son.[19a]

On the other hand, although that act of faith of Mary was purely the result and the effect of God's grace-laden decree determining that He would enter the world

18. S. J. Ridderbos, *De theologische cultuurbeschouwing van Abraham Kuyper,* Kampen, 1947, p. 28.

19. "Through a special grace and privilege granted by God Mary is, in view of the merits of Jesus Christ, the Savior of the human race, chosen to remain free from all stain of original sin." Bull "Ineffabilis Deus," December 8, 1854, Denziger, no. 1641.

19a. Both the title of this section and the text of this paragraph play on the Dutch term *voorwaarde,* which can mean *condition* and, if spelled as *vóór-waarde* ("pre-value"), can refer to a value realized in anticipation. Ed.

through a human being, one belonging to our race, it is also true that it was Mary's own act. Her personal insertion, her own struggle was involved in that act. But this should not disturb the conscience of a believer, for in a dialogue between God and man, the free response of faith in no way affects the sovereign activity of God's grace. On the contrary, that very response is a constant actual gift of God that becomes man's personal action.

Mary's Act of Faith Is Her True Greatness

The mystery of our being-Christian is the reflex experience of the solidarity of God's Son with our sinful humanity that He sanctified through utter obedience in our stead and for our benefit. He desired to experience personally our extreme estrangement from God. Particularly in His temptation in the desert and in Gethsemane He had an existential experience of the attraction of sin. But precisely in that temptation, He struggled with our will that rebels against God, and led it back to the Father. He experienced the temptation as an invitation of the Father to establish the universal salvific power of His obedience against the universally destructive power of the first man's disobedience.

Mary's life was not an idyllic life lived closely to the Son of God; but it was a subjective, living association with the "cruel" obedience with which the Son of God passed as Savior through her and our human existence. For that purpose she followed our road of unconditional faith, of not seeing and not understanding. And on that road she too had to learn obedience.

"We poetically attribute to the historical Mary a sort of miniature 'intuitive vision-of-God' of which neither Scripture nor the true tradition of faith says a single word, and that is contrary to the honest account especially of Luke's Gospel; and in so doing we undervaluate her true

greatness, namely, her life of faith."[20] Scripture gives no
foundation for the naively exaggerated representation of
Mary as knowing that her Child was the Son of God when
she heard the message of the angel: "He will be great,
and will be called the Son of the Most High; and the Lord
God will give to him the throne of his father David, and
he will reign over the house of Jacob for ever; and of his
kingdom there will be no end" (Lke 1:32-33). The whole
testimony of Scripture about Mary is in conflict with
such a certitude.

Mary, in line with the Old Testament expectations,
could understand by those words only that her Child was
to be the Messiah who had been announced for centuries,
and that He would deliver His people from their sinful
situation.

Along the same line also is the fact that Mary could
not have conceived that redemption from sin without
connecting it with the restoration of the national greatness of the Jewish people; and this is confirmed by the
explicit prophecy that He would receive the throne of
David and that this would be an eternal kingship. Mary
does not stand isolated from the Apostles who, in spite of
all the events to the contrary, continued to struggle with
that nationalistic hope to the very last.

It was against the suggestive background of those centuries old expectations and intense desires, that the actual life of the Mother of the Messiah ran its course.
Mary saw the clear outline of her way of life. But she was
asked to make an act of uncomprehending faith when, at
the great moment of her life for Him to whom the throne
of David was promised, "there was no place for them in
the inn" (Lke 2:7) and she was obliged to flee to Egypt
(Mt. 2:13-15).

20. Schillebeeck, *Maria, Moeder van de verlossing*, p. 23.

The seriousness of her conflict of faith appears outwardly first of all when the evangelist records: "his father and his mother marveled at what was said about him" after he had recalled the words of Simeon to Mary: "Behold this child is set for the fall and rising of many in Israel, and for a sign that is spoken against" (Lke 2:33-34).

And all certainty concerning the religious traditions and expectations of her people, with which she had so greatly identified herself was shaken by the words she heard in the Temple after her quite natural anxiety: "Did you not know that I must be in my Father's house?"

She knew from that moment that her fidelity to Christ required of her that she should walk through the mist of faith and without knowing where she was going: "And they did not understand the saying which he spoke to them, . . . his mother kept all these things in her heart" (Lke 2:40-51).

Mary also became acquainted with the reality of temptation in her faith. Her faith would have lost the inner dynamism of a constantly renewed surrender if she had not had to struggle all her life in order to bind her will to God's will as it manifested itself concretely in the life of her Son. The words "O woman, what have you to do with me? My hour has not yet come," addressed by Christ to Mary at the wedding feast of Cana do not sound to a Christian like an expression of annoyance that was caused by Mary's lack of trust in God. Here Mary gave witness to the hard reality of her faith, of her availability with respect to God's Kingdom, in contrast with her own insight and desires, by immediately replying to the temptation: "Do whatever he tells you" (Jn 2:4-5).

Mary has followed her Son with a constant disposition of willing surrender, whatever might be the way He was led by His Father in a self-sacrificing obedience. If Scrip-

ture testifies about Him, that He is "to sympathize with
our weaknesses" and that "in every respect (He has) been
tempted as we are, yet without sinning" (Heb. 4:15),
then no Christian can fail to see the estrangement from
God of our human existence. And this applies also to
Mary.

She too in following her Son experienced in her own
life the rebellion of our will against God. The force of
that temptation in her life of faith is delineated in a
passage of the Gospel about which there has developed
an endless controversy among divided Christians:

> While he was still speaking to the people, behold, his
> mother and his brothers stood outside, asking to speak
> to him. But he replied to the man who told him, "Who is
> my mother, and who are my brothers?" And stretching
> out his hand toward his disciples, he said, "Here are my
> mother and my brothers! For whoever does the will of
> my Father in heaven is my brother, and sister and
> mother" (Mt. 12:46-50; cf. Mk 3:31-35; Lke 8:19-21).

Here Mary felt the same tension between the rights of
her maternal love for her Child and the will of the Father
that governed Christ's whole life unto an utmost detach-
ment from everything. She experienced it also another
time when Christ replied to the very human remark,
"Blessed is the womb that bore you and the breasts that
you sucked!" by making an unmistakable correction
which forcefully emphasized the opposition: "Blessed
rather are those who hear the word of God and keep it"
(Lke 11:27-28).

Mary's Son constantly offered Himself to the will of
the Father and this meant an ever-renewed personal sacrifice of the mother from whose faith the utmost was
demanded. But she remained faithful to Him in spite of
everything. She continued to follow Him unto the bitter
end when the faith of the Apostles was no longer able to
bear the short-circuiting between their high-strung expec-

tations and the bloody rejection of Christ by His own People. They fled, but, "by the cross of Jesus were His mother . . ." (Jn 19:25).

Mary experienced in all its fierceness the paradox of her faith in Christ. She stood in the impenetrable darkness of the mystery taking place in front of her: He of whom the Angel had told her: "The Lord God will give him the throne of his father David and he will reign over the house of Jacob for ever; and of his kingdom there will be no end" (Lke 1:32), was now hanging on the Cross following the destructive judgment by His People: "Away with him, crucify him! . . . We have no king but Caesar" (Jn 19:15). In Him the faith of all Israel was extinguished.

But there stood Mary, with the confidence of Abraham who in his son offered the sacrifice of his faith as father of a great People. But no angel came to her to prevent the ultimate consequence of her act of faith. Neither did she know concretely to what limit God would bring her sacrifice of faith. Her faith reached even beyond the frontier of a visible failure. Hence it is more true of her than of Abraham that "in hope he believed against hope. . . . No distrust made him waver concerning the promise of God, but he grew strong in his faith as he gave glory to God, fully convinced that God was able to do what he had promised. That is why his faith was 'reckoned to him as righteousness'" (Rom. 4:18-22). The words of Jesus on the Cross, "woman behold your Son . . . behold your mother," have always been understood by the Fathers in the sense that Mary was the symbol of the Church as the community that believes in Him.

3. **THE MARIAN DOGMAS AS STRUCTURES OF THE SALVIFIC CHRIST MYSTERY**

Mary's true greatness lies in her complete self-giving in faith, as a subjective experience of being saved in

Christ, in her humanity. In her life of total surrender, the reality and power of our humanity saved in Christ is made manifest.

It is not on the basis of isolated texts of Scripture that the Church in a believing reflection has wished to outline a number of concrete aspects of Christ's salvific work for us, in her teaching about Mary, *but she has done it on the basis of the whole revelation of Christ in the Bible.*

Mary is the one who is eminently redeemed, because the fullness of the plan of salvation that Christ has desired to realize in His living solidarity with our sinful humanity becomes manifest in her life of faith.

If it is true that Christianity is the reception of God, and that it is this not only in an abstract ideal way but in the concreteness of history, in His human word, in His grace that irradiates the world, in short in man's corporeity, it then becomes evident that the divine maternity is the most perfect case in Christianity of a reception of God in a concrete corporeity. This must not be understood, however, in reference to a motherhood conceived in a narrow sense, as a purely biological event; it must be seen as something that lays claim to the whole corporeal and spiritual being of the Blessed Virgin.

Hence the search for a perfect Christian who accepts salvation in Jesus Christ thus leads to a simple and yet all-embracing image of the holy Virgin. All that faith knows about the realization of redemption, about salvation, grace, the fullness of grace became a reality in Mary.[21]

21. Karl Rahner, *Maria, Moeder van de Heer,* Deurne, 1961, pp. 44-45; Cf. E. Walter, *Maria, Mutter des Glaubenden,* 2nd ed., Freiburg, 1957; R. Guardini, *The Mother of the Lord,* 1958; Cl. Dillenschneider, *Marie dans l'économie de la création rénovée,* Paris, 1957; W. Meyer–A. Muller, "Maria als Bild der Gnade und Heiligkeit," in *Begegnung der Christen,* pp. 573-600; J. H. M. Hupperts, "Naar een oecumenische toenadering in de Mariologie," *Standaard van Maria,* vol. 40 (1964), pp. 82-112.

In that light, Mary's unique place in the order of salvation can be expressed in the following words, using dogmatic terms: Just as we subjectively receive the objective gift of the Savior by our faith that is exteriorized in the physical reception of the sacraments (*per fidem et sacramenta fidei*), so is Mary saved through her faith that is exteriorized in the bodily reception of the Fundamental Sacrament, which is the Man Jesus Christ.[22]

We see then that it is necessary for Mariology to receive a Christocentric resourcement starting from the faith of the ancient Church. The Church was unacquainted with any veneration of the person of Mary before the Council of Ephesus.[23]

The positive significance of that silence of the first centuries lies in this that whoever has the Church has Mary also. In those days the theology concerning the Church was particularly rich and fruitful. And also in piety, in more lyrical expressions, the Church to a great extent had the position that Mary now occupies. History records the fact that during a centuries-long process, the figure of Mary has slowly acquired the place in Christian thought and prayer that originally belonged to the Church.

During the first centuries Mary was not forgotten nor lost, but she was hidden and preserved in the theology concerning the Church; that is, Mary was there where her dignity and greatness is not smaller, but where the doctrine about her remains "in the middle of the Church" (*in medio Ecclesiae*), and does not inevitably run into a dead end. Here we must once more recall the parallel between Eve and Mary, which is probably the oldest post-biblical element of a theological doctrine about Mary.[24]

22. E. Schillebeeckx, *Maria, Moeder van de verlossing*, p. 72; cf. G. Kreling, "Maria," *Ned. Kath. St.*, vol. 55 (1959), p. 141.

23. E. Hendrikse, "Maria, Kerkelijke leerontwikkeling," *Theol. Woordenboek II*, 3086-3124.

24. A. Müller, "Problemen en perspectieven der huidige Mariologie," *Theologisch Perspectief* II, Hilversum, 1959, p. 106.

It was after Ephesus that patristic theology, in its reflection upon the book of Revelation (12:1-13) arrived at an explicit believing attention to Mary and at a veneration of Mary as the personification of the Church.[25] All titles that were once given to the Church, were from then on transferred to Mary.

Mary becomes isolated from the Church and is given an independent attention to the extent that the Church mystery is experienced in an impersonal way, as a hierarchy. Religious reflection must recognize that the salvific significance of Mary lies in the fact that she was eminently redeemed, and this must be seen as rooted in the mystery of the Church; in this mystery man experiences his being-redeemed in Christ in personal belief and as sharing this privilege with others. Marian veneration can avoid obscuring the Christ mystery only when it is seen within the Church mystery.

It is precisely because of the uniqueness of Mary's affirmative response that she is the image and symbol of the Church. Are we not justified in saying that the fact that Vatican Council II included the Schema "On the Blessed Virgin Mary Mother of God" as a chapter of the *Constitution on the Church* (October 29, 1963) is a historical event of ecumenical importance, for it said: "Therefore she is also hailed as a pre-eminent and altogether singular member of the Church, and as the Church's model and excellent exemplar in faith and charity. Taught by the Holy Spirit, the Catholic Church honors her with filial affection and piety as a most beloved mother" (no. 53).

In Mary's act of faith as the subjective experience of her being-redeemed in Christ, the Spirit achieved the objective salvation of all mankind through the Incarnation of the Son of the Father:

> The Father of mercies willed that the consent of the predestined mother should precede the Incarnation, so that just as a woman contributed to death, so also a woman should contribute to life. . . . Rightly therefore the holy Fathers see her as used by God not in a passive way, but as cooperating in the work of human salvation through free faith and obedience. For, as St. Ireneus says, she, "being obedient, became the cause of salvation for herself and for the whole human race." (*Constitution on the Church,* no. 56).

In Mary's response "Be it done according to thy word" we hear a resounding of the Church's act of faith. Hence if we wish to appreciate the salvific importance of Mary we must always consider it within St. Paul's vision of the Church: "Christ loved the Church and gave himself up for her, that he might sanctify her, having cleansed her by the washing of water with the word, that he might present the church to himself in splendor, without spot or wrinkle, or any such thing, that she might be holy and without blemish" (Eph. 5:25-27).

The Second Vatican Council has shed a clear light on the ecclesial dimensions of the Marian mystery:

> Through the gift and role of divine maternity, Mary is united with her Son, the Redeemer, and with His singular graces and offices. By these, the Blessed Virgin is also intimately united with the Church. As St. Ambrose taught, the Mother of God is a model of the Church. . . . The Church, moreover, contemplating Mary's mysterious sanctity imitating her charity, and faithfully fulfilling the Father's will, becomes herself a mother by accepting God's word in faith. For by her preaching and by baptism she brings forth to a new and immortal life children who are conceived of the Holy Spirit and born

of God. The Church herself is a virgin, who keeps whole
and pure the fidelity she has pledged to her
Spouse. . . .

Seeking after the glory of Christ, the Church becomes
more like the exalted model, and continually progresses
in faith, hope, and charity, searching out and doing the
will of God in all things (*Constitution on the Church*,
nos. 63-65).

It follows that full ecumenical attention should be paid
to the new direction in which the Council desires to guide
a believing consideration of the Marian mystery:

This Synod earnestly exhorts theologians and preachers of the divine word that in treating of the unique
dignity of the Mother of God, they carefully and equally
avoid the falsity of exaggeration on the one hand, and
the *excess of narrow-mindedness* on the other. Pursuing
the study of sacred Scripture, the holy Fathers, the doc-
tors, and liturgies of the Church, and under the guidance of the Church's teaching authority, let them rightly
explain the offices and privileges of the Blessed Virgin
which are always related to Christ, the Source of all
truth, sanctity and piety.

Let them painstakingly guard against any word or
deed which could lead separated brethren or anyone else
into error regarding the true doctrine of the Church. Let
the faithful remember moreover that true devotion consists neither in fruitless and passing emotion, nor in a
certain vain credulity. Rather, it proceeds from true
faith, by which we are led to know the excellence of the
Mother of God, and are moved to a filial love toward our
mother and to the imitation of her virtues (*Constitution
on the Church*, no. 67).

It is against that background that we interpret the
privileges of Mary as aspects of the Christ mystery that is
accomplished in the Church, such as her Immaculate
Conception, Virginity, Sanctity, Assumption, cooperation
in redemption and the bestowal of grace.

A. *The Immaculate Conception*

In the full reality of her salvation through Christ, Mary is said to have been immaculately conceived on the basis of our predestination in the First-born of all creation, of the one who has kept the world of man in the grasp of God's salvific plan against the power of sin: "He (the Father) chose us in him before the foundation of the world, that we should be holy and blameless before him" (Eph. 1:4).[26]

Mankind is not primarily a biological fact that is based on the participation in one and the same nature. It is a community of persons that has unity in virtue of one common vocation and destiny. It is in the realization, codetermined by others, of the human vocation to be together with God in Christ that we must situate original sin.

The figure of Adam in his unsalutary function can be explained only in Christ who, as the First-born of all creation, is not only the permanent foundation of all human existence ("without him was not anything made that was made") but also realizes in all men continuous orientation to God ("the life was the light of men"). The first origin of man in the primitive time of his existence and mankind's self-realization in and through the evolution of his history is the beginning of the realization of the incarnation of God's Son.

Adam is the type of the human community in which the coming about of the Christ mystery is codetermined by the others; but in him that being-together of God and man in the Covenant was broken. Man's actual history is the experience of the estrangement of the entire human

26. Cf. H. Fortmann, "Maria's Onbevlekte Ontvangenis, vrucht van Christus' heilswerk," *Het Schild*, vol. 31 (1954), pp. 199-204. E. Longpré, *La Vierge immaculée. Histoire et doctrine*, Paris, 1945.

community from God, a situation that made man power-less and sinful. Man can realize himself only in commu-nity with others: he was unable to respond to his voca-tion of life in Christ in that sinful community of a broken Covenant.

And yet, the People of Israel did not live exclusively in helpless sinfulness, without any other light than the promise of the Messiah who was to come. When we look at the Old Covenant in the light of the mystery of Christ who represents both sinful and redeemed mankind, we see that Covenant as the coming of God, whose salvific plan for creation had been upset, in Christ. The believing Israelite could recognize his existence as being "both just and sinner" in that as yet veiled Christ mystery of the Old Covenant. He could see his existence as sinful because of his real connection with the powerless and sinful com-munity of his people. But he could see it at the same time, as objectively but still incompletely justified through his real relationship with Yahweh in the Cove-nant. He experienced his existence as one who was be-ginning to be redeemed in Christ from sin.

It is that salvific event of the descent of God's Son, in solidarity, into the Covenant history of His People, that the Church, after centuries of reflection upon the experi-ence of faith in the Christ mystery, has confessed in her dogma of the Immaculate Conception of Mary: "At the first moment of her conception, by a singular grace and privilege of the onmipotent God, and in view of the mer-its of Christ Jesus, Savior of the human race, she was preserved immune from the stain of original guilt" (Den-ziger, no. 2083).

But if we wish to realize the salvific meaning of that dogma, we must avoid relating that dogmatic declaration exclusively to the person of Mary as an isolated individ-ual. The salvific dimensions of that dogma become visible only when we place it within the broad context of the Christocentric realization of the salvific plan of the Father.

For that dogma is actually dealing with the final healing of the whole people of God of the Old Testament in the revelation of God in the Man Jesus Christ who was a child of His people. This mystery is tersely expressed in the scriptural words: "born . . . of God" (Jn 1:13), and "when the time had fully come . . . born of woman" (Gal. 4:4).

The Church looks at that scriptural declaration and it is in that light that she considers the personal privilege of Mary's immaculate conception as the culmination of the salvific activity of the Old Testament:

> She stands out among the poor and humble of the Lord, who confidently await and receive salvation from Him. With her, the exalted Daughter of Sion, and after a long expectation of the promise, the times were at length fulfilled and the new dispensation established. All this occurred when the Son of God took a human nature from her, that He might in the mysteries of His flesh free man from sin (*Constitution on the Church,* no. 55).

This expresses her belief that the New Testament is the fulfillment of the Old Testament: "Think not that I have come to abolish the law and the prophets; I have come not to abolish them but to fulfill them" (Mt. 5:17). Hence when we proclaim our faith in the Apostolic Creed in "Jesus Christ . . . born of the Father . . . born of the Virgin Mary," we know in the light of that salvation history that there is question of something more than a biological happening: in her the Spirit of the Father overshadows the earthly reality, desiring to make in it the tabernacle of His Son.

The dogma of the Immaculate Conception is the expression of our belief that every man by virtue of his predestination in Christ is called to salvation in Christ.

B. *Virginity*

Throughout her life as a Virgin, Mary is the manifestation of the unexpected and unmerited mystery of God's sovereign grace at work in the sending of His Son, as well as the manifestation of the total readiness and availability of her faith. The mystery-of-grace of the Incarnation, as God giving Himself, has as counterpart the virginity of Mary as the image of man who receives in faith. To the sovereign fact of being "born of God" (Jn 1:13),[27] there must correspond the perfect readiness of Mary's act of faith expressed in the words" "Behold the handmaid of the Lord."

By reflecting upon the Virgin's "be it done to me," as expressing the willingness of the consecrated people of God to be available for God, tradition has understood Mary's reception of the Holy Spirit as a declaration that her whole life was at God's disposal. At the same time, however, that virginity "before, during and after childbirth" expresses a declaration of faith in the salvific event of her motherhood of God's Son through the power of the Holy Spirit.

In this respect theology should avoid entering into biological considerations, and Christian piety should renounce asking too curious questions about that unique mystery of divine motherhood. The most we should say is that in that virginity, through the overshadowing of the Holy Spirit, there took place an eminent experience of being children of God, which belongs to all men who are not born "of blood, nor of the will of the flesh, nor of the will of man, but are born of God."

27. J. Guitton, *La Vierge Marie*, Paris, 1940.

C. Sanctity

On the basis of that sublime experience of her being redeemed by Christ as a human being, a sanctity that surpasses that of all men is attributed to Mary: "No one born of God commits sin; for God's nature abides in him, and he cannot sin because he is born of God" (1 Jn 3:9). If Scripture testifies in such strong words to the reality of Christ's salvific action in overcoming sin, that total redemption from sin certainly should apply to her who received Him as the fruit of her womb.

The message of the angel to Mary must be placed in the whole context of salvation history. It can, then, be understood only in virtue of the salvific announcement of the wondrous birth of Isaac, Samuel, John the Baptist, and the vocation of Isaiah and Jeremiah.

Mary is called the "favored one," the "chosen one" (*kecharitomenē*) because she is invited to accept a task in the salvific action of God with His Covenant people, and because in virtue of that invitation she is capable of fulfilling that task. "She conceived her Lord first in her spirit and then in her body."[28] Just as in Christ, Mary's functional and personal sanctity go hand in hand.[29]

In the overshadowing of Mary by the Holy Spirit the salvation that was already at work in the Old Covenant began to be fulfilled, and that salvific reality came among us in a human form: "To all who received him, who believed in his name, he gave power to become children of God; who were born, not of blood nor of the will of the flesh nor of the will of man, but of God" (Jn 1:12-13).[30]

28. Pope Leo I, *Christmas Homily*, P.L. 54, 190.
29. B. van Iersel, "Schetsen voor een bijbels Mariabeeld," *De standaard van Maria*, vol. 32 (1956), pp. 203-233.
30. Cf. J. Schmid, "Jo. 1, 13," *Biblische Zeitschrift*, N. F. 1, 1957, pp. 118-125: "To all who received him he gave power to become children of God; to all who believe in him, who are not born of blood, nor of the will of the flesh nor of the will of man, but who are born of God."

This coming of God's Son in the womb of the Virgin Mary is the redemption of all mankind, that came to a head in His getting hold of the spirit of her who was the source of His human life. In Mary Jesus received his human mode of existence from believing Israel, in which existence He experienced His life of union with the Father. The emphasis here must fall fully on the salvation-historical perspective: the entire Old Covenant is the pre-realization of the incarnation of God's Son, of the Messiah's birth from the holy remnant of the people of the Covenant, of the conception of the Son of the Most High from the virginal *anaw,* the consecrated poor of Yahweh.

Mary's sanctity is the concentrated experience of the salvific event that was already begun in the long history of the people of the Covenant. The holiness of her life was a growing toward and living by the salvific event that took place in her life at the message of the angel. This holiness the Church must accept, for the conception of God's Son must not be thought of as another case of a miraculous overpowering of a pagan mother-of-god; but it is the culmination of Yahweh's Covenant activity for His people. In her holiness we see the culmination of the Godward strivings of the prophets and the devout in Israel who felt ever more profoundly and intimately the saving nearness of Yahweh.

Mary's consent to the angel's message was the first human response to the incarnation of the Word, the first explicit believing experience of the fulfillment of God's coming to all men.

D. The Assumption

But Mary too experienced the reality of her redemption by Christ in the darkness of faith. She too lived by the expectation expressed in the words: "When Christ who is our life appears, then you also will appear with him in glory" (Col. 3:4) for "if we have been united with him in a death like his, we shall certainly be united with him in a resurrection like his. We know that our old self was crucified with him so that the sinful body might be destroyed, and we might no longer be enslaved to sin" (Rom. 6:5-6).

We are redeemed in Christ even with respect to our bodies. Of that certainty that by Christ's salvific actions the death of the body has also been overcome and that our redemption shall have its accomplishment even in the bodily experience of His glorified humanity with the Father: "when he appears we shall be like him as he is" (1 Jn 3:2)[31]—of that certainty of faith the Church has given testimony in her doctrine concerning Mary's Assumption into Heaven.

Hence, also, that aspect of believing reflection needs to be placed in a clear Christological light. For when we say that eternal happiness will consist in the contemplation of God, we must understand this properly.

Man as a creature cannot see God: "No one has ever seen God; the only Son, who is in the bosom of the Father, he has made him known (Jn 1:18). The Man Jesus Christ can testify: " 'No one comes to the Father but by me. If you had known me, you would have known my Father also; henceforth you know him and have seen him.' Philip said to him, 'Lord, show us the Father, and we shall be satisfied.' Jesus said to him, 'Have I been with you so long, and yet you do not know me, Philip? He who has seen me has seen the Father" (Jn 14:6-9; cf. 17:24).

Jesus Christ is in His glorified existence with the Father the full human realization of the love that the Father has for every man: "For God so loved the world that

31. M. Jugie, *La mort et l'Assomption de la Sainte Vierge*, Rome, 1944.

he gave his only Son, that whoever believes in him should not perish but have eternal life" (Jn 3:16). In the human encounter with the glorified Lord in word and sacrament we can constantly discover the believing response of our daily life as a participation in His glorified humanness with the Father.

On earth, we still experience that being-like-to-Him in the darkness of faith. But in eternity we shall fully experience our being redeemed in Christ as men, according to our human and individual possibilities: "See what love the Father has given us, that we should be called children of God; and *so we are.* . . . Beloved, we are God's children now; it does not yet appear what we shall be, but we know that when he (the glorified Man Jesus Christ) appears *we shall be like him,* for we shall see him as he is" (1 Jn 3:1-3).

Our eternal happiness will consist in an ever new and hence always marvellous experience of being-redeemed in Christ in our human existence: "And we all, with unveiled face, beholding the glory of the Lord, are being changed into his likeness from one degree of glory to another" (2 Cor. 3:18). We shall experience our human existence as He experiences His human life as glorification of the Father. "This is eternal life, that they know thee the only true God, and in Jesus Christ whom thou hast sent" (Jn 17:3), as God in human form. St. Paul saw being-a-Christian as a solidarity of life with the glorified Lord—on earth in an as yet eschatological tension, and later in a full experience—and expressed this vision in the following words: "In fact Christ has been raised from the dead, the first fruits of those who have fallen asleep. . . . For as in Adam all die, so also in Christ shall all be made alive. But each in his own order: Christ the first fruits, then at his coming those who belong to Christ" (1 Cor. 15:20-23).

In Christ the whole creation is brought to its fulfillment, to the full realization of God's plan of salvation. In Him we are redeemed, even as to what is corporeal in us. Of this the Church has given witness in her confession that Mary "at the end of her earthly course was assumed to heavenly glory in body and soul" (Denziger, no. 3903). But this profession must be fully seen in the light of the scriptural testimony: "But our commonwealth is in heaven, and from it we await a Savior, the Lord Jesus Christ, who will change our lowly body to be like his glorious body, by the power which enables him even to subject all things to himself" (Phil. 3:20-21).

In accepting the dogma of Mary's Assumption, we speak in virtue of the faith in our own resurrection in Christ in a way that also glorifies our body:

> As was the man of dust, so are those who are of the dust; and as is the man of heaven, so are those who are of heaven. Just as we have borne the image of the man of dust, we shall also bear the image of the man of heaven. . . . For this perishable nature must put on the imperishable, and this mortal nature must put on immortality. . . . Then shall come to pass the saying that is written: "Death is swallowed up in victory. O death, where is thy victory?" . . . But thanks be to God, who gives us the victory through our Lord Jesus Christ (1 Cor. 15:48-52).

E. Mary as Co-redemptrix and Mediatrix of All Grace

An Authentic Scriptural Protest Against the Traditional Catholic Veneration of Mary

We see, then, that a renewed reflection upon the salvific meaning of the incarnation of God's Son offers a possibility of bringing the divided Christians closer together and making them understand those aspects of Christ's salvific work that are summed up in the dogmatic declarations of the Catholic Church concerning Mary.

But there opens up a definitely unbridgeable chasm when the question of believing in Mary as co-redemptrix and as mediatrix of all graces appears in the controversy.

That is why it is important for the unity of the Church, that both sides in the controversy should make use of clear words and carefully examine the means for a rapprochement regarding that matter.

Catholics cannot expect the Reformation to make even one step toward a rapprochement with respect to the central thought of its believing testimony in which its followers feel obliged to proclaim absolutely the one and only Mediatorship of Christ:

> Regarding that point the Reformation is most sensitive. One very essential element of the Reformation testimony is the fact that Jesus Christ is absolutely the only one in whom a Christian takes refuge in his existential plight of sin and misery. . . . This part of the testimony of the Reformation is in no way weakened in our time insofar as the Reformed Christians are concerned.[32]

The traditional Catholic reflection upon the part of Mary in our salvation starts from the dialogue with the angel of God, in which there was question of *our* salvation. On the basis of Mary's free consent to become the mother of our Savior and her sharing in Christ's sacrifice, especially as she stood underneath the Cross, Catholic theology attributes to Mary an objective cooperation (Mary as co-redemptrix) and a subjective redemptive part (Mary as mediatrix of all graces).[33]

32. W. H. van de Pol, *Het getuigenis van de Reformatie,* Roermond, 1960, p. 114.
33. C. X. J. M. Friethoff, *Volledige Marialeer,* Hilversum, 1953, pp. 169-274; A. Janssens, F. Tummers, P. Ploumen, *Maria in de leer der Kerk,* Den Bosch, 1940, pp. 111-120; J. Lebon, "Comment je conçois, j'établis et je defend la doctrine de la médiation mariale," *Ephem. Theol. Lov.,* vol. 16 (1939), pp. 655-744; Cl. Dillenschneider, *Le mystère de la Co-rédemption mariale,* Paris, 1951.

A few theologians go to extremes in advocating Mary's special role in our redemption, making Christ and Mary together the *one* principle and source of redemption: beside Christ—who is true man but not a human person —there stands Mary, who as a human person is the representative of all mankind.[34]

A Catholic in his dialogue with Reformed Christians could angrily dismiss such an exaggeration of Mary's place in Christ's salvific work, if he need not to admit that his own actual veneration of Mary is determined by a practical monophysitism that undervalues the salvific function of the Incarnation and sees Christ too exclusively in His divine dignity. In such a religious perspective and attitude of life, Mary then comes to bridge the distance between Christ and man.

It is on the basis of Scripture itself that the Reformed Christian steadfastly protests against that overshadowing of Christ by such Marian claims, and that he refuses to yield even when a Catholic hastily adds to his defense of Mary's titles of co-redemptrix and mediatrix, that "all this is in subordination to Christ." Scripture testifies too clearly to the unique value of the incarnation of God's Son and to the all-sufficiency of His salvific work to permit it to be overshadowed by giving Mary a place of her own in the realization of our salvation: "There is one mediator between God and men, the man Christ Jesus, who gave himself as a ransom for all" (1 Tim. 2:5).

Christ is the Grace-giving Church; Mary is the Grace-experiencing Church

It is only from the Christological center of the salvific event that there comes a road on which divided Chris-

---

34. E. Druwe, "Mediatrix nostra," *Tijdschrift voor Geest. Leven* I, 1945, pp. 217-245, 230-234; H. M. Koster, *Die Magd des Herrn*, Limburg a.L., 1947.

tians can meet. The Son of the Father, in His solidarity with our sinful human existence, was "for our sake made to be sin" (2 Cor. 5:21), in order to restore God's salvific plan for man, as the obedient man, in our place and behalf: "a body thou hast prepared for me . . . lo, I have come to do thy will, O God" (Heb. 10:5-6). "He himself partook of the same nature, that through death he might . . . deliver all those who through fear of death were subject to lifelong bondage. Therefore he had to be made like his brethren in every respect" (Heb. 2:14-17).

In our glorified human nature Christ represents the whole of mankind with the Father; this is not true of Mary. The mediatorship for all men must be attributed exclusively to Christ, and not at the same time to Mary. The act of faith by which we subjectively realize that we are saved in Christ as men, we perform in virtue of His power. We do not owe it at the same time to Mary. Our objective and subjective redemption then, comes continuously and exclusively from God's purely gratuitous initiative of love in the sending of His Son.

If then a Christian wishes to reflect, on this biblical foundation, upon his believing attitude toward Mary, he will find that there are two aspects of Christ's salvific work that determine her eminent place within redeemed mankind.

In the first place, a human action remains inalienably the possession of a person. The act of faith which a redeemed man performs by the power of the glorified Lord is not Christ's act, but the free personal act of that man. Man is the subject of that act which is entirely a gift of God. That is why the free consent of faith is by its very nature implied in the experience of our being redeemed in Christ. In this sense, being-a-Christian always includes a human cooperation which is correlative in salvific power to the grace that is given. The act of faith is the gift-of-grace of the free personal surrender to the redemption that is accomplished by Christ. The fact that grace operates everything does not mean that grace alone is active. "Without faith it is impossible to please him (God). . . . By faith Abel offered to God a more acceptable sacrifice than Cain, through which he received approval as righteous, God bearing witness by accepting his gifts; he died, but through his faith he is still preaching" (Heb. 11:6, 4). That is why St. Paul, conscious of being redeemed by Christ was able to declare: "By the grace of God I am what I am, and his grace toward me was not in vain" (1 Cor. 15:10).

In the second place, an act of faith is never an isolated deed of an individual man, but it blossoms within the whole community of faith (the idea of the Covenant). In experiencing your being-saved-in-Christ "You are the body of Christ and individually members of it. . . . For by one Spirit we were all baptized into one body—Jews or Greeks, slaves or free—and all were made to drink of one Spirit. . . . To each is given the manifestation of the Spirit for the common good" (1 Cor. 12:27; 12, 7). The individual believer, in his living union with the glorified Lord, stands in a living union with the whole believing community of the Church, and the power of Christ's grace in him has a real influence and significance for all other believers.

This biblical idea of the believing community being the Body of Christ must form the starting-point for determining Mary's place in the Christian life of faith: *in her exemplary believing response "Be it done unto me according to Thy word" she represents the Church throughout her life as the community of faith that is with Christ.*

Christ and Mary stand on a totally different level: Christ is the new Israel that *brings* salvation, the Church that *brings* grace, the Church as salvific *instrument.*

Mary, on the contrary, is the new Israel that *receives* salvation, the Church that *experiences* grace, the Church as *community* of salvation.

In her believing response "Be it done to me according to Thy word," which epitomizes her whole life of surrender to Christ, Mary is the first human being who believes in Christ and experiences her being-the-Church. And this believing act has a real influence on, and significance for all believers. She could have said about her response to the message of the angel, as the most radical and eminent believer: "At this moment I rejoice because I can suffer for You and am permitted to complete in my flesh what is lacking in Christ's afflictions for the sake of his body, that is, the church" (Col. 1:24).[35] And what she is permitted to "complete" is the self-giving surrender by which Christ can realize His salvific coming to mankind.

If a Catholic, however, basing himself on the place Mary occupies in the Church, thinks he is permitted to call her co-redemptrix and mediatrix of all graces, he should know that all terms which even remotely suggest that Christ and Mary are on the same level, are not only misleading, but clearly also a distortion of the Bible's testimony about Mary. The Reformed Christian has the right to misunderstand them on that account and we are giving him a valid reason for his continued protest against the Catholic Church.

But here also the Second Vatican Council has wished to open an ecumenical perspective:

> We have but one Mediator, as we know from the words of the Apostle: "For there is one God, and one Mediator between God and men, himself man, Christ Jesus." . . . The maternal duty of Mary toward men in no way obscures or diminishes this unique mediation of Christ, but rather shows its power. For *all* the saving

35. H. Coathalem, *Le parallelisme entre la Ste. Vierge et l'Eglise dans la tradition latine jusqu'à la fin du XIIe S.*, Rome, 1954.

influences of the Blessed Virgin on men originate, not
from some inner necessity, but from the divine pleasure.
They flow forth from the superabundance of the merits
of Christ, rest on His mediation, depend entirely on it,
and draw all their power from it. In no way do they
impede the immediate union of the faithful with Christ.
Rather, they foster this union (*Constitution on the
Church*, no. 60).

4. AN ECUMENICAL CONFESSION

By that believing reflection upon the most controversial issue about Mary, the Catholic Church wishes to
make an ecumenical step that will make possible the
rapprochement of the divided Christians.

A new dialogue with the Reformation has become possible because the Catholic Church desires to stress the
following points in her interpretation of her dogmas concerning Mary:

1. The veneration of Mary in the course of centuries
developed from the theology about the Church as a believing community that lives by Christ as her glorified
Lord; and Mary as the prototype of mankind that is
redeemed through faith in Christ may never be isolated
from that community.

2. With respect to Mary's maternity as a foundation
for venerating her, it is not primarily a question of a
biological event but of an act of faith leading to a total
surrender of her person to God. Scripture primarily reveals to us a message of salvation.

3. Faith is a condition of our being-saved in Christ
that is constantly given to us by God, but it is, at the
same time, one that is experienced by man.

4. In the Marian dogmas it is not primarily a question
of the personal privileges of Mary, but of the concrete
aspects of the salvific work that Christ has achieved for
the benefit of all men. All those aspects are eminently

realized in Mary who, through her faith in being-redeemed in Christ, is the Mother of God's Son. But when
the Church professes those facts she must bring out that
those gifts of faith were also tasks to be fulfilled and that
those gifts are offered to all men.

5. The Church can arrive at a clarification of those
aspects of our salvation in the exemplary life of faith of
Mary, not on the basis of isolated scriptural words concerning Mary, but by taking into consideration the whole
Christ-revelation that is found in the Bible.

If this is so and the Catholic Church has made this
step of ecumenical significance, the Reformed Christians
in their turn will have to make their own the words of
Berkouwer, not only in their theological thinking but in
their practical life of faith:

> The Reformation also showed great respect in the way
> it has spoken about Mary. Bavink, for instance, who
> expressly accuses Rome of deifying Mary, speaks of
> Mary as the favored one among women and he sees how
> the whole preparation for the Incarnation is concen-
> trated and achieved in the election and favoring of Mary
> as the Mother of Jesus. Mary is the blessed one among
> women. She received an honor that was not granted to
> any other creature. She far surpasses all men and angels
> because of the unmerited grace that was given her. He
> who refuses to acknowledge this does not take God's
> incarnation seriously.[36]

But even if we come to understand one another and
recognize the salvific significance of Mary, it will remain
ecumenically important that we do not try to force one
another to adopt a certain uniformity in our veneration
of Mary; such a uniformity would do violence to the
fullness of the Christ mystery as well as to the freedom
of the children of God.

36. B. C. Berkouwer, *Conflict met Rome*, p. 218.

EPILOGUE

LET US LEARN TO LIVE TOGETHER IN SPITE
OF OUR DIFFERENCES

The Church of Jesus Christ in a State of Change and Tension

In the Church of Jesus Christ we meet and often enter into conflict with imperfect ways of being-a-Christian; we encounter the religious opinions and practices of other local Churches, and we might be prompted to protest violently because we find it impossible to feel at home with them.

But we are not permitted to abandon other Christians and other Churches. We can learn from them to correct our own one-sidedness of which we are sometimes unaware, and they can also enrich us.

Sincere impatience born of faith that looks forward to the fullness and the purity of the Church of Jesus Christ, and a temptation to impose our way of being-the-Church as the norm for all, must be tempered by the charitable readiness to tolerate other Christians and Churches in their way of life; and we must permit them to witness to Christ according to the way they are inspired by the Gospel.

For centuries we have been the Church engaged in a strong monologue with respect to one another. Now we must learn to be the Church in a dialogue with one

465

another. Might this not be the ecumenical significance of the dark week with which the third session of Vatican Council II came to a close? The ecumenical movement could have suffered great harm—also in the other Christian Churches—if the great majority in the Catholic Church had not borne the rapidly rising heat of that week. Because of the progress in dialogue, the local Churches in the Catholic Church have clearly manifested their solidarity by unanimously accepting that which could be attained at the time.

Differences cannot be talked away; we can only strive together to live-them-away. This the majority has done because it was profoundly aware of its ecumenical responsibility toward the other Christian Churches.

The Spirit of ecumenism asks all Christians and all Churches to live together in the one Church of Jesus Christ, in spite of their differences. The pressing need for that dialogue must generate uneasiness and a deep concern in all Christians and all Churches at this critical hour of salvation history. Frontiers that one might consider closed in principle must be broken open, for we ought to keep in mind that all our human differences have already been definitively overcome in Christ. What a vast perspective is opened to all the ecumenical efforts of the Churches by the words: "The earth is the Lord's and the fulness thereof, the world and those who dwell therein" (Ps. 24:1).

In the past so filled with apologetic battles, the Churches, entrenched in self-satisfied monologue, contented themselves with inviting the return of the others. Today we have dialogue everywhere because the Catholic Church has recognized the churchly character of other Christians groups. But the negative attitude that has been overcome in ecumenical encounters with Christians still influences our approach to many people who desire to live by earthly standards and values. In the past we have branded such people as "outside the Church" and when the Churches enter into dialogue with them it might be only in order to find out how we could make them accept what we have developed in our isolation and monologue.

We have lived in separate ghetto Churches; we are now running the risk of creating an isolated inter-church ghetto because of our negative approach toward those who are "outsiders"; such an attitude makes us powerless with respect to "the world."

The unity of the Church of Jesus Christ can be realized only through a common dialogue of Christians with that world. Vatican Council II has described the Church as the instrument of the most intimate unity of *all* men and, by this means, of their unity with God. The Church can be fully the salvific instrument of Christ's active presence in this world only if she enters in open communion with *all men*, and this means also with worldly men who possess their own proper values which they are able to contribute for making the world-wide human community the Church of Jesus Christ. "In my Father's house are many rooms" (Jn 14:2), that is, there are rooms for all.

The Way That Was Given Us to Walk Together

When a group of mountain-climbers has reached a summit that had never been "conquered" before, and one of them is giving an account of the exploit he feels obliged to express a word of thanks to all the members of the team. Not only because there was a common effort and courage but especially because of the presence of a true *esprit de corps* was success achieved. They had been able, literally speaking, to lean constantly upon one another and had pulled one another upward. All are now grateful to the other members of the expedition.

When other members now read the account given by one they may wonder why certain aspects of the journey were not described in greater detail. They may even remark that certain events were not mentioned or were not accurately described. The only excuse the narrator can offer is that the journey was so thrilling that he was unable to absorb everything at the same time. After all, this was the first time that this mountain top had been reached. And although he is fully aware of the incompleteness and perhaps one-sidedness of his impressions, he nevertheless dares to present his own record. This record will require additional writing of course, for this sort of thing by its very nature demands "supplements."

At the end of the road we have traveled together, we offer this book to our fellow-Christians of the Reformation who in true ecumenical reflection have been willing to make the journey with us. And now we are waiting for their own record and account for the benefit of our common ecumenical cause.

INDEX OF NAMES

469

INDEX OF SUBJECT MATTER

472